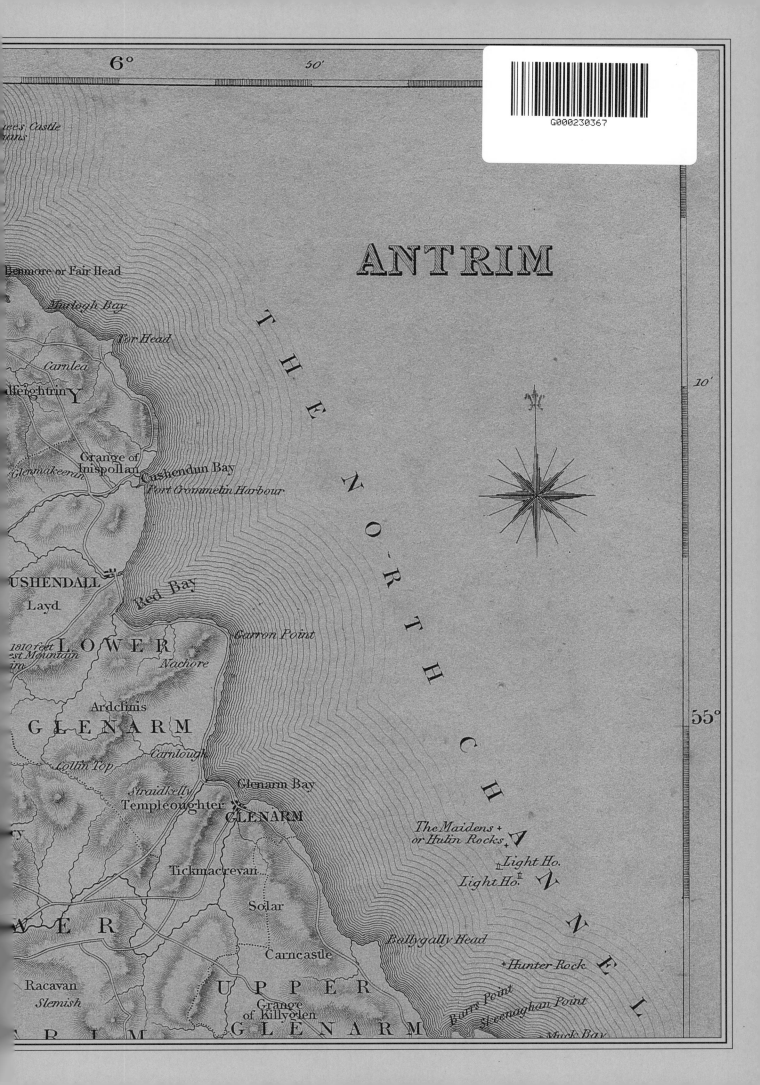

BUILDINGS OF COUNTY ANTRIM

BUILDINGS
OF
COUNTY ANTRIM

by

C E B BRETT

with photographs by

MICHAEL O'CONNELL

A joint publication of the
ULSTER ARCHITECTURAL HERITAGE SOCIETY
and the ULSTER HISTORICAL FOUNDATION

BELFAST

First published 1996
by the
Ulster Architectural Heritage Society
185 Stranmillis Road, Belfast BT9 5DU
and the
Ulster Historical Foundation
12 College Square East, Belfast BT1 6DD
Reprinted 1997

Typeset in 10/11 Baskerville
Designed by Della Varilly
Printed in County Antrim by Nicholson & Bass, Ltd

ISBN 0 900457 47 3

A catalogue record for this book
is available from the British Library

Leslie Hill Bally money

Frontispiece: ~~Hillmount House, Cullybackey~~ (79). Photograph: Michael O'Connell
End-papers: Map of County Antrim, 1837 (from S Lewis: *Topographical dictionary*)

DEDICATED

- on the one hand, to
Maurice James Craig,
doyen of Irish architectural historians;

- on the other hand, to
the memory of Emyr Estyn Evans,
geographer, folklorist and archaeologist;

- in the hope that I may find standing ground
somewhere between the two of them

CONTENTS

"It is not just the thatch and the whitewash and the cylindrical gate-post which speak of our unofficial, workaday selves; there are also scutch mills, linen factories, warehouses, hotels, bridges and chimneys, railway stations, breweries and distilleries, convents and colleges, nineteenth century Catholic churches, twentieth century parochial halls, mill towns, music halls, opera houses, workers' houses, schoolhouses. We have inherited all these and more as an important part of our environment also, and it would be effete, even if it were physically and psychologically possible, to deny them a real place in that formal architectural language which ... is being spoken to us all the time."

Seamus Heaney

'From Maecenas to MacAlpine', in 'One hundred and fifty years of architecture in Ireland', Dublin, RIAI, 1989, p 70.

ACKNOWLEDGEMENTS

My thanks are due to a great many people who have helped me during the two years it has taken me to compile this book.

I have made much use of the Linen Hall Library, Belfast, and am especially grateful to John Killen, Gerry Healey, and Mary Delargy of that excellent institution. I have also been a very regular visitor to the Public Record Office of Northern Ireland, and my thanks are particularly due to Ian Montgomery and Michèle Neill, and to the reading-room and search-room staff, for their patience in dealing with my, sometimes importunate, inquiries. I am grateful also to Terence Reeves-Smyth of the Monuments and Buildings Record, Belfast; to Karen Latimer of the Architecture and Planning Library of the Queen's University of Belfast; to W A Maguire of the Ulster Museum; to Sally Skillen of the Library of the Ulster Folk and Transport Museum; to David Griffin of the Irish Architectural Archive, Dublin; to Brian Mackey of the Lisburn Museum; and to Peter Marlow of the National Trust.

Many individuals have helped me with information, and I am grateful to them all; but I am especially indebted to Eddie McParland of Trinity College, Dublin; to Alistair and Ann-Martha Rowan; and to Donald Girvan, who has been unfailingly generous with his rich stores of local knowledge. Belinda Jupp's files on the heritage gardens of Northern Ireland, in the Monuments and Buildings Record, were of uncommon value. Gordon Wheeler, editor of the publications of the UAHS, has been immensely supportive and helpful. For typing and secretarial assistance, I am deeply grateful to Sally Lowry, as also to Belinda Conlan who helped out during Sally Lowry's absence. I am grateful, too, to Della Varilly, designer, for her diligence and professionalism.

I have preferred to use modern photographs where possible; but in some cases trees have grown up, telegraph poles or bungalows been planted, or circumstances otherwise altered so as to make a picture from the archives preferable. For older illustrations, I have to thank the Public Record Office of Northern Ireland for permission to reproduce the map on page 182, and, with Lord Dunluce, the drawing on page 101; the Trustees of the Ulster Museum for permission to reproduce the R J Welch photographs on pages 4, 18, 20, 46, 73, 94, 161, 214, 273, 276 and 279; the Trustees of the Ulster Folk and Transport Museum for permission to reproduce the W A Green photographs on pages 8, 12, 22, 23, 186, 256, 277, 281, 291, and 293; and the Monuments and Buildings Record, Hill Street, Belfast, for permission to reproduce crown copyright photographs on pages 70, 76, and 286. The other older illustrations are separately acknowledged in the captions: I am grateful to all those institutions and individuals who have allowed me to make use of them. I am exceedingly grateful to the Trustees of the Marc Fitch Fund for a handsome grant towards the cost of the new illustrations. But, most of all, I am grateful to Michael O'Connell for all the pains he has taken with his specially taken photo-graphs which contribute so much to this volume. All the colour photographs are his. I must also thank Jim McCall both for taking the aerial photographs, and for taking me up with him.

It became clear, well before the compilation of this book was complete, that the inclusion of adequate illustration would call for sponsorship or support from outside individuals and bodies, in addition to the substantial investment falling to be made by the Ulster Architectural Heritage Society and, to a lesser extent, the Ulster Historical Foundation. I am extremely grateful to all those listed below for their generous contributions:

The Pilgrim Trust
Department of the Environment for Northern Ireland
Esmé Mitchell Trust
The Marc Fitch Fund
The Belfast Society
School of Irish Studies Foundation
Antrim Borough Council
Lisburn Borough Council
Newtownabbey Borough Council

Finally, I must thank most heartily all those who devoted so much time and trouble to showing me their homes, or the buildings in their care, and to digging up old letters, cuttings and photographs to illuminate their history.

C E B B

INTRODUCTION

My main purpose in writing this book has been to fill a gap; perhaps more gaps than one. The biggest gap has certainly been the lack of any serious account of the architecture of County Antrim as a whole. True, publications of the Ulster Architectural Heritage Society,[1] compiled between 1969 and 1978, in great part by the pioneering Donald Girvan, covered much of the northern parts of the county, though not Larne, Newtownabbey, or the Lagan valley. True, the publicly available statutory Lists of buildings of special architectural or historic interest, prepared since 1970, today cover all the District Council areas concerned, including in their various categories some 1500 buildings within the old boundaries of County Antrim. But the statutory Lists are cryptic in the extreme; in most cases, they contain neither descriptive nor historical information; they are unaccompanied by illustrations; their classification system is confusing; and, though copies may be inspected by the public, they are not available for purchase.

A volume on North-east Ulster in the Pevsner-Penguin series is awaited, but I understand its appearance is not likely for some time. There is no equivalent of the splendidly authoritative volumes of the English and Scottish Royal Commissions on Ancient and Historical Monuments. There is no Victoria County History, nor any equivalent in contemplation that I know of.

In 1980, Estyn Evans, in his introduction to W A McCutcheon's The Industrial Archaeology of Northern Ireland,[2] remarked that, in the 1960s, it had been " decided to concentrate on separate county surveys after the model of those published for Great Britain, and to begin with County Down. The admirable survey of County Down was published in 1966".[3] Very unhappily, no companion volume for any other county has appeared in the thirty years since then, nor does any such publication appear to be in prospect, although some groundwork has been done but remains unpublished. Like Nikolaus Pevsner, Estyn Evans was a man who got things done; one who saw to it that a project, once embarked upon, was brought to a successful conclusion. Had he been still living, I feel pretty sure that we should, by now, have had similar surveys for at least two other Ulster counties. Had Antrim been one of them, I should not have been impelled to write this book.

The basic tools of the trade of the architectural historian, and of the conservationist of the built environment - above all, the fundamental descriptive inventory on which all else depends - are still lacking in most parts of Northern Ireland in respect of historic buildings, though not in respect of ancient monuments. This volume is therefore, first and foremost, an attempt to plug this particular gap so far as County Antrim is concerned. But it is not, and does not pretend to be, itself an authoritative inventory; it is more in the nature of a personal anthology. I hope, however, that it may constitute a useful contribution towards an eventual inventory, insofar as each individual entry is as complete as I have been able to make it.

There is a second gap which I have consciously attempted to fill. To most people, buildings are less interesting than are those who once lived in them, or made use of them. Those who are interested in local history are not always those who are keen on architecture. In general, and for obvious reasons, purist architectural historians (and their editors) mostly exclude gossip about the inhabitants of the buildings about which they write. This is discouraging for the very numerous enthusiasts for local history. I share the interests of the latter, and rate highly the importance of oral tradition, anecdote and the entertaining sidelights of history, which I think often - and for many people - can bring old buildings to life. And I follow Mark Girouard in believing that architectural history and social history should go hand in hand. Accordingly, I have done my best to include, whenever it came my way, interesting material about the owners, the occupiers, the tenants, the lodgers, and the visitors, as well as about the buildings themselves.

I think I have identified a third gap, in Ireland, between the territory of the architectural historian proper, and that of the folklorist and geographer. Maurice Craig, Eddie McParland, Alistair Rowan, and Paul Larmour are primarily interested in the architect-designed building as a work of art. Estyn Evans, Kevin Danaher, Alan Gailey and Jonathan Bell have been more interested in vernacular buildings as an expression of "the local folk tradition", rather than in aesthetic terms. "Truly vernacular buildings will never have seen the hand of an architect - they were never planned on paper, but simply built according to the prevailing style of the region":[4] which till now, has mostly meant thatched cottages, and the simpler kind of farmhouse.

In England, the no-man's land containing intermediate buildings between stately home and cottage has been explored by scholars such as Maurice Barley and R W

Brunskill; in Ireland, this is almost virgin territory, apart from some useful groundwork by Paddy and Maura Shaffrey. The gap was clearly identified by Alan Gailey in 1984 in the opening chapter of his book on Rural Houses of the North of Ireland;[5] and its significance was re-emphasised in an important article in 1993 by Philip Robinson;[6] but to identify a gap is not to stop it up. Although I set out with no such deliberate intention, I find that I have, in this book, made a start on plugging this third gap, by describing a considerable number of unlisted but important vernacular buildings which are not really very grand, but much grander than just rustic cottages. Indeed, I have come to the view that it is these buildings which constitute the greatest wealth, the greatest built asset, of County Antrim.

What is a building? I have taken a robust view, with which not everyone will agree, as to what constitutes a "building". Broadly speaking, I have used the word to include anything erected by human agency: from a holestone to an obelisk: from a dolmen to a rope bridge: from a tombstone to a windfarm.

What is County Antrim? (I have taken it as axiomatic that buildings within the boundaries of the City of Belfast are excluded). A very ancient territorial entity; surrounded for the most part by water - the North Atlantic, the North Channel, Belfast Lough, the river Lagan, Lough Neagh, and the river Bann. It is the postage stamp on the top right-hand corner of the map of Ireland. However, it seems that, since the local government changes of 1972, the county of Antrim no longer has any administrative, only a ceremonial, existence: on the one hand, as the territory within which a Lord Lieutenant represents the Queen; on the other hand, as the territory within which the GAA organises Gaelic sporting teams and contests. It is to be doubted whether many members of the GAA would recognise the Lord Lieutenant if they met him, even wearing his peaked cap and striped belt. It is equally to be doubted whether every Lord Lieutenant would recognise the county colours so exuberantly displayed when Antrim wins through to a major contest at Croke Park.

The administrative functions of the former Grand Jury, then of the County Council, were redistributed in 1972 amongst the 26 new district councils - but their boundaries pay scant respect to historical integrity. The county today includes the whole of the territory administered by the District Councils of Ballymoney, Moyle, Ballymena, Antrim, Larne, Carrickfergus, and Newtownabbey; but only one ward of Craigavon, two wards of Coleraine, and 12 out of 23 wards of Lisburn. Neither barony nor townland boundaries are now officially recognised, except for conveyancing purposes. Since 1972, census, population, and many other statistics can no longer be related to their comparables of the previous three centuries. All this poses problems for the architectural historian, and represents a triumph for the short-term view over the historical one.

As I have said, this is an anthology rather than an inventory; so I must state the criteria I have employed in deciding which buildings to include, which to exclude. Such decisions are, unavoidably, highly subjective. The selection is entirely my own. I have tried to include build-

ings which seemed to me to be of especial architectural, or artistic, or historic significance; or which I particularly liked, for any or no good reason; or which amused me; or which seemed to me particularly interesting, even if I did not much like them; or which appeared to me to represent the vernacular tradition in an important way. Perhaps exclusions are easier to explain than inclusions. I have excluded buildings which are no longer there, however attractive they may once have been; I have also excluded those which have been so much altered as to have lost, in my view, their original character.

Although this book describes buildings designed by Robert Adam, John Nash, William Vitruvius Morrison, Edward Blore, and other notable architects, the predominant architect is Anon. That said, there is a healthy amount of creditable work by local practitioners, of whom Charles Lanyon, for much of his professional career county surveyor and architect, naturally stands out. I have described most, but not all, of his surviving work in the county.

I expect that I shall be told that some of my inclusions, and exclusions, are too subjective. In particular, I have not included many buildings designed after about 1890. And a prejudice on my part may be thought to have unfairly excluded prominent buildings such as Drumalis, Cairndhu, Carnfunnock, Magheramorne, and Runkerry; all the works of S P Close or R M Close, father and son. The truth is that I do not care for any of these; they seem to me of little merit; though I have included one vertical exemplar of the work of the Close practice, the Chaine memorial: which I hope will make some amends. There are not many 20th-century buildings, either. I will leave it to the generation which comes after mine to pass considered judgement on the buildings of my contemporaries.

The county has suffered considerably from the Troubles of the years since 1969. The historic heart of Lisburn, in particular, has been smashed by successive bombs. Ballycastle and Cushendall lost their principal hotels, both buildings of architectural significance, by fire-bombs. Some other counties have suffered worse, but the damage has been pretty widespread, rivalled only by the redevelopment of the centres of Antrim and Ballymena, and the continuing exploitation of the former green fields around Carrickfergus and Newtownabbey. Large areas of the countryside have been infiltrated by inappropriate new houses and bungalows in a great variety of non-traditional styles, though fortunately, so far, most of the Glens and most of the coastline remain relatively - I emphasise the word relatively - unspoiled.

One side-effect of the Troubles has been a wariness of publicity. Fears of organised burglary have also had an effect. Three owners of important houses made it an express condition of my writing about them that I should make no mention whatsoever of the interiors, still less of the contents. Three owners of less important houses refused me permission either to photograph, or to mention, their houses at all. In each case I have complied with their wishes, which (unlike Sir Nikolaus Pevsner, who had some sharp words for those who refused him) I find quite understandable, especially in the case of elderly persons living alone. For this reason, contrary to the usual custom in works about buildings, this book contains almost no interior views; almost no descriptions of interior features; and no ground-plans.

I have looked at the exteriors of all the buildings

recorded in this book, and at the interiors of roughly two-thirds of them: where I was not invited in, or could not readily obtain access, I left it at that. For people are well entitled to privacy in their own houses. Buildings form a very important part of our common heritage, and it is right that the public should have access to information about them. But householders have their rights too. There is, at present, no stately home in county Antrim regularly opened to the public. I owe it to the owners, who have shown me so much kindness and courtesy, to urge readers of this book not to trespass, or intrude where they are not wanted; but to content themselves with visits to castles, monuments and churches that are open to the public; or the view of a private house from the public roadway.

The division into chapters is fairly notional: I have not greatly fussed myself over questions of demarcation. I have tried to provide the basic information on address, townland, parish, District Council area, and grid reference, which a researcher is likely to need; but it should be remembered that boundaries can be moved, and parishes restructured over the years. The grid references represent my own estimates based on the 1:50,000 Ordnance Survey maps. I am afraid that some mistakes will inevitably have crept into these geographical particulars. Moreover, changes will certainly have taken place since I started compiling the book, and looking at the buildings, in January 1994; there is always an unavoidable time-lag between the record date on the ground and the date of publication.

I have sought to indicate whether a building is listed, and, if so, in which category; and whether a building lies within the boundaries of a conservation area. But these things can change, and any reader with a special interest in a particular building would be wise to check its current status with the Environment and Heritage Service.

The system of grading employed is confusing. It is said that the grading system used in Northern Ireland is similar to the Scottish system, though different from that used in England and Wales. I have been permitted to see, and quote from, a draft leaflet designed to explain the grading criteria: "Buildings listed by the Department are divided into three categories, A, B+ and B". "The listed building gradings are not statutory, but are used as a management tool to help the Environment Service in administering levels of grant to owners of listed buildings." "Since 1987 the Environment Service: HMB have been banding category B buildings into two groups namely B1 and B2". In addition, it seems that Q is used to identify a particular kind of thatched property for grant purposes; IA is used to indicate significance in terms of industrial archaeology.

The entries are arranged, within each chapter, very roughly in order of date - or guessed-at date: though I have not followed the rule strictly, and have departed from it where it seemed more telling to describe or illustrate particular buildings in juxtaposition or by contrast; or where a degree of rearrangement facilitated the lay-out of the photographs.

The dating of Irish buildings, especially of Irish vernacular buildings, is an exceptionally difficult task. As Henry Glassie puts it, "Houses are constantly rebuilt. Scholars accustomed to traditions in which rebuilding is rare or neatly periodic become frustrated by the impossibility of assigning dates to Irish houses. New houses contain early stone corners; homes expand and shrink and shift over old sites, continually absorbing diverse materials

into their walls."[7]

In the absence of documentary evidence it is almost impossible to date with confidence a vernacular building within a local tradition that lasted, with surprisingly few changes, from around 1720 until around 1870. There are some helpful details - banisters and rails, glazing bars, panelled doors, window-shutters - but, so far as my experience goes, every one of them can lead to delusive conclusions. Where the building history of a house seems to cover a wide span, I have endeavoured to assess its, so to speak, centre of gravity: but the process has often been an arbitrary one. And documentary evidence is not always so helpful as might be supposed.

Amongst the earliest sources are maps; Taylor and Skinner's Roads of Ireland, "surveyed 1777, published ... 14th Novr 1778", is a most valuable starting-point: it shows the seats, and surnames, of the principal gentry; the houses, like the churches, being however delineated in a very stylised form. It was quickly followed by James Lendrick's county map, commissioned by the Grand Jury: "the survey was carried out in 1780, published at the beginning of 1782".[8] Lendrick was himself a member of the Grand Jury, for a time county treasurer, and agent for Lord O'Neill's Shane's Castle estate. His map contains information, by way of key numbers, as to 193 "Noblemen and Gentlemen's Seats", and as to 82 "Bleach Yards", though it is confusing in its arrangement and difficult to use. It also contains numerous townland names, but these do not seem to imply that a house of the same name existed in 1780. And there is no way of being sure (without corroborative evidence) that a gentleman's seat, shown as existing in 1780, is the same as that still standing today: for sometimes, manifestly, it is not.

Lendrick's map, in turn, was overtaken by a revised version by his son-in-law, James Williamson, published in 1808. Comparison of these two maps is useful; Williamson's changes and additions are readily identifiable: but the unanswerable question remains, how far was he recording new houses built since 1780? How far simply remedying his father-in-law's omissions? Mention should also be made of William Wilson's The Post-Chaise Companion: or Traveller's Directory through Ireland first published in 1784, with new editions in 1786, 1803 and 1813. This contains no detailed maps, but a number of passing references to gentlemen's seats. I have in this book quoted on occasions from the edition of 1803.

A number of useful works were published in the early years of the 19th century. The three volumes of Shaw Mason's Statistical Account, published 1812 to 1819, include descriptions of several County Antrim parishes. James Dubourdieu's Statistical Survey of the County of Antrim, also published in 1812, contains a mass of interesting information, very little of it, however, about modern buildings, in which the author was not much interested. At this period, numerous travellers wrote their Irish travel books, which contain occasional snippets of useful information: the most valuable being that of Anne Plumptre, which enables us (for the first time) to date Rockport, Cushendun, with exactitude, to the year 1813.

A particularly helpful visitor to Ireland was the slightly mysterious A Atkinson, 'late of Dublin', whose two volumes on Ireland Exhibited to England, published in 1823, in fact record information collected during a prolonged visit in 1817: the whole of the second volume is devoted to County Antrim, and it is an invaluable source of information, especially about the mills and mill owners of that period, although he did not hesitate to quote without acknowledgement from the works of Shaw Mason and Dubourdieu. His later volume of 1833 is much less useful, though it does fill up a few gaps.

The next group of invaluable source material comprises the first Ordnance Survey maps, the Ordnance Survey memoirs, and the first set of Valuation books, all dating from 1829 and the ensuing few years. The value of the maps is self-evident; but a map cannot tell the inquirer whether the building denoted is a cottage, a skyscraper, or something in between. These maps, of course, have been a standard source of information ever since their first publication. But their usefulness is greatly enhanced when the maps are collated with the memoirs, prepared at much the same time, now in the process of publication in full by the Institute of Irish Studies at the Queen's University of Belfast. Twelve volumes for County Antrim have appeared to date. There are still a number of volumes to appear; the material they will contain is available on computer print-out in the Public Record Office, and has been made use of in this book; but references are unavoidably incomplete when they relate to parishes as yet unpublished.

A number of scholars have already made use of the unpublished memoirs, but only a very few (notably the industrial archaeologist, Fred Hamond) have made extensive use of the almost contemporary manuscript Valuation books calendared as 1B in the Public Record Office.[9] They are not easy to work with; unless the researcher knows beforehand the parish and townland, and the name of the occupier, of the building whose description he seeks, he may be forced to retire defeated. Their system of categorisation is highly confusing, and does not seem to have been consistently applied. Some volumes, and some of the key-numbered maps, are missing, as are (quite often) page numbers and exact dates. Nevertheless, I believe that, by collating information derived from the first valuation with information derived from the Ordnance Survey maps and memoirs, I have been able to assemble a considerable volume of information not previously known even to specialists in the field.

The later, so-called "Griffith" valuation of 1859-60, calendared in the Public Record Office as 2B, and the still later series running on into the 1930s, calendared as 12B, have also provided much invaluable information. But it should be remarked that the Valuation books are more helpful for large houses, less helpful for cottages, shops, or modest terrace houses in towns, or villages, unless independent evidence of identification exists.

During the interval between the valuations of 1830 and of 1860, a number of useful books appeared; in particular, Samuel Lewis's two-volume Topographical Dictionary of Ireland (in editions of 1837, 1838, and 1847) and the three-volume Parliamentary Gazetteer of Ireland, published in 1845-6, both of which are generally informative about certain kinds of buildings - especially churches and glebe-houses, since the information was largely collected from the clergy - and reliable. Dr J A Pilson's Annals of the County Antrim, annexed to his History of Belfast published in 1847, are also useful.

I have of course made use also of family papers, cuttings and title deeds wherever I have come across them; and of the standard and local works listed in the Bibliography. I am afraid I may have missed a considerable number of local history leaflets and such-like publications of recent years: not all of these seem to find their way onto the libraries' shelves or into their catalogues, and it would be useful if their authors or publishers could make a practice of presenting copies to the Belfast Central, Queen's, and Linen Hall libraries, if no others.

As I have explained, this book is more of an anthology than an inventory, though I have tried to make each entry for an individual building as complete and free-standing as possible. For this reason, the references are collected together at the end of each entry, not relegated to separate footnotes at the end of the volume. I hope that it will constitute a useful groundwork upon which others can build: and that it will encourage those who are entrusted with the care of our historic buildings to intensify their own programmes of research and, especially, of publication.

Perhaps I may end on a personal note. The Brett family hailed from Lecale in County Down, until my infant forbear Charles Brett was brought by his widowed mother, in 1758, to Belfast; which has, since then, been the centre of gravity of my family. However, for nearly twenty years now I have lived in south Antrim. Neither of my grandfathers was born in the county. Both my grandmothers were born and brought up in houses described in this book: Harriet Agnes Brett, née Traill, in Ballylough (118); Josephine Mary Carter, née Richardson, in Springfield (95). Both sprang from extensive families, and the countryside is fairly liberally sprinkled with cousins of near or far degree. I have known parts of the county, especially the sea-coast, all my life; family holidays have been spent both on the north coast, and in the Glens. It has been a great pleasure systematically to explore the parts of the county less well known to me, and to discover quite unsuspected delights, as well as some disappointments: at the end of one lane, an enchanting house; at the end of another, an odious villa; at the end of one lane, a hospitable cup of tea; at the end of another, a pack of savage dogs. But the delights have outweighed, if not out-numbered, the disappointments.

In short, the compilation of this book has been enormously various and enjoyable: and I end by offering my thanks to all who have made it so. It will inevitably contain errors, for which I alone accept responsibility: I shall very much welcome corrections, in the hope that, if there should ever be another edition, it may prove possible to rectify them.

C E B B
31 December 1995

References: 1. UAHS Lists and Surveys, 'Lisburn', 1969; 'Antrim & Ballymena', 1969; 'West Antrim', 1970; 'Glens of Antrim', 1971; 'North Antrim', 1972; 'Rathlin', 1974; 'Carrickfergus', 1978. 2. W A McCutcheon, 'The industrial archaeology of Northern Ireland', 1980. 3. 'An archaeological survey of County Down', 1966. 4. P Robinson, in 'Perspective', July/August 1993, p 53. 5. A Gailey, 'Rural houses of the north of Ireland', 1984. 6. P Robinson, op cit. 7. H Glassie, 'Passing the time', 1982, p 390. 8. J H Andrews, 'Commentary' on facsimile edition of Lendrick's map published by Linen Hall Library, Belfast, in 1987. 9. T Parkhill, 'Valuation records in the Public Record Office of Northern Ireland', in 'Ulster local studies', XVI, 1994, pp 45 - 58.

ABBREVIATIONS

BNHPS	Belfast Natural History and Philosophical Society
BNL	*Belfast Newsletter*
CEMA	Council for the Encouragement of Music and the Arts
DPJ	*Dublin penny journal*
GJ	Grand Jury
HEARTH	Hearth Housing Association and Revolving Fund
HMNI	*Historic monuments of Northern Ireland*
HMSO	Her Majesty's Stationery Office
IB	*Irish builder*
IGS	Irish Georgian Society
JRSAI	*Journal of the Royal Society of Antiquaries of Ireland*
MB	Monuments and Buildings Record of Northern Ireland, Belfast
NIE	Northern Ireland Electricity
OS	Ordnance Survey
OSM	*Ordnance Survey memoirs*
PG	*Parliamentary gazetteer of Ireland*
PRONI	Public Record Office of Northern Ireland, Belfast
PSAMNI	*Preliminary survey of the ancient monuments of Northern Ireland*
QUB	Queen's University, Belfast
RCB	Representative Church Body of the Church of Ireland, Dublin
RHA	Royal Hibernian Academy, Dublin
RIA	Royal Irish Academy, Dublin
RIBA	Royal Institute of British Architects, London
RIAI	Royal Institution of the Architects of Ireland< Dublin
TCD	Trinity College, Dublin
TD	Lewis's *Topographical dictionary*
UAHS	Ulster Architectural Heritage Society
UJA	*Ulster journal of archaeology*
VAL	Valuation books

Throughout the text, figures appearing in parentheses
refer to the entry numbers for other buildings discussed

CHAPTER ONE

ANTIQUITIES,
FORTIFICATIONS AND RUINS

Reused holestone in Layde churchyard (13). Photograph: Michael O'Connell

1

ANTIQUITIES, FORTIFICATIONS AND RUINS

The county of Antrim is rich in archaeological material - that is, very roughly speaking, human artefacts or buildings of any period earlier than 1700 AD. There are at the time of writing 27 historic monuments in state care, 263 scheduled for protection but not in state care. Unlike buildings of later periods, excellent records of both classes are available in the Monuments and Buildings Record, Belfast. The foundation for this collection was laid between 1935 and 1940, when Estyn Evans and H C Lawlor, with a handful of colleagues on the Ancient Monuments Advisory Council, compiled the invaluable Preliminary Survey - often referred to as PSAMNI[1] - covering the whole of Northern Ireland. In County Antrim, they visited and described over 200 monuments. There are now marked-up maps, files and reports on some 5,000 sites, large and small, scheduled and unscheduled. But there is still, for County Antrim, no publication remotely comparable to the splendid Archaeological Survey of County Down[2], published thirty years ago in 1966.

I have selected twenty of these earlier buildings or monuments to serve as an introduction to the main part of this book. I have chosen examples which seem to me likely to appeal directly to the eye and the imagination. Archaeological sites can be extraordinarily baffling, even boring, for the uninitiated. One of the earliest dwelling sites ever uncovered in Ireland has recently come to light in Ballygally: but there is extraordinarily little to show for it. Concavities and voids, post-holes, souterrains and adits, seem always less interesting than solid convex structures, be they dolmens, standing stones or fortifications. The paucity of evidence renders many antiquities less striking and dramatic than later works. I recall Estyn Evans asking me why I found prehistory less interesting than history. My reply was, through an absence of imaginative powers: as a short-sighted person afflicted with ingrowing toenails, I was and am unable to conceive of life before the invention of spectacles and nail-scissors. I suspect I am not alone in this deficiency.

I have confined myself, therefore, to a handful of the most visible of prehistoric, early Christian and medieval antiquities. Even the most dramatic monuments of these early periods are enigmatic enough; there remains uncertainty as to the exact use of round towers, and as to the debatable boundary-lines between raths, cashels, crannogs, mottes, and their respective landlords and tenants.

It is only with the arrival of the Normans that we reach slightly firmer ground, and written records. Carrickfergus Castle (15) is the first building in the county to be reasonably well documented. It is also much easier than most of its predecessors to admire and enjoy. Dunluce Castle (18) is equally approachable: though I suspect that many visitors associate both with medieval jousting, feasting, and knights in armour; not wholly inappropriate to the keep at Carrickfergus, but historically out of place at the much later Dunluce. Whether the present mode of displaying these monuments assists or impedes the imagination is a matter for the individual.

Apart from Ballygally Castle (20), which could just as well be in Scotland as in Ireland, and the uninteresting stumps at Olderfleet and Whitehead, Antrim lacks the tower-houses which are so common in County Down and in several other Irish counties. Although it is possible that vestiges of some early settlers' houses lurk beneath thatch or corrugated iron, I know of none; nor do I know of any cruck dwelling in the county, save a tiny example, roofed in corrugated iron, at Trummery, Magheragall. Antrim is not, and probably never has been, well-wooded; moreover, it is of all the Ulster counties the one where Scottish influence has been strongest, English influence weakest. But wood and wattle structures there must once have been. As my sardonic great-uncle Thomas L'Estrange wrote over a century ago to his friend George Benn, the historian of Belfast: "When Henry the Second of England spent his Christmas in Dublin in AD 1172, there was not any stone house in which to receive him. He passed the time of his dismal visit in a pavilion constructed of 'smooth wattles'. The Irish of that time had not any stone houses, any coined money - written literature - navigation - foreign trade - nor (I suspect) agriculture."[3] So much for the mere Irish: but then my uncle was a Westmeath man of Norman ancestry.

References: 1. 'PSAMNI', 1940. 2. 'Archaeological survey of Down', 1966. 3. Letter of 18 March, 1874, D 3113/7/72 in Benn papers, PRONI.

The Holestone, Doagh

1. The Holestone is just what it says it is: a stone with a hole through it. It could be by Barbara Hepworth, but is not. The relevant questions are: who made the hole? when? why? But nobody to date has propounded a satisfactory answer to any of them. All we can say for sure is, it has stood where it stands for quite a long time.

It is a large slab of whinstone, set up on end, "about 5 ft high, 6 ft 8 ins in circumference at base, 10 ins thick, pierced with a smooth-sided hole ...... [which] will permit the passage of the hand of a woman but not that of the average man" (Dr Chart, in PSAMNI). Girvan hazards the guess that it is "probably of the Bronze Age", upon what evidence he does not say. O'Laverty prognosticated over a century ago - "A quarry, which is being worked on the rocky eminence on which stands the Holestone, it is to be feared will, at no distant day, cause its destruction"; but this has not yet occurred. Evidently the quarrymen stayed their hands, leaving the Holestone curiously isolated on top of a near-circular platform of stone, encircled with whins, on a hill-top with a splendid view all round. Well worth the scramble.

As to its use, M'Skimin says "it is still deemed a place consecrated to the meeting of lovers; and when they join hands through the stone, the pledge of love and troths there given is sacred". O'Laverty asserts that, according to the Book of Ballymote, "such stones were at times used for the purpose of chaining to them culprits about to be put to death". He adds that holestones occur frequently in early Christian graveyards which had previously been used for pagan interments: several souterrains have been found in the vicinity.

H C Lawlor, in his younger days, waxed positively romantic about this monument. Having established that a souterrain had been discovered nearby in 1929; and that

souterrains could confidently be dated to the 4th century AD; he observed: "A close intimacy with the district of which the Holestone is the approximate centre ... reveals the fact that the country is in some districts practically honeycombed with these underground dwellings; but nowhere so much as in the immediate area surrounding Doagh ... Why did their builders not utilise the Holestone? Within a couple of hundred yards of it on either side are two souterrains with a hundred or more of these long stones used in the roofs. Here was a suitable stone immediately to hand, and yet they would not disturb it? ... To this day" - (1930) - "through all the changes of race and peoples that have occurred in County Antrim, the tradition that the Holestone is a betrothal, if not a marriage, token, remains unbroken, and couples from all the district round still plight their troths by clasping their fingers through the ring or hole in this stone. Here, then, appears the probability that the souterrain builders refrained from using the Holestone, because it was sacred in their pagan religion, if not actually a deity."

M'Skimin tells a diverting tale of a man whose hand got stuck in the hole, who was threatened with liberation by gunpowder, but was rescued, despite the swelling of his wrist, by the application of vinegar: an event said to have occurred in 1802.

Photograph: Michael O'Connell.
Situation: td, Holestone; Parish, Kilbride; District Council, Antrim; Grid ref. J 242 906.
References: Scheduled monument, not in state care. S M'Skimin, in DPJ, 1830, p 340; J Boyle, OSM, 1836-9, J Bleakly, 1838, J R Ward, 1835, Antrim, XI, pp 138, 147, 154, 156; O'Laverty, 'Down and Connor', III, 1884, p 189; H C Lawlor, in 'Irish naturalists' journal', September 1930, p 105; PSAMNI, 1940, p 38; Cox, 'Kilbride', 1959, p 64; Girvan, 'West Antrim', UAHS, 1970, pp 20, 31.

Mount Druid Megalith, Ballintoy

2. Above and behind Mount Druid house, Ballintoy (100) to which it lends its name, on a knoll, looking out and down over White Park Bay, a group of basalt stones which may be a passage tomb.

"This altar is situated about the middle of an enclosure approaching to circular shape and seeming to have stood 37 feet in diameter, and formed by a circle of moderate-sized stones set round in the ground ... The altar is a large stone approaching to a triangle in shape. It measures 7 and a half feet long on the west side, 6 feet on the east, and 5 and a half on the south side" (Fagan, 1838). Excavated in 1939 by John Mogey, one of Estyn Evans's star pupils, the result written up by him in the Ulster Journal of Archaeology. An impressive site.

Photograph: R J Welch, Ulster Museum W01/08/12. Wood engraving: DPJ, 1833-4, p 381.

Situation: td, Magheraboy; Parish, Ballintoy; District Council, Moyle; Grid ref. D 037 438.

References: Scheduled monument, not in state care. DPJ, 1833-4, p 381; T Fagan, OSM, 1838, Antrim, IX, p 26; O'Laverty, 'Down and Connor', IV, 1887, p 334; PSAMNI, 1940, p 5; J Mogey, in UJA, 3rd series, 1941, pp 49-56.

Dolmen and Druid's Cottage, Ballylumford

3. The dolmen, and the cottage orné before whose front door it stands at the roadside so unexpectedly, are as unlike each other, yet go together as well, as melon and Parma ham. The 'dolmen' or 'cromlech' appears to be a small megalithic single-chambered portal tomb (or possibly what remains of a passage grave), with a well-balanced and well-shaped cap-stone. The cottage appears to be of around 1840, stuccoed and painted yellow, with strong coved eaves; quoins, doorcase and dripstones picked out in dark red. It is one-and-a-half-storey, five-bay, to the front, with an attic window in the central peak above the doorcase; but is in fact a considerably larger house than it looks, with a two-storey return extending down the sloping ground at the rear. It does not figure in the woodcut or Samuel M'Skimin's description of the 'Druid Altar' in the Dublin Penny Journal of December 1832, but that is not altogether conclusive evidence, for the artist's viewpoint is looking towards Larne. The listers say the cottage is 20th century, but this is not credible, the more so as it appears, just as now, in a woodcut of 1883: and Mr Gray says, in the accompanying text, "a cottage has been built adjoining the cromlech, so that the latter stands within a few yards of the front windows - a circumstance that has, doubtless, served to preserve the monument up to the present".

It is a pity that the person who chose, at whatever date, to site his house where he did should not be known: though the Ordnance Survey Memoir of 1839 does say, "this is the most remarkable relic of antiquity in this district: it is situated on the farm of Thomas McIlwain and at the south end of his house"; and Egerton, in 1906, says "previous to the erection of this house, the spot which the monument occupies was the garden of the cottage - the

old residence". Alternatively, as a member of the Historic Buildings Council is popularly supposed to have remarked to a colleague on the Historic Monuments Council, "What a silly place to put a dolmen!" All very droll and delightful.

Photograph: Michael O'Connell. (See also colour-plate XIa). Wood engraving: DPJ, 1832-3, p 209.

Situation: 91, Ballylumford Road, Islandmagee; td, Ballycronan Mor; Parish, Islandmagee; District Council, Larne; Grid ref: D 431 016.

References: Dolmen, scheduled monument in state care; cottage, listed B1. DPJ, 1832, p 209; J Bleakly, OSM, 1839, Antrim, III, p 100; W Gray, in JRSAI, XVI, 1883-4; Borlase, 'Dolmens of Ireland', I, 1897, pp 269-270; Egerton and Bigger, 'Guide for tourists', 1906, p 20; Donaldson, 'Islandmagee', 1927, p 17; PSAMNI, 1940, p 35; HMNI, 1983, p 71.

Antrim Round Tower

that lie at some distance from the town" (Dubourdieu). The conical roof was repaired, and parts of the walls re-pointed, in 1819 by Mr Clark, owner of the adjacent mansion. Its site is most attractive, amidst immemorial lawns, rooks, and trees.

The Rev. Hamilton appositely wrote in 1784, "The round towers of Ireland are alone sufficient to show, that there were public monuments in Ireland before the arrival of the English, which were original in their kind, and not inelegant in their structure." Received opinion, after years of debate, seems to have settled down to the view that round towers served a dual purpose as bell-towers and as places of refuge. Both propositions strain credulity. Why build a 90-foot belfry just to shake a hand-bell out of an upper window? There is little evidence for any better class of bell. Why make a place of refuge so prominent that it can be seen for miles? Why have wooden, not stone, floors; wooden, not stone, stairs; wooden, not metal-faced, doors; when the application of fire would turn the whole place into a roaring chimney? But I have no better explanation to offer.

I have heard an irreverent, and perhaps biased, theory that some early monks asked Saint Patrick to design them a well that would provide a never-failing supply of holy water. He drew them a set of plans accordingly. However, being unfortunately illiterate, the monks read the plans upside-down; and the round towers of Ireland are the result. The same thought, in more poetic form, occurred also to Tim Robinson: writing of the stump of a round tower on Aran, he describes its investigation as "a matter of sounding the great well-shaft its absence sinks into the sky."

Samuel M'Skimin, writing in 1833, says "Tradition ascribes the erection of this Tower, as well as others in the north of Ireland, to the celebrated architect 'Gobban Saer', or 'Gobban the Builder'", and adds, helpfully, "who is believed, in this part of the country, to have been a woman". The Goban is recorded also to have brewed an ale which kept all who partook thereof from illness and death.

George Petrie, in 1845, also roundly ascribes this very tower at Antrim to "the celebrated architect, Goban, or, as he is popularly called, Goban Saer, who flourished early in the seventh century". He adds: "I have already alluded to the historical evidences which prove that the Goban Saer was no imaginary creation ...... it would appear from a very ancient authority, namely, the Dinnsenchus, preserved in the Books of Lecan and Ballymote, that he was the son of a skilful artisan in wood, if not in stone also; and that this artisan was, if not a foreigner, at least very probably of foreign extraction, and that the Goban himself was probably born at Turvy, on the northern coast of the County of Dublin ......" Petrie and M'Skimin today stand discredited amongst serious archaeologists; can the latter be sure that they will fare better with posterity?

4. A very fine Irish round tower; the only others in the county are the stumps at Armoy and on Ram's Island in Lough Neagh. HMNI says, defensively, "not closely datable but a 10th or 11th century date seems likely"; Dr Craig agrees. The tower is all that survives of an extensive monastic site, possibly connected with St Comgall; Dr Hamlin remarks that, when Bangor Abbey was plundered by the Vikings in 824, his relics were brought here. But this Abbey, too, was plundered in 1018, 1147, and 1164.

The literature on the tower is very extensive, and on occasions pretty speculative. It is 93 feet high; it has its doorway (4 feet high and 2 feet wide) at a height of 7 feet 6 inches from the present ground level; a carved cross above the lintel; and eight windows. Although it now has no floors or stairs, there must originally have been some crude system of ladders and landings. The walls have not the smooth, geometrical sophistication of later masonry: the contrast with the nineteenth century towers at Jordanstown (65) and Larne (265) is instructive. "The stones used in the building are of coarse grained basalt, and have been taken from a quarry on the high grounds,

Photograph: Michael O'Connell.
Situation: In grounds of Steeple House, Steeple Road; td, Parkhall; Parish, Antrim; District Council, Antrim; Grid ref. J 155 876.
References: Scheduled monument in state care. Hamilton, 'Antrim', 1784, p 43; Dubourdieu, 'Antrim' 1812, p 599; S M'Skimin, in DPJ, 1833, p 18; Petrie, 'Ecclesiastical architecture of Ireland', 1845, pp 382, 401; Reeves, 'Ecclesiastical antiquities', 1847, p 63; J Boyle, OSM, 1838, Antrim, XI, pp 30-32 (also excellent illustrations); UJA, 1st series, IV, 1856, p 131; O'Laverty, 'Down and Connor', III, 1884, p 249; PSAMNI, 1940, p 42; A E Hamlin, PhD thesis, 1976, in MBR; Craig, 'Architecture of Ireland', 1982, p 31; HMNI, 1983, p 71; Robinson, 'Stones of Aran', 1995, p 54.

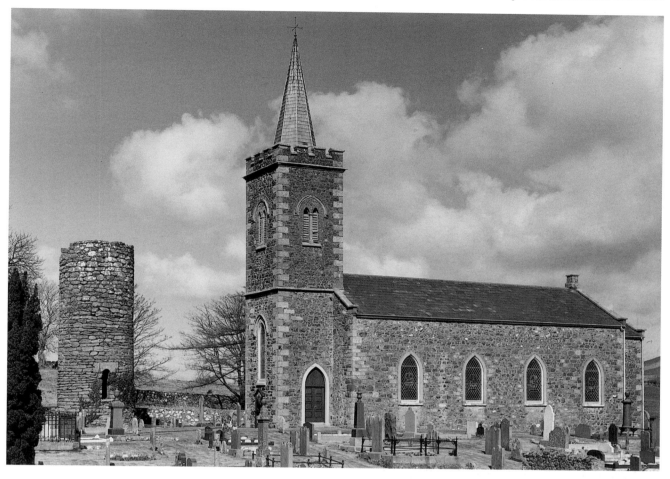

Armoy Round Tower

5. Neither the topless stump of the probably 10th-century round tower, nor the very plain little parish church, the latter dedicated to St Patrick, is of much interest by itself; but their juxtaposition is charming.

In 1838, the stump had some kind of roof, and housed the bell. "An attempt was made to pull the whole down and use the stone for building the Glebe House. This happened about the year 1805 but it was resisted by the parishioners and the monument consequently preserved. It is now repaired in every part and used as a belfry for the church. Its height is greatly diminished by the accumulation of the graves ... the original floor is 6 feet below the surface of the ground. The stones of the wall are all large, grouted, and carefully fitted into one another ... Each stone has been chiselled wherever necessary to suit the curve of the circle and great numbers completely so from end to end ... Nowhere does the curve of the circle meet with any interruption" (Stokes). "The door is semi-circular headed, having the arch cut out of one block and ornamented with an architrave also cut on the same lintel-stone, it follows the curve of the arch" (O'Laverty). "Lower masonry neatly fitted, long, narrow, slabs of schist with some spalls, dressed to curve" (Hamlin).

"The church, which stands on an eminence and within a few feet of an old round tower, is a very plain edifice in good order and comfortably fitted internally. It is 60 feet long by 22 feet wide and would accommodate 300 persons. It was rebuilt in 1820" (Boyle). The square black-stone tower, added in 1846, when the chancel was added and the church lengthened by a bay, carries a rather squat octagonal spire; the windows in the west wall of the tower and the louvred belfry openings are dressed in old brick, whereas the east window of 1963 is dressed in uncomfortably modern brick. The vestry was added in 1869. The nave is of four bays.

The graveyard contains many good tombstones much older than the church; the gates, and relationship to the rectory, are nicely judged; but alas, the old glebe-house of 1805 has been demolished and a bungalow substituted. It must have been a sociable arrangement when the rector of Armoy lived here, and the rector of Loughguile in Turnarobert House, a stone's throw away. When the foundations of the tower were excavated by Mr Getty in 1843, those present included the Rev. Mr Harvey of Turnarobert, and Mr Edward Benn of Glenravel. Lavens Ewart says "there is a legend that Saint Patrick himself preached in Armoy church, which is not improbable, as he is said to have baptised Aengus MacNissi, who died in 513 and was the first Bishop of Connor."

Photograph: Michael O'Connell.
Situation: Glenshesk Road, Armoy. td, Turnarobert; Parish, Armoy; District Council, Moyle; Grid ref. D 079 333.
References: Round tower, scheduled monument, not in state care. Church, Listed B. J Boyle, OSM, 1835, and J Stokes, 1838, Antrim, IX, pp 4, 6; J Getty, in UJA, 1st series, IV, 1856; O'Laverty, 'Down and Connor', IV, 1887, p 449; S R Kirker, in JRSAI, XXIX 1889; H C Lawlor, in PSAMNI, 1940, p 15; Ewart, 'Down & Connor & Dromore', 1886, p 60; Girvan, 'North Antrim', UAHS, 1973, p 37; A E Hamlin, PhD thesis, in MBR, 1976, HMNI, 1983, p 149; M'Cahan, 'Local histories', 1988.

Altagore Cashel, Cushendun

6. The only cashel, or dry-stone fort, in the county; very dramatic when seen from the hill-top beyond the Torna-mona Burn in the slanting light of morning or evening. The circular enclosure has an internal diameter of fifty feet, and walls ten feet thick - compare the far better known Grianan of Aileach in Donegal, with an internal diameter of seventy-seven feet and walls 13 feet thick, not so very much larger. The walls are still, in places, six to ten feet high. Lieutenant Robe, writing in 1831, says "Circular, the interior being 66 feet in diameter. The wall is about eight feet high, built of large loose stones and without mortar, and about 20 feet thick". Inside, there is a long curving wall chamber or souterrain; and projecting stones built into the wall to provide steps. In the complete absence of literary references, it is as hard to date as the comparable dry-stone forts at Staigue, Dun Aenghus and the Grianan: possibly early iron age? Professor Alcock of Glasgow has suggested features in common with the Scottish dun at Castle Haven, Kircudbright.

The received wisdom seems to be that this is merely a variant on the usual form of rath. George Petrie, commenting on J Stokes's Memoir on Ancient Topography for the parish of Billy, asserts roundly "By the word cashel, all over Ireland, a stone fort is understood, in opposition to a rath, which is of earth. The dun is sometimes of the one and sometimes of the other, and fragments of both." It seems odd that dry-stone-wall enclosures of this kind are so unusual. Certainly, Lieutenant Robe was right in describing it as "very singular".

Photographs: W A Green, Ulster Folk Museum WAG 1537; Michael O'Connell.
Situation: To the east of the Tor road, close to Tornamona bridge; td, Tornamoney; Parish, Culfeightrin; District Council, Moyle; Grid ref. D 249 349.
References: Scheduled monument, not in state care. T C Robe, OSM, 1831, Antrim, IX, p 40; G Petrie, OSM, Billy, 1838, Antrim, V, p 55; PSAMNI, 1940, p 16; notes in MBR.

Crannog, Fair Head

7. One of the best-preserved crannogs in Ireland, and on an enchanting site, in the middle of Lough na Cranagh: happily, in the ownership of the National Trust. Lawlor's crisp description is unbeatable: "Oval in shape, approximately 120 by 90 feet. Faced towards the lake by a dry-built revetment rising 5 to 7 feet above the water level. It has escaped the fate of others in positions isolated, and is practically free from vegetation, except for two stunted and weather-beaten trees. It has never been satisfactorily examined, and no estimate of its period can be given" (1940).

Thomas Fagan, however, was less inhibited. On 3rd January 1839, he wrote: "About the centre of this lake stands an island approaching to circular shape and said to contain about half a rood of ground and composed chiefly of rocky substance, but at some former period enclosed round the edge by a stone wall mixed with clay or other soil. The surface of the rocky substance composing the island is also said to have been strewed over to some depth with clay which, on the whole, rendered it a handsome pleasure ground ... The whole erections are said to have been instituted by a McDonnell, one of the Scotch chieftains who some centuries past was proprietor of a large tract of the grounds along the Fair Head, where he also had his place of abode.

However, at a subsequent period, and during the existence of the Penal Code, this once island of pleasure was occasionally occupied as a seat of Roman Catholic worship, till at length a boat which was conveying the clergy and congregation from the mainland was upset with a large number who were on board and consequently perished in the bowels of the lake ... A subsequent disaster by burning stripped the whole island of its fleury and verdant garb, and also reduced the parapet from its original size

and appearance, as the fire took away the dry soil intervening between the stones. Yet its ruins, situated in the middle of a large and handsome sheet of water, contribute much to the interesting scenery along the Fair Head."

Brian Williams, in a report of 1994 in the MBR, remarks that the crannog has three possible landing places, one certainly an original feature, an indent built into the perimeter wall; also a notch capable of providing some shelter for a moored boat.

Photographs: Michael O'Connell; Jim McCall.
Situation: In the middle of Lough na Cranagh, north-west of the Fair Head car park; td, Cross; Parish, Culfeightrin; District Council, Moyle; Grid ref. D 179 428.
References: Scheduled monument, not in state care. T Fagan, OSM, 1839, Antrim, IX, p 81; H C Lawlor, in PSAMNI, 1940, p 8; Brett, 'Glens', UAHS, 1971, p 54; HMNI, 1983, p 149; Gallagher and Rogers, 'Castle, coast and cottage', 1986, p 46; M'Cahan, 'Local histories', 1988; B Williams, report, 1994, in MBR.

Dundermot Motte, Glarryford

8. "A splendid motte with perfect surrounding trench, no doubt much filled up by centuries of falling leaves from surrounding trees. It is 525 feet in circumference, 40 feet in height with flat circular top 70 feet in diameter. It will thus be seen that the gradient of the sides is practically 12 in 14. The bailey, apparently large and formidable, existed in 1814 when Shaw Mason wrote. The measurements there given are subject to error". So enthused the usually unemotional H C Lawlor in 1940; he was quite right, and the site remains quite unspoiled. Shaw Mason's correspondent, the Rev. William Mayne, found the place enigmatic. "On the top it is surrounded by a very deep foss; another foss is cut from that one, towards the west, so far as the declivity extends, which lands it at the low ground, constantly inundated in time of flood from the Main ... It does not appear that it had any defence but by water; nor during the time it was inundated, does it appear how any person got either in or out of it ..." Reeves deduced that this was the Fort of Dermot, but no other evidence as to its builder seems to have survived. J Stokes of the Ordnance Survey remarks, "No ancient articles have been found in it ... It is most remarkable for its name, which seems to have given a designation not only to the townland but to the district also." Samuel Lewis says in 1837 that, "towards the bridge over the Ravel, two parallel branches from the fosse inclose another area of a quadrangular form, now called "the Parade"."

The appearance of the motte is much enhanced by its surroundings - the dome of mature trees surmounting the mound, which mark it out from afar; the curling course of the Clogh river, close to its junction with the river Main; and the graceful arch and handsome stonework of Glarryford bridge: all quite close to, but for the most part unnoticed by, travellers on the main road north from Ballymena to Ballycastle.

Photograph: Michael O'Connell.
Situation: North of the road from Glarryford to Clogh; td, Dundermot; Parish, Grange of Dundermot; District Council, Ballymena; Grid ref. D 061 133.
References: Scheduled monument, not in state care. Mason, 'Statistical account', 1814, I, p 250; J Stokes, OSM, 1835, Antrim, IV, p 33; Lewis, TD, 1837, I, p 572; Reeves, 'Ecclesiastical antiquities', 1847, p 73; O'Laverty, 'Down and Connor', IV, 1887, p 45; PSAMNI, 1940, p 24; notes in MBR.

Derrykillultagh Rath, Glenavy

9. An unusually attractive large rath, with a single low circular stone-faced bank, "query: a counter-scarped rath?", some fifty yards in diameter, enclosing a large open area; and growing from the bank itself, a ring of some sixty mature and semi-mature trees, mostly beeches: all set in a broad pasture-field, the farm buildings concealed amidst more trees some distance to the east.

There is perhaps little to distinguish this from hundreds of similar raths in the county, but the circlet of trees is so handsomely shaped that it makes a striking impression on the passer by. And yet, it is not mentioned in the Ordnance Survey Memoirs; nor in PSAMNI; nor in HMNI; nor in Mallory and McNeill.

Photograph: Michael O'Connell.
Situation: To north-west of Lisburn Road, Glenavy; td, Derrykillultagh; Parish, Ballinderry; District Council, Lisburn; Grid ref. J 183 702.
References: Not scheduled, not in state care: site 63.22. Field record of 1978 in MBR.

Ballywalter Motte, Doagh

10 (left). A striking small fortification, plainly man-made, almost certainly Norman, probably of about 1200; not large enough for occupation save during a brief emergency. On a strategic ridge-top site, overlooking the Six Mile Water valley; on the farm formerly owned by the Shaw family, and marked on the 25" map as "Shaw's Fort". "Circular earthen mound with steep scarp. Much eroded at base and just below the top, which is generally flat, but much disturbed" (Williams). A six-foot-wide ditch encloses the site. Traces of post-holes are said to have been found. The height is over 15 feet, the diameter of the base between 60 and 90 feet and of the summit around 40 feet. This is just about the average size for a Norman motte in Ulster. "There was an old church and graveyard on the farm of Mr George Shaw, near the fort or mound near his house, in which a quantity of human bones was discovered . . . with old coins of silver . . . with old brass spurs and old brass stirrup irons" (Bleakly).

In 1213 Pope Innocent III confirmed the Knights Hospitallers in possession of the Terra Walter de Logan; and in 1333 Ralph Logan held "Waltirtown" in knight's fee from the estate of William de Burgo, late Earl of Ulster. There is no evidence of a bailey, but there was probably some sort of hall on the ridge nearby. Dr McNeill considers this very probably a Norman "manorial centre" and the ecclesiastical ownership may be significant. It may or may not be associated with the group of six raths nearby in the townlands of Ballypalady and Ballyhartfield. In his memoir of the nearby parish of Ballylinny, Boyle remarks, under the heading "Ancient Topography", that "A village is said to have stood in the townland of Ballyhone, as some of the walls still remain standing. This village is said to have extended to Shaw's Fort in Ballywalter."

Photograph: Michael O'Connell.
Situation: South of road from Templepatrick to Larne; td, and Parish, Grange of Ballywalter; District Council, Newtownabbey; Grid ref. J 265 883.
References: Scheduled monument, not in state care. Reeves, 'Ecclesiastical antiquities', p 67; Inquisition of 4 November 1333; J Bleakly, OSM, 1838, Antrim, I, p 27, and J Boyle, 1838, Antrim, XII, p 26; Field record, MBR, by B Williams, September 1978. For Ballypalady raths, see PSAMNI, 1940, p 46; and D Waterman in UJA, 3rd series, XXXV, 1972, pp 29-36.

The Mound, Antrim

11. In 1838, Boyle wrote "Close to the north side of the castle is a mount 37 feet high and 51 yards in diameter at the base and 12 at the summit. It seems to be one of the old Danish mounds commonly met with in the country". Almost certainly a conversion of a Norman motte into a garden mound in the manner fashionable in the late 17th century: though in 1978 Brian Williams of the Archaeological Survey recorded his opinion that it was originally constructed as a landscape feature. The motte was probably the "Castle of Antrim" for which the Irish Pipe Roll of King John recorded, in 1211, wages of £21.6.8 for two knights, 12 armed archers, and six foot-soldiers, with a similar sum for their victuals. Later the site of a specially constructed oak armchair, placed there by the first Lord Massereene; of a long gun, "Roaring Tatty", last fired at the battle of Antrim in 1798; then of a flag-pole; all at the top of a clock-wise spiral path flanked by clipped yew hedges. Along with the canals, round pond, parterres and wilderness, it is at present undergoing energetic restoration after years of neglect.

If the mound was indeed there before the castle, it is remarkable that the latter was built (in 1613) so close to it, since the mound must have greatly over-shadowed it, and deprived the rooms on the north side of all privacy: though the principal rooms looked south over the river. "The summit of the mount, which overlooks the loftiest turret of the Castle, is perfectly level, and planted round the edges. From thence a charming view is had of the terrace gardens, the town beneath, and round tower beyond; the park, the hills of Muckamore, the hospitable house of the Venerable Chaine, the ruins of Shane's Castle, Cranfield Point, and the hills of Feeva" (O'Neill, 1860).

Rebuilt in 1663 with corner towers and a row of gables, incorporating a great Jacobean mannerist doorway (now dismantled and in store), the castle was enlarged and castellated about 1813: Bence-Jones says, "as a solid 3 storey Georgian Gothic castellated mansion, designed by John Bowden, of Dublin, faced in Roman cement of a pleasant orange colour". I know of no evidence for the attribution to Bowden, which seems unlikely, and the "Roman cement", "coloured to imitate the ancient stile of building", was not added until 1823. Nicely described in 1953 by that distinguished stylist, T F O Rippingham: "the front of the house now appears as a somewhat repellent facade in the pseudo-gothic style of 1813, done in stucco over the original brickwork, but incorporating a very interesting collection of stones salvaged from earlier periods ... starting at the top, there is a bust of Charles I (hardly earlier than 1661); a panel of Arms (Massereene with a female hatchment); a cartouche (with an inscription); an overdoor (in which the cornice does not fit the console); a carved lintel (with mermaids most excellently sculpted); and a doorway (in which the jambs do not fit the enclosing pilasters) ... the work of an antiquary or dilettante, not of an architect". The castle was gutted by fire in 1922 (see page 71). The park was colonised by Americans and Belgians during the second World War, leaving the bases of many Nissen huts to be removed. The walls of the castle, still standing until 1970, were demolished as dangerous by the Antrim and Ballymena Development Commission in that year. A slim octagonal turret was added in 1887, and now alone survives, looking more than a little absurd. It will look even odder if the Antrim Borough Council carries out its threat to build new Council offices beside it. In the meanwhile, the Council's extensive restoration of the gardens and of the mound or motte, if motte it be, is warmly to be welcomed.

Church and St Colman's Well, Cranfield

12. A place of great antiquity, and a numinous one; in a way, an antiphon to Layde (13).

The ruins of the simple stone chapel, probably 13th century, stand amidst tomb-stones of lesser, but considerable, antiquity, on a knoll looking out over the broad expanse of Lough Neagh. The harbour and car-park below are screened by thorn hedges; nearby, the holy well in a rocky cleft of the bank is likewise overhung by thorn trees fluttering with votive rags. "The architecture is very rude. None of the stones are hewn except the doorway and corner stones. They were placed in the wall in the same form as when lifted from the shore . . . The windows are lined and arched with a kind of hard and large square brick, much closer in the grain than those used in the present day" (Hannyngton, 1835).

Little is known by way of hard fact: the church was recorded under the name of Crewill in the Taxation of 1291, but described as "decayed" by 1662, following the departure of the first recorded preaching-minister, the unfortunately-named Thomas Cowturd. The well had been associated both with St Colman and with St Olcan, and had been a place of pilgrimage for many years for those living around the Lough, particularly in May and June. "It is fine spring water and produces crystals. The country people assemble and take them out on May morning. They believe them to grow only on May Eve. These they take to America: their tradition is that no ship can be wrecked in which they are" (Hannyngton). However, around 1828, the clergy felt obliged to put an end to the pilgrimage because it had turned into a scene of riot and drunkenness. Since 1978, the tradition has been revived in the somewhat different form of an open-air Mass, incorporating a blessing of the boats of the fishermen. The accounts of church and well, and their respective associations, by O'Laverty (in 1884) and by Patrick O'Kane (in 1991) are both rewarding.

Photograph: Michael O'Connell.
Situation: On the shore of Lough Neagh, south of the road from Randalstown to Toome; td, Parish, Cranfield; District Council, Antrim; Grid ref. J 055 853.
References: Scheduled monument in state care. T C Hannyngton, OSM, 1835, Antrim, VI, p 32; O'Laverty, 'Down and Connor', III, 1884, p 316; F J Bigger and W J Fennell, in UJA, 2nd series, IV, 1898, p 48; PSAMNI, 1940, p 42; Girvan, 'West Antrim', UAHS, 1970, p 22; O'Kane, 'Sweet Drummaul', 1991, pp 13, 21.

◁

Photograph: W A Green, Ulster Folk Museum WAG 971.
Situation: In Castle Gardens, Antrim; td, Parish, District Council, Antrim; Grid ref. J 146 867.
References: Scheduled monument, not in state care. Irish Pipe Roll, 1211-12, cited in 1941 supplement to UJA, p 54; estimate, 16 June 1823, T 2519/4/2024, in PRONI; J Boyle, OSM, 1838, Antrim, XI, pp 12, 36; O'Neill, 'Antrim Castle', 1860, p 31; memorandum by T F O Rippingham of 18 November 1953 in MBR; Girvan, 'Antrim and Ballymena', UAHS, 1969, pp 6, 7; Bence-Jones, 'Burke's guide', 1978, p 6; Smyth, 'Antrim', 1984, pp 14, 15.

Layde Church and Churchyard, Cushendall

13. The former Parish Church, referred to in 1288 as "Ecclesia de Leyde", by 1622 in ruins. Richard Dobbs, in 1683, writes of "Coshandall ... the church of Layd harde by without roofe, seemes to have been a handsome country church with a square steeple aboute 30 foot high, stands in a bottome near the sea, noe howse within a quarter of a mile; this pleasant dry ground under the mountaynes". Rebuilt about 1696, the date inscribed on a stone in the east wall; in use until 1790; by 1800, and ever since, in ruins again. Reeves says "A stone which had been in the east wall bears the date 1696; but this must refer to the repair or restoration of the church in that year, as the general character of the building, and the fact that the graves outside are nearly five feet higher than the floor inside, indicate a much earlier date." "It is situated in a site of

great beauty, in a little valley overlooking the sea, and is surrounded by vaults and headstones of different dates; many are to members of the McDonnell family, some of the 17th century. A most peaceful and evocative place" (Brett). Lieutenant Chaytor, writing in 1832, says "a ruin ... which is called the Old Church, around which is situated the chief burial ground of the parish ... From a stone lately found in this ruin it appears to have been either built or rebuilt in the year 1638. Divine service was performed in it until 45 years ago." Whether there were really two rebuildings in 1638 and 1696 is unclear.

The inscriptions have been painstakingly recorded, and published, by the excellent Glens of Antrim Historical Society. The most curious tomb is the first to meet the eye by the gate, a kind of small holestone, perhaps derived from the form of an ancient High Cross, evidently re-used in 1861 to mark the grave of Frank McDonnell of Legg.

Lieutenant Chaytor adds the delightful information: "This parish is said by tradition to have derived its name from a Scottish lady called Lydia, who eloped with a young man and landed on a rock in the townland of Layd, from which that townland, as well as the parish, takes its name. From this she proceeded to Knocklayd, to which place she was pursued and overtaken, hence the name of that mountain."

Photographs: Michael O'Connell.
Situation: East of the coast road from Cushendall to Cushendun; td, Glebe; Parish, Layde; District Council, Moyle; Grid ref. D 245 289.
References: Scheduled monument in state care. R Dobbs, D 162/6 in PRONI; Reeves, 'Ecclesiastical antiquities', pp 82, 298; J Chaytor, OSM, 1832, Antrim, IV, p 41; F J Bigger and W J Fennell, in UJA, 2nd series, V, 1899, pp 35-46; S D'Arcy, in JRSAI, LX, 1930, pp 192-3; PSAMNI, 1941, p 17; Brett, 'Glens', UAHS, 1971, p 38; McCallin and Delargy, 'Survey of Layde graveyard', [1992].

Bonamargy Friary, Ballycastle

14. The ruins of a small monastery said to have been founded so late as 1509 by Rory McQuillan; burned out in 1584 in an attack on English troops quartered there, repaired, and occupied by the Third Order of Franciscans Regular until the mid-17th century. An alternative local tradition, cited by Fagan, has it that the abbey was founded by Phelimy or Felix McCormick of Glenshesk, "better known as Phelimy-na-Mocht, being a father to the poor", in order to exorcise the ghost of a person he had murdered.

Whilst it is distressing to see a building of so late a date roofless and ruined - compare the very many far earlier buildings still intact in England - yet it must be said that Bonamargy lacks the magical qualities shared by the ruined churches at Layde (13) and at Cranfield (12). This is largely because it is divided on the one hand from the seashore, on the other from the river, by a busy main road and an equally busy (and very intrusive) golf course.

The buildings are dramatic enough; for the most part, of squared yellowy-brown sandstone blocks, with many small flat stones packed in between them by way of galleting. These are relieved by masons' carved stonework of high quality, but no great awareness of changing tastes over the water. Indeed, the four-light Jacobean window in the south wall of the McDonnell Chapel has much in common with the East window of St John's church in Islandmagee (21).

There are numerous interesting tombstones in and around the buildings: the most uncommon being that of the skilled stonemason himself, "Alexander McDonnell wrought this monument for his family, 1764"; and the curious small holestone, resembling that at Layde (13) more than that at Doagh (1), traditionally believed to mark the grave of Julia McQuillan "the black nun". The site is well presented to the public.

Photographs: Michael O'Connell.

Situation: South of the road from Ballycastle to Cushendall; td, Bonamargy; Parish, Culfeightrin; District Council, Moyle; Grid ref. D 126 408.

References: Scheduled monument in state care. T Fagan, OSM, 1839, Antrim, IX, pp 59-66; F J Bigger and W J Fennell, in UJA, 2nd series, IV, 1898, p 9; O'Laverty, 'Down and Connor', IV, 1887, pp 468-470; HMNI, 1983, pp 72-73; Mallory and McNeill, 'Archaeology of Ulster', 1991, p 296.

Carrickfergus Castle

15. The grandest castle in the county, and in the province: a noble building on a notable site; in occupation for military purposes from 1177 until 1928. For most of this period, the castle and the walled town of which it was the heart formed a single defensible entity. Unhappily, the Marine Highway of the 1950s cut off the castle from the town, in the process destroying the outer defences; and the massive cubes and cylinders of the Kilroot power station (256) now overshadow the castle walls and keep. Moreover, great expanses of car-covered tarmac extend almost up to the walls. The latter retain, nonetheless, an impressive presence, especially seen from the east or from the harbour.

The castle covers the whole of a sill of basalt projecting from the shore, in which it proved possible to bore a deep fresh-water well, in proximity to a tolerable, if rather shallow, harbour. As Richard Dobbs succinctly remarked in his manuscript notes of 1683, "In the castle of Carrickfergus is one of the finest arches I ever see ...... likewise a draw well in the low vault of the Castle wrought through the rock of a considerable depth ...... the sea surrounds the Castle three parts out of four ...... the port or kay cost £1,400: a vessel of 100 tons has layn in it". Here the Anglo-Norman John de Courcy placed the central stronghold of the territory he had conquered, most of the counties Antrim and Down, at a place which enjoyed easy communications by sea with Dublin, Scotland, and England, as well as North Antrim and his other castle at Dundrum. He was a great builder: in the twenty-five years from 1177, he built not only Carrickfergus and Dundrum castles, but also Grey Abbey, Black Abbey (now demolished), and Inch Abbey, not to mention Downpatrick cathedral and St Nicholas's church in Carrickfergus (24). It is a wonder how he found the stonemasons and crafts-

men; some at least seem to have been brought over from Lancashire and Cumberland.

The building history of the castle over so long a period is complex, but consistent. It is mostly built of local basalt, with dressings of red sandstone and, later, creamy Cultra stone; and, from the Tudor period onward, thin bricks, particularly in the gun-splays. The massive keep, 90 feet high with four storeys and basement - these rooms were designed as much to provide domestic comfort and, even, splendour, as for pure defence - and the inner curtain, date from 1177-95; the middle curtain, 1217-22; the outer curtain, probably 1226-42; the original gatehouse, 1315. In these years, the castle changed hands several times: Hugh de Lacy ejected de Courcy in 1203 and was in turn ejected by King John, who spent ten days in the castle in July 1210 before taking ship across the Lough to Holywood. He left behind a garrison of 10 knights, 16 men-at-arms, 5 crossbowmen, 4 watchmen, 4 door-keepers and a chaplain. De Lacy sought to take back the castle by siege in 1224; and it surrendered to Edward Bruce, after a long siege, in 1315. "By the second quarter of the 15th century, Carrickfergus was isolated between the O'Neills of Clandeboy and the MacDonnells of the Glens from the nearest area (Lecale and the southern Ards) which claimed to be English". Though often in disrepair, it seems to have provided an effective refuge, and occasionally stronghold, for garrisons of varying size until the invention of heavy artillery: in 1496, it was successfully (if nervously) held by only 6 men at a time when Sir John Mor MacDonnell of the Isles, with 1,000 Scots and kerns, was roaming uncomfortably close to Carrickfergus. By the Tudor period, Carrickfergus had become one of the key bases for expansion in Ulster.

By 1555, the garrison comprised 1 warden, 12 arquebusiers, 12 bombardiers, and 5 archers: sign of the growing importance of gunners. The gatehouse was rebuilt, and gunports inserted, in 1561-7, when the constable, Williams Peers, who had in effect "started with a late medieval Irish tower house and bawn" proceeded to make them "defensible by the new weapon of cannon", incidentally "using brick almost for the first time in Ulster". During the Irish wars of the 17th century, the castle was an important base. In 1601, although unlike other forts in Ireland it had no demesne to supply it, Carrickfergus had to accommodate 800 foot and 125 horse. In the 1640s, it changed hands three times, having served first as a place of refuge, then as General Monro's base against the royalists in Belfast. At the end of the century, it was captured by Schomberg for King William, after a week's siege, in 1689; but by 1698, when the Williamite wars were over, the garrison was reduced once again, this time to the minimum force of one storekeeper costing £36.16.5 per annum.

By then Belfast, whose harbour could accommodate much larger ships, had surpassed Carrickfergus in importance. Carrickfergus castle continued to be used as a military headquarters because of the expense of building a modern fortress at Belfast, estimated by Thomas Phillips, in 1685, to cost £42,000. In 1714 barrack buildings were constructed within the walls; during the '45 rising the castle was garrisoned by militia, and by a volunteer company from Belfast. On 21st February 1760, the town was forced to surrender, for want of ammunition, to a French force of 800 men landed by Thurot: who retired shortly thereafter. Subsequently, the garrison consisted of around 180 men, mostly recruits, or guarding French prisoners of war.

The castle was considerably modernised during the Napoleonic wars. Around 1802 the old barracks were demolished (except for the officers' quarters, now caretaker's residence). Between then and 1820, many adaptations - vaults, parapets, embrasures, and other artillery works - were undertaken. Once again the castle reverted to a mere powder magazine; in 1839, of its 31 guns 30 had been dismounted, and it was manned only by 1 master gunner and 2 invalids. In 1855, its fortunes looked up: it became the headquarters of the Antrim Artillery, and a battery of 64-pounder rifled guns on swivelling carriages was installed. Thereafter, the castle declined gradually until it served as little more than an ordnance depot and general military store, though four 6-inch guns were added shortly before 1914 for coastal defence purposes. The castle was declared an ancient monument in 1928; part of it was used as an air raid

shelter during the second World War; a military museum occupied the keep until the mid 1980s. At this point, it was decided to modernise the presentation of the castle to the public. A garrison of some 30 coloured dummies, of all periods, was installed; a modern staircase was introduced in the keep, and a shop and tea-room built in the outer ward. Opinions on these changes are divided: some care for, others do not care for, this mode of presentation. It does not really much matter, for Carrickfergus castle has reserves of dignity amply sufficient to endure, and survive, the revolutions of passing fashion.

Photographs: Michael O'Connell; Ordnance Survey of Northern Ireland.
Situation: Townland, parish, and borough of Carrickfergus. Grid ref. J 415 873.
References: Scheduled monument in state care; in conservation area. M'Skimin, 'Carrickfergus', editions of 1811, 1823, 1909, passim; J Boyle and S M'Skimin, OSM, 1839-40, Carrickfergus, as yet unpublished; E M Jope, Guide, 1957, 1966; Campbell and Crowther, 'Carrickfergus', UAHS, 1978, p 11; McNeill, 'Anglo-Norman Ulster', 1980, pp 9-18; McNeill, 'Carrickfergus Castle', 1981, passim; Robinson, 'Carrickfergus', 1986.

The White House, Whitehouse

16. A bizarre 17th-century survival in 20th-century outer suburbia: the remains, now cut down to a single-storey, of a formidably fortified house perhaps of three, four, or even five storeys. This was the "little pyle" in 1574 of a Mr Brunker, "a soldier who had seen hard service under Essex and Perrott". In 1839, it was used as barn and stabling by the local farmer; today, it is a gospel hall. It appears that until the roadway of Whitehouse Park was driven in between, this and the tall, probably 18th-century, house opposite - possibly that which appears in the Nixon print of 1780? - both formed part of the courtyard group of buildings associated with the bawn. Thomas McTear, born 1800, writing in 1882 his recollections of boyhood, says "This house is very old, and is now just as it was described when William III landed at Carrickfergus in 1688." And this is footnoted: "Behind the Whitehouse are the ruins of an old fortified plantation house or bawn."

"The existing remains of this house not only bears the appearance of great antiquity, but also of great strength. Its original height was either 4 or 5 storeys, but has been unroofed and lowered to its present height about 70 years since ...... No arch work appears in any part of the building. Strong oak lintels were used in all cases over the doors, windows and fireplaces" wrote Thomas Fagan in 1839. Alan Gailey, who may not have been aware of Fagan's evidence, disbelieved in its skyscraper character: he describes it as "a three-unit two-storey house with gable hearths, squat circular towers at the front at each end, and a rear round-ended stair projection. Pistol loops in the towers and the small number of ground-floor window openings indicate the builder's concern with defence. Similarly defended with pistol loops in both sides at ground-floor level, and in both gables at upper-floor level". Dendrochronology indicates that the timber used was felled early in the 17th century.

It consists of a rectangular building, 70 feet long, with two large and formidable roofless circular towers at the south-facing corners, flanked by an enclosing wall of a fascinating speckledy texture, ending in a square pillar of dressed ashlar blocks, and with a projecting half-tower at the rear. The random stonework now has the original loups and windows blocked by bricks or by breeze blocks. The central entrance has been turned into a (quite pleasing) window for the hall behind, and a new doorway has been broken through the stonework on each side. The facade is ornamented by pious texts, painted in yellow on sheets of brown plywood, and ventilators.

It is said that King William III spent in this house the night of 14th June, 1690.

18

Bishop's House, Kilroot

17. "A stone house buylte by Mr Homstone the late Bishop of Downe at a place by the Sea syde called Kilroote and a stone walle aboute it 10 foote high repaired by the nowe Bishop" (1610). The name of this bishop was, in fact, Humpston: he was consecrated in 1602, and died at Kilroot in 1606. In a terrier of 1622, quoted in 1839, "Ecclesia Killneagh alias Kilroot decayed; the rectory possessed by the bishop as a mensal belonging to his lordship's vicar, Edward Brice"; and described by James Boyle as "held under the bishop by Edward Bruce Esquire, a lineal descendant of the Edward Brice referred to in the terrier, and whose family had for nearly a century occupied Kilroot House, now almost in ruins. This mansion was also for some time the residence of the bishop." "The building was occupied for nearly 200 years by the Brice family, who were the last known occupants. The building was still roofed at the beginning of this century" (Rankin).

In 1683, Richard Dobbs noted "To the east of Carrickfergus about a mile stands Killroot, now the mansion howse of the Lord Buishop of Downe & Connor, not farre from the sea, though noe buishop has lived there since Buishop Echlyn whoe was (as I take it) aboute the latter end of King James ...... what vessel soever comes into the Lough and has sight of the Bishop's House is free at this point." Bishop Echlin died in 1635, but for some time before that had preferred to live at his house known as the

Abbacy, at Ardquin in the Ards.

A very strange, gaunt, three-storey, rubble-stone ruin: thin and elongated like a tower-house which has been squeezed in a vice: built apparently in the first decade of the 17th century, with bawn, within the bounds of a much more ancient church and graveyard; there was also a bullaun stone. The house measures 60 feet by 24 feet; its arched round-headed openings have red brick dressings; the bawn has partly disappeared, and a former farmhouse, now apparently office building for the salt mines, occupies part of the site. Difficult of access - surrounded by ferocious 'Keep Out' notices - and almost impossible to interpret, it is nonetheless a curiously impressive, though puzzling, even sinister, ruin. Two circular flankers survive; on the lower courses of stone of that nearer the road is superimposed a dovecote of brick, slates, and mortar, probably of quite early date: the mortar has proved much more durable than the bricks, so creating a curious but attractive reticulated pattern.

Photograph: Michael O'Connell.
Situation: Fort Road, Kilroot; td and Parish, Kilroot; District Council, Carrickfergus; Grid ref. J 450 895.
References: Scheduled monument, not in state care. T 811/3 of 1610, and R Dobbs, 1683, D 162/6, in PRONI; J Boyle, OSM, 1839, Antrim, X, pp 68,69; PSAMNI, p 51; Rankin, 'Parish of Kilroot', 1982, p 3.

◁

Photographs: R J Welch, Ulster Museum W01/76/B; Jim McCall.
Situation: On north west side of Whitehouse Park, Macedon; td, Whiteabbey; Parish, Carnmoney (until 1840; now Whitehouse); District Council, Newtownabbey; Grid ref. J 356 817.
References: Listed B. J Boyle, OSM, 1839, and T Fagan, 1839, Antrim, I, pp 68-9, 96; OS maps, 1833, 1857; O'Laverty 'Down and Connor',

III, 1884, p 2-3, for a very full description; Thomas McTear, 'Recollections', in UJA, 2nd series, V, 1899, p 164; E M Jope, in UJA, 3rd series, XV, 1960, p 111; Armstrong, 'Newtownabbey', [1978], pp 249-252; Craig, 'Architecture of Ireland', 1982, p 124; Gailey, 'Rural houses', 1984, p 191; Larmour, 'Belfast', 1987, p 101; notes by Hugh Dixon in MBR.

Dunluce Castle

18. One of the most striking attractions of the north coast, a highly romantic ruin on a highly dramatic site. "An insulated perpendicular rock of one hundred feet high, standing proudly among the boiling waves which foam around and wash its sides, and separated from the mainland by a precipitous chasm of about twenty feet wide, and nearly a hundred feet deep".

"At first sight it only presents an unseemly pile of ruins, like those of a village destroyed; but on a nearer approach, its situation becomes truly striking, and indeed majestic" (Sir Richard Hoare, 1807). "If it stood inland, on a level field, the ruin would scarcely attract a glance, unless, perhaps, on account of its extent; for as a building, there is nothing fine or beautiful about it" (H D Inglis in 1835).

"As a military position the site is very ill chosen; at least it could make no stand against artillery, being completely seen into from ground not a quarter of a mile distant ...... it might be a very good situation for a prison" (Lt Robe, 1832). There seems to have been no well within the castle which, presumably, relied on rainwater stored in the lower courtyard. There appears to have been quite a sizeable town to landward of the castle, now completely disappeared - the present buildings there are not earlier than the late 17th century.

The 100 foot high rock was probably a defensible site long before the invention of artillery: both the name, and the existence of a souterrain, indicate occupation at an early date. O'Laverty suggests "it is probable that shortly after Bruce's invasion the cyclopean walls of the Celtic dun were swept away, and their stones used in the erection of the Castle." The Norman refortification, of about 1300, probably had four (or possibly five) corner towers linked by a curtain; but documentary evidence is wanting. According to Boyle, there was "a tradition the first founder of this place was a McKeown". In 1513 the castle belonged to the McQuillans (perhaps the hibernicised version of the Norman name de Mandeville). By 1565 they had been displaced by the McDonnells, who briefly surrendered it to Shane O'Neill in that year, but they were back again two years later. In 1584 Sir John Perrott took the castle with the aid of artillery, but as soon as he was out of the way the McDonnells returned. Sir James McDonnell rebuilt and refortified the castle, installing three of the guns saved from the wreck of the Armada ship Girona in 1588. He was "a close friend and kinsman of James VI of Scotland, whom he frequently visited", and was described by a court chronicler as "ane bra man of person and behaviour, but had not the Scots tongue nor nae language but Erse".

In 1610, Carew and Chichester reported "From thence we went to Dunluce where Sir Randall McDonnell hath buylte a fayre stone walle about the whole rock within which he hath erected a good house of stone with many lodgings and other roomes. The towne of Dunluce consists of many tenements after the fashion of the Palle peopled for the most part with Scotishmen". In 1638 Randal McDonnell, eldest son of the first Earl of Antrim, who had been expensively brought up in England and had married a very rich wife, widow of the Duke of Buckingham, found it necessary to retrench; in that year he and his Duchess moved to Dunluce as an economy, and made it their principal residence for three years; this must have been the very peak of its importance. One stormy night in 1639, a great chunk of the servants' quarters fell into the sea, taking with it nine servants, one of them (by tradition) the castle cook. In 1641 the castle was unsuccessfully besieged. In 1642 General Monro, having accepted the hospitality of the Earl of Antrim, took him prisoner after dinner and proceeded to plunder Dunluce of its valuables. This account H A Boyd disbelieves on the strength of a pamphlet of 1642, which suggests that, Monro having sent a trumpeter, one thousand men, two troops of horse and two field pieces to the castle gate, Lord Antrim sensibly surrendered before dinner. However that may be, an "Inventory and Appraysement", dated 9 March 1645, of the items of furniture removed by the family to Chester in 1641, amounted to the enormous sum of £989.15.3. By 1665, the castle had been so far wrecked that Lord Antrim had to live for a while at the nearby Ballymagarry House; but by 1671 he was back again. On 23 February, 1671, St Oliver Plunkett, Archbishop of Armagh, was his guest, and a better-mannered one than General Monro: in a letter to Rome the saint said "I was with him for three days at his house in Dunluce; it is a noble building; the palace is perched on a high rock which is lashed on all sides by the sea; it is twelve miles distant from the largest of the Hebrides".

The gate-house, very much in the Scottish style with corbelled pepper-pot turrets, was probably built between the artillery siege of 1584 and 1600. Access was by a narrow drawbridge over the twenty-foot cleft between rock and mainland; now a permanent wooden foot-bridge. Parts of the original curtain walls, having fallen into the sea, were replaced by 17th-century work. Inside the south wall there stand the remains of an extraordinary mid-16th century renaissance open loggia in the Italian style, but facing north: evidently copied from a Scottish original. Between the loggia and the seaward courtyard stand the walls of what was a large and luxurious 17th-century two-storey manor house, Lord Antrim's 'palace' as the archbishop called it, whose great hall, 70 feet by 23, had three great bay windows facing west towards Benevenagh and Inishowen. Beyond this were kitchen, servants' quarters, and the place where the landslide occurred.

The surviving buildings on the mainland, beyond the converging walls leading to the drawbridge, were (according to Mr Young) "erected by Randal, second earl, to accommodate his retainers, who, in consequence of the

frightful catastrophe which took place at their quarters on the rock, refused any longer to live there". The alternative version is that they were built "because the widowed Duchess of Buckingham, whom the second earl married, disliked, quite understandably, the bleakness of the old fortress" (Girvan).

A forty-foot souterrain runs underneath the north-east tower. The rock is pierced by a sea-cave through which it would have been possible to supply the castle when under siege. Scratched on one of the stones of the gatehouse wall there is a crude representation of a galley of the kind common in the Irish Sea and North Channel in the late 16th century.

The McDonnell family abandoned Dunluce late in the 17th century in favour first of Ballymagarry, burned down in 1750, and then of Glenarm (86); the castle thereafter fell into decay; and was presented by Lord Antrim to the state in 1928. It is now, on the whole, well presented, apart from an absurdly inappropriate entrance through a sort of knorman knight-ride mixture of iron and timber. The visitor is greeted also by an ungrammatical notice disclaiming liability for his injuries; an excellent model of the castle in its prime; a largely irrelevant audio-visual display which credits the Scots across the way with golf as well as whisky; and a curious use of the McDonnell coat of arms to indicate the whereabouts of the lavatories. Was this authorised by the current Earl, one wonders?

A disastrous night at Dunluce Castle

Photographs: R J Welch, Ulster Museum W01/44/6; Jim McCall. Tail piece: Angela Antrim, reproduced by permission of Hector McDonnell.
Situation: North of the road from Bushmills to Portrush; td, Parish, Dunluce; District Council, Coleraine; Grid ref. C 905 414.
References: Scheduled monument in state care. T 811/3, of 1610, in PRONI; 1645 valuation, copy in MBR; Hoare, 'Journal', 1807, pp 205-209; Dubourdieu, 'Antrim' 1812, p 609; Inglis, 'Ireland in 1834', 1835, p 232; T C Robe, OSM, 1832, and J Boyle, 1835, Antrim, V, pp 102, 108, 113-115; Hill, 'Macdonnells of Antrim', 1873, p 137; O'Laverty, 'Down and Connor' III, 1884, pp 274-286; Lawlor, 'Dunluce and the Route', 1919; Boyd, 'Dunluce parish', 1937, p IVB; PSAMNI, 1940, p 2; Girvan, 'North Antrim', UAHS, 1972, p 19; Angela Antrim, 'Antrim McDonnells', 1977, passim; HMNI, 1983, p 74; H Dixon, Guide card, 1985; McCahan, 'Local histories', 1988; M Meek, Guidebook, n.d., passim; H MacDonnell, in JRSAI, CXXXII, 1992, p 109.

Dalway's Bawn, Kilroot

19. Built about 1609, soon after the grant of letters patent from James I to John Dallwaye of Carrickfergus in 1603: by 1610, Carew and Chichester say "we sawe a ffayre Bawne 15 foote high with 2 rounde flankers buylte by the sd Dallawaye upon his owne lande at Brade Island, within w'ch Bawne he hath errected a pritie house of tymber after the English manner tatched for the pr'sent but entended to be slated." A detailed account of the bawn by Alfred Lee published in the UJA in 1858 gives an excellent ground plan, showing a curtain wall 133 feet long between the front towers, each 30 feet high with an internal diameter of 12 feet; and quotes in full an agreement of 1632 with William Miller, mason, for 'putting up 4 staircases in the 4 turretts at £8 apiece', and other work, including chimneys, 'pidgion holles', and windows of freestone.

This very full account is glossed by no less a person than Dr John O'Donovan, who remarks that "the term 'Bawn' for a cow-fortress, or enclosure for cattle, would appear to have been more generally used in the Highlands of Scotland than in Ireland". Lee says that "in its original state it was capable of affording shelter for 200 head of cattle". The "pritie house" has disappeared; but the bawn still very much houses cattle, and its agricultural use greatly impedes the understanding of the site. One of the four corner towers has completely disappeared; one is invisible from the road. The others, still inhabited in 1940, have been somewhat altered; the roofs were, until very recently, neglected; some of the loopholes and mullioned windows, and the central arched entrance with iron ring above it, have been closed up; the curtain walls have been raised by thinner upper walls; but the frontage to the road still gives a better idea than any other site in the county of the original appearance of an early 17th-century planter's bawn, and one with exceptionally large and fine corner towers.

Photographs: W A Green, Ulster Folk Museum WAG 1764; Jim McCall.

Situation: On the road from Carrickfergus to Ballycarry; td Bellahill or Ballyhill; Parish, Kilroot; District Council, Carrickfergus; Grid ref. J 443 914.

References: Scheduled monument partly in state care. T 811/3, 1610, in PRONI; A Lee, in UJA, 1st series, VI, 1858, p 125; C H Mallock, OSM, 1831, and J Boyle, 1839, Antrim, X, pp 57, 70-71; O'Laverty, 'Down and Connor', III, 1884, p 88; Egerton and Bigger, 'Guide for tourists', 1906, p 60; PSAMNI, 1940, p 40.

Ballygally Castle

20. Built in 1624-5, almost certainly by John Shaw of Greenock, this High House "has so much in common with other houses in Renfrewshire that it might as well have been built in Greenock. A simple rectangular tower rises to a steeply-pitched roof and a characteristically theatrical skyline of high chimneys, cone-topped bartizans supported on corbels, and elaborately gabled dormer windows..... The only feature which would mark Ballygally as an Ulster castle is the presence of a bawn with corner flankers" (Dixon); although "there remains room for doubt as to the original relationship of the Castle to its enclosure, its outbuildings, and (before the construction of the coast road) the sea." It is clear, from the early photographs, that the little circular turrets with conical roofs at the corners of the walled garden are not the original flankers, but are ornamental late-Victorian summerhouses. Lady Louisa Kerr, in 1844, noted "Formerly the approach to the Castle on the land side appears to have been through an avenue of trees, leading from the south and along the banks of a stream called Weyburn - this approach entered the courtyard of the castle through a large stone gateway now in ruin."

Of four storeys, with walls five feet thick, pierced with loups for musketry. The original hall doorway, inscribed **GODIS PROVIDENS IS MYN INHERITANCE**, with coat of arms and the initials J S and I B, is inside not outside the building since alterations of 1760. These initials, and armorials, are usually now interpreted as those of John Shaw and Isabel Brisbane; but Lady Louisa is quite firmly of the view that they commemorate the marriage of James Shaw of Ballygally with Jane Blair of Killyglen; and Boyle thinks the lady was Elizabeth Busby. The noted Belfast schoolmaster David Manson started his career here as tutor to the Shaw family. In 1814, the residence of Rev. Thomas Alexander. In 1834, the valuation shows the castle as belonging to Archibald Blair - "Castle rented by coast guard at £24 per annum, Government having expended 2 or £300 on it". "Shaw's Castle . . . and the

property attached to the amount I believe of 600 to 800 pounds a year remained in the possession of [Shaw's] descendants until about 12 years ago, when it became the property (by purchase) of Mr Agnew of Kilwaughter, the last of that house of Shaw having become embarrassed in circumstances from failure in mercantile or other pursuits . . . This Castle has been of later years modernised, and is now the dwelling of the chief officer of the coastguard for the prevention of smuggling, from which it would appear that it has been subject to a complete reversal of destiny, having been supposed at one time to have been a stronghold for smuggling" (Boyle).

In 1875, the local historian, the Rev. Classon Porter, was living there, and wrote to his fellow-historian George Benn "The house or, 'beg its pardon', the "castle", is quaint and old-fashioned but that I like, and it is very warm and comfortable, the walls being 5 or 6 feet thick, so that we never feel the greatest storm that blows, and the air is so pure and bracing that I really think my health is better here".

Since 1940, part of an hotel, the additions to the northward being unobjectionable; though more lurid, Disneylike proposals, were fortunately disallowed in 1984.

"A unique example of a C17 Plantation Castle surviving intact, inhabited and unchanged, apart from the insertion of sash windows" (Bence-Jones). On the shore below the castle, John Betjeman insisted on paddling when en route to stay with Lord Antrim at Glenarm.

Photograph: W A Green, Ulster Folk Museum WAG 1140.
Situation: Coast road, Ballygally; td. Ballygally; Parish, Carncastle; District Council, Larne; Grid ref. D 372 078.
References: Castle, bawn walls and towers listed A. VAL 1B/150, p 70, Lady L Kerr 'Album of Glenarm Castle and its vicinity', 1835 onwards, D 3560/1, and Benn papers, D 3113/7/190, all in PRONI; J Boyle, OSM, 1835, and T Hore, 1833, Antrim, III, pp 6, 11; W J Fennell, in UJA, 2nd series, VII, 1901, p 2; PSAMNI, 1940, p 29; Dixon, 'Introduction', 1975, p 22; Notes by H Dixon, 1985 in MBR; Bence-Jones, 'Burke's guide', p 22.

Angel prayer-desk, St Patrick's Church, Jordanstown (65). Photograph: Michael O'Connell

CHAPTER TWO

CHURCHES AND CHAPELS

Christianity in Antrim goes back to Saint Patrick, whose associations with Slemish mountain are well known, who may have preached at Armoy, and one of whose teeth is said to be buried under the altar of the tiny chapel dedicated to him at Derriaghy (36). He seems to have organised the early church on the basis of numerous small, local, bishoprics, gradually amalgamated over the years. Today, both the Roman Catholic and the Church of Ireland dioceses of Connor are almost co-extensive with the county of Antrim, except for a small part which belongs to the diocese of Dromore.

The great Saint Bernard of Clairvaux did not, according to O'Laverty, think well of the people of Connor; when, in 1124, Saint Malachi was placed over them as bishop, "it was not to men but to beasts he had been sent; ... he had never met such a people, so profligate in their morals, so uncouth in their ceremonies, so impious in faith, so barbarous in laws, so rebellious to discipline, so filthy in their life, Christians in name but Pagans in reality":[1] and so on. These painful strictures seem to have been meant for all the then residents of County Antrim, except, presumably, those living in the parish of Aghalee. Lawlor thought all this was a result of their addiction to holestones.[2] Fortunately, Saint Malachi was successful in civilising them swiftly.

Notwithstanding the Reformation on the one hand, and the Tudor and Jacobean settlements of Ulster on the other, the people of the Glens and of Rathlin remain predominantly Roman Catholic, largely no doubt because of their close links with Kintyre and the Hebridean islands. The people of the Lagan valley remain largely episcopalian, Methodist or Quaker, for that was an area of English settlement. For the rest, the county is predominantly Presbyterian as a result of the influx of successive waves of Scottish lowlanders.

The earliest churches still in use, and still wearing the original roof, go back no farther than the late 16th or early 17th century; and even they are few enough. However, many later churches and chapels may well incorporate older stones, or even the complete side-walls of nave or chancel. And successive churches have sometimes been built on the same site, often amidst the graves of an ancient burying-place.

When Dr Daniel Beaufort wrote in 1792, he counted in Antrim (including Belfast) 73 parishes, 41 churches, 10 glebe houses, and no episcopal palace.[3] The number of Church of Ireland churches was considerably augmented during the ensuing forty years by the Board of First Fruits in Dublin, sometimes to designs of John Bowden. The modest parish church at Ballintoy (38), of 1811, adapted from his designs, is exceptionally well documented for its date. A second wave of new churches, this time to the designs of the county surveyor Charles Lanyon, was built at the instance of the energetic Church Accommodation Society in the 1830s and 1840s. Another wave of buildings in the second half of the century is attributable to the highly original partnership of Welland and Gillespie, architects to the Church Commissioners: there are fine examples of their work at Doagh (61) and Derriaghy (62). Thereafter, only W H Lynn's church in the Celtic Revival style at Jordanstown (65) deserves to be singled out.

The Church of Ireland has, on the whole, built smaller but more numerous churches, whilst both Presbyterians and Roman Catholics have built fewer but much larger ones. A handful of Roman Catholic chapels, rather surprisingly, survive from the years before the final repeal of the penal laws and the Catholic Emancipation Act of 1829, but for economic reasons the ensuing wave of church-building followed slowly, and unfortunately, was architecturally rather undistinguished: the best of the county's Roman Catholic churches are those at Whitehouse (59), Ballycastle (63) and Moneyglass (64).

The Presbyterians seem never to have had classical meeting-houses in County Antrim comparable to the many delightful examples in County Down, but it is hard to be sure, for they are great modernisers and rebuilders, any sentimental attachment being usually to the congregation rather than to its building. The outstanding exception is John Millar's Grecian church in Antrim town (47). There are, however, meeting-houses of considerable charm at Randalstown (34), Crumlin (46) and Dunmurry (33). The Moravian churches at Gracehill (31) and Ballinderry (32) are also worthy of particular note.

References: 1. O'Laverty, 'Down and Connor', V, 1895, p 65. 2. H C Lawlor, in 'Irish naturalists' journal', III, 1930, p 105. 3. Beaufort, 'Memoir of a map', 1792, p 110.

St John's (C of I) Church, Islandmagee

21. Perhaps of 1596, more probably of 1609, a charming simple little Jacobean church in a walled graveyard full of trees, daffodils, and old headstones, looking west over Larne Lough. In 1683 Richard Dobbs remarked "there is a handsome church much out of repair, but no church-men, all presbiters." Lewis says "a small edifice, rebuilt in 1827 on the foundations of an ancient and more extensive structure on the margin of Larne Lough".

Boyle says: "The original church as remembered consisted of an aisle 88 feet long and 28 feet wide ... attached to its western end and northern side was another aisle of less dimensions. In the year 1828 the latter aisle and 28 feet of the former were taken off and the present neat-looking church formed of the remaining portion ... The original church must have at one time been a building of some consequence, to judge from the superior quality of the white oak and that of the cut sandstone sold on its alteration. The square windows, divided into 4 lights by heavy stone mullions and surmounted by label mouldings, are precisely similar to those of Antrim church ..."

However, the present structure, cut down from its length as first built, does not quite correspond to the description, though it seems to be largely original. There are five-light windows at east and west end; and three-light windows in each of the side walls: compare with Ballinderry and with Antrim (25, 23). The slated roof is of lower pitch than usual and, from the upstands at the gables, looks as though it was originally thatched. The walls, which are covered in yellow-grey smooth plaster, are propped up by very large buttresses, dating from the early nineteenth century restoration. There is no spire or tower, just a neat little belfry, added at some date after 1840. A two-storey porch-cum-vestry was added in 1988 at the west end of the nave, reasonably appropriate in itself but unfortunately masking the original round-headed door-way and five-light window in the west wall. Also, the modern horizontal Celtic window signed "Solaglass Caldermac", just where one might have expected that a view of the Lough would be most welcome, is not entirely appropriate; all the other windows have clear glass in iron diamond-pattern lattices, and very nice too.

Somebody has erected improbable notices pointing the way to "St John's Church: AD 1595": as though a Christian church could conceivably date from 1595 BC!

Photograph: Michael O'Connell. (See also colour-plate IIa)
Situation: Ballyharry, Islandmagee; td Ballyharry; Parish Islandmagee; District Council Larne; Grid ref. D463 980.
References: Listed A. R Dobbs, D 162/6 in PRONI; Lewis, TD, 1837, II, p 28; J Boyle, OSM, 1840, Antrim, III, pp 20, 44; PSAMNI, 1940, p 35; Donaldson, 'Islandmagee', 1927, p 99; H Dixon, notes in MBR.

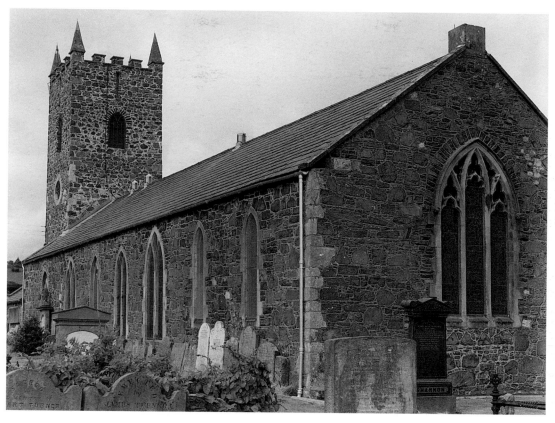

St Cedma's (C of I) Church, Larne

22. Saint Cedma, a saint not in the calendar, is locally believed to have been the father of St Comgall, and a Magheramorne man. There seems here to have been a very ancient friary; re-founded at some time in the 15th century by the Third Order of St Francis. In 1609, seventy years after the dissolution of the monasteries, the parish of Larne and Inver was reorganised. In 1657, a Cromwellian Commission reported that the church was in good repair. The modest but very charming tower is clearly dated 1778 on a stone above the arch, now blocked up, in the western wall; but in 1826, the then spire was found to be unstable; it was taken down and the square tower in that year raised to "about the height of the original tower and spire". Above the more modern pointed door, built into the north wall of the tower, there is a long-chinned head with leaves instead of a beard; and in the north wall of the nave, there is a single slit window with cusped head and label moulding, a Tudor rose set into the wall below, a very worn red sandstone head (that of St Cedma?) above. There is also a grotesque animal in the east wall: all these seem to be early stones re-used in later re-building.

Surprisingly, all the Ordnance Survey Memoir has to say is "the church stands just outside the town and is sufficiently large for the 3 parishes of Larne, Inver and Raloo, to which it is attached".

In 1837, Lewis wrote "the church, for the repair of which the Ecclesiastical Commissioners have recently granted £186, is a spacious edifice with a spire"; but ten years later, he wrote that "the church has been so disfigured with plaister, as to have lost all originality of character". "So late as the year 1840, the church contained a few remnants of Jacobite architecture, with its high oak canopied pews and rudely carved text of scripture and quaint inscriptions. When the church was remodelled in that year, the whole were swept away" (Ewart). In 1860 the vestry was built and the east window inserted. That the church still retained something of its old character is evident, however, from the view expressed in 1886 by the diocesan architect (Thomas Drew) that this was a specimen of "an early type of church peculiar to Ulster" instances of which might be seen at Billy, Carrickfergus, Dromore, and Ballywillin.

The tower, with its corner pinnacles, simple battlements, and emphatic corner quoins, has an oculus below a pointed arch in each of three faces, all ornamented with curly modern ironwork; unlike the chancel, which has been over-pointed, the tower retains its original mortar, and is correspondingly much more congenial than the hard blackstone and pointed windows of the Victorian work in the nave and chancel. Font by S P Close of 1878. There is an excellent signed window of 1927 by Wilhelmina Geddes.

The church stands in an uncommonly pleasing stone-walled graveyard, full of exceptionally fine tombstones going back to the 1680s, with a nice lych-gate; but alas, now over-shadowed in its cul-de-sac by ill-judged tower blocks of flats and road flyover.

Photograph: Michael O'Connell.
Situation: Inver Road, Larne; td Inver; Parish, Inver and Larne; District Council, Larne; Grid ref. D 397 024.
References: Listed B+. W R Boteler, OSM, 1833, Antrim, III, p 125; Lewis, TD, 1837, II, p 25; 1847, I, p 688; Ewart, 'Down & Connor & Dromore', 1886, pp 69, 94; Bassett, 'Antrim', 1888, p 369; Fair, 'To this you belong', [1980], passim.

All Saints (C of I) Church, Antrim

23. 1596: the date inscribed on a stone in the north wall. "Church and walls newly erected" according to the 1622 Visitation; "Church in Repair, and stands conveniently for Resort" according to that of 1657: which contradicts Lewis's statement that "the church was destroyed by fire in 1649, and remained in ruins until 1720 when it was rebuilt". The gateposts, with round knops, are inscribed 1733. Dr D A Beaufort saw it from outside on 22nd November 1787 and remarked "The church is very ancient and from its small casement windows must be very gloomy within". In 1816, the tower and spire were added, and the doorway moved. By 1825, the church was once again "in a dilapidated state", but this was rectified by an energetic new curate. The second transept and vestry were added in 1869 "by the Ecclesiastical Commissioners, and they bear the stamp of the work of that body"(!); altered in 1892 to designs by S P Close.

Externally, the church is of random stone, rather badly over-pointed in places, with three-light Jacobean cusped and mullioned windows with dripstones. There are defensive loopholes in the north and east walls: no longer discernible from inside; in 1837 six were noted, but only three are visible now. It is not easy to decide whether they were designed for use by standing or kneeling marksmen. The east wall has a large three-light window of 1870; at some date the stonework here has been crudely patched, using bricks and fragments of roof-slate. The tower and spire, with corner finials, four-way clock, and heavy buttresses, of large squared blocks of black ashlar, are rather ungraceful. They have been attributed to John Bowden, who may possibly at the time have been working at Antrim Castle; if so, they are rather below par for his work; but the evidence for his involvement in work at Antrim is exiguous.

The interior is dark but pleasant, with a simple gallery carried on cast iron columns with palmetto capitals. There is a very good Flaxman memorial to the 4th Lord Massereene, d.1816, with weeping classical figures; a flamboyant gothic one to the 10th Lord Massereene, d 1863, by J R Kirk of Dublin, showing him laid out in the robes of the Order of St Patrick; and two lesser monuments by the irrepressible Harry Hems of Exeter, one incorporating a virtuoso carving in brown marble of a full-size violin and bow - plus masonic instruments.

Photograph: Michael O'Connell.
Situation: Church Street, Antrim; td, Town Parks; Parish, and District Council, Antrim; Grid ref. J 149 866.
References: Listed A; in conservation area. D A Beaufort, Ms Journal, 1787, III, p 46, in TCD Library; Lewis, TD, 1837, I, p 38; J Boyle, OSM, 1838, Antrim, XI, pp 33-35; M H F Collis, in UJA, 2nd series, III, 1897, pp 30, 90; PSAMNI, 1940, p 45; Girvan, 'Antrim & Ballymena', UAHS, 1969, p 5.

24. An imposing cruciform church of great antiquity, at the heart of the town, in a walled churchyard. The original pro-cathedral, probably built by John de Courcy about 1180, on Cistercian lines, was enlarged and completed by the 'architect' Robert le Mercer in 1306; he was responsible for the unusually long choir. But by the early 16th century the church was a roofless burned-out shell, with only piers and other fragments surviving; it was not until 1614 that Sir Arthur Chichester entrusted a very drastic reconstruction to the master mason Thomas Paps: this is, in essence, the present church. Many other changes were to follow. Most conspicuously, the old steeple had to be taken down, and Dr Beaufort noted in his journal on 23rd November, 1787, "The venerable church has lately been adorned with a very elegant modern steeple and spire": with its classical doorcase topped by a Palladian window, it is a handsome piece of Georgian work, having a good deal in common with the steeple of the church (26) at Ballycastle of 1756. Unfortunately, the inappropriate modern clock faces on the spire give ominous warning of the unhappy state of the interior.

Some few parts of the interior stonework have merely been over-pointed, with cement not mortar; but far worse, both transepts, and large parts of the nave and choir, have been completely covered in a kind of cushion-faced crazy paving cementwork; even in the vicinity of the memorials (of all dates and great interest) of which the church is full: even in the Chichester transept,

St Nicholas's (C of I) Church, Carrickfergus

where "the most elaborate and exquisite monument of its type surviving in Ireland," of marble and alabaster, stands (see page 286). A baptistry, font, and modern window presenting St Nicholas as Santa Claus were installed in 1951 in the south porch. There is a 17th-century Flemish window on the theme of baptism, imported from the private chapel of Dangan, Co. Westmeath, "lately the seat of the Marquis Wellesley", to which the rest of the glass is inferior. A number of clustered columns and arches sprout incomprehensibly at various points on the walls; there is an early piscina; much of the original tracery has been reasonably sensitively renewed, but Tudor brickwork has been unforgivably replaced by Portland stone; the roof of the Chichester transept is a barrel-vault, but the rest of the roof is of timber, not original, presumably the work of Sir Thomas Drew. The floor level is three feet higher than that of the Norman building. It is surprising that the church has been so badly messed up, considering the stature of the architects concerned with the fabric: Sir Thomas Drew, S P Close, R M Close and Denis O'D Hanna, amongst others; but Maurice Craig expresses a very general view when he writes that it has been "recent-

ly robbed of virtually all its character by injudicious 'restoration'". If the town wishes to attract 'cultural tourism', as now seems to be its policy, it will not only need to find means of having the church more often unlocked, it will also have to assist in undoing much of what has been done in the name of 'restoration': William Morris would have had a thing or two to say.

The War Memorial gateway and bell-tower of 1962, by Denis O'D Hanna, incorporating a sandstone gateway of 1831, are at first glance not unattractive in a kind of poor-man's-Lutyens style; but the structure is of cement, not stone, and unsatisfying in consequence.

Photograph: Michael O'Connell.
Situation: Market place, Carrickfergus; td, Parish, District Council, Carrickfergus; Grid ref. J 415 872.
References: Listed A; in conservation area. D A Beaufort, Ms Journal, 1787, III, p 49, in TCD Library; M'Skimin, 'Carrickfergus', 1811; Atkinson, 'Ireland exhibited', 1823, II, p 112; Drew, 'The ancient church of St. Nicholas', 1882; Mitchell, Guide, 1962; Potterton, 'Irish church monuments', UAHS, 1975, p 88; Campbell and Crowther, 'Carrickfergus', UAHS, 1978; McNeill, 'Anglo-Norman Ulster', 1980; Craig, 'Architecture of Ireland', 1982, p 149; Speers, 'Under the big lamp', 1989, pp 10-12.

'Middle Church' (C of I), Upper Ballinderry

25. The old, or first, church in the parish was at Portmore, near Lough Beg. Bishop Jeremy Taylor worshipped there, but in 1666 decided to erect the so-called Middle Church (superseded by the newer church in 1824) on a more convenient site. In the event, the bishop died in Lisburn of a fever in August 1667, and the Middle Church was not consecrated until 1668. "The original roof-shingles were replaced by Aberdovey slates in 1791" (Evans and Turner). By 1838 it was "falling fast to decay and is now merely preserved for antiquity's sake and the accommodation of funeral services." In 1902, the rector Canon Sayers, the antiquarian F J Bigger, and the architect W J Fennell undertook a major programme of restoration, paid for, in memory of Samuel Walkington, by his widow. Our gratitude is due to these pioneer conservationists; but their zeal slightly outran their discretion.

Externally, the church is very simple, with a curiously geometrical bell-cote, an external staircase giving access to the gallery, and windows "on the old fashion, the casing of wood, strong and clumsy" (1838). In these square openings, the restorers inserted panes of bottle-bottomed glass which, with the walls roughcast in a kind of brownish pebbledash, the roof of greenish slates, and the reddish-brown woodwork, combine to provide a somewhat off-putting appearance. As Maurice Craig puts it: "In truth it is rather an ordinary little building, moving us more by its illustrious associations and its box-pews and pulpit of oak rather than by much architectural character. The hand of the restorer has been heavy upon it, filling the very late Perpendicular windows with bull's-eye glass." As Estyn Evans and Brian Turner remarked in 1977, "regrettably, it is not now white-washed" - as it had been until its restoration.

The interior is much better, with oak three-decker pulpit with sounding board and candlesticks, pews, panelled gallery, and communion table. "In no country church

could better examples of the conditions under which worship was held" (three) "hundred years ago be found - the great family pews, high and uncomfortable, the old central pulpit in three stages rising one above the other; the wide stone-paved aisle, the small red-tiled chancel, and the bell-cot on the west gable". There is a wall cupboard dated 1668; a chest dated 1706; a hatchment with the arms of Jeremy Taylor; a candlestick - and a candle - for every pew; four long-handled collecting-pans; a bell of 1955, and a tablet in memory of the Higginson clan who gave it.

A note on Jeremy Taylor may be helpful to those who know his name, but cannot quite remember why. An intellectual English divine, a chaplain to Charles I, he was deprived of his living under Cromwell, and whilst in retirement in Wales wrote two best-sellers of the day, 'Holy Living' and 'Holy Dying'. In 1658 he retreated to live at Portmore with his patron, Viscount Conway. On the restoration, instead of being recalled to England as he might have preferred, he was appointed Bishop of Down and Connor, so that to him fell the uncomfortable duty of depriving thirty-six parishes of the covenanting or Presbyterian Ministers who, under the Commonwealth, had usurped their tithes and pulpits. The troubles of his episcopate no doubt shortened his life. He was 54 when he died; he was buried in the cathedral at Dromore.

Photograph: Michael O'Connell.
Situation: Off road from Upper to Lower Ballinderry; td, Cluntiriff; Parish, Ballinderry; District Council, Lisburn; Grid ref. J 152 672.
References: Listed B+. T Fagan, OSM, 1838, Antrim, VII, pp 50, 51; F J Bigger and W J Fennell, in UJA, 2nd series, III, 1897, pp 13-22; W J Fennell, scrapbook, 1902, PRONI, D 1878/1/4; PSAMNI, 1940, p 581; Welch, 'Ireland's eye', 1977, p 161; Craig, 'Architecture of Ireland', 1982, p 149; T Neill, in 'Lisburn Historical Society journal', VII, 1989, pp 41-43.

26. Though not the parish church - according to Ewart, "the Incumbent of Ballycastle church is Chaplain of a Donative Chapelry" - this handsome mid-18th century building is probably the best church, architecturally, in the county. The porch inscribed '1756', 'Fear God honour the King', with pediment borne on fluted Doric semi-engaged columns. Above this, a Venetian window; above that, a large clock-face; then a balustrade at the foot of the fine hexagonal spire, with circular openings, topped by ball finial and weathervane. On the south face of the tower, a prominent sun-dial. Maurice Craig describes this church, like that at Moira, Co. Down, as "a respectable piece of classicism" but remarks that "the clock-face, like that of Shandon, is wildly out of scale: otherwise, as at Shandon, it could not be read at any distance."

In 1831, "the principal building in the town is the church, a neat stone structure with a handsome spire. The stone made use of is the sandstone from the collieries, which is very well adapted for architectural purposes. It was built in 1756 at the sole cost of Mr Boyd, who endowed it with 50 pounds per annum ... It is a chapel of ease to the parish, and the presentation to the chaplaincy is in the gift of the proprietor of the Boyd estate" (Lt Robe). Hugh Boyd was an active and enterprising landlord, who developed the town's harbour, glassworks and coal mines; he was a colonel only in the local militia, not a genuine military man; unfortunately, his initiatives died with him. "From the terms of Colonel Boyd's will it appears that he expected it would become the parish church ... It is said that the first service held in the church was Colonel Boyd's funeral service" (Ewart). This is odd. H A Boyd says that work was started in 1752, and completed at 1756, at the sole expense of Col Hugh Boyd, and at a cost of £2,769.4.7^{1}/2; but Col Boyd died on 15 June 1765 and "was buried in Ballycastle Church on the same day in which it was consecrated". So, as H A Boyd remarks, it seems to have been nine years old before it was consecrated: which, he surmises, was due to a delay in completing its endowment.

The interior is rather plain, apart from the very fine classical pedimented doorcase in the west wall. The ceiling is a shallow vault, with a feathered rosette, surrounded by Greek key pattern and festoons. Substantial alterations were made about 1875.

The initials 'LM' and a broad arrow are carved to the left of the doorcase; in 1971, I thought this might be the signature of mason or architect; but I am informed that the arrow is an Ordnance Survey bench-mark. It is tempting to attribute this church to Christopher Myers, the architect of Glenarm Castle, who is known to have been in Ballycastle in 1754, working on the harbour works for Mr Boyd. But there seems to be no evidence for this; and, if Myers was indeed the architect, it would not have been in character for him not to have boasted of it.

Holy Trinity (C of I) Church, Ballycastle

Photograph: Michael O'Connell.

Situation: The Diamond, Ballycastle; td, Town Parks; Parish, Ramoan; District Council, Moyle; Grid ref. D 116 408.

References: Listed A; in conservation area. Hamilton, 'Antrim', 30 July 1784, edition of 1822, p 26 ; Rev. Connolly, in Mason, 'Statistical account', II, 1816, p 512; T C Robe, OSM, 1831, Antrim, IX, p 89; Lewis, TD, 1837, I, p 127; Ewart, 'Down & Connor & Dromore', 1886, p 63; Boyd, 'Ramoan parish', 1930, pp 90-100 and 111-112; Brett, 'Glens of Antrim', UAHS, 1971, p 46; Craig, 'Architecture of Ireland', 1982, p 213.

Christ Church (C of I) Cathedral, Lisburn

27. The tall, slim, elegant spire of Lisburn Cathedral accurately pin-points the heart of the town, visible for miles. From close up, the Cathedral is almost invisible, its back turned to the site of the old Castle, the graveyard amidst which it sits hemmed in by the unappetising backs of the shops of Castle Street, Market Square and Bridge Street.

The original small church built in 1623 was destroyed in the rising of 1641; its successor was destroyed in the great fire of 1707. Rebuilding started almost immediately; the nave is of this rebuilding, of random blackstone, with brick relieving arches over the four pairs of cusped and pointed windows, divided by (later) buttresses, on each side. The 75-foot tower, of 1674, survived the fire; originally it was topped by a cupola. Dr Beaufort noted, on 26 November 1787, "The church is large and very neat - On the tower is a wooden louvre; and on its four sides are painted in black and white the four evangelists". No view of this appears to survive.

Of random blackstone (over-pointed in places), with white ashlar quoins, the tower is now topped by four corner pinnacles and the very fine 96-foot octagonal spire, with three roll-mouldings at its base, added in 1804 by David McBlain of Limavady. Fagan says "The steeple of the cathedral, Lisburn, is locally said to have been raised from 20 to 30 feet above its original height, and the present spire of cut stone erected on it in 1804. Cost is said to

be 1500 pounds, defrayed jointly by the parish and the Marquis of Hertford, engineers, David and James McBlane." The gallery, borne on cast-iron columns, was inserted in 1824. Clock and bells were a gift from the Marquis of Hertford in 1796: "the hour is proclaimed loquaciously with eight tongues". According to an inscribed tablet, the vestry dates from 1718, though it does not look it. The exterior of the church is generally in excellent shape, except for the unworthy toilet block beside the vestry of, apparently, cement blocks.

"The interior of the cathedral is spacious and all its fixtures executed with permanence and taste, which together with its splendid organ, gives it a venerable appearance" (1837). Today the interior is a curious mixture of old and new, light and dark. The roof-timbers, gallery-front and seating, and the (very fine) carved bishop's throne of 1893 (by Jones and Willis of Birmingham) are all dark rich brown, as the whole interior used to be. However, there is much modern and comparatively pale woodwork - new pews, new pulpit, new prebends' stalls, harmonium; red fitted carpet up the aisle and on the seats of the pews. There is a fine east window of 1950 commemorating the Barbour family; the side windows, the Wallace family; the organ dates from 1790. The cathedral is rich in memorial tablets, of which the most striking are that of 1780 to Williams Dobbs, with sea-battle, by Edward Smyth, and that of 1862 to General Nicholson, with land-battle, by

J H Foley. They are all well placed, spaced and cared for, save for the unfortunate Rev. Saumarez Dubourdieu, 1812, whose bust fell from its place on the wall in 1987 and now lacks its plinth.

In 1662, Charles II granted a charter erecting the church into the episcopal seat of Down and Connor for ever, since Downpatrick cathedral was then 'ruinous and laid waste'. Doubts arose as to the validity of this charter, so in 1952 a Bill was introduced into the General Synod to the same general effect but limited to the Diocese of Connor. Presumably St Anne's Cathedral in Belfast, not to mention the cathedral churches of Downpatrick and Dromore, and the ex-cathedral church of St Saviour in Connor, find themselves none the worse off. But "the whole cathedral hierarchy seems to sit lightly on the shoulders of Christ Church, which is really little more than a parish church providing shelter for a homeless chapter" (Galloway)!

Photograph: Michael O'Connell.
Situation: Market Square, Lisburn; td, Lisnagarvey; Parish, District Council, Lisburn; Grid ref. J 262 643.
References: Listed A; in conservation area. D A Beaufort, Ms Journal, 1787, III, p 56, in TCD Library; Bayly, 'Lisburn', 1834, pp 25-26; T Fagan, OSM, 1837, Antrim II, pp 24-25; Carmody, 'Lisburn Cathedral', 1926, passim; Brett and Dunleath, 'Lisburn', UAHS, 1969, p 6; Potterton, 'Irish church monuments', UAHS, 1975, pp 46, 80; Galloway, 'Cathedrals of Ireland', 1992, pp 164-6; current guide to Cathedral, no author, no date.

Trinity (C of I) Church, Aghalee

28. A simple little rustic church, with a stumpy copper spire. "It is locally said that this church was built about 1686 ... The exterior of the church, with its handsome spire and large Gothic windows, are all in good order and, from the handsome eminence on which they are situate, surrounded by lofty sycamore and other forest trees, commands a majestic appearance and an ornament to the neighbourhood" (1838). "The church is a small plain edifice, built in the reign of Charles II, and in substantial repair" (1847). It was, in fact, consecrated in May 1667.

The original roof, of oak shingles, was replaced by slates in 1792. But in 1827, the roof was again replaced, and the walls raised by six feet, and the spire was added to the original tower. The nave has two pairs a-side of coupled pointed windows: there is a very small chancel, of 1899; the walls were roughcast in 1923. The square tower has four diminutive corner pinnacles, and the octagonal spire, 21 feet high, is topped by ball, stalk, and weather-vane with the date 1827 cut out.

The interior is plain and cheerful. The gallery, with its frilly front, is carried on cast-iron columns, and in turn carries the organ. There are pine pews, a modern pine reredos, six nice brass chandeliers, and a well-lettered stone commemorating M. Iohn Usher who died in 1757.

The one extraordinary feature of this otherwise not very exciting little church is the unique form of stopper employed at the ends of all the dripstones over doors and windows: at first glance, resembling a stylised bunch of grapes, on closer inspection like nothing so much as a wasp's nest.

Photograph: Michael O'Connell.
Situation: Off road from Soldierstown to Aghalee; td, Poobles; Parish, Aghalee (diocese of Dromore); District Council, Lisburn; Grid ref. J 145 629.
References: Listed B. Lewis, TD, 1837, I, p 16; 1847, I, p 14; T Fagan, OSM, 1838, Antrim, VII, p 30.

First Presbyterian Church, Broughshane

29. A T-shaped church, probably built 1720, the date on the sun-dial, perhaps incorporating parts of an earlier church of 1655; an inscribed panel proclaims "This church was reconstructed 1929-30, the original walls being retained". The reconstruction was by Young and Mackenzie. The question how old, or how new, the building may be, is a comparatively subjective one: as Maurice Craig puts it, in such cases "continuity inheres in the congregation rather than the fabric". The history of the congregation says "July 19th, 1931, was a day of rejoicing and thanksgiving, when the reconstructed Church was opened for public worship. With the exception of portions of the walls, the bell, and the clock, which had been a gift to the congregation in 1757, the building was entirely new." In 1835, J R Ward of the Ordnance Survey wrote "a plain, stone building ... The last repairs and putting the building in its present state cost 850 pounds, which was defrayed by public subscription. It will accommodate 1,100 persons; the average attendance is 800. This is supposed to be one of the earliest settlements of Presbyterians in Ireland." In 1837, Samuel Lewis described it as "a spacious handsome building with a cupola containing a bell".

It has three galleries, each reached by an external staircase sheltered by the oversailing eaves of the main roof: and a central peak, with bell, above the sundial and inscription. "The traditional T-plan ... is rendered extraordinary by the external exposed staircases leading to the galleries and themselves supporting the elaborate overhanging eaves of the roof - a very interesting conception", says Girvan. It seems that the staircases are original, but not so the overhang of the roof. The church is situated in an old and attractive graveyard, the cause of much dispute when the landlord, Mr O'Neill, threatened to plough up "the meeting-house green" rather than let it be used for burials. Many handsome memorials, the most prominent that to Robert Stewart, DD, 1783-1852. Six Corinthian columns support a domelet sheltering a draped urn which has an inscription on each side of the square plinth: ... "where his influence extended litigation was unknown": all kept very neatly painted in cream and bronze, not (presumably) by the legal profession. Girvan describes the cupola as "slightly pointed and looks like an egg-cosy".

Photograph: Michael O'Connell.
Situation: Main Street, Broughshane; td, Broughshane Upper; Parish, Racavan; District Council, Ballymena; Grid ref. D 151 067.
References: Listed B+. Minutes of Presbytery of Antrim, 1671-1691, transcript in PRONI, D2861/F/3E; E Durnford, OSM, 1832, J Boyle, 1835, and J R Ward, 1835, Antrim, IV, pp 87, 91, 97; Lewis, TD, 1837, II, p 479; Girvan, 'Antrim & Ballymena', UAHS, 1969, p 31; Craig, 'Architecture of Ireland', 1982, p 212n.

Duneane (C of I) Church, Duneane

30. On a site remote from any village, amidst rolling farmland, a rustic white-painted church with sky-blue trim: at the end of a lane guarded by two successive sets of conical-capped gate-pillars, and pairs of clipped yews.

Built in 1729 on the site, and in the graveyard, of a much older church, going back to the 13th century. In 1836, "a simple little building 50 feet long and 19 wide, and containing accommodation for 227 persons. It was erected in 1729. It is perfectly plain. On its western gable is a little arch, from which is suspended a bell. It is not in good order." And: "There is no steeple or tower on the church. The only ornament is a bell which is on the west end of the church, put up at the expense of the parish and cost £7."

It is in excellent order today, if not quite unaltered - the church was enlarged, though not greatly, around 1857. The pointed windows are Georgian-Gothick lattice-glazed; the simple bell-cote is unaltered; there is a slate sundial, inscribed 'Duneane Church', set into the south wall.

Photograph: Michael O'Connell.
Situation: Off road from Milltown to Moneyglass; td, Lismacloskey; Parish, Duneane; District Council, Antrim; Grid ref. J 013 909.
References: Listed B. Taylor and Skinner, 'Roads', 1778; J Boyle, OSM, 1836, and J Bleakly, 1837, Antrim, VI, pp 100, 118; O'Laverty, 'Down and Connor', III, 1884, p 333.

Moravian Church, Warden's House and Manse, Gracehill

31. "Ballykennedy, or Grace-hill, ... owes its origin to the Rev. John Cennick, who, in 1746, founded here an establishment of Moravians ... the village consists of 39 family residences, of which the greater number are small cottages, exclusively of the chapel, and the two principal houses for unmarried brethren and sisters respectively, which occupy three sides of a quadrangle, of which the area is ornamented with shrubs ... the chapel is a neat and commodious building" (Lewis, 1837). In fact, Cennick died in London in 1755, and never saw the settlement he had projected.

The Moravians were recognised by the English Parliament as "an ancient Protestant Episcopal Church" by Act of Parliament of 1749. Their communities in England and Ireland were derived from foundations in Georgia and the Carolinas in the 1730s, but ultimately from the 'mother' community at Herrnhut in Saxony, founded in 1722. Planning of the community at Gracehill started in the 1750s; by 1760, Mark Berry, a young carpenter from Ballinderry was helping the Swedish Brother Jorde with the plans. In the same year, the Committee inspected a new house at Harryville, Ballymena, lately built by one John Bligh, and concluded "he appears by his work to be a good Architect and a man of a good Character". He was employed to advise on the materials to be used: for there were difficulties in finding suitable freestone, slates, timber, and brick clay. But most of the work seems to have been executed by the Brothers themselves "without any Hurt or Danger, which is a matter of Thankfulness to us". The whole venture was financed by

an indefinite loan of £2,000, at 5% interest, from Herrnhut, on the security of a bond given by six leading members of the congregation.

The foundation stone of the central inter-connected group was laid on 12th March 1765, the Building Overseer at that time being John Reinhard Schloezer, one of the guarantors, and the church was opened for worship on 6th November of the same year. The house on the right hand side was the original manse, that on the left the home of the Warden, but during the intervening years the two have more than once exchanged functions. The earliest buildings must have been of a plain and simple vernacular, suited to the skills of the congregation. The ceiling of the church was only put in in 1767. An organ was introduced in 1781. The church was extensively "renewed and enlarged" in 1798. Until 1842, it had "a hard clay floor": this was replaced by a wooden floor (now carpeted) in a major restoration in 1842, when the present

delightful pulpit was installed. The organ was rebuilt, and new seating (made by John Christie, cabinet maker, of Ballymena) substituted for the previous backless forms in 1866. The present cupola dates from the 1920s; it cost £453, from "Messrs Dowling of Belfast", its predecessor (erected about 1880) having been discovered to be dangerous - "It wasn't taken down a minute too soon". In 1948, the rendering of lime and sand was stripped from the rubble walls, which were then "cement plastered and stone finished", the result being not quite so happy as might have been wished; the texture and colour are somewhat disagreeable, unworthy of so fine a group of buildings.

Externally, the church has three tall round-headed windows to the front, and two doorcases with smaller round-headed windows above them. Each doorcase is of carved timber, painted black and white, with fluted pilasters, acanthus leaves, dentils and a delightful wreath with ribbons - Girvan says of bay leaves, but I think I detect acorns or oak apples. Mark Berry was the first Master Carpenter, later Warden, but this work is by oral tradition attributed to a Swedish brother named Rev. Jons Fredlizius, 1751-1816, who was a skilled wood-carver. Craig says, "The two doors are believed to have been for the two sexes ... such an arrangement, with two doors and the liturgical focus in the centre of the long back wall ... is common to all the "nonconformist" groups, including the Catholic." The house at each end is two-storey, with two bays of windows facing the garden square, and the doorway being at the side.

Internally, the church has two galleries at the ends - one for males, one for females - carried on simple cast-iron columns; under each gallery, a door giving direct access to the adjoining house. There are three brass chandeliers. The finest feature of the interior, however, is the magnificent 'tulip' pulpit of 1842, with its twin curving staircases, white-painted balusters and twisting mahogany handrails.

At the rear of the house to the left, a row of five covered archways, presumably for the accommodation of traps or carriages; and a long garden. To each side of the group, a pathway leads through the trees to the remarkable hill-top graveyard, where the grave slabs are laid out in due order, from the foundation of the settlement to the present day, males on one side of the central path and females on the other: it is curious that, over two-and-a-half centuries, the females buried here have been noticeably more numerous than the males. Lewis, in 1847, remarks that the burial ground "has an air of peculiar quiet and repose". He also observes, strangely, that "Camomile is reared by some of the inhabitants with advantage." Apparently, John Rea of

Camomile Hill made a living from camomile flowers, employing the children of Gracehill to harvest his crop and rewarding them with meals and New Testaments.

Gracehill features in practically every travel book or gazetteer relating to County Antrim, almost invariably depicted in a flattering light. However, Atkinson, visiting in 1817, wrote "its aspect would, in our view, be much more light and graceful, if its slender area had not been planted with a single tree. With this description of ornament ... the interior of the village is however most heavily and ungracefully crowded ..."

It is still, in my view, charming; as well as being a declared conservation area, it contains no less than 16 listed buildings, of which only the chapel is represented here. Modern buildings have encroached on every side of the central village, but without disastrous ill-effects.

Photographs: Michael O'Connell.
Situation: 21, 23 and 25 Church Road, Gracehill; td, Ballykennedy; Parish, Ahoghill; District Council, Ballymena; Grid ref. D 074 019.
References: Listed A; in conservation area. Journals and diaries of the Ballymena congregation, 1757-1765, of the Gracehill congregation, 1765 to the present day, original Bond of 1 December 1763, all in the care of the minister; Atkinson, 'Ireland exhibited', 1823, II, pp 190-3; T C Robe, OSM, 1833, and J Boyle, 1835, Antrim, VIII, pp 2, 3, 10, 18, 19; Lewis, TD, 1837, I, p 140; 1847, I, p 134; PG, II, 1846, p 282; Girvan, 'Antrim & Ballymena', UAHS, 1969, p 28; Ingham, 'Gracehill', 1977, passim; Craig, 'Architecture of Ireland', 1982, p 230; Blair, 'County Antrim characters', 1993, pp 52, 53, 90, 91; 'Moravian history magazine', No 8, 1995, pp 9-11; White, 'History of Gracehill Moravian Settlement', 1996: and information from her.

Moravian Church and Manse, Lower Ballinderry

32. "The original chapel, built here" around 1755 "was thatched and constructed at the expense of the English and other foreign Moravian congregations. However, in 1821, it was rebuilt and slated, furnished with a valuable organ, and various improvements made on and about the place, at an expense of about £700 ... it is said to have been a very handsome edifice and to be much admired by all for its style and cleanliness ... But in 1835, on Easter Sunday morning, the chapel with all its furniture was consumed by accidental fire. The present chapel was subsequently erected and opened for divine service on the 16th June 1836". It seems likely that neither the 1836 nor the 1821 rebuilding greatly altered the form of this, modest enough, place of worship. "A house and 2 good gardens" go with the ministry: "the buildings and place is altogether in neat order and form an ornament to the village in which it is situated" (1838). In the Valuation book compiled in the same year, the "Moravian Chapple" is valued at £10.3.1, and the dwelling of the Rev. James Chambers at £9.17.10.

The oddity is, that the manse (very sensibly) is built end-on to the church, and under the same roof, so that the minister may step from his home through a communicating door directly into the pulpit. "Sometimes the body of the church and the house of the priest or minister form a continuous building with an unbroken roof-ridge. Though visually dissimilar, this is no doubt a continuation of the tradition of the residential west end as seen, for example, at Taghmon, Co. Westmeath ... The Moravian Church at Ballinderry and the Methodist Church in Castlebar are just the same ..." (Craig). (But compare Ballyhamage House (112), where a similar arrangement was disallowed by a Church of Ireland bishop).

Of cream-washed stucco, the side walls roughcast, the church and manse stand between a most agreeable garden, and a modest graveyard, each with nice old yew trees. The gable of the church has a simple bell-cote, and a modest porch; there are three round-headed Georgian-glazed windows on each side. Inside, the gallery, with organ, is carried on four rather grand Ionic columns. The pews are of pine. The manse is two-storey, with Georgian-glazed windows throughout, but modern door-cases on three sides. Nonetheless, an uncommonly pleasing group.

Photograph: Michael O'Connell.
Situation: Off Portmore road, Lower Ballinderry; td, and Parish, Ballinderry; District Council, Lisburn; Grid ref. J 128 677.
References: Listed B. T Fagan, OSM, 1838, Antrim, VII, pp 47, 48; VAL 1B 167, in PRONI; Craig, 'Architecture of Ireland', 1982, p 225.

▷

Photographs: Michael O'Connell.
Situation: Glebe Road, Dunmurry; td, Dunmurry; Parish, Drumbeg; District Council, Lisburn; Grid ref. J 291 689.
References: Listed A. T Fagan, OSM, 1837, Antrim, II, pp 122-3; D O'D Hanna in 'Arts in Ulster', pp 39, 40; Dixon, 'Introduction', 1975, p 49; Brett, 'Roger Mulholland', UAHS, 1976, p 12; Craig, 'Architecture of Ireland', 1982, p 210.

Non-Subscribing Presbyterian Church, Dunmurry

33. This church dates from 1779, though the congregation was founded in 1676. "Situated on a very handsome site in the village of Dunmurry, it is an oblong structure, 1-storey high and slated ... The interior is spacious, well-lit, and all furniture in good order" (1837). "You might expect to find it in Salem or Williamsburg, USA. It is essentially Puritan and Non-Conformist ... in scale and conception it is utterly foreign to the English church ... it has a domestic beauty far more in common with the farmyard than the church" (Hanna, 1951). This church has been tentatively attributed to Roger Mulholland of Belfast, architect.

The church is built of random brown-black stone with much galleting, the plinth, eaves-course and tablet surrounds of red sandstone, the Gibbsian-blocked architraves to windows and doors, and the little console brackets supporting the cills, of ashlar. There are twin doors, pedimented, served by a single wide flight of six stone steps; above each door, an inscribed tablet, "This house was rebuilt at the expense of the congregation of Dunmurry, 1779" and "Reverend James Stouppe AM, Minister." The round-headed windows have Georgian-style glazing, but at only 13 large panes to each window, these do not look original. The central window is of Victorian stained glass.

The interior is very nicely painted in a cool pale grey; box-pews complete; five tiers of raked box-pews in the two galleries, borne on simple wooden columns; pedimented internal doorcases with charming (modern) gilt-on-black musical cherubs and oak-apples in the tympana; octagonal pulpit, with nice fan-shaped corner panels, clerk's seat below, curving bannisters,

organ above in arched recess. Four well-matched white-on-black-marble wall memorials of 1856, 1863, 1865, and 1895. The upper storey of the vestry at the rear is later, though its ground floor seems to be original; both have been rendered. The flat ceiling is modern, but the slated roof is tall and steeply pitched.

"The general layout may be compared with the Presbyterian Church at Corboy, Co. Longford, with the Moravian Church at Gracehill"(31) "and with the Catholic Church at Kildoagh, Co. Cavan. In all of these the focus of interest is, or was, in the centre of the long back wall, and it is more than likely that the two doors were originally set aside for the two sexes" (Craig).

Old Congregation Presbyterian Church, Randalstown

34. This elliptical church was built in 1790; the hexagonal porch was added, and the galleries were inserted, around 1830; the "minister's annexe" was added, the walls and roof were raised, and 18 oculus windows were inserted, in 1929. Yet, miraculously, the parts combine to form an almost completely seamless and harmonious whole, and it is almost impossible to differentiate the stonework of 1929 from that of 1790 in the exterior walls; although the alteration of the pretty glazing-pattern of the Georgian-Gothick pointed windows is regrettable. It appears that the then Minister, Rev. F G Bell, organised the transport by horse and cart of suitable matching stones from ruined cottages near the shores of Lough Neagh. His son, Sir Ewart Bell, then a small boy, recalls that the supervising architect was a Mr Graham, from Belfast; and that every meal-time at the Manse was spent discussing ways of raising the needful £6,200.

"The Presbyterian meeting is situated in a hollow on the opposite side of the road from and within a few yards of the church. Its form is rather singular, being that of an elipse, the major diameter of which is 88 and the minor 48 feet" ...... "The erection of this meeting house (in 1790) cost the congregation £600. In 1828 it was newly roofed by them at an expense of £200, and between the years 1830 to 1832 £1,054 was expended in erecting the porch and gallery" (1838).

The original conception must surely owe something to the elliptical First Presbyterian church in Rosemary Street, Belfast, completed to the designs of Roger Mulholland in 1783. Indeed, it is not impossible that he had some hand in the Randalstown church, though that is pure conjecture; and there may be some obscure relationship with the somewhat later Unitarian church in Crumlin (46). It has been suggested that it may owe more to St Andrew's church in Edinburgh, designed by Andrew Frazer, chief engineer of Scotland, who "generously insisted on relinquishing the competition premium in favour of a drawing-master named Robert Kay, whose design had

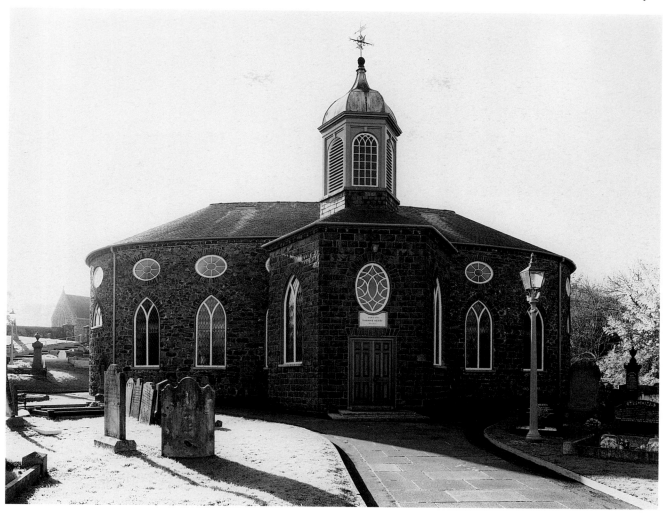

been commended" (Colvin). But, despite the close connections of Co. Antrim presbyterianism with Edinburgh at this period, this derivation seems to me improbable, given the sophisticated classical inspiration and detailing of St Andrew's - Corinthian portico, Adamesque plasterwork ceiling, and cupola (superseded by a spire).

The church is built of brownish basalt blocks, mostly rubblestones though some, principally in the porch, squared, and with some galleting, particularly in the lower courses. The hexagonal porch is of square basalt, topped by a graceful cupola, with a delightful oval window above a panel inscribed "Built in 1790, Thomas Henry, Minister"; inside the porch, a handsome double staircase gives access to the galleries, which were very dark and low when first inserted in 1830, lighted only by the very tips of the pointed windows, but are now light and airy thanks to the slightly flattened oculi with frosted glass (renewed 1988); below, there are pointed windows, cast-iron fluted columns carrying the gallery, fine pews and pulpit, and

two subsidiary doorways (with Gothick fanlights) as well as the nicely-curved Minister's room, with internal stair up to the pulpit, so tactfully added in 1929. In the late 1950s, the sexton's cottage in front of the church was demolished, and a new boundary wall built using stone salvaged from the ruins of Ballymena Castle - the gate-pillars are constructed from its chimney-stacks!

Photographs: Left: before 1929, courtesy Mr T Nicholl; right: Michael O'Connell. (See also colour-plate Xa)
Situation: Between road from Randalstown to Portglenone and that to Ahoghill; td, Ballygrooby; Parish, Drummaul; District Council, Antrim; Grid ref. J 078 909.
References: Listed A. J Boyle, OSM, 1838, Antrim, VI, p 42; Girvan, 'Antrim & Ballymena', UAHS, 1969, p 25; Youngson, 'Classical Edinburgh', 1966, pp 84-5; Colvin, 'Dictionary', 1978, p 322; information from Mr Tom Nicholl, and from Sir Ewart Bell.

St James's (RC) Chapel, Aldergrove

35. A charming, early, cruciform chapel, roughcast and whitened, with Gothick-glazed pointed windows, an oculus window above the porch, and a plain cross atop each gable. Almost everything is white-painted, inside and out, save for the slate roof and black-painted splashband. The gallery, with railings like bannister-rails, is later but congruous; also white-painted. There is a fine high altar. Altogether a delightfully simple, austere, uncluttered little church.

As to its date, Girvan follows Boyle who, writing in 1838, describes it as "a plain edifice built of stone and kept neatly, roughcast and whitened - floor of earth - no gallery: erected 1816". But O'Laverty is quite specific; the first chapel at Aldergrove was erected by Father Crangle, who died in 1814; "which was enlarged and altered into the present church, erected by Father McMullan in 1824. It was dedicated under the invocation of St James", but is known to Girvan as St Mary's.

Photograph: Michael O'Connell.
Situation: In Aldergrove village; td, Ballyquillin; Parish, Killead; District Council, Antrim; Grid ref. J 136 798.
References: Listed B. J Boyle, OSM, 1838, Killead, as yet unpublished; O'Laverty, 'Down and Connor', II, 1880, pp 329, 333; Girvan, 'West Antrim', UAHS, 1970, pp 10, 27.

St Patrick's (RC) Chapel, Derriaghy

36. A tiny rural church, only two bays deep, with a three-light east window, rendered and painted grey; a little unfortunately, roofed with tiles not slates; and an even tinier cottage, for sacristan or caretaker; in an old graveyard well furnished with trees.

"The original house" - of 1745 - "was 48 feet long and thatched. It was maliciously burnt at the last rebellion in Ireland and when subsequently rebuilt" (in 1802) "it was slated and reduced in length ... In 1836 the walls was raised three feet and a new roof put on." The earlier chapel was the work of Father Hugh O'Donnell, a native of the Glens, who had been educated at Salamanca, and in later life it was he who erected St Mary's in Chapel Lane, Belfast, opened with ceremony in 1784. This chapel was burned by the 'Wreckers' in 1798, rebuilt by Father O'Donnell's curate Father Devlin. The church is dedicated to St Patrick one of whose teeth is said to be buried under the altar.

Photograph: Michael O'Connell.
Situation: Off Barnfield Road, Derriaghy; td, Lagmore; Parish, Derriaghy; District Council, Lisburn; Grid ref. J 265 685.
References: Not listed. T Fagan, OSM, 1837, Antrim, II, p 104; Barr, 'Derriaghy', 1974, pp 90-92.

Church (RC) of the Blessed Virgin, Feystown

37 (left). A simple, low, white-painted church in a broad stone-walled graveyard high on the hillside of Crockandoo: a striking more-than-lifesize statue affixed to its south-facing gable, visible from afar, and not disimproving from close up.

Dedicated in 1828 - the year before Catholic emancipation - by Dr Crolly. Lieutenant Hore, writing in 1830, says "there are 2 Roman Catholic chapels, one in the townland of Harphall close to the sea to the north, and one in the townland of Clady on the east side of the parish. This last will soon be a ruin, as there is another just finished very near it on the roadside, to supply its place." This must be Feystown chapel, despite the slight discrepancy in dates. The chancel and sanctuary added in 1878. Three Gothic windows a-side in the nave, two lancet windows a-side in the chancel; a plain, well-painted barn-church interior with gallery; a reproduction of the 11th century Ardclinis crozier in the door of the altar-rail. (This crozier, or bishop's crook, was entrusted to the Galvin family of Straidkilly, Glenarm, for sake-keeping in the mid 18th century; in 1961 their descendant sold it to the National Museum in Dublin and gave the proceeds to the parish to pay for a major renovation of the church). The roof is topped by a nice little bell-cote with cross on top. At the rear, there is a cottage-like vestry with low slate roof and prominent chimney. The gable-end statue of the youthful St Patrick, looking across the hills to Slemish, with staff and flying cloak, is by Angela Countess of Antrim; the model was her younger son, Hector McDonnell, the painter, then aged 15.

Photograph: Michael O'Connell.
Situation: At Feystown, on road from Craigyhill to Glenarm; td, Clady; Parish, Tickmacrevan; District Council, Larne: Grid ref. D 316 101.
References: Not listed. T Hore, OSM, 1830, and J Boyle, 1835, Antrim, IV, pp 123, 129; O'Laverty, 'Down and Connor', IV, 1887, p 584; McKillop, 'Glenarm', 1987, pp 8, 40-41; information from the model.

Parish Church (C of I), Ballintoy

38. Not only is this, internally and externally, one of the prettiest churches in the county, it is also one of the best documented. "Began pulling down the old church on 2nd April 1812; the first stone of the new one laid on 14th April 1812; the building finally completed (down to the varnishing of the pews) on 15th December 1813." Planning had started in 1810, when a first £100 was levied on the congregation. In September 1811 John Bowden, the Dublin architect to the Board of First Fruits, supplied plans and elevations. On 28th February 1812, the rector, Rev. Robert Traill, signed a contract with "Henry Clark of Turnarobert Esq and Henry Wynn, Carpenter, of Dervock" for the erection of the church to the plans and specifications made by John Bowden, to be completed by May 1813, at a fixed price of £993.5.6. An unsigned and undated specification, probably that referred to in the contract, also survives.

In fact, it seems that Mr Traill and Henry Wynn took it upon themselves to depart substantially from Bowden's plans. Between them, they ran up considerable extras: the final cost of church and spire came to £1324.11.6 of which £800 was contributed by the Board of First Fruits, £367.15.9 raised from the parishioners, £75.15.6 came from the sale of materials from the old church, and £80.18.3 was contributed by Mr Traill himself. "Henry Wynne, architect" whose name is engraved on a stone below the altar, received payments totalling £233.19.7 between April 1812 and May 1814. The weather-cock for the spire cost £4.11.3. On 1st August 1814, three Commissioners certified to the Bishop of Down and Connor that, after inspection, they found all in order - "the roof well timbered and slated with the best ton slates ... the seats commodious ... all neatly finished and painted ... the church is neat, the steeple handsome and well executed." No other work by Henry Wynne (or Wynn) seems to be known. He is presumably a carpenter-styled-architect in the same way as his near contemporary, Roger Mulholland of Belfast. It seems unlikely that this is the same person as the Henry Wynne of Belleisle, near Dervock, who was living in New Orleans in 1821; but it is not impossible.

There is room for doubt whether the existing tower is that of the earlier church, or a new one of 1813. Bowden's elevation purports to show the old tower re-used - tower 42 feet high, spire 25 feet, weathercock 4 feet; steeple, 10 feet square inside, 15 feet square outside. On the other hand, his drawing looks very little like the present tower; and the contract documents suggest that Mr Clark and Mr Wynn were to take down the old tower, being careful not to allow its removal to cause damage. In any event, the spire or steeple erected in 1813 ("a conspicuous object in so bleak a view, and ... a useful landmark to mariners" - PG) was blown down on 28th December 1894. Fortunately, though now irreparably cracked, the old bell still survives, inscribed "Archibald Stewart gave me; Charles his son recast me Anno 1686; and Archibald the son of Charles recast and augmented me, Anno 1718" A curious sundial was added in 1817.

According to Thomas Fagan in 1838, "This edifice is 1-storey high and slated, and situated on the ruins of an ancient one, which was overhauled and rebuilt and enlarged by attaching an aisle to the north side in 1813 ... The steeple and spire stands between 70 and 80 feet high, including a vane on the top - the steeple seems to be nearly square and measures 17 and a half feet across the front outside and about 50 feet in height, with a pinnacle of cut stone on each corner, and lit by 3 oval windows and 1 flat arch. And over the entrance door, engraven on a cut freestone, the following inscriptions: "Samuel Thompson, Masons, William Finey, April 1733". The steeple is said to be built to the old church at the above period. The spire is composed of wood and plaster, and slated on the surface and topped with a large round ball and vane." All this is puzzling, and not easy to reconcile either with the documentary or the built evidence.

The church is T-shaped, harled, and white-painted, standing out amidst its flock of gravestones on its little plateau half-way between the village and the harbour. The tower has very rudimentary pinnacles, linked by a low curving parapet, almost Moorish in feel, with uncommonly small openings. Between the two wide windows in the south wall is mounted a finely carved tombstone of 1723. The north wall contains a single segmental-headed window, lighting both transept and gallery, with 34 panes above and 20 below, the plain glass looking out to seaward.

Internally, the church is painted in a subtle mixture of white and cream, both contrasting with the varnished pine of ceiling and pews. There are two galleries in the transept. There is a good font of 1864; a lovely hexagonal hour-glass pulpit ornamented with cut-out shamrocks and quatrefoils; and a chancel arch carried on a pair of rather showy Tuscan columns.

Photograph: Michael O'Connell. (See also colour-plate XIVa)
Situation: North of Ballintoy village; td, Ballintoy demesne; Parish, Ballintoy; District Council, Moyle; Grid ref. D 039 449.
References: Listed B+ (Girvan accords it an A, and so would I). Original vestry minute books and building contract, specification and drawings in the custody of the rector; copy drawing in T 1124, letter to Thomas Camac of 13 October 1908 in T1177/11, in PRONI; J Boyle, OSM, 1835, and T Fagan, 1838, Antrim, IX, pp 15, 19; Lewis TD, 1837, I, p 119; PG, I, 1845, p 149; Ewart, 'Down & Connor & Dromore', 1886, p 62; Girvan, 'North Antrim', UAHS, 1972, p 30.

Old Parish Church (C of I), Ballymena

39. Most attractive: a historical feature of the town in considerable contrast to the bleak and overbearing new parish church of 1881 nearby.

"The church was built in 1707 (the ground being given by Sir Robert Adair), Mr Ballantine, architect. In 1798 it was used for a barrack and the woodwork consumed for fuel. In 1822 the tower was built at a cost of £320, £100 of which was advanced by the Board of First Fruits, to be repaid by instalments" (1835). The draft memoir of 1834, by various hands, reads somewhat differently: "Built by Mr Ballantine, the exact cost cannot be found out. In 1707 the body was built in a plain form like the meeting houses of the present day. In 1798 it was used as a barrack and very much injured by all the woodwork being used as fuel. In 1822 the tower was built by William Dean and cost £320. This sum was advanced by the Board of First Fruits, to be paid by instalments levied off the parish. [Insert note by Boyle: The Board only sent £100, the rest was subscribed. It is now 1834 and the whole sum has not yet been repaid.] ... Many more persons would attend if there were a few free seats. Many poor people remain absent, not wishing to intrude on their more wealthy neighbours." I know nothing either of Mr Ballantine or of William Dean.

Of the original church only the pinnacled tower survives, with louvred opening, elliptical plaque, and built up pointed doorway: and the crow-stepped west wall of the nave, propped by red brickwork. Tower and wall now provide, from the back, an extraordinary kind of columbarium with memorials, many now damaged, inset in the recesses. Surrounded by gravestones; approached by a path, lined by five lime trees a-side, between dignified stone gate-pillars with good iron gates.

Photograph: Michael O'Connell.
Situation: Off Church Street, Ballymena; td, Townparks; Parish, Kilconriola; District Council, Ballymena; Grid ref. D 106 035.
References: Not listed at all, though Girvan awards it an A. J Boyle, OSM, 1835, and draft memoir, 1834, Antrim, VIII, pp 94, 116; PG, II, 1846, p 571; Ewart, 'Down & Connor & Dromore', 1887, p 65; Girvan, 'Antrim & Ballymena', UAHS, 1969, p 17.

St Patrick's (C of I) Church, Cairncastle

40. "The church is a very plain little building 60 feet long and 24 feet wide, and would accommodate about 120 persons. It stands in the townland of Ballygalley and was erected on the site of the former one in the year 1815. This church has a very low spire" (1835).

"The Church, a small plain edifice with a lofty spire, was built on the site of a former church, by aid of a loan of £350, granted in 1815 by the late Board of First Fruits". (1837: note the difference of opinion as to the loftiness of the spire). The previous church seems to have dated from about 1650; the Visitation of 1622 reports "Ecclesia de Carnecastle, noe church, but the wals faln to the ground"; the site is of great antiquity, and is mentioned in the 1291 Taxation of Pope Nicholas IV.

A pleasant little rubblestone church, with a charming tower and spire: the former modestly fortified, with a louvre'd oculus on each face (that facing the road off-centre);

the latter is, unusually, a slated octagonal spire, topped by a nice nautical weather-vane. There are paired lancet windows, with lattice glazing, in the nave; a three-light window above the altar. The chancel, of rather later date and blacker stone, has a flag-pole attached to the wall.

As O'Laverty says, it is "beautifully situated, nestling under the Sallagh Braes"; the graveyard is an uncommonly pleasant one, with many old gravestones of interest, and a finely carved Celtic cross in memory of Rev. Classon Porter (d. 1885), the local historian of the district.

Photograph: R J Welch, Ulster Museum W01/28/11.
Situation: Off road from Kilwaughter to Cairncastle; td, Ballygalley; Parish, Kilwaughter; District Council, Larne; Grid ref. D 360 071.
References: Listed B. J Boyle, OSM, 1835, Antrim, III, p 3; Lewis, TD, 1837, I, p 264; Ewart, 'Down & Connor & Dromore', 1886, p 98; O'Laverty, 'Down and Connor', IV, 1887, p 580.

St John Baptist (C of I) Church, Bushmills

41. "A handsome edifice ... on the site of an ancient church, which was a ruin in 1625" (Lewis). "It is very neatly fitted up internally and can conveniently accommodate 200 persons ... There are few country churches kept in such extremely nice order and repair as this" (Boyle). "Largely by the efforts of" the Rev Charles McDaniel Stewart, vicar from 1804 to 1826, "the present church at Bushmills was built, divine worship having been previously held at the old church at Dunluce". The Parliamentary Gazetteer records, with meticulous exactitude, that it was built in 1821 "at the cost of £1200, of which £830.15.4½ gifted by the late Board of First Fruits, £276.18.5½ lent by that Board, and £92.16.1¾ was raised by subscription." (which seems to leave 9.11¼ over): "sittings 350; attendance 200."

Of carved basalt, with simple pointed dripstones framing the three principal windows in each side wall: little square lattice windows lighting the gallery. The tower (attributed by the listers to John Bowden, on what evidence they do not say) has the date '1821' in a lozenge. Rather unusual corner pinnacles with recessed channels, and very attractive triple-ribbed string-courses: but the knops are missing from two of the four pinnacles. The chancel and transept are later than the rest. The interior contains a gallery borne on four cast-iron columns, a pulpit of 1875, and many memorials to members of the Macnaghten and Montgomery families. Girvan awards this church an 'A'.

Photograph: Michael O'Connell.

Situation: Priestland Road, Bushmills; td, Magheraboy; Parish, Dunluce; Grid ref. C 939 405.

References: Listed B; in conservation area. J Boyle, OSM, 1835, Antrim, V, p 109; Lewis, TD, 1837, I, p 585; PG, II, 1846, p 158; Pilson, 'History of Belfast', 1846, p 158; Stewart, 'Three hundred years in Innishowen', 1929, p 307; Boyd, 'Dunluce parish', 1937, p VII; Girvan, 'North Antrim', UAHS, 1972, p 18.

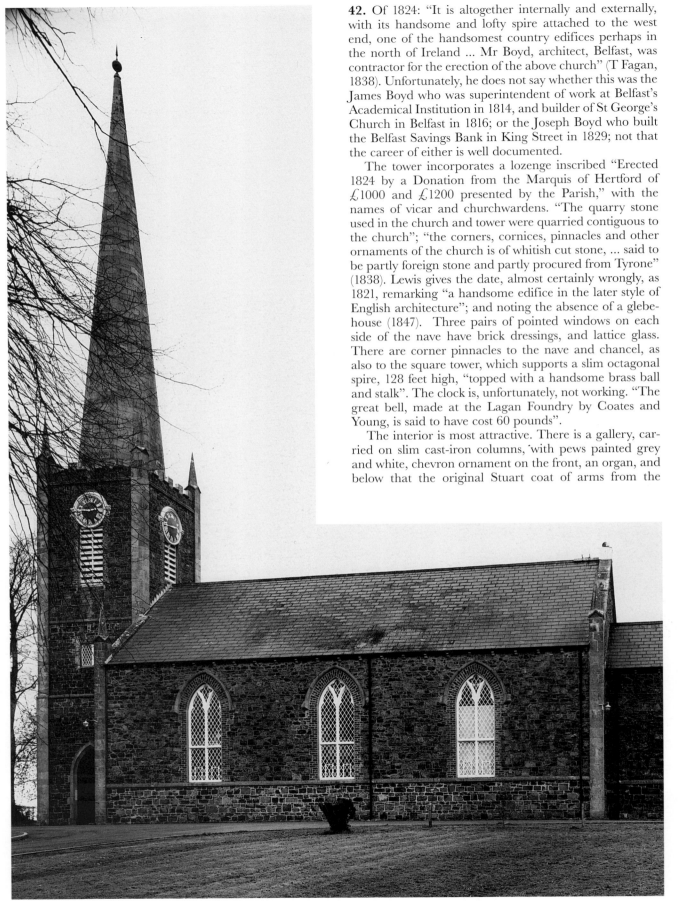

42. Of 1824: "It is altogether internally and externally, with its handsome and lofty spire attached to the west end, one of the handsomest country edifices perhaps in the north of Ireland ... Mr Boyd, architect, Belfast, was contractor for the erection of the above church" (T Fagan, 1838). Unfortunately, he does not say whether this was the James Boyd who was superintendent of work at Belfast's Academical Institution in 1814, and builder of St George's Church in Belfast in 1816; or the Joseph Boyd who built the Belfast Savings Bank in King Street in 1829; not that the career of either is well documented.

The tower incorporates a lozenge inscribed "Erected 1824 by a Donation from the Marquis of Hertford of £1000 and £1200 presented by the Parish," with the names of vicar and churchwardens. "The quarry stone used in the church and tower were quarried contiguous to the church"; "the corners, cornices, pinnacles and other ornaments of the church is of whitish cut stone, ... said to be partly foreign stone and partly procured from Tyrone" (1838). Lewis gives the date, almost certainly wrongly, as 1821, remarking "a handsome edifice in the later style of English architecture"; and noting the absence of a glebe-house (1847). Three pairs of pointed windows on each side of the nave have brick dressings, and lattice glass. There are corner pinnacles to the nave and chancel, as also to the square tower, which supports a slim octagonal spire, 128 feet high, "topped with a handsome brass ball and stalk". The clock is, unfortunately, not working. "The great bell, made at the Lagan Foundry by Coates and Young, is said to have cost 60 pounds".

The interior is most attractive. There is a gallery, carried on slim cast-iron columns, with pews painted grey and white, chevron ornament on the front, an organ, and below that the original Stuart coat of arms from the

Parish Church (C of I), Upper Ballinderry

Middle Church (25), inscribed 'CR [Carolus Rex]: Dieu et Mon Droit', removed to this church in 1859 after repainting and gilding by Anne Coates, of 49 Castle Street, Belfast, at a cost of £6. The pine pews are pleasing, and there are box-pews at each front corner, flanking the pulpit and reading desk, of white marble, of 1915. The good east window dates from 1863. Everything is neat, well-painted, and seemly.

The church is attractively sited on a knoll at the head of a lime avenue.

Photograph: Michael O'Connell.
Situation: Off road from Upper Ballinderry to Lower Ballinderry; td, Ballyscolly; Parish, Ballinderry; District Council, Lisburn; Grid ref. J 160 673.
References: Listed B. T Fagan, OSM, 1838, Antrim, VII, pp 51-52; Lewis, TD, 1847, I, p 108; Ewart, 'Down & Connor & Dromore', 1886, p 61.

Methodist Chapel, Islandmagee

43. A very pleasing simple little preaching-box; the plaque over the door is inscribed "Wesleyan Methodist Chapel MDCCCXXIX". "In the erection of their place of worship the young congregation received friendly support from the Presbyterians of the district and the neighbouring farmers carted the materials free of cost. It was opened for public worship on Sunday, 13th September 1829". The little Methodist community here dates back to the visit in 1800 of an "eccentric but devoted young American evangelist," the Rev. Lorenzo Dew. The chapel, however, is quite un-American. Three bays wide, four bays deep, its walls are of painted stucco with contrasting quoins; all the openings are round headed: the front door is surmounted by a nice geometrical-Gothick fanlight, but alas, the Georgian glazing bars in the windows (shown in Donaldson's illustration) have been removed: it would not

be too late to restore them. "The chapel will accommodate about 450 persons at 14 inches to each sitter" - more cramped than tourist class air travel? "Total number at present in society or class, 25, all from Island Magee" (1840).

Modestly sited in a stone-walled and grassed enclosure on the spine of the peninsula, "all planted round with alder trees at the same time the house was built"; but these last have all gone.

Photograph: Michael O'Connell.
Situation: Middle Road, Islandmagee; td, Ballymoney; Parish, Islandmagee; District Council, Larne; Grid ref. D 463 002.
References: Listed B. J Boyle, OSM, 1840, and J Bleakly, 1839, Antrim, III, pp 21, 78; Donaldson, 'Islandmagee,' 1927, p 129.

St Colman's (C of I) Church, Dervock

44. "The Parish church ... is an extremely neat edifice with a handsome, square tower. It is stone finished externally and comfortably fitted up inside. The framework of the roof is metal. It was erected on the north side of the town in 1831 and cost £1,200. Its dimensions are 60 feet long by 24 feet wide, and it would conveniently accommodate 180 persons. There is a small but handsome gallery containing 2 private seats" (Boyle). "A spacious and handsome structure, in the later English style of architecture, with a lofty square embattled tower crowned with pinnacles: being too small for the congregation, it is about to be enlarged by the addition of transepts, which will give it a cruciform character" (Lewis). "The architecture of the church is Gothic; renovated in 1857, and again in 1878" (Ewart). "The builder of the church, Mr Hans Wood, is reputed to have fallen from the tower, to meet an untimely death at the age of 27" (Johns).

A charming, prickly, church in the Irish tradition of its period: a spare pinnacle, taken down when the vestry was added in 1935, stands near the door. The pinnacles themselves are unusually elegant, with ball and chevron ornament; carved quatrefoil panels are inset in the faces of the tower parapet. Inside, there are some good memorials to members of the local gentry, the best of them, by Thomas and Edward Gaffin of London, showing three marble angels bearing an 11-year-old girl up to heaven; and a very large pulpit of 1878 borne on six pink marble colonettes.

The patron saint is not just any old St Colman, he is St Colman Muilinn of Derrykeighan, said to have been a miller at Dervock about AD 460. The site for the present church was controversial: "one party favoured building on the old spot hallowed by so many memories, but another favoured its erection at Dervock. These discussions were shortly afterwards abruptly terminated by a charge of gunpowder blowing up the old building ... Tradition still tells the name of the perpetrator, who was merely a tool in more influential hands" (Camac, 1908).

Photograph: Michael O'Connell.
Situation: Castlecat Road, Dervock; td, Ballyratahan Lower; Parish, Derrykeighan; District Council, Ballymoney; Grid ref. C 977 321.
References: Listed B. J Boyle, OSM, 1835, Antrim, V, pp 82, 83; Lewis, TD, 1837, I, p 453; Ewart, 'Down & Connor & Dromore', 1886, p 89; Camac, 'Derrykeighan parish', 1908, p 34; Girvan, 'North Antrim', UAHS, 1973, p 35; Johns, 'Derrykeighan', 1981, pp 5-9.

Gartree (C of I) Church, Gartree

45. According to James Boyle, in 1838, "Gartree church is a sort of chapel of ease - a plain but very neat structure with a neat square tower about 30 feet high, ornamented at its summit by neat stone pinnacles - seven neat Gothic windows with cutstone label mouldings". Built in 1831 at the cost of £1,200 at the instance of Sir Hercules Pakenham of Langford Lodge. In a later entry Boyle adds "the architect who built Gartree church was Mr. Edward Sands an Englishman".

No such architect is known; the architect of the castellated Langford Lodge itself, built in 1821 but now gone, was James McBlain. Presumably, the reference should have been to James Sands, a pupil of Lewis Wyatt, who did work in Carlow in 1824, for Lord Downshire and the Montgomerys of Rosemount in the 1840s, and for Lord O'Neill at Shane's Castle around 1848. Gordon Wheeler has drawn my attention to the resemblance between the Gartree tower and the upper sections of the tower at Down Cathedral, completed in 1829 by Thomas Alfred Cobden and James Sands "of Carlow and London" to (much modified) designs by William Farrell.

The church is sited in a delightful graveyard, with many Irish yews, looking out over Lough Neagh and the hangars and runways of the wartime aerodrome. It is approached through a charming stone archway, with pin-nacles and quatrefoils, erected 1832 in memory of Sir Hercules's agent Captain Armstrong: "Reared to Arms and Conversant with Camps/It could not be expected/that he would have understood/or regarded with interest/the Toils and Difficulties of Farmers"; but he did; "and lowered the high rate of Rent laid on/the Farms during the French War to/one more proportionate to the Produce/of Land in Peaceful Times".

The church is of random basalt, with a pretty square tower, very sharply pointed pinnacles in the Irish manner (especially on the buttresses), diamond-pane windows, and a family pew with its own fireplace and front door. The interior is appropriately furnished in pitch-pine; the old gas-lamps have been retained and converted; there is a generally military atmosphere - many monuments with white marble trophies on dark backgrounds; there is even a military window of 1905.

Photograph: Michael O'Connell.
Situation: Up a lane, north of the road from Crumlin to Gartree Point; td, Gartree; Parish, Killead; District Council, Antrim; Grid ref. J 099 758.
References: Listed B+. J Boyle, OSM, 1838, as yet unpublished; Lewis, TD, 1837, II, p 134; Ewart, 'Down & Connor & Dromore', p 92; Girvan, 'West Antrim', UAHS, 1970, p 10.

First Presbyterian (Non-Subscribing) Church, Crumlin

46. The datestone over the door says 1835. It is hard to believe so late a date, yet the church was, in fact, only opened on 17th September 1837. It seems that the Rev. Alexander of Crumlin, who since 1801 had conducted the prestigious Crumlin Academy, was present at the first meeting of the Remonstrant Synod of Ulster, held in 1830 in Rosemary Street, Belfast; and very probably decided to model his new church on the elliptical First Presbyterian Church there, designed by Roger Mulholland fifty years earlier; in particular, the horseshoe-shaped gallery with its double bow, and the ship-shaped pattern of pews below, are almost identical. Unfortunately, Mr Alexander, who retired on 1st March 1837, died only six weeks later, too soon to see his church completed, having been succeeded by Rev. George Hill, the eminent local historian, who in his turn retired on health grounds (he had lost his voice and could no longer preach) in 1850 to become Librarian to Queen's University.

James Boyle, in 1837, says "the meeting house is situated on the south side of the town. The former house, near which it stands, was erected in 1723. It presents a plain but substantial appearance. It measures 58 feet long and 24 feet wide. It contains a gallery, and would accommodate 800 persons. the expense of erecting it will amount to £1000, to be defrayed by subscription." And: "the minister, the Reverend Nathaniel Alexander, receives £100 regium donum and £30 stipend".

Externally, the church is of random blackstone with brick dressings, an elongated octagon housing an internal ellipse, with a porch (rather than portico, despite the simple pediment) tacked onto the front. The upper windows are round-headed with radial glazing-bars, the lower ones segmental-headed with a pretty geometrical glazing-pattern; both are, surprisingly, set back in rectangular recesses. The very plain doors (no fanlight) open into a lobby with a fireplace facing the entrance, a door on each side giving access to the body of the kirk, and a spiral staircase with curly banister-rail in each re-entrant. Inside the church itself, the gallery is borne on Ionic columns, the plaster painted to simulate brown marble; there are pleasing oil lamps; and the whole composition focuses on a hexagonal white-painted 'tulip' pulpit, balanced on a slim stem, with a miniature curly staircase at each side. The ceiling, unfortunately, has been somewhat altered, not for the better; and the delightful old harmonium and its case have been abandoned, dismantled, in a corner of the gallery; but this is a building of much distinction, set a long way back from the village street in an ample graveyard.

Photograph: Michael O'Connell.
Situation: South of Main Street, Crumlin; td, Ballytromery; Parish, Camlin; District Council, Antrim; Grid ref. J 148 762.
References: Listed B+. OS map, 1832; J Boyle, OSM, 1837 (?), Antrim, VII, pp 66, 69; 'Northern Whig', 26 September 1837; 'Bible Christian', new series II, No. IX, November 1837; Girvan, 'West Antrim', UAHS, 1970, p 8; information from Dr J W Nelson.

First Presbyterian Church, Antrim

47. A most uncommon Greek Revival church to designs by John Millar of Belfast. The decision to build was taken in January 1832; in January 1833 the journal of Rev. Robert Magill records that "Mr Millar architect from Belfast visited Mill Row with the view of drawing out a plan of the intended new meeting house"; the date in the pediment is 1834, but the roof was only just going on in July 1835; "the house was only opened for divine service" on 18th June 1837. James Boyle reports "The entrance front at its northern end is in the Egyptian style and has a handsome and massive appearance ... It is an airy cheerful and comfortable place of worship well designed and executed". The erudite Donald Girvan described it as follows: "The dominant feature is a recessed entrance porch with a segmental ceiling, supported by two heavy and incredibly archaeological Doric columns, copied from the portico at Thoricus" (unearthed in 1812, and published in 1817 in The Unedited Antiquities of Attica by the Dilettanti Society). However, he now thinks the design is derived from that of the puzzling, unfinished, Temple of Apollo on Delos, published in volume III of Stuart and Revett's Antiquities of Athens, 1794, upon which Revett had based the columns of his church at Ayot St Lawrence, Herts, of 1778-9. "The whole front is surmounted by a plain pediment and impressively sited at a considerable distance from the road". The building was designed for a congregation of 2000 and cost £3,000. The interior, of less interest, was considerably altered in 1903 after a fire.

The present colour-scheme is sophisticated but uninhibited: the recess is painted terra-cotta brown, the outer walls pale yellow, the plinth, quoins and outer door-case grey, the columns and remaining details off-white. The result is most satisfying.

John Millar, an irascible and somewhat eccentric architect, was trained by Thomas Hopper and would have had access to his library. He was responsible for the Third Presbyterian Church in Belfast in 1831, as also those at Portaferry and Castlereagh, before emigrating to New Zealand. Since he is only mentioned once in Mr Magill's journal, it seems likely that he was responsible only for the design, not the supervision, of the work at Antrim.

Photograph: Michael O'Connell.
Situation: Church Street, Antrim; td, Town Parks; Parish, Antrim; District Council, Antrim; Grid ref. J 152 864
References: Listed A; in conservation area. Diary of Rev. R Magill, D 2930/9, 10, 11, 12, 13, in PRONI; J Boyle, OSM, 1838, Antrim, XI, p 8; West, 'First Presbyterian Church, Antrim', 1902; IB 1903, p 2050; Girvan, 'Antrim & Ballymena', UAHS, 1969, p 6; P Larmour, in 'Perspective', September 1994; C E B Brett in 'Ulster architect', September/October 1994.

Presbyterian Church, Crumlin

48. Built in 1839; labelled "Ecclesia Scotica" in a square panel above the door; signed "MILLAR ARCHITECT" in the underside of the lintel just above the door (note that the capital A's both lack cross-bars). Despite the complete departure from his usual Grecian style (47), this must certainly be the work of Thomas Hopper's Belfast pupil, John Millar.

Externally, the central door is contained in a three-storey tower topped by slim pinnacles that are like spiky knops. To the right, a cylindrical projection houses a spiral staircase to the gallery, with tall slim newel post and long curly hand-rail. There is no balancing projection to the left. The simple hall church is four bays deep, buttresses alternating with tall pointed diamond-pane windows. The gallery is carried on Doric columns; the front displays a pattern of large quatrefoils. The 'swallow's nest

pulpit' (as Girvan calls it, for all I know with technical correctness) is high up in the facing wall, a doorway below and a doorway at the back of it, with elaborate mouldings and consoles.

Surprisingly, there is no mention either of this church or of this congregation in the Ordnance Survey Memoirs of 1839-40. The church is nicely complemented by two little Gothic cottages, each with three pointed windows, which frame the entrance from the street.

Photograph: Michael O'Connell.
Situation: North of Main Street, Crumlin; td, Ballytromery; Parish, Camlin; District Council, Antrim; Grid ref. J 152 763.
References: Listed B. Watson, 'Glenavy, Camlin & Tullyrusk,' 1892, p 43; Girvan, 'West Antrim', UAHS 1970, p 8; P Larmour, in 'Perspective', September 1994; CEB Brett, in 'Ulster architect', September/October 1994.

49. "The chapel, which accommodates 360 persons, was opened by licence on 28th of July 1840; and was consecrated on 29th June, 1843" to the designs of Charles Lanyon, £716.16.0 having been granted by the Down and Connor Church Accommodation Society for that purpose. "It has since been enlarged and otherwise improved by the addition of two transepts, chapel, etc., - over £2000 being laid out on it" (apparently also to Lanyon's design). "The total cost would, therefore, be about £3000. It is now a cruciform shape, style modified Gothic, and has stained glass windows in chancel and transepts" (1886). One of the most successful of this group of sixteen churches, all designed free of charge by young Mr Lanyon, in this instance to serve "the villages of Whitehouse and Whiteabbey ... both containing large and extensive manufactories ... [and] ... much in want of a place of public worship according to the rites of the Church of England and Ireland, owing to their great and increasing population."

A surprisingly large church, remarkably little altered: the exterior of squared basalt blocks with sandstone trim, the pinnacles of the tower particularly effective. Internally, chancel, transepts and nave all retain their original handsome pitch-pine ceilings and cross-beams. The original baptistery is now a tiny chapel, just inside the west door. The stone chancel arch is carried by a pair of nicely-carved angels. There are many Victorian memorial brasses and tablets, and every single window is filled with rich dark Victorian stained-glass, so the church must today be much darker than it was 150 years ago; but it is a kind of agreeable Gothic gloom which suits the building very well.

The little schoolhouse, also by Lanyon, cost £300; it was used as a NAAFI for the troops at Merville House nearby during the second World War, and demolished thereafter to make way for a larger, modern, church hall.

St John's (C of I) Church, Whitehouse

Photograph: Michael O'Connell.
Situation: Shore Road, Whitehouse; td, Parish, Whitehouse; District Council, Newtownabbey; Grid ref. J 346 803.
References: Listed B. 'Last report of the Down and Connor Church Accommodation Society', 1843, p 21; Ewart, 'Down & Connor & Dromore', 1886, p 107.

Craigs (C of I) Parish Church, Cullybackey

50. A pretty little rural church, its appearance much enhanced by the numerous yew trees in the surrounding walled graveyard, and by its site close to Craigs bridge and the river, the stone schoolhouse (222), and Craigdun Castle (96). As Samuel Lewis remarked in 1847, "the church and school-house correspond in architecture and, though separated from each other by the high road, are connected by the plantations in which they are embosomed, so as to form one picture of repose scarcely to be equalled in this part of the country."

"The church was one of several built by the Diocesan

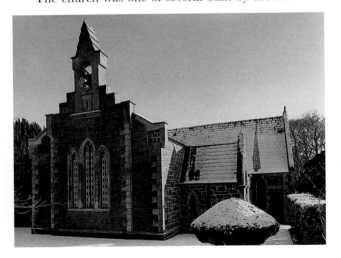

Church Accommodation Society between the years 1838 and 1843". Its foundation stone was laid in 1840; it was consecrated in 1841; "the expense was £760.12s.5d., of which all but £50 was given by the Society: and the accommodation provided is for 300 persons". "It was designed by Sir Charles Lanyon, and originally consisted of a nave and small chancel, with a porch and vestry. In 1870 two transepts and a south aisle were added, under the superintendence of Thomas Drew, architect. Some of the details in the additions then made were taken from old Irish churches". In 1888 the little vaulted chancel was enlarged and timber-panelled at the expense of Edmund McNeill of Craigdun Castle "in memory of six infant children, folded by the Good Shepherd".

The church is topped by a pleasing bell-cote. Lanyon's original work is of squared blackstone, with reddish ashlar trim; but regrettably, Drew built the extension of random, not squared, blackstone; which is a bit disconcerting.

Lithograph: Church Accommodation Society report, 1843. Photograph: Michael O'Connell.
Situation: At Craigs cross-roads, on road from Cullybackey to Glarryford; td, and Parish, Craigs; District Council, Ballymena; Grid ref. D 045 079.
References: Listed B. 'Last report of the Down and Connor Church Accommodation Society', 1843, p 27, with illustration by Thomas Turner; Lewis, TD, 1847, I, p 418; Ewart, 'Down & Connor & Dromore', 1886, pp 87, 88; Girvan, 'West Antrim', UAHS, 1970, pp 28, 29; Boyd, 'Craigs, Dunaghy and Killagan', 1991, p 10.

St John's (C of I) Church, Glynn

51. Lavens Ewart says tersely: "The Church is a plain structure of cut stone, without chancel or transept, with porch in the centre. It is built close to the site of an old abbey founded by St. Patrick". Its rector in 1896 did not think much more of it: "Though neatly built of cut stone, the Church does not present any features of architectural interest." Cost £800; consecrated 1841, to the plans contributed free by the youthful Charles Lanyon, with the aid of a grant of £233.16.2 from the Diocesan Church Accommodation Society. According to the Visitation of

1820, "Vicar resides in Derry; no church; no glebe; no manse; no clerk; no schoolmaster." In 1843, the Church Accommodation Society Report remarks that "The whole clerical income of the Vicar of Glynn is only £31.10s. rent-charge; augmented to £72 by a grant from Primate Boulter's Fund". For once, the generally reliable Parliamentary Gazetteer of 1846 is out of date: its entry for Glynn states categorically "There is neither church, meeting house nor chapel".

The steeply sloping graveyard, of great antiquity, is

reached by a lane that runs through the green tunnel of the glen. The plan and elevation are almost identical with those of Lanyon's slightly later church at Glenoe (52), but the material is blackstone. The contrasts are harsher, the feeling more Jacobethan. There are lattice-paned lancets with wide surrounds; a curious cross formed of interlinked circles above the ogee doorway into the porch; no tower or spire, only a slightly stylised bell-cote. There is some distressing modern cement-work at the rear.

Photograph: Michael O'Connell.
Situation: To the south of the village of
  Glynn; td, Parish, Glynn; District Council, Larne; Grid ref. D 408 997.
References: Listed B. Visitation of 1820 in PRONI; 'Last report of the Down and Connor Church Accommodation Society', 1843, p 19, with illustration by Thomas Turner; PG, II, 1846, pp 274-275; Ewart, 'Down & Connor & Dromore', 1886, pp 33, 94; R C Oulton, in UJA, 2nd series, II, 1896, p 180.

Raloo (C of I) Parish Church, Glenoe

52. Like that at Glynn, "designed by Mr, now Sir, Charles Lanyon, who placed his time and professional services gratuitously at the disposal of" the Down and Connor Church Accommodation Society. "The cost of the erection of a small church, having accommodation for 200 persons, was £436; of which £311 was granted by the Committee". Consecrated 18th August 1842, very thoroughly restored in 1980.

A pretty little church on an elevated wooded hill-top, looking out over the village and the valley; the golden-grey stone is much less harsh than the blackstone employed at Glynn (51), and well suits the more conspicuous site. The cross over the porch has been simplified, so have been the windows with their neat modern lead lattices, otherwise the designs are closely similar. There is at all times the lovely sound of falling water from the glen, owned by the National Trust, just below.

When Boyle wrote in 1840, the church was in the course of being erected on the site of a "very pretty ornamental cottage, the property of Miss McClaverty of Glynn. It was until 1834 celebrated for the taste of its construction and the beauty of its situation, and was the scene of numerous Pic Nic parties from the neighbouring towns." But it was not only the picnic parties that were put out: "Sectarian feelings are carried to some heights here, and the members of the Orthodox or Trinitarian and the Unitarian Presbyterians regard each other with any other than Christian feelings ... The prejudice against episcopacy is very bigoted, so much so that the contemplated erection of a church in Glenoe is a subject of much annoyance to the Presbyterians".

Photograph: Michael O'Connell.
Situation: In Glenoe village; td, Bally-willin; Parish, Raloo; District Council, Larne; Grid ref. D 394 968.
References: Listed B. J Boyle, OSM, 1840, and J Bleakly, 1840, Antrim, XII, pp 98, 105, 121, 127; 'Last report of the Down and Connor Church Accommodation Society', 1843, p 31, with illustration by Thomas Turner; Ewart, 'Down & Connor & Dromore', 1886, pp 33, 81.

Dunluce Presbyterian Church, Bushmills

53. Datestone of 1845: the Parliamentary Gazetteer of 1847 merely remarks, "The Presbyterian meeting house is attended by 360". An uncommonly interesting church, as Girvan points out, awarding it an 'A' and suggesting a 'strong resemblance' to Crumlin Presbyterian Church (48) of 1839, which is signed by John Millar. For my part, I do not see this resemblance; and in fact, the Coleraine Chronicle, recording the opening of the church on 27th July 1847 by Dr Henry Cooke, no less, observes: "The church was built in 1845-6 by Mr Daniel McIlroy of Bushmills to plans and specifications furnished by Mr Lanyon." So far as I know, though he designed many churches for the Church of Ireland, he designed only one other - for the non-subscribing congregation at Holywood - for the Presbyterians. The arrangement may have arisen as a result of Lanyon's commission at Dunderave House (91) near by. Dunluce in fact resembles his little church at Hollymount, near Seaforde in Co. Down, completed in 1840 for Lady Harriett Forde, though there are minor differences of detail, such as the proportions of the windows, and the omission of the central pinnacle. Larmour points

out that, of Lanyon's buildings in "the Tudoresque vein", Ballymena Court House (220), Hollymount and Dunluce share, with variations, the central feature of "a perpendicular traceried window over a Tudor arched opening."

A cruciform church, with porch and stairs to the gallery (added in 1860) in the front section, with its "surprisingly sophisticated Gothick front", buttresses, tracery and pinnacles. The body of the kirk is six bays deep, the windows with quoin-like surrounds. At the rear, a tactful additional of 1995 by W Atkinson of Ballymoney: the whole group of stucco, prettily painted.

Photograph: Michael O'Connell.
Situation: In Priestland Road, south-west of Bushmills, just over the boundary between Moyle and Coleraine; td, Walk Mill; Parish, Dunluce; District Council, Coleraine; Grid ref. C 938 402.
References: Listed B; outside conservation area. PG, II, 1846, p 158; Coleraine Chronicle, 7 August 1847; 'Last report of the Down and Connor Church Accommodation Society', 1843, p 18; Girvan, 'North Antrim', UAHS, pp 17, 18; Mullin, 'Presbytery of Coleraine', 1979, p 171; P Larmour, in 'GPA Irish arts review', 1989-90, p 204; Mullin, 'Dunluce Presbyterian Church', 1995, p 34.

54. A pleasant, nicely-painted, barn-church reached by ten steps down from the road: the entrance flanked by a tiny cottage. White-painted roughcast (judging from the photographs in Mr Blair's book, the white paint must be of quite recent date) with contrasting architraves and quoins. Circular window, divided into petal-like compartments, in the gable, above the round-headed doorcase; a round-headed window on either side; and round-headed windows in the side walls; late-Georgian style glazing throughout. The service of dedication was held on 21 August 1842, the preacher being the then moderator, Dr Stewart of Broughshane; the Rev. William Orr was minister from 1841 to 1865, when he died young, leaving a widow and seven children, the youngest still (as lawyers put it) *en ventre sa mère*, and was buried in the churchyard immediately behind his own pulpit. He was succeeded by the Rev. J S Mairs, an ally of the Rev. Armour of Ballymoney in the Tenants' Right movement.

Inside, a raked gallery on cast-iron columns. The minister's room was added, quite unobtrusively, in 1929. At the time of writing, there is no minister.

Presbyterian Church, Dunloy

Photograph: Michael O'Connell.

Situation: On east side of main street, Dunloy; td, Dunloy; Parish, Finvoy; District Council, Ballymoney; Grid ref. D 017 195.

References: Not listed. 'Banner of Ulster', 2 September 1842; McLean, 'Dunloy past and present', 1990, p 43; Blair, 'In the midst of the village', 1991, passim; Ms history compiled by Mrs Sally Wallace, in possession of Mrs Sarah Filor.

55. A somewhat strange church, not without a character very much of its own, on a sloping site close to the riverbank. The earlier church of 1760 was rebuilt in 1841, and then "completely renovated" in 1903. It is hard to be sure which parts are of which date. The 'body of the kirk' is stuccoed, with stone buttresses, three bays long, the tracery of the windows curiously asymmetrical in what seems an attempt to mix the Tudor and the rococo styles. There are strange curly ornamental iron brackets projecting upwards at the eaves.

The oldest feature of the church, however, appears to be the tower, which has had added to it four tall corner pinnacles, linked by arches, through which can be seen a central conical spire. This, the entrance front, and a kind of oriel window to the side of the church, are of squared blackstone with ashlar dressings. There is a triple window on each side of the entrance front above the wooden porch. The listers suggest that the renovation of 1903 was probably to the designs of Vincent Craig, which would explain some of the idiosyncrasies of the building.

Presbyterian Church, Armoy

Photograph: Michael O'Connell.

Situation: Off main street, Armoy village; td, Moyaver Lower; Parish, Armoy; District Council, Moyle; Grid ref. D 068 327.

References: Listed B. Girvan, 'North Antrim', UAHS, 1972, pp 36, 37; H C Waddell, 'Armoy Presbyterian Church', no date.

Christ Church (C of I), Ballynure

56. A simple church by Joseph Welland of Dublin, built 1854-6, at a cost of £2,000, to replace the old church in the ancient graveyard across the road, supposed to have been Jonathan Swift's first cure. Of blackstone, with ashlar dressings and belfry; tall five-light pointed-arch east windows, and two-light windows in the north and south walls. There is a particularly nice little quatrefoil window of chequered multi-coloured glass high in the west wall. According to Lavens Ewart, "The decorative painting of the chancel contains some well-executed copies of ancient Irish Ecclesiastical ornamentation, and the chancel is provided with two coronas of burnished brass." The timber ceiling (a replacement after an accidental fire in 1973) painted black. The church contains a number of simple but good memorials to members of the Dobbs family. It is nicely set in a neat, grassy, walled enclosure, with direct access to the rectory on one side and the old schoolhouse on the other.

Photograph: Michael O'Connell.
Situation: On Church Road, from Ballynure to Ballyeaston; td, Toberdowney; Parish, Ballynure; District Council, Newtownabbey; Grid ref. J 315 937
References: Listed B. Ewart, 'Down & Connor & Dromore', 1886, p 68.

Presbyterian Church, Finvoy

57 (right). The old thatched church on this site, of 1690, was demolished in 1845, and the new one, built at a cost of £1,023.13.1½, was inaugurated with a thundering sermon on 6 January 1847 by Dr Henry Cooke, no less. The lecture hall was added in 1875, with a room up stone steps for the Sunday School, and accommodation below for thirty horses (the equivalent of a modern church car-park). Both were the work of the energetic Rev. Andrew Todd, whose obituarist wrote in 1891 - "when one considers the improvements which have taken place in ecclesiastical architecture since 1845, the edifice which Mr Todd built - so neat, so accommodating, so modern in its arrangements - is a monument not only of his zeal, but of his exquisite taste and artistic skill. There are few parishes which have a finer church building, better school accommodation, or a statelier lecture hall than the parish of Finvoy."

A most attractive group, tall church with its tall slim windows complemented by good trees, tactful extension at the rear, and adjacent church hall of 1963: all of stucco, with quoins, very well painted cream, white and brown, looking uncommonly neat and trim. The central doorway is flanked by a pair of narrow Gothick-glazed windows, a shallower one over the door; there are four similar tall windows in each side wall; the sashes must be exceptionally well balanced. The box-pews inside are unusually handsome: there is a good gallery carried on cast-iron columns: and the pulpit is flanked by twin stairs with curly mahogany hand-rails, and pretty iron-filigree balusters. The church was extensively renovated in 1958.

Photograph: Michael O'Connell.
Situation: South of Finvoy village, off the main road to Rasharkin; td, Mullans; Parish, Finvoy; District Council, Ballymoney; Grid ref. C 958 178.
References: Listed B. Girvan, 'North Antrim', 1972, p 52; Thompson, 'Story of Finvoy Church', 1990, passim.

Killymurris Presbyterian Church, Glarryford

58. A slightly gaunt barn-church of 1860; stucco, quoins, six very tall slim pointed windows in each side wall, two higher ones flanking the principal door and lesser window above in the gable facade. The top ornamented by a minimal bell-cote and a rather larger copper ventilator shaped like a witch's hat.

This large church, set in an attractive old graveyard, dominates a rather bare landscape near the head-waters of the river Main.

Photograph: Michael O'Connell.
Situation: Off main road from Cullybackey to Dunloy; td, Dromore; Parish, Rasharkin; District Council, Ballymena; Grid ref. D 052 133.
References: Listed B. Datestone in gable.

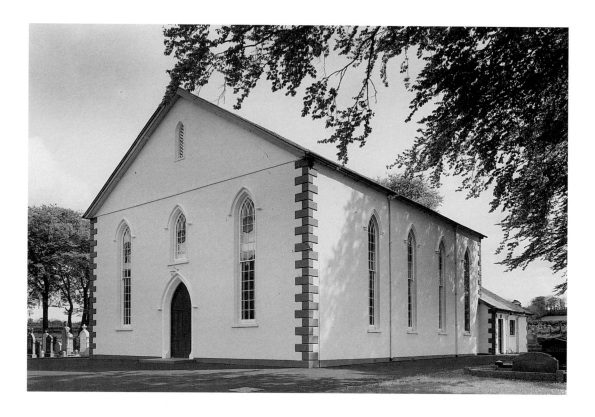

St Mary, Star of the Sea (RC) Church, Whitehouse

59. A tall and handsome Gothic Revival church on a bluff overlooking Belfast Lough; of 1865-7, by John O'Neill, architect; his "first ambitious exercise in architectural design, probably commissioned in late 1861". The very tall tower and spire, built under the supervision of J J McDonnell but possibly to the original designs of O'Neill, completed only in 1899. At 180 feet high, it receives unfair competition from the two 15-storey tower blocks of flats built nearby by the NI Housing Trust at Rush Park in 1963.

The walls are of black basalt, the dressings of white sandstone, giving - especially in the quoins of the buttresses to the tower - a curiously chessboard effect. The belfry has very tall double Gothic open arches, flanked by triple rows of slim engaged columns, housing the peal of ten bells. Slim octagonal pinnacles at the corners of the tower guard the base of the spire. The interior is cool, airy, well-painted, and blessedly free from *bondieuserie*. The attractive high altar and reredos of white Caen stone, by Thomas Earp of London, with red marble columns and the figures of eight saints, have happily survived the changes in the liturgy. Wooden gallery supporting organ-loft; good pine pews; a portrait of Father Patrick Ryan, who built the church, hanging above the altar-rail on the south wall; nicely detailed in every particular.

Photograph: Michael O'Connell.
Situation: 305, Shore Road, Whitehouse; td, Parish, White House; District Council, Newtownabbey; Grid ref. J 351 813.
References: Listed B. 'Builder', 25 March 1869; O'Laverty, 'Down and Connor', III, 1884, pp 20, 21; Armstrong, 'Newtownabbey', [1979] p 287; Larmour, 'Belfast', 1987, p 102; J J Tracey, MA dissertation, 1987, 'Buildings of John O'Neill', in library of QUB, pp 127-129.

St Joseph's (RC) Church, Glenavy

60. A rural church of blackstone, by John O'Neill of O'Neill and Byrne, consecrated on 13th September 1868. The listers call it "a good example of the Gothic Revival style with careful attention to massing and detail." The church stands on the site of a previous chapel, burned by "the Wreckers" in 1798. There is a square tower, topped by a conspicuous spire with alternating bands of plain and fish-tail slates, and louvred openings. The porch has a very handsome broad cusped arch and colonettes. The nave is of five bays, the chancel of two; there is a large five-light west window, the east window is three-light.

The white marble altar has been successfully detached from, and moved to stand in front of, its reredos. The interior is very simple, plain, pleasant and unassuming. The roof has stencilled interlace ornament.

Photograph: Michael O'Connell.
Situation: Ballymacricket cross-roads, south-west of Glenavy village; td, Ballymacricket; Parish, Glenavy; District Council, Lisburn; Grid ref. J 149 718.
References: Listed B. O'Laverty, 'Down and Connor', II, 1880, pp 332-3; Totten, 'Glenavy parish', 1980, p 24; J J Tracey, MA dissertation, 1987, 'Buildings of John O'Neill', in library of QUB, pp 136-138.

St Bride's (C of I) Church, Doagh

61. A charming little church of 1868 in the highly idio-syncratic style sometimes employed by Welland & Gillespie, architects to the Ecclesiastical Commissioners. Rather optimistically described as "in the Early English style", it is orthodox in its cruciform layout, but not in its detailing nor in its use of materials. The main walls are of squared rock-faced black basalt, divided by two bands of rock-cut red stone; the quoins of the buttresses are of pink sandstone; the remaining dressings of white sandstone. No wonder a commentator at the consecration, before the stonework had mellowed, remarked that the exterior made "a brilliant, highly-coloured picture".

The spire is octagonal but from a distance seems to curve, like Gaudi's steeples in Barcelona or a Hindu tem-ple, because of a visual distortion caused by angle ribs which terminate some way below the top. There is a beau-tifully crisp Gothic-cusped bootscraper-niche on each side of the nicely detailed pointed doorway at the foot of the tower. Spire and plate-tracery alike are punctured by cir-cular holes of various sizes: the result is faintly reminiscent

of Gruyère cheese. The gable of the nave is topped by a delightful weather-cock-salmon.

Inside the doorway, there are some mildly exotic sur-prises, starting with a naked faun, putto or cherub playing the pan-pipes in the porch (attributed to the Larne sculp-tor Frank Wiles, 1910). Various pictures, carvings and ornaments lend the otherwise rather undistinguished inte-rior its character. They include the font brought from Ballyhamage (112) with a modern cover on which three naked infants disport themselves; a large Italian (or French?) print of 1725; a small Greek icon; lead, bronze and wooden religious reliefs; tiles; early bibles; a pestle and mortar; a weaver's shuttle; and a polished brass bowl planted with cactuses.

Photograph: Michael O'Connell.
Situation: North of Doagh, on the road to Kilbride; td, Ballyhamage; Parish, Doagh; District Council, Newtownabbey; Grid ref. J 255 904.
References: Listed B. Drawings in RCB Library, Dublin; Cox, 'Kilbride', 1959, pp 17-26; Girvan, 'West Antrim', UAHS, 1970, p 18.

Christ Church (C of I), Derriaghy

62. One of the strikingly original churches produced by "Mr Gillespie, Architect to the Ecclesiastical Commissioners", of Welland and Gillespie; consecrated in 1872, cost £3,600.

The graveyard stands on a steep declivity: an earlier church on the site belonged in 1204 to the Benedictine Priory of St Andrew (commonly known as Black Abbey) in the Ards peninsula. The present church is an extraordinary exercise in three-dimensional geometry. The very slim tall square tower and spire stand at 45 degrees from the axis of the nave, presenting a right-angled corner to anyone facing the central doorway. The lower part of the tower is clothed in Virginia creeper; the tall louvred openings have amplifiers where bells are expected; the spire, like a rocket ready to be launched, has various patterns of ornamental carving, including Celtic interlace. The bell-tower is balanced, on the other side of the porch, by a squat round turret. The two are linked under the eaves of the porch by ornate carved stone vegetables with nesting birds. Above the lean-to slated roof of the porch is a great circular window of plate tracery, incorporating cusped circles of three diminishing sizes in the Venetian-Gothic manner admired by Ruskin, and providing an unintended columbarium with many convenient niches for passing pigeons. The west wall is topped by a remarkable upstanding crow-stepped gable.

The side walls are executed in the same yellowish-grey stone, random laid, with tall four-light windows on each side, and a great six-light east window with ten cusped circles at the top. The roof of the nave slopes steeply: that of the, much narrower, chancel, even more so; the geometry of their junction is masterly.

The interior is simple but extremely impressive, largely because of the great span of the high, boat-shaped, wooden roof - a kind of stone tracery re-expressed in pitch-pine, the ribs resting on finely-carved stone corbels. The gallery, with staircase in the turret flanking the porch, is original; the organ chamber however was added in 1904. The glass, good of its kind, is all very harmonious and appropriate. The pitch-pine pews are handsome and said to be quite uncommonly comfortable. The only discordant note in an otherwise most pleasing church is the reredos of 1972.

Photograph: Michael O'Connell.

Situation: Just up-hill from Derriaghy cross-roads; td, Parish, Derriaghy; District Council, Lisburn; Grid ref. J 275 679.

References: Listed A. Reeves, 'Ecclesiastical antiquities', 1847, p 46; drawings in RCB library, Dublin, Folio 7; O'Laverty, 'Down and Connor', II, 1880, p 336; Ewart, 'Down & Connor & Dromore', 1886, p 88; Dixon, 'Ulster architecture', 1972, p 20, pl. 87; Barr, 'Derriaghy', 1974, passim; 'Oldest register of Derriaghy', 1981, p xii.

St Patrick and St Brigid's (RC) Church, Ballycastle

63. A striking church whose spire is visible for miles: built on "an elevated piece of table-land, immediately adjoining, but rising high above, the streets of the town." Started in 1870, dedicated on 9th August 1874; to the designs of Father Jeremiah Ryan McAuley, "at that time curate at Cushendall", who had trained as an architect under Thomas Jackson, and taken orders in 1858. The stone was quarried near the Pan Rocks, and is now of a yellowish butterscotch colour. The stone mason was Charles Darragh, who dressed the first stone of the church laid on 7th June 1870, and the last stone of the spire on 17th July 1890. The spire was added in 1890, whether or not to Fr McAuley's design does not seem to be known. "The style of architecture is Gothic of the twelfth century. The western facade is very imposing" (O'Laverty).

The character of the church was considerably altered in 1993, when it was "extended and re-ordered" to designs by Paddy Byrne, architect. Although they almost double the building's size, his two transepts, with slightly raked pews, fit in very well with the old, both internally and externally. The "re-ordering" has also been skilfully accomplished: the fine old Caen stone high altar remains in place, but now behind a screen of brass and glass, with a modern square central altar at the 'crossing' of nave and transepts. In general, the ancient and the modern mix comfortably, especially in the side chapels; though there is a degree of discordance between the colourful modern glass in the transept windows, and the 19th-century Stations of the Cross. Otherwise, the architect has done an admirably sensitive job.

Photograph: Michael O'Connell.

Situation: 9 Moyle Road, Ballycastle; td, Town Parks; Parish, Ramoan; District Council, Moyle; Grid ref. D 112 407.

References: Listed B. O'Laverty, 'Down and Connor', IV, 1887, pp 432-435; Brett, 'Glens of Antrim', UAHS, 1971, p 50; inscriptions in the church.

Our Lady of Lourdes (RC) Church, Moneyglass

64. On a prominent site overlooking an important cross-roads, a most imposing and conspicuous church with a very tall four-storey bell tower, and a broached spire above it. The composition derives much of its effect from the contrast between the dark squared blackstone of walls and tower, and the near-white ashlar of the limestone trim and spire.

The two-door porch has a Gothic arch embracing tracery windows, and a statue of the Virgin carried on a central cluster of colonettes. The interior is tall and dignified. The whole church, completed so late as 1925 to the designs of the Belfast architect J J McDonnell, is Victorian in feeling; hardly surprising, for he had learned his profession in the 1880s - Larmour considers the chapel of Clonard Monastery, Belfast, approximately contemporary with the death of Queen Victoria, to be his masterpiece.

Inside, the very fine white marble high altar, surprisingly, remains, as do the side-altars and various ecclesiastical furnishings, shown up well against the dark red of the east wall, and the heavy brown marble columns which carry the weight of the transept roofs. The stained glass is by Meyer of Munich; there is a richly-coloured tiled floor. There are one or two discomforting contrasts: between the very conservative Stations of the Cross, and the large globular light fittings which alternate with them; between the traditional Gothic confessional boxes, and the very modern heating panels which flank them. But on the whole, the effect is harmonious and satisfying; and the tactful detailing does much credit to the skills of J J Brennan & Co., the architects for the major restoration of 1992.

Photograph: Michael O'Connell.
Situation: At Moneyglass crossroads, on the main road from Ballymena to Toome; td, Ballymatoskerty; Parish, Duneane; District Council, Antrim; Grid ref. J 017 934.
References: Listed B+. Girvan, 'West Antrim', UAHS, 1970, p 22.

St Patrick's (C of I) Church, Jordanstown

65. Built in 1866-1868, to designs by Lanyon, Lynn and Lanyon - Sir Charles Lanyon was a parishioner (see The Abbey, 93) but this delightful church, one of the finest examples of the Celtic Revival, was built to the designs of his younger partner W H Lynn. "The First Attempt in Modern Times to revive the Ancient Ecclesiastical Architecture of Ireland" (1868): and one of the best. "The general style of the building is of the tenth century. The material is white sandstone, slightly relieved with red, for the exterior; and red and black brick lining, with sandstone dressings, for the interior. The pillars supporting the arches are of blue limestone" ... "A round tower, 14 feet 6 inches in diameter at the base and 73 feet high, is introduced as a material part of the structure ... on the ground floor is placed the vestry, the upper portion forms the belfry": as in St Finian's at Clonmacnoise, the special study of General James Smythe, brother of the then Archdeacon. There is a rather un-Irish semi-circular apse.

The porch contains an enchanting tympanum stone carving by Rosamund Praeger of Saint Patrick as a shepherd boy on Slemish mountain: 1933, in my view her finest work. The interior roof and pews of pitch-pine, but the nave and side aisle are divided by round stone arches carried on fat columns with Celtic cushion-shaped capitals. In 1894, the Torrens family added eight arches of Caen stone very richly carved with Celtic motifs, on each side of the altar, the panels filled with richly coloured mosaics, an extraordinarily happy mixture of the Celtic and the Byzantine. The altar is surmounted by a reredos or tabernacle of crunchy, crispy, crackly Derbyshire marble, beautifully cut. The apse contains four original windows of Sts Patrick, Comgall, Brigid and Columba, by Clayton & Bell of London, much superior to most of the other and later glass. The church furnishings are of exceptional merit, particularly the font, and a marvellous pair of prayer-desks supported by angels, one with a palm, one with a trumpet, of 1912, by Purdy & Millard, the former figuring in the photograph on page 24.

Photograph: Michael O'Connell.
Situation: On Jordanstown Road, just north of the railway line to Larne; td, Parish, Jordanstown; District Council, Newtownabbey; Grid ref. J 356 844.
References: Listed A. Anon, 'Notice of St Patrick's', 1868, in MBR, passim; Dixon, 'Introduction', 1975, p 66; Sheehy, 'Rediscovery of Ireland's past', 1980, p 66; Larmour, 'Belfast', 1987, p 101; W McCappin and D Rodgers, Guidebook, 1993, passim.

St Joseph's (RC) Church, Dunloy

66. A surprising composition of cones and cylinders rising out of a hillside above the village of Dunloy: circular church in the contemporary idiom, with an ornate cross at its apex, flanked by a modern version of an Irish round tower, both 1994, by Tracey and Mullarkey of Derry.

As 'Perspective' remarks "Joe Tracey is perhaps unique among Irish architects in having designed a round tower for a 20th century purpose". The 75 feet high tower, constructed of blocks of yellowish stone like butterscotch (Drumquin sandstone), incorporates not only the bell at its summit, but a ceremonial entrance to the vestry for the clergy. It looks very convincing from below the hill, but closer to, some features cause uneasiness: it seems not quite tall enough for its girth; the rectangular openings at the top seem rather too large; the twelve-foot high entrance combines six-foot-wide projecting monolithic dripstones with an uncompromisingly concrete ceiling.

The main entrance, also of yellow-stone side walls framing wide doors, leads into a great circular tent-like hall, the centre depressed, with tiers of seating all round. The roof is carried on 22 red-painted iron columns; the ceiling bulges downward like canvas; the space is lit principally by a clerestory all round, and a central roof-light.

In addition, there is stained glass of various dates at ground-floor level, the most striking being the three great windows of 1953 by the Earley Studios, unexpectedly (for Dunloy) incorporating the stylised figures of English martyrs with others, brought here from the previous church (now demolished).

The furnishings are of above average merit. The drum-shaped stone altar is rather heavy, but the font, with its fishes and dappled pebbles, is delightful; and the dark woodwork of prayer-desk, throne, and lectern complements the intricate pattern of pale woodwork of the curving pews: the detailed designs being those of the architects, since the designer Ray Carroll unhappily died before completing more than a few preliminary sketches.

Altogether, an interesting, exhilarating, even inspiring composition: though perhaps not to be taken too seriously.

Photograph: Michael O'Connell. (See also colour-plate VIIa)
Situation: To the south of the village of Dunloy; td, Dunloy; Parish, Finvoy; District Council, Ballymoney; Grid ref. D 017 190.
References: 'Perspective', May/June 1995, p 24; Ulster architect, May / June 1995, p 13.

Plasterwork ceiling, Red Hall, Ballycarry (69). Photograph: MBR

CHAPTER THREE

GRAND HOUSES

The dividing line between really 'grand' houses and middling ones is not an easy one to draw. I suppose, however, that most connoisseurs of grandeur would accept Galgorm Castle (67); Castle Upton (68); Castle Dobbs (70); Glenarm Castle (86); Red Hall (69); Leslie Hill (72); presumably Benvarden (77), which could make up 33 beds, accommodate a household of 50, and still not need to buy or borrow one article; and, a latecomer to the stakes, Dunderave (91). It is interesting that of these eight houses, five are still owned and occupied by descendants of their original builders. It is also interesting that every one is still in private hands. Although the National Trust has very substantial holdings in the county, particularly along the coastline, they do not include a single 'stately home' opened to the public. Nor, indeed, is there any mansion-house generally open to the public, apart from occasional openings for charity: not so many even of these since the Troubles, and since the arrival in Ireland of specialised self-propelled fine-art burglars.

With only a few exceptions, the houses of County Antrim seem never to have been quite as grand as some of those in Fermanagh or Armagh. Certainly, I know of no undiscovered house of the quality of Castlecoole. A certain austere Scottish homeliness has mostly prevailed over the more exotic display of Palladian, Grecian or even renaissance styles. But there are some fine buildings still, despite a formidable roll of losses over the years.

One of the first, and worst, losses was the great Elizabethan house at Carrickfergus, built about 1611 by Sir Arthur Chichester, of which no trace remains: it was demolished early in the 18th century, when "the late Marquis of Donegal, with his wonted liberality," gave "the grounds upon which stood the ruins of his castle of Joymount" to the Grand Jury for their new court house.[1] Fire, sometimes accidental but too often deliberate, has been a constant enemy. Shane's Castle was destroyed "by an accidental fire which broke out in one of the bed or dressing rooms on the 20th May 1816, at about 6 or 7 o'clock in the evening. The castle had been very gay at the time and a large party was assembled there that day. So rapid was the progress of the devouring element that scarcely anything was saved".[2] Lisanoure Castle, seat of the MacCartney family, was destroyed by an accidental(?) explosion of gunpowder stored there in 1847 (see page 103). The Antrim family's subsidiary seat at Ballymagarry, just south of Dunluce, derelict for many years, has finally disappeared within living memory.

On the dreadful night of 20th May 1922, "flying columns of the IRA carried out a series of burnings, raids and seizures on an unprecedented scale. The following were amongst the residences destroyed:- Shane's Castle, near Randalstown" (the Victorian replacement for the older house, a very fine building by Charles Lanyon); "Crebilly House, near Ballymena" (also by Charles Lanyon); Garron Tower (90) was also burned down that night; Drumnasole (88) "was sprinkled with petrol somewhat hastily and set alight, but the caretaker and his family, after an exciting few minutes, succeeded in getting the flames under control". On the same night, £2000 was stolen from the Northern Bank at Cushendall, several police stations were attacked, and Killagan railway bridge blown up: all this, allegedly, to coincide with the disbandment of the old Royal Irish Constabulary.[3]

A few months later, on 28th October 1922, Antrim Castle was burned down during a ball. "Somehow the grand staircase in the entrance hall caught fire. As the fire rapidly spread through the rectangular, box-like building, orders were issued that the water-storage tanks in the attic should be punctured. Curiously, these tanks ... were discovered to be empty! The servant, whose job it was to ensure the tanks were kept well supplied, was also discovered to be missing, along with his suitcases; and was later reputed to be a Sinn Feiner".[4] Cushendun House was to follow in 1926.

And then, there is the long list of houses which, for one reason or another, have deteriorated apparently beyond the point of no return - Moneyglass (another Lanyon house, seat of Squire Bumper Jones); most recent and perhaps saddest, Clare Park (see page 300), originally a McDonnell house, then seat of the McGildowny family, on its magnificent cliff-top site outside Ballycastle. There is also the roll-call of gentlemen's seats and grand bathing-lodges along the north fringes of Belfast Lough, now almost all knocked down to meet the insatiable demands for offices, indus-trial sites or private housing - Longwood, Macedon, Hazelbank, Abbeylands, Thornfield and Scoutbush amongst others.

So, the sequence which follows is shorter than it might have been; but it still contains a respectable muster of fine houses whose merits are less widely appreciated than they perhaps deserve.

References: 1. M'Skimin, 'Carrickfergus', 1811, p 59. 2. J Boyle, OSM, 'Drummaul', 1838, Antrim, VI, p 48. 3. 'Ballymena Observer', 26 May 1922. 4. Smyth, 'Antrim', 1984, pp 78-9.

Galgorm Castle

67. Built by Dr Alexander Colville between 1627 and 1645. By the latter date, house and bowling-green were certainly complete; sited within the protective walls of the bawn built in 1619 by Sir Faithful Fortescue, a nephew of Sir Arthur Chichester, close to the site of an older fort occupied by Rory Og McQuillan in 1610. The remains of an early church stand close by the entrance to the bawn. In 1758, when the house was occupied by Dr Peter Leslie, rector of Ahoghill, Mrs Delany wrote "Galgorm ... is old and in the castle style, with battlements round the court, large dark rooms, more venerable than pleasant." Agreeably, spelled 'Gillgorum' in Taylor and Skinner's Roads of Ireland, of 1778. In 1833, "an antiquated looking building ... built partly in imitation of an ancient defensible residence;" but in 1834, "at present it is under thorough repair by the noble proprietor the Earl of Mountcashell ... the good taste of the peer is evinced, by having, in the alterations, no change of appearance made ... but for the windows, which are not now of small diamond-shaped panes, set in lead and strongly stauncheoned with iron. The antique and commanding appearance of the place has outwardly undergone no alteration. It has a low, double roof, the gables of which are formed as represented in the above engraving" - which clearly shows the curly parapets as at present: so that the refurbishment of the 1850s suggested by Dixon and Girvan must in fact have been considerably earlier. The large Georgian-glazed windows, with brick surrounds, must also have been inserted in the thick walls (no doubt with great difficulty) before 1834. In 1837, "The castle of Galgorm, built by the celebrated Dr Colville, is a handsome square embattled structure, now the seat of the Earl of Mountcashel: the whole of the rooms are wainscoted with Irish oak." But by 1854, the fashion had changed,

and J B Doyle thought it "an inelegant and stiff-looking-building of no peculiar or historical interest whatsoever"! In 1859, the Valuation book described it as "a very fine concern ... the principal building has been almost renewed by the present occupant": valued at no less than £100.

The three-storey-on-basement house is built of rubble stone on the characteristic 17th-century double-pile plan: the central spine wall, seven feet thick, rises to two long chimney stacks, one with thirteen flues and chimney-pots, the other with eleven - there is a slight kink in the middle of the house, which is not exactly symmetrical. The place was sold up by the Encumbered Estates Court in 1850, and bought by Dr William Young, whose descendants still live in the house. Sir Charles Lanyon is said to have designed the front door and some of the internal door

cases, but of the original interior woodwork, only the Jacobean oak staircase remains: the oak panelling and floors were removed by Lord Mountcashel before he went bankrupt. Since 1988, both Castle and outbuildings have been thoroughly (and admirably) overhauled; the Court-yard Business Centre is now comfortably ensconced in the outbuildings.

Photographs: Michael O'Connell. Wood engraving: DPJ, 28 June 1834.
Situation: 190, Galgorm Road, Ballymena; td, Galgorm; Parish, Kilcon-riola; District Council, Ballymena; Grid ref. D 082 022.
References: Listed A. Delany, 'Letters from Georgian Ireland', 1991, pp 149, 150, letter of Mrs Delany, 8 October 1758; Taylor and Skinner, 'Roads', 1778, p 18; T C Robe, OSM, 1833, Antrim, VIII, p 2; D PJ, 28 June 1834; Lewis, TD, 1837, I, p 637; Doyle, 'Tours in Ulster', 1854, p 179; VAL 2B/1/64A, p 63, in PRONI; Girvan, 'Antrim & Ballymena', UAHS, 1969, p 22; Dixon, 'Introduction', 1975, p 27; Bence-Jones, 'Burke's guide', 1978, p 130; Pierce and Coey, 'Taken for granted', 1984, p 162; Young family papers.

Castle Upton, Templepatrick

68. In 1610: "we beheald materialles sufficient to finish a faire Castle alreadie buylte two stories high with two greate Towres or flankers the worke of Humfrey Norton Lieutenant of the Lo: Deputies foot companie, at a place called Tymple Patricke upon the said Sir Arthur Chiches-ter's lande by the River of Sixmylewater. He means to buyld a strong bawne of lyme and stone about it towards w'ch said Sir Arthur gives 100 li ster and a lease of the

lands for many yeares at a small rent." The oldest surviv-ing parts of the castle are the two round towers, NE and SW, the east wing, and the doorcase inside the porch with datestone of 1611.

In 1625 the Nortons sold the castle to Captain Henry Upton, an officer of Cornish extraction, MP for Carrickfergus in 1634, who changed its name; and it remained in the occupation of his descendants (later

Viscounts Templeton) until the deaths of two sons in the first World War. The remnants of the original Castle are embedded in a complex structure of which parts date from the remodelling of Robert Adam, parts from the remodelling of Edward Blore, and parts from a series of 20th-century modifications: and it is not always easy to tell t'other from which. In 1787, Dr Beaufort called it "Lord Templetown's Castle Upton, a large embattled building, partly castle and partly modern, all whitewashed". Writing in 1915, Sadleir and Dickinson consider this "in some respects a house of peculiar interest ... that part which formed the 17th century dwelling was really a transition between a castle and a house; the battlements and the small splayed windows in the ground floor are suggestive of the former, while the fireplaces and the upper windows are more in keeping with the latter." In the forty years between 1923 and 1963 the estate underwent various vicissitudes, including military occupation and the stripping of trees by a timber merchant; also, saddest of all, the loss of the fairy-tale conical tops to the towers.

In 1838, Boyle summarised matters as follows: "The present Castle originally consisted of a quadrangular building with a larger circular tower at its NE and SW angles, and in 1798 an addition of a wing containing some very fine apartments was made by Lord Templetown on the north side of the Castle - The appearance is somewhat baronical and interesting and its extent rather considerable. Of three floors and basement, the towers, four storeys with conical roofs with vanes, and with ornamen-

tal little machicolated towers at its other angles, give to the building a singular and pleasing effect - which however is not increased by its having been roughcast and whitened. Current improvements to the Castle, which is let, are by an architect Mr Blower of London." And, at a later date, he added: "In the basement storey there are numberless little appartments of almost every variety of form. Throughout the old part of the Castle, the rooms are generally small, but in the new part there are several very fine apartments, still in an unfinished state ... several casts of Italian marbles in alto relievo ornament the walls ... Since 1798 none of the Templetown family have resided here ... but Lord Templetown is now carrying out improvements on a large scale." (Sadleir and Dickinson drily comment - "owing to the mansion being broken into, and plundered of a large quantity of plate, on 1st July 1798", the first Viscount resided thenceforth in England). In 1835, before Blore began work "Lord Templeton's house", offices and stables were valued at £60.6s.0d; but in 1862, at £200, with the comment "a very old concern, remodelled - now in excellent order".

Although it is no longer whitewashed, one must agree with Boyle that the harling, though it serves to unite the old and the even older, is rather dreary: it is a pleasant surprise to come upon the great cutstone oriel window, borne on six little arches, and the rubble-stone wall, tower and turret on the north (or back) facade. But both the main mass of the Castle proper, and the roofline of the extensive double courtyard of the stables (designed by Robert

Adam in 1788-9), suffer from the absence of the original roof-cones. A considerable number of drawings by Robert Adam, dating from 1783 to 1789, survive in the Soane Museum. As King says, "Adam's 1783 work at Castle Upton was exceptional in that he made no attempt to produce symmetrical facades". Two years later, after the death of the first Viscount Templetown, he produced a delightful scheme - alas, not proceeded with - for a "Riding Room or Great Room for Exercise" opening off the dining room. The battlements, where they survive, are something of a puzzle; those on the stable-block are of what Girvan calls "Adam's distinctive machicolated cornice, copied from Roman fortifications", executed in brick; but the same theme appears in the work usually attributed to Blore, and it seems that he may, with somewhat surprising modesty, have deferred to Adam in this respect. Of the Adam work, the most exciting is the restless rhythm of the stables complex, best seen when slanting sunlight casts strong shadows: "Adam's finest stable courtyard", according to King.

The best of Blore's work - apart from the drawing-room oriel window already mentioned - is in the interior; particularly the quatrefoil plasterwork in some of the ceilings. The house is full of disconcerting mixtures of the work of different periods: the staircase, already fitted in by way of a kind of zany dogleg, has one 18th-century bannister-rail, and one 19th-century, with the grain of the wood running cross-wise in the former, lengthwise in the latter. The foot of the staircase in the main hall terminates in a magnificently extravagant triple whorl of mahogany on each hand. There is a ballroom, rebuilt in the late 20th century, but incorporating a very fine chimneypiece from the Earl-Bishop of Derry's house at Downhill. Strangest of all, there is a charming dining-room with Blore's characteristic interlinked quatrefoils, and Maltese crosses, in the ceiling, and a series of eleven plaques of differing shapes and sizes, with mythological figures rather in the style of Flaxman or Thorwaldsen: too late, one would think, for Robert Adam, too early, one would have said, for Blore, especially if these are the "alto relievo casts" mentioned in the Ordnance Survey Memoir (see colour-plate IXb). Perhaps a clue lies in the fact that the Viscountess Templetown

of the day was one of Wedgwood's best customers?

James Boyle was much impressed by the "magnificent entrance, somewhat resembling a barbican, in the Saxon style of architecture. It is punched granite, with white porphyry quoins, mouldings, and pinnacles ... The whole is of a superior style of architecture and workmanship ... the plan by Edward Blower Esquire and the officiating architect Mr Charles Lelam, both of England".

The grounds are charming, many fine trees have survived the timber-merchant's axe, and the paddocks around the house are enlivened by peacocks, fallow deer, and guanacos (a kind of ornamental llama).

Known to the Ordnance Survey, if to nobody else, as "Upton Park".

Photographs: R J Welch, Ulster Museum W01/88/3; Michael O'Connell.
Situation: 97 Antrim Road, Templepatrick,; td and Parish, Templepatrick; District Council, Antrim; Grid ref. J 227 858.
References: Listed A. T 811/3, of 1610, VAL 1B/129A, p 17, and VAL 2B/1/10, p 77, all in PRONI; Taylor and Skinner, 'Roads', 1778, p 280; D A Beaufort, Ms Journal, 1787, III, p 46 in TCD Library; Adam drawings in Sir John Soane's Museum, XLVIII, Nos 29 to 39; Blore drawings in the Victoria & Albert Museum, 8731 to 9; J Boyle, OSM, 1837, Templepatrick, as yet unpublished; Sadleir and Dickinson, 'Georgian mansions in Ireland', 1915, pp 92-95; O'Laverty, 'Down and Connor', III, p 235; PSAMNI, 1940, p 46; Girvan, 'West Antrim', UAHS, 1970, pp 14-16; Bence-Jones, 'Burke's guide', 1978, p 78; Pierce and Coey, 'Taken for granted', 1984, p 176; C Kinahan, 'Castle Upton', n.d., [1986?] passim; King, 'Complete works of Robert and James Adam', 1991, pp 223, 328.

Red Hall, Ballycarry

69. Red Hall is an architectural jack-in-the-box: its rather dull exterior conceals a whole bundle of surprises.

From the front, it appears a three-storey, three-bay, Victorian stuccoed house, with single-storey wings, a clumsy portico, a rather fussy square turret, plate-glass windows (many of them false), and chimneys not in the expected places. Once inside, the stranger finds himself in a long, low hallway with ceiling plasterwork in the style of around 1830. Off the hall to the right is a charming large, tall, sunny drawing-room of 1793, with coved ceiling plasterwork, and a (later) Italian marble chimney piece; at the other end of the hall, a dining-room evidently of similar date.

Next, the visitor discovers the ball-topped newel-post of a very handsome oak staircase, clearly early 17th-century; its levels and landings fail however to fit the window-openings in the thick walls of its tower-house - can it have been fitted into a still older, perhaps 16th-century, tower? After this, he may feel faint at the discovery that two (only) of the first-floor bedrooms have lavish figurative and floral plasterwork ceilings, in the robust but fairly primitive style of the 17th century; which nonetheless incorporate half-life-size figures of a gentleman and his lady dressed in the style of around 1730 (see also page 70); whilst the wooden panelling, mouldings, door-cases and so forth constitute a strange mixture of 17th- and 18th-century fashions. Just to help matters, dendrochronology seems to indicate that the roof-timbers date from the second half of the 17th century. Due to the slope of the site, the basement is at ground level at the back of the house: here the main walls are battered, and there are various puzzling early doors and door-cases. Odder still, the small, square Victorian turret perched on the roofline turns out to be perched on top of a mysterious four-storey turret of much earlier date, with consistently in-curving walls, like - but probably in fact not

- a latrine tower; possibly built to house a (totally disappeared) spiral staircase.

The earliest document relating to the house is a lease of May, 1609 of the "Readhall" and other lands, from the West Countryman John Dalway to a Scotsman, William Edmonstone, shown as 'Edmonston Bart.' on Taylor and

Skinner's map of 1777. In 1784 they were sold (for £24,500) to the Ker family, of Portavo and Montalto in Co. Down, whose family letters evidence the additions of 1793. In the 1798 rising, the Islandmagee men "knew that the owner of Red Hall, Richard Gervase Ker, had a plentiful store of weapons ... At the entrance they were received by the butler, who informed them that Mr Ker was not at home (he had prudently withdrawn to Carrickfergus). They broke open the gun-room and distributed the muskets found there, only to discover that, before his departure, Mr Ker had had the foresight to remove all the firing-pins".

Following his visit in 1817, Atkinson waxed both lyrical and pious, at great length, about the beauties of the demesne. "This seat of Richard G. Ker Esq may be considered as the most respectable feature of a valuable property on which this gentleman chiefly, if not solely, resides. It is also a beautiful and graceful improvement of that portion of the Antrim coast, but from its low position on the shore, you do not, in your perambulations through this otherwise interesting demesne, enjoy the pleasures of an open and extensive prospect" ... "We have been compelled to acknowledge, that Red-hall cannot boast of a towering position: and it remains for us to notice ... those charming shades that are suited to meditation, and those beauties of lawn and forest, which combine, with a silent and serene sky ... to raise the thinking soul in gratitude to the great author of this earthly temple, who has taught his creatures to decorate it;" - and so on, for another whole page.

In 1835 "the house is a tolerably spacious mansion consisting of a central portion with 2 wings ... It presents a plain *stone-finished*" (my italics) "front and is without any architectural ornament ... It was rebuilt by the late Mr Ker about the year 1807", but if the date of 1801 for the water-colour of the house is correct, the rebuilding must have been some years earlier. In 1837 "An elegant mansion with a fine demesne". In 1869 the County Antrim estate (but not the County Down estate) was sold through the Landed Estates Court: the purchaser of the house was a Mr John McAuley, who was probably responsible for encasing the Georgian work of the Kers, visible in Frances Ker's water-colour, in a more up-to-date Victorian skin. According to Pierce and Coey, "the tower is thought to have been added after 1869 by the McAuley family who were also responsible for the external plaster and the red, painted finish" - but of this I have been able to find no documentary confirmation. In 1902, it passed to an English woollen merchant called WJ Porritt, who died in 1918 of eating infected oysters on board the Stranraer steamer. After his death, it was bought but not lived in by George Reade; much of the land was sold off; the house stood empty for some years, until bought by Vice-Admiral McClintock in 1927. During the second World War it was requisitioned for military use.

The townland, before 1609 called 'Irewe', seems to have been renamed for the house, not vice versa; but this is paradoxical, for the house seems first to have been painted red only about 1870: some traces of which painting remain.

No scholar has yet produced a convincing account of the building history of this extraordinary house: certainly the most enigmatic in the county.

Photographs: Michael O'Connell; MBR. Water-colour: Frances Ker, courtesy of D J R Ker.
Situation: 30 Red Hall Drive, Ballycarry; td, Red Hall; Parish, Templecorran; District Council, Larne; Grid ref. J 450 951.
References: Listed A. Taylor and Skinner, 'Roads', 1778, p 13; Letters, D Ker, in Rome, to R J Ker, of 29 June, 17 October, and 21 December 1793, D 2651/2/74, 81, 84 in PRONI; water-colour of 1801 by Frances Ker, in possession of D J R Ker; Atkinson 'Ireland exhibited', 1823, II, p 102; J Boyle, OSM, 1835 and 1840, Antrim, X, pp 85, 91; Lewis, TD, 1837, II, p 603; O'Laverty, 'Down and Connor', III, 1884, p 94; Egerton and Bigger, 'Guide for tourists', 1906, p 63; PSAMNI, 1940, p 38; Dowlin, 'Ballycarry', 1963, p 23; Bence-Jones, 'Burke's guide', 1978, p 241; Pierce and Coey, 'Taken for granted', 1984, p 162; Lyons, 'Illustrated incumbered estates', 1993; Stewart, 'Summer soldiers', 1995, p 95; information from owners.

Castle Dobbs, Kilroot

70. Secluded in its walled and wooded parkland demesne, south-facing with a glimpse of sea and the ships, Castle Dobbs is a classic example of the 18th-century Irish country house. I cannot improve on Professor Rowan's summation: "For its date, c 1750 to c 1754, it is quite without an equal in Ulster while its perfect Palladian plan with flanking wings - if from a pattern book source - is hard to match in a house of this scale anywhere in Ireland". However, it does have its idiosyncratic features: above all, the absence of an architect; and the thin Victorian veneer in which parts of it are encased.

In 1610, "One John Dobb buylte a fayre castle within two myle of Knockfargus called Dobbes Castle about w'ch he entends to buylde a bawne of stone ...... This Castle is buylte upon parte of Ensigne Dallawayes lande". In 1683 Richard Dobbs referred to "the small castle built by my grandfather" (still standing, in ruins) and wrote "my home in a few years may be remarkable for the orchards and gardening around it"; there was an intermediate house, of which only foundations remain. The present house was built by Arthur Dobbs, late surveyor of the Irish Works, later Governor of North Carolina. Pococke remarked in 1752 "Mr Dobbs is now building on a very fine spot on rising ground". The surrounding oak trees had been planted before the house was built.

As successor in office to Sir Edward Lovett Pearce, Arthur Dobbs had acquired a respectable architectural library. One of the books he is known to have owned was James Gibbs's A Book of Architecture, of 1728. Plate 64 was "a Draught done for a Gentleman in Essex", proba-

bly never built, a simplified version of his design for Ditchley in Oxfordshire. That plate is missing from Dobbs's copy. It appears that Castle Dobbs was loosely based upon this design, though, visually, the appearance differs considerably because the basement storey is at ground level, not sunk or concealed.

Basically, this is a rather large 7-bay 2-storey double-pile house, on a substantial basement, with two 5-bay 2-storey wings without basement, linked by courtyard quadrants lit by pairs of oval lunettes. The south-facing facade, with 33 windows, but no other opening, door, porch, or portico, is formidably austere. The simple pediment on the south facade, the hipped roof with four solid chimney-stacks, consort a bit uncomfortably with the Victorian frills below. Much of the original internal joinery, and some fine plasterwork, survive. James Boyle in 1839 said "the house is a spacious old-fashioned looking mansion, the entrance front presenting in its central building and two projecting wings a somewhat Elizabethan appearance. It is three storeys high and presents a plain rough-cast and whitened front - plantations, grounds and house are in a very neglected state".

It seems that, in the mid-19th century, the Dobbs of the day first embarked upon, and then recoiled from, a programme of Victorian 'improvements'; probably to designs by Charles Lanyon, probably about 1850. The results are curious; the ground floor of the central section of the main, south, facade, has been encased in vermiculated rustication; there are similar rusticated details applied to the west wing, but not to the east wing of the entrance

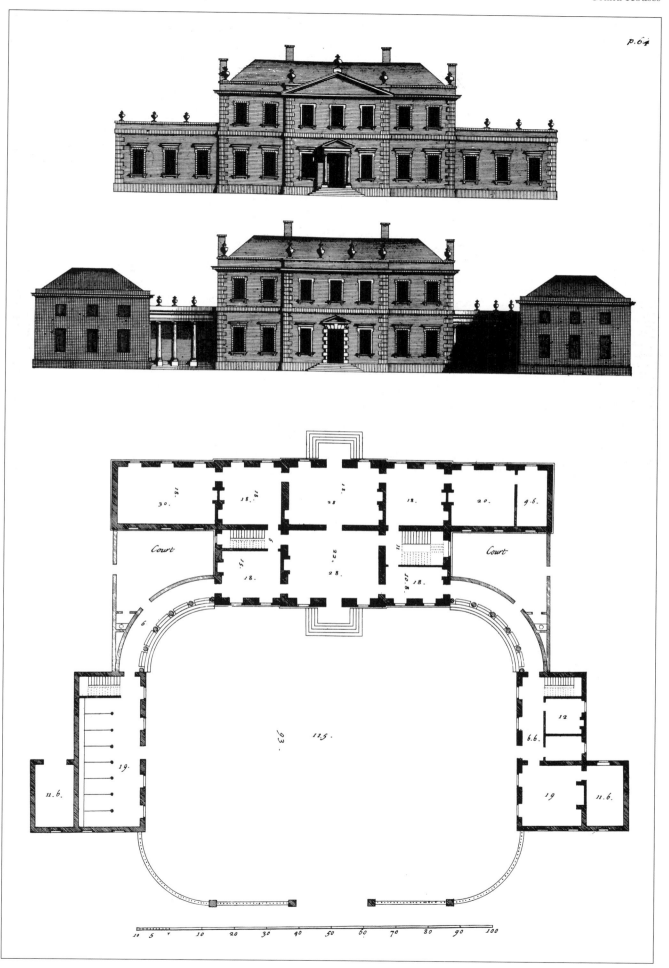

front; plate glass has been substituted for the former thick, early, glazing-bars in the windows of the piano nobile on the south front. But on the entrance front, the original glazing survives; and to this front has been added, in the 19th century, a remarkable double staircase of reddish stone, which leads to a veranda borne on Ionic columns giving access to the 'front' door: there is no direct means of access to the principal rooms from the principal facade (unlike Ditchley).

Despite these incongruities, the house has a kind of brooding dignity, and a sense of over-riding integrity, which render it one of the most important buildings in the county.

It is still owned and occupied by descendants of its original builder.

Photographs: Michael O'Connell. Engraving: Gibbs, 'A book of architecture', 1728, pl 64.
Situation: Dalway's Bawn Road, Kilroot; td, Dobbsland; Parish, Kilroot and Templecorran; District Council, Carrickfergus; Grid ref. J 445 908.
References: Listed A. T 811/3 of 1610, and R Dobbs, D 162/6, of 1683, in PRONI; Gibbs, 'A book of architecture', 1728, pl 64 and p xvii; Pococke, 'Tour in Ireland', 1891, p 112; Taylor and Skinner, 'Roads', 1778, p 13; J Boyle, OSM, 1839, Antrim, X, p 59; Young, 'Belfast and province of Ulster', 1909, p 253; Bence-Jones, 'Burke's guide', 1978, p 66; Pierce and Coey, 'Taken for granted', 1984, p 163; notes and reports by H Dixon and A J Rowan in MBR.

Beardiville House, Coleraine

71. There must have been some kind of house at Dunmull, or Beardiville, when Francis Macnaghten took a lease from the Earl of Antrim in 1709. The puzzling armorial plaque above the front door is dated 1715. A slightly crude survey of 'Berdivile' of 1712, by Thomas Roe, shows 'house, orchard, garding, stead, and meadow or moss'. Girvan thinks the present house not so early, suggesting that it was rebuilt about 1750. For my part, though there are some internal features that are certainly later, I find a date of around 1710 convincing enough, given the narrow windows, only two panes wide, in the 17th-century manner found also at Springhill, the heavy chimney-stacks, and the handsome oak staircase. The house is two-storey on basement, of five bays, with a central porch of Tuscan columns: the walls are roughcast and painted white; the roof is hipped, and the dormer windows shown in old photographs have been slated over. A single-storey range to the west has long, later, Georgian-glazed windows: otherwise, the house has, externally more of antiquity than of elegance. At the rear, the master's mistress's cottage in the yard has been restored as flats; though the outside staircase from his bedroom has disappeared, as has a former basement chapel, and the entrance to a tunnel said to have gone all the way to Dunluce Castle.

Since the parish of Ballywillin is part in County Antrim, part in County Londonderry, the house (perversely) appears in the Londonderry Ordnance Survey Memoirs, where, in 1835, C W Ligar wrote "the house is good and commodious but old fashioned. It was until 1833 the residence of the late Edmund A Macnaghten Esquire. It then passed into the hands of his brother Sir Francis W Macnaghten, from whom it is rented by the present resident, James Leslie Junior Esquire ... owing to the low situation of the house and demesne, the view is confined in every direction." In the Valuation book of 1833, the main house is classified 1A: the valuation, quite a high one, was £38. In 1856 there are two entries, one showing James White as occupier, one James Leslie, when house, offices and two gate-lodges, no doubt including the Victorian wing now demolished, were valued at £68.18.0; though the house was shown as 'vacant' in 1858.

Edmund Macnaghten of Beardiville, who never cut his nails or his hair, is said to have been known as 'Beardy', "though of course this could equally well have been derived from his property" - or is it just a later invention? His elder son Edmond, barrister and MP, may or may not have married his housekeeper, by whom he certainly had a daughter Mary Anne, who married Captain Hannay of Ballylough. After Edmond's death in 1831, the property passed to his brother Francis - for particulars of whom, see Dunderave (91). In 1845, Beardiville passed to Hugh Lecky, who had married in 1837 a Miss Hutchinson, and the Macnaghten interest in the property was finally extinguished only by a deed of exchange in 1884. Hugh Lecky's grandson, also Hugh, went to live in the apple-house in the walled garden around 1939, abandoning the big house which was shut up; after his death without issue in 1962, the house continued to lie empty until it was bought in 1965 and painstakingly restored by the present owner's father.

Photograph: Michael O'Connell.
Situation: 2 Ballyholme Road, Cloyfin, Coleraine; td Beardiville; Parish, Ballywillin; District Council, Coleraine; Grid ref. C 901 373.
References: Listed B1. Taylor and Skinner 'Roads' 1778, p 272; C W Ligar, OSM, 1835, Londonderry, XII, p 33; VAL 1B/137, pp 14, 76, VAL 2B/1/30A, p 1, and T 2992, all in PRONI; Macnaghten, 'Clan Macnachtan', 1951, pp 79, 86, 87, 103; Girvan, 'North Antrim', UAHS, 1972, pp 15, 33; Pierce and Coey, 'Taken for granted', 1984, p 114.

Leslie Hill, Ballymoney

72. If Castle Dobbs is the grandest mid-Georgian house of south Antrim, Leslie Hill, of almost the same date, is certainly the grandest in the north of the county: even with its wings clipped. It is unusual in that it can be dated with considerable exactitude. On 8th October 1758, Mrs Delany, coming from Dr Peter Leslie, rector of Ahoghill, who seems that year to have rented Galgorm Castle, stayed with his third son, James Leslie, "married and settled in this neighbourhood. We went to them in an inconvenient time, their house unfinished and full of company, but they crammed us in, and it was better than any inn we could go to."

Like Castle Dobbs (70), Leslie Hill seems to have been built from a pattern-book (not yet identified in this case, however): Dr Craig remarks that its doorcase is "straight out of the pattern-books and without solecisms". The main block of the house is a double cube, with a tall and rather austere facade: the three central bays break forward, separately quoined, and support a pediment incorporating a half-oculus. The house is seven bays wide, three storeys on basement; the glazing-pattern of the window-sashes is rather unusual: nine over nine panes on the principal floor; but nine over six on the floor above, six over three in the attic and the basement, the upper sash being in each case the larger one. The broken pediment of the doorcase is borne on two Doric columns; there is a semi-circular fanlight. The dressed stonework of the doorcase, and of the eaves-course, has been (for many years) dis-

creetly painted; the walls have been (for many years, probably always) encased in good-quality 'Roman' cement. There are nine broad stone steps up to the platform outside the front door, which is supported on heavy blocks of rusticated ashlar: below the platform are cobble-floored wine-cellars which outdo in generosity even those of Ahoghill glebe-house (106): but this arrangement seems not to have been original, for there is evidence that there was once a low side-door under the steps from which footman or horse-holder could dart out directly from the basement to greet a visitor.

The three-bay two-storey pavilions, and the blank-arcaded passages which linked them to the house, seem to have been original, for they appear in very early pictures of the house, and even on the map in the Road-Book of 1778. They were demolished, by reason of rampant dry rot, in 1955. But neither was really part of the house proper; for, as at Springmount (78), one contained kitchen, servants' hall, and servants' bedrooms over, so freeing all the bedrooms in the main block for the family and their guests; while the other, despite its sophisticated appearance, in fact housed stables, loose boxes and tack-rooms, with lofts for hay and grooms above them.

The front of the house faces roughly north-east, looking out over the park, and a lake excavated in the mid-19th century. In 1833, the valuers found Leslie Hill a problem. It was initially placed in category 1B, and, with its offices, valued at £105.18.6, despite the comments "House old and not in modern style, also too large." This is followed by another note: "Mr Griffith says this house should not be more than £85 and reducing it from £105.18.0 would about bring it to that nearly". The outcome of this mystifying operation was a valuation of £56.14.0! James McGann of the Ordnance Survey, writing in May 1835, says "the house is large and roomy, the ornamental grounds are extensive, and the plantings are very judiciously and handsomely arranged ... In the summer the appearance of the place is greatly improved by the luxuriant foliage of the numerous fine trees which surround it". The back of the house, facing south-west with a splendid view out over the valley of the Bann, contains the finely-proportioned large drawing-room and dining-room.

Two much smaller but charming rooms, sitting-room and library, flank the splendid square hallway, with its six fine shouldered doorcases, floor of stone flags, and twin-arched screen. The staircase is comparatively modest; there is a long passage running along the central spine of the house on each of the upper floors. The central attic bedroom, behind the pediment, contains a couple of surprises - the half-oculus turns out to give extra light to a high, vaulted ceiling; which has as its centrepiece a por-

trait head in stucco of an individual with large nose and larger ear - Girvan has unkindly suggested that this may be a portrait of James Leslie, builder of the house!

For nearly 250 years, the house has remained in the ownership and occupation of the builder's family, if not always by direct descent. The family, a mainly clerical and military one, has provided many high sheriffs for the county, as well as deans, archdeacons, and even a rear-admiral. The farm buildings are now open to the public, but not the house.

Photograph: Michael O'Connell. (See also colour-plate I)

Situation: The avenue debouches on the Old Coleraine Road, Ballymoney; td, Ballypatrick; Parish, and District Council, Ballymoney; Grid ref. C 935 260.

References: Listed A. Delany, 'Letters from Georgian Ireland', 1991, p 150, 8 October, letter of Mrs Delany, 1758; F Sloane, Survey, 1765, p 25, in possession of owner; Young, 'Tour in Ireland', 1780, p 53; Taylor and Skinner, 'Roads', 1778, p 19; VAL 1B/142B, p 149, in PRONI; J McGann, OSM, 1835, Antrim, V, p 9; Young, 'Belfast and province of Ulster', 1909, pp 235, 408; Girvan, 'North Antrim', UAHS, 1972, p 45; Craig, 'Classic Irish houses', 1976, p 29; Bence-Jones, 'Burke's guide', 1978, p 184; Pierce and Coey, 'Taken for granted', 1984, p 162.

Seaport Lodge, Portballintrae

73. It is curious, indeed paradoxical, that so important and prominent a Georgian house should have so Victorian an appearance: but the nicely-cut sandstone painted white, like stucco, combined with the plate-glass in the ground-floor windows, lend this house a deceptively 19th-century air. In fact, it seems to have been built by James Leslie soon after Leslie Hill (72), that is, between 1758 and 1775. By 1776, it must have been habitable, and

occupied by one of James Leslie's brothers, for on 4th August of that year Arthur Young recorded: "Accompanied Mr Lesly to his brother's at - within 3 miles of the Giant's Causeway, where I had the pleasure of learning several particulars concerning the country upon the coast." It is clearly delineated, very much as it now stands, on a map of 1780 by James Williamson, Land Surveyor and Draughtsman, Ballymena, still at Leslie Hill. But this is odd: for Seaport appears on Williamson's 1808 revision of his father-in-law's map of 1780 of the whole county, but not on the latter.

It is a wonder that a younger son of a clergyman could afford to build, in quick succession, two such splendid houses as Leslie Hill and Seaport, however up to date his farming activities. It is probable that, in the process, he much overstrained the family finances. James Leslie must have had a nasty shock when, on 12 February 1794, Barry Yelverton, Chief Baron in Dublin, conveyed to Archdeacon Traill Seaport, Portballintrae, and many other townlands, by reason of the fact that James Leslie "was outlawed in a plea of debt at the suit of said Archdeacon Trail"; but the matter was somehow patched up. Local tradition has it that the building of Seaport was spread over many years. The foundations were cut out of the rock, and there is extensive underbuilding, including remarkable vaulted cellars. The house seems to have been originally designed only for summer use, without fireplaces or servants' quarters. At some date unknown, chimneys serving the downstairs rooms were installed at the four corners of the house, chimneys serving the upstairs rooms between them, all incorporated in the roof-top balustrade. Still later, the corner chimneys were boxed in, and new larger fireplaces and chimney stacks inserted in the spine wall - one stack is still surmounted by a surviving chimney-pot made of cut slates bound together, as at O'Hara Brook (74) and Wheyburn (128). The two-storey service wing appears, from dates found carved on its wall-plates, to have been added in 1827.

In 1807, Dr Beaufort admired "the small port Ballintray ... not far from it on the west bank of the river Mr Leslie has built a very neat Lodge of cut stone and called Seaport". James Boyle, writing in 1835, says, "Seaport Lodge, the summer residence of James Leslie

Esquire, is situated on the seacoast. It was built about the year 1790. The house is 2-storey, commodious and tasteful in its style of architecture and appearance. Its situation, though exposed and unprotected, is admirably calculated for that of a bathing lodge." The Valuation book of 1833 gives a ground plan, showing the extension to the rear and the three bay windows, classifying the house 1A and commenting "settled this at £45 it being too good for a bathing lodge and not likely to get a tenant if vacant." In 1859, this was reduced to £40, of which £17.6.2 was added "for situation as a watering place", but with the note, "Houses on this coast require more to keep them in repair than in an inland ordinary situation" - how true!

The house faces east, looking across the bay towards the Causeway headlands. The ground-floor windows and central door all round-headed, all but those in the entrance bow tripartite and divided by pilasters; these windows were originally Gothick-glazed, but the plate glass was substituted by Colonel Douglas Leslie at the turn of the century. The upper windows are square, eight-over-four-pane sashes, with architraves. Above them, below the cornice, runs a restrained and most attractive band of fluting. The hipped roof is invisible behind a high ornamental balustrade which incorporates the tall slim chimney stacks which punctuate the roof-line. The standard of the stone-carving is extraordinarily high. It seems that, about 1980, the owners sought to remove the paintwork but found the sandstone beneath so multi-coloured that it was decided to repaint the walls after all. Internally, the central bow contains a most elegantly detailed elliptical hallway, with a similarly shaped room (said to have been a chapel) in the basement below, and a similarly-shaped small sitting room above. In many ways, this is the most desirable 18th-century house in the county.

The house remained in the ownership of the Leslie family until this century: its present owner bought it in 1984 from Hume Stewart Moore of Moyarget.

Photograph: Michael O'Connell. (See also colour-plate XVa). Water-colour: courtesy Mr J Leslie.

Situation: 40, Seaport Avenue, Portballintrae; td, Ballintrae; Parish, Dunluce; District Council, Coleraine; Grid ref. C 922 422.

References: Listed B+. Taylor and Skinner 'Roads', 1778, p 272; James Williamson, map, 1780 at Leslie Hill; Young, 'Tour in Ireland, 1780, p 139; D A Beaufort, 'Tour', 1807, p 21, Ms 4033 in TCD Library; T C Robe, OSM, 1832, and J Boyle, 1835, Antrim, V, pp 105, 110; VAL 1B/140 p 131, VAL 2B/34A, pp 1, 104, D 4081/1/16, all in PRONI; Bence-Jones, 'Burke's guide', 1978, p 256.

▷

Photograph: Michael O'Connell. (See also colour-plate IIIa)

Situation: Set well back, at the end of a long avenue, off Bann Road, Ballymoney; td, Enagh Lower; Parish and District Council, Ballymoney; Grid ref. C 925 246.

References: Listed B. Lease of burying ground of 1749; Taylor and Skinner, 'Roads' 1778, p 19; J McGann, OSM, 1835, Antrim, V, p 9; Young, 'Belfast and province of Ulster', 1909, p 235; Girvan, 'North Antrim', UAHS, 1972, p 45; Bence-Jones, 'Burke's guide', 1978, p 228; Pierce and Coey, 'Taken for granted', 1984, p 114; 'Clergy of Connor', 1993.

O'Hara Brook, Ballymoney

74. A most attractive house, but a most puzzling and confusing one: nothing is quite what it seems. A long, low, house of two storeys, without cellar or attics; ostensibly symmetrical, but the symmetry is delusive. Oral tradition, traceable back only to the 1890s, has it that this was originally a coaching inn; but this may be a myth resulting from the bewildering multiplicity of small rooms. Analysis is not made easier by the fact that the house is presently divided into two dwellings for separate generations, with the drawing room in one half, the dining room in the other.

The owners, who know the house better than anyone else, think the eastern wing to the right (unlike the western one a double cube in depth) may have been the earliest part, with the original entrance through a fanlighted doorway in the gable; and that the break forward of the central block, incorporating the staircase, was a later addition. But I wonder: to me (as to Girvan, and as also to Pierce and Coey) it seems that the four-bay central block, with its two off-centre pyramidal gables, may have been a decidedly different double-cube house, at right angles to the present long axis. Certainly some of the internal detailing, such as shutters or their absence, and the masking of the lower panes of the windows, could tend to confirm this of the east wing, though not the drawing room in the west wing.

From the front, the house reads as three four-bay two-storey blocks, the central block advancing: all clad in Roman cement, with V-channelled quoins of reddish sandstone, and knops (twentieth century though very appropriate) at each corner. The off-centre doorcase is housed in a later porch, serviceable rather than beautiful. The central block has very tall Georgian glazed windows, of nine panes over six, on the ground floor; above, rather squat ones, of six panes over three. The two wings are somewhat lower. A low parapet seeks, not wholly without success, to unify the composition. Instead of chimney-pots, pointed slates are set on end on top of the stacks, as at Wheyburn, Ballygally (128). The conservatory was added to the facade, a bit incongruously, in 1901; it incorporates what might be a considerably earlier oval fanlight.

The hall contains a most peculiar L-shaped staircase, the bottom step just inside the front door on the right, which has the air of having been removed from somewhere else; there is also a very strange narrow gallery with bannister rails, leading nowhere. Yet the ceiling of the upper landing is barrel-vaulted, and contains a nice little piece of floral stucco work as centrepiece. The dining room faces north, out across the Ballymoney river, yet is the best room in the house; it has simple shutters of an effective but unsophisticated kind, and built into their recesses a po-cupboard. The drawing room faces south, being placed in the west wing, and has a most unusual cornice moulding of hundreds of, apparently, goose-eggs.

Entered from the rear part of the central double-cube, there is an enchanting little square single-storey cobbled yard with the slates sprouting prize-winning cushions of green moss. Apart from porch and conservatory, there have been two or three other minor extensions. But the house retains its indomitably individual character.

It must have been named for the family that first built and owned it. One George Teatte had married Catherine, only daughter and heiress of Cormack O'Hara of Co. Cavan, and changed his name; his grandson Henry O'Hara was described as 'of O'Hara Brook' in 1749. In 1835, James McGann justly remarked "The house is only 2-storeys high, but its lowness is compensated for by its length ... The situation of the house is low and contiguous to the Ballymoney river. The general appearance of the place, however, is interesting and picturesque". Charles O'Hara, the owner in 1835, had three sons and two daughters, but none of them had children. Charles O'Hara's youngest daughter had married the Rev. William Armstrong, rector of Scarva, who in 1867, "retired from the active ministry ... to manage the O'Hara Brook estate" for his mother-in-law. His wife inherited, but died aged 48 in 1889, her husband having predeceased her, when the estate was sold for £6,300, to Captain J S Cramsie of Bannfield, whose forbears had settled in Ballymoney about 1709, and prospered there. His descendants have lived here for the past century.

Manor House, Rathlin Island

75. A long low two-storey range of buildings overlooking the harbour, the earliest dating from the mid 18th century: built soon after the Rev. John Gage had bought a long lease of the island for £1,750, in 1746, from the Earl of Antrim, then in financial difficulties. In 1838, the seat of "the Revd Robert Gage, the rector and landlord of the island, is a good modern house, pleasantly situated at the head of Church Bay and enjoying a southern prospect and beautiful view of the northern coast of Antrim. There is a tolerable garden near the house" (Boyle).

The western gable is marked by an imposing entrance, perhaps of 1790, incorporating a kind of Gibbsian surround in red sandstone, with a rectangular fanlight, and a round oeil-de-boeuf window above it. Then comes the main range of the Gage family living quarters, six bays of tall Georgian-glazed windows above and below. Next, a slightly lower seven-bay range, incorporating three pairs of coupled windows, those below in segmental-headed recesses, probably the earliest part of the complex, built before 1760 to provide workspace for weavers; and a modern porch, replicating with creditable accuracy that at the western gable, though its proportions are, perforce, not quite the same. Then a long low range of stables and outbuildings with ventilation slits but no windows; a formal archway of squared limestone, dated 1819; and then a large and handsome hipped-roof stone barn, with extensive lofts. There are good cutstone details, such as the eaves mouldings, many apparently by two masons, John McIlroy and his son William, brought over from Ballycastle in June of 1820, who were not always sober enough to be at work.

The Gage family, with regret, moved out of the Manor House in 1975; after a period of increasing dereliction, it has been well restored, over a lengthy period, with the intention of providing a variety of services to the islanders and visitors. At the date of writing, these include restaurant and kitchen, guest-rooms, community meeting room, workshops, clinic, and fire-engine house, with an underwater exploration centre in the barn. However, it is no easy matter for a population of only 100 to support institutions such as these, even with substantial aid from outside, and the future remains somewhat uncertain. Most of this work was carried out for the Rathlin Island Trust by Hegarty, Masterson and Doherty of Derry. Internally, the work has been executed to a high standard, and incorporates some intriguing wood-carvings by an island sculptor, Paddy Burns. Externally, the former reddish Roman cement has been replaced by a much whiter cement render, which is perhaps a pity; five chimney stacks have, somewhat mysteriously, become six; but otherwise, the whole range looks very well, despite the sea-change which has taken place in its function.

Photograph: Jim McCall.
Situation: Overlooking the harbour in Church Bay, Rathlin Island; td, Church quarter; Parish, Rathlin; District Council, Moyle; Grid ref. D 145 511.
References: Listed B+. D508 and T1833/7, in PRONI; Lendrick, map, 1780; J Boyle, OSM, 1838, Antrim, IX, p 131; Catherine Gage, Ms history of Rathlin, 1851, pp 142, 143; Brett, 'Rathlin', UAHS, 1974, p 11; Bence-Jones, 'Burke's guide', 1978, p 140.

76. A splendid tall Georgian house, the listers thought of 1860, but I think of early 18th-century date, named after, and for two centuries the seat of, the White family. On the face of it, it hardly seems to justify a place amongst the Grand Houses of the county; but old pictures show it surrounded with ornamental gardens, lake, and swans; and the standing of the White family in the county was such that I cannot bring myself to describe it as a Middling House.

It seems that Fulke White, a Greek-speaking royalist from the West Riding of Yorkshire, sought refuge in Ireland about 1650, and at first set up a classical school in the town of Antrim; but this did not answer; in 1685 it is recorded that "Mr. Fulk White, having no scholars come to him, quit all hope of a Philosophy School." However, he arranged to be ordained, and was installed as Presbyterian minister of First Broughshane in 1687. His fortunes by then somehow restored, he soon after bought 180 acres of land upon which he built the house he called White Hall, just possibly the house still standing, although the present house seems more likely to have been a replacement of about 1750 for the original one. In 1709, "by reason of his age and craziness", he was "not able to perform the requisite duties" as minister; but means were found to preserve him from premature retirement. He died in 1716. Both his sons were preachers; one married a Miss McCollum of Lemnalary, the other a Miss Donaldson of Drumnasole, and the family ultimately thereby came to own extensive property in the county.

The house stands, behind a screen of trees rendering it invisible from the road, on a hillside looking south-west down the Braid valley towards Ballymena. A flight of ten wide ashlar steps, with an iron handrail on each side, leads up to the central doorcase, with segmental-headed arch; reeded columns divide the sidelights from the door. Three triple windows in the upper floor, and two in the basement, retain their Georgian glazing, but not so the triple windows on either side of the doorcase. A pair of dramatic eagles flap their wings at the front gable-ends; they would look more at home if they had piles of quoins to perch on. (One wonders, could these be the "pair of bath-stone eagles which are quite new" auctioned by the creditors of Bernard O'Neill of Lemnalary on 1st September 1762, together with a post-chaise, a pair of horses, and an eight-day clock?) Now slated, the roof may originally have been thatched, judging by the gable upstands. Internally, there is a fine stone floor in the hallway, and an unusual glazed screen giving light to the staircase at the rear; some good panelling in the doorways. There is an excellent U-shaped range of stone outbuildings at the rear.

The house and outbuildings were described in quite exceptional detail in the first Valuation book, as they stood, property of James White Esq., on 27 October 1836 - House, Basement, Return Pantry, do, Return, Kitchen, Return, Passage, Turf house, Dairy, Shed, Stables, Office, do, Wash House, Coach House, Gate Ho dwg, Cow house, do, do, sheds in Haggard (arched) - being together valued at a total of £53.11.2; deduct for large amount, £4.0.4; add for neatness of situation, £4.19.0; deduct for distance to market and post town, £6.16.3; result, £47.13.8.

The most eminent member of the White family was Sir George White, VC, who lived from 1835 to 1912, and was a hero both of the Afghan wars and of the siege of Ladysmith. His brother-in-law, according to Camac, "was a Crimean Veteran whose memory will long be held green by lovers of the leash for the many pleasant days spent in 'Coggyhill' testing the longtails."

The property was finally sold by the last of the White family in 1947; the father of the present owner purchased it in 1955. Although still occupied, it is unfortunately in considerable disrepair, and likely to deteriorate quickly unless substantial repairs are undertaken, soon.

White Hall, Broughshane

Photograph: Michael O'Connell.
Situation: 24 Tullymore Road, Broughshane; td, Correen; Parish, Skerry; District Council, Ballymena; Grid ref. D 153 080.
References: Listed B. Taylor and Skinner, 'Roads', 1778, p 21; Lendrick, map, 1780; VAL 1B/15A, p 20, and White family documents and transcripts, D2861/A/3 and E1, T3054/C/2; all in PRONI; Atkinson, 'Ireland exhibited', 1823, II, p 448; J Boyle, OSM, 1835, Antrim, IV, p 111; Camac, 'Derrykeighan parish', 1932 reprint, p 54; J G Kenny, in 'The Glynns', XXII, 1994, p 37.

Benvarden House, Dervock

77. A long, low, complicated, attractive house, divided only by its lawn from the River Bush. Two-storey, stucco, nicely painted pale grey, the main block of 16 bays, with an alternation of canted and curved bays facing the river, a simple pediment added to the south (entrance) front, a service wing striking off at an angle, and a complex multiplicity of chimney-stacks.

"In May 1636 the land was leased by Lord Antrim to Daniel Macnaghten, who had been living at Ballymagarry" (Girvan); "formerly the residence of the Macnaghten family, and then consisted of a small thatched cottage. It came into the possession of the late Mr Montgomery in the year 1797, and was soon after thrown down and rebuilt" (Boyle). John Macnaghten was hanged in 1761 for shooting one Mary Anne Knox of Prehen whilst trying to abduct her. His only daughter Cassandra later married an army officer called Joseph Hardy, for whom James Williamson surveyed the demesne in 1788. In the same year, Hugh "Split Fig" Montgomery, fruit merchant, waistcoat seller, and descendant of a Glenarm family who had gone out to Virginia, returned to Belfast with a somewhat mysteriously acquired fortune. He was one of the founders of the Northern Bank, owned property in Coleraine and Kentucky, a grand house in Donegall Place, Belfast, and in 1797 bought Benvarden too, and set about 'improving' it. In particular, he added a wing, whose ground-floor rooms had taller ceilings (but the first-floor rooms had lower ones, since he respected the roof-line) at each end of the facade: one containing dining-room, the other drawing-room or ball-room.

Parts of the earlier house may or may not have been incorporated in the new one; the central five bays, with the delightful hall and staircase, seem to be no later than

mid 18th century. In 1805, Hugh Montgomery "has made the Benvarden house a great work - twelve bed-chambers - a Ball Room 26 feet long, with dining room and drawing room and very extensive offices of all sorts - a garden pretty well of 1³/₄ acres" (Rev G Macartney). In 1807, Dr Beaufort "crossed the river Bush again at Ballyvarden where there is a very large house of Mr Montgomery with planted demesne and a very neat new porter's lodge". Hugh Montgomery died in 1822 (not, as Bence-Jones and Chambers say, 1832), and was succeeded by his eldest son, who lived here till 1873.

The valuers of 1833 rather surprisingly complained "not a very fine situation", and "very large", putting a figure of £90.19.4 upon house and offices. (In 1859, this dropped to £60, but, rose again to £80 in 1864). Boyle, in 1835, says "Benvarden, the seat of John Montgomery Esquire, is beautifully situated on the river Bush ... The house is of an oblong form, 2-storeys high and perfectly plain in its architecture. The library, dining and drawing rooms are spacious and lofty, and the bedrooms numerous". (They had need to be; when in 1830 the Viceroy, the Duke of Northumberland, came to stay with his wife and entourage, "altogether we made up thirty three beds, and had a Household of fifty souls, and did not require to borrow or buy one article". The Duke "wore the blue ribbon always, and at dinner the Star and Garter, which charmed the children").

The central block of the south front was refaced about 1850. On John's death, the house passed to his only remaining son, Robert, a survivor of the charge of the Heavy Brigade at Balaclava, who soon busied himself taking out all the glazing bars, adding a further service wing, and building the delightful cast-iron bridge over the river, 124 feet long on its square blackstone abutments, which

cost him £1000. Since then, the house has been little altered, except in consequence of a serious fire in 1940, when the ball-room (or drawing-room) was extended to its present length of sixty feet by the removal of an internal wall; and reproduction plasterwork, of very high quality, was subsequently inserted. In the first part of this century the house was covered in bushy creepers and ivy; this has, happily, been removed, and it is now clean-shaven.

The best part of the house is the oldest central section, especially the delightful arched entrance-hall with wine-cellar beneath (reached by a curved concealed door) and staircase-landing with balustered elliptical light-well and lantern above.

The outbuildings and gardens are very fine, and in fine order: the great curved-walled-garden is beautifully kept up; the bell in the stableyard is inscribed 'Glasgow, 1781'.

Photograph: Michael O'Connell.

Situation: 36 Benvardin Road, Dervock; td, Benvardin; Parish, Derrykeighan; District Council, Ballymoney; Grid ref. C 947 331.

References: Listed B1, out buildings B. Taylor and Skinner, 'Roads', 1778, p 270; D A Beaufort, 'Tour', 1807, p 17, Ms 4033 in TCD Library; J Boyle, OSM, 1835, Antrim, V, p 109; Macnaghten, 'Clan Magnachtan', 1951, pp 66, 79-83; Girvan, 'North Antrim', UAHS, 1972, p 21; D 572/18/80, VAL 1B/140, p 79, VAL 2B/1/34B, p 11, and VAL 12B/4/5A, p 70, all in PRONI; Chambers, 'Faces of change', 1984, pp 85-87; Bence-Jones, 'Burke's guide', 1988, pp 40-41; Pierce and Coey, 'Taken for granted', 1984, p 161; Dean, 'Gate lodges', 1994, p 5; family papers in possession of owners.

Springmount, Clough

78. A very fine large 18th-century gentleman's farm-house, the main block of five bays, two tall storeys on basement, with steps up to the front door: original glazing bars complete, but segmental-headed doorcase a later replacement. Originally either white-washed, or yellow-washed like the gate-lodge and pillars, but the back (with half-round-headed windows lighting the half-landings) roughcast, the front encased, in the 1930s, in a kind of Roman cement, with quoins and architraves. The two lower, subsidiary hipped two-storey wings, are most imposing from the front - each has glazing-barred windows, with four narrow panes in each sash above, eight below. But these are deceptive: they do not form part of the main house. That to the left contained stabling, loose-boxes, and hayloft over; that to the right still contains the kitchen and servants' rooms over. The house enjoys the luxury of three staircases, the principal one broad and impressive. There are attics in the central block, lit by small windows below the chimney-stacks which top each gable: the roof was thatched until, after a fire about 1900, this was replaced by slates.

The Springmount property originally belonged to the Allen family of Lisconnan, Dervock (139) and of Allenbrook, Larne. About 1746 Mary Allen married William Higgin-son of Nappan, in the Largy, so the house could date from around 1750; but internal evidence - in particular some surviving decorative work in the Adam style -would suggest a somewhat later date for the present house, perhaps around 1780, though there may well have been an earlier one on the site. The Road Book of 1778 shows here a 'Bleech Mill - Allen Esq', suggesting that the Higginson husband had not yet built the big house; but, Lendrick shows John Allen junior in 1780, (Williamson

deletes the word "junior" in 1808), as owner of a Gentleman's Seat, not just a bleach yard. In 1807, Dr Beaufort thought Springmount "a good-looking seat, with much wood." In 1814, the Rev. William Mayne, in his account of the parish of Dunaghy for Shaw Mason, wrote: "The first place, worthy of notice, like a gentleman's seat, is Springmount, anciently Drumatickle; the house is three stories high with a wing to each end, a story and a half high: it stands on a gentle acclivity, with a spacious lawn between it and the road."

In 1835, James Boyle (who was not ashamed to borrow from Shaw Mason) wrote "Springmount (formerly Drumastickle), the residence of Major John Higginson DL ... was built about the year 1780 and consists of a basement and two upper storeys. It is rather large and the apartments are spacious. There is a wing attached to each end of it, and in front of one of these is" (no longer) " a handsome conservatory or greenhouse, containing some rare and valuable plants." However, in December of the same year, 1835, the valuer deducted no less than £8.7.2 from the valuation of the property at £25.1.6 "for unpleasant situation, bad roads, uninteresting neighbourhood"! By 1861, the owner was shown as John O'Neill Higginson Esq; the buildings were still valued at £25, and 139 acres of land at £74. But the Higginsons retained their interest in the Glens; 'Major Higginson' lived at Glendun Lodge (154) in 1834; Charles Henry Higginson evidently bought Rockport, Cushendun (155), as a holiday house in 1874, and after his death in 1889 his widow and family (including his daughter Agnes, known to the family as Nesta, and to the public as Moira O'Neill the poet) went to live there permanently. Springmount was sold to Hamilton Ross, a comparatively young man, originally from Drumnagrove near Clough, who had made a fortune in India as timber and tea merchant. His son John Louis Ross succeeded him in 1919; and his grandson, the present owner, succeeded to the property in 1965.

Photograph: Michael O'Connell.
Situation: 49 Springmount Road, Clough; td, Springmount; Parish, Grange of Dundermot; District Council, Ballymena; Grid ref. D 075 141.

References: Listed B. Taylor and Skinner, 'Roads', 1778, p 20; Lendrick, map, 1780; D A Beaufort, 'Tour', 5 November 1807, Ms 4033 in TCD Library, p 31; Williamson, map, 1808; VAL 1B/1/157, pp 32, 54, VAL 2B/1/46B, p 22, VAL 1B/133, VAL 12B/2/8A, in PRONI; Mason, 'Statistical account', I, 1814, p 246; J Boyle, OSM, 1835, Antrim, IV, p 30; Girvan, 'West Antrim', UAHS, 1970, p 33; Pierce and Coey, 'Taken for granted', 1984, p 116; Dean, 'Gate lodges', 1994, p 28; information from present owner and from Wing Commander John Higginson.

Hillmount House, Cullybackey

79. "The Hills were among the earliest of the linen merchants to establish a mass bleaching plant". Hillmount, a fine three-storey Georgian mill-owners' house, was built by one of this family perhaps about 1720, probably around 1760, certainly before 1778. Shown as the seat of Mr John Hill in Lendrick's map of 1780, and Williamson's revision of 1808. It seems that the Hills prospered during the Napoleonic wars, adding the handsome single-storey bow-fronted bays at either side, and excavating the lake in front of the house when "the material taken out was distributed in such a way as to suggest to the stranger the remains of extensive earthworks". But by 1825 Mr Hill had failed; he was imprisoned for debt in Carrickfergus Gaol, and it was there that the purchase of the house, bleach-green and mill was negotiated by Dr William Young, one of the ubiquitous Youngs of Ballymena. The Hillmount property was occupied by Robert Young, the buying partner in the family firm, who had to ride 50 or 60 miles a day; he was a man beloved of children, who used to slip pennies through a slit in the window sash to the beggars who waited outside for them at breakfast time. His unmarried sisters, Miss Elizabeth and Miss Mary, used in wintry weather to take their exercise by walking up and down the hall wearing long sealskin coats. Robert Young having died without issue in 1872, the Hillmount property was sold in 1885 to the Frazer and Haughton families. Shaw, in 1913, says,

"The Messrs Frazer occupy Hillmount House, which is ... surrounded by ornamental plantations".

In 1833, the house ("residence of Robert Young") had been described as two-storey; if the third storey was added later, the work was remarkably well done; but the house appears much as now in an oil painting which looks earlier than this. There is a very full description of it on 2nd June 1836 in the Valuation books for that year, Dwelling, 48 feet long, 26 feet wide, 27 feet 6 inches high £13.10.10; Kitchen or addition 12 feet high, £1.3.6; laundry, 15.10d; North Wing, 26 feet 6 inches long, 29 feet wide, 14 feet high, £5.9.1; South Wing, same measurements, same value; stables etc £7.10.7; giving a grand total of £35.8.11: to which may be added £26.12.0 for the engine house, lapping room, lower engine house, and stable. In 1860, the "House, offices and gate lodge" were valued at £66: "a fine substantial house in excellent repair and favourable situation".

The chimneys are at the gable-ends; the gables are topped by crow-stepped upstands which indicate a possible earlier thatched roof. The whole facade is encased in an unusually high-grade stone-coloured stucco, covered in ancient Virginia creeper; the main block is five bays wide, with triple windows in the middle, and a doorcase framed by reeded engaged columns, and geometrical glazing bars in side-lights and shallow fanlight.

There are many elegant details inside and out: the keystones have pretty little balls atop; the quoins are nicely reversed where the side bows overlap the main facade; the stone window-sills are supported on pairs of neat little consoles; there are no downspouts on the front, the rainwater is carried away round the sides. Inside, there is restrained reeding in the woodwork of window-and door-cases, and even in the unusual projecting chair-rails. Best of all, the shutter-cases in the bow-windows of the grand rooms in the flanking bays (here not, as more commonly, used for services) have radially reeded fans or fillets in the triangular space where vertical meets horizontal: the detail so much admired by Dr Craig in his Classic Irish Houses. Hillmount also has some disconcerting naivetés, such as the single knop at one corner. But on balance, a house of unusually high quality. See also the frontispiece (page ii).

Photographs: Michael O'Connell. (See also colour-plate IIIa)
Situation: 72 Hillmount Road, Cullybackey; td, Craigs; Parish, Craigs, formerly Ahoghill; District Council, Ballymena; Grid ref. D 047 073.
References: Listed B1. Taylor and Skinner, 'Roads', 1778, p 18; Lendrick, map, 1780; Williamson, map, 1808; T C Robe, OSM, 1833, Antrim, VIII, p 12; VAL 1B/1/155, pp 9-10, and VAL 2B/1/45, pp 28 et seq., in PRONI; Bassett, 'Antrim', 1888; Shaw, 'Cullybackey', 1913, pp 190-142; H C Lawlor in 'Fibres and fabrics journal', March 1942, p 68; Girvan, 'West Antrim', UAHS, 1970, p 28; Craig, 'Classic Irish houses', 1976, p 37; unpublished memoirs of W R Young; information from Mr J W Frazer.

Seapark House, Carrickfergus

80 (right). A pleasant, stuccoed, two-storey Georgian seaside house of 1804, now unfortunately almost submerged in later additions, some Victorian, some more recent. Shown on Williamson's map of 1808.

In 1817, "the seat of Thomas Ludford Stewart" (who had become rich as Lord Donegall's agent) "comprises a handsome new-built house, and 30 acres of demesne, ornamented with young plantations. It stands ... in a low position on the shore, and commands an interesting level view of the town and spire of the church, which form a noble group of architecture in this water view ... had this villa been sufficiently exalted above low water mark, instead of a legal claim to the character of an humble beauty; its harmony of prospect and position would have raised it to the very summit of perfection in the perspective history of this fine district" (Atkinson).

Boyle described it, in 1840, as "the residence of Very Rev. John Chaine, Dean of Connor and Rector of Carrickfergus ... it occupies a delightful situation on the shore of the Lough ... The house is a very neat-looking and comfortable residence. The garden and offices are suitable as to extent. Sea Park was originally erected in 1804". Mr Chaine, a son of William Chaine of Bally-

craigy, was much beset by creditors, with whom he compounded twice; in 1847 he had to flee to France; in 1855 they finally caught up with him, just after he had resigned his living, in August 1855. Apparently, he then adroitly exchanged livings with the Rev. George Bull of Claughton in Lancashire, where John Chaine died in 1862.

The original house seems, from the early plans, to have had two segmental bays facing east, looking out towards Carrickfergus, Scotland, and sunrise, and two facing west, looking up the Lough to Belfast, the Cave Hill, and sunset; with the entrance in the narrow front looking due south. A 50 year lease of it was bought in 1852 by John Owden of Richardson, Sons and Owden. He was an Englishman of Huguenot descent, but not a Quaker: "an elderly, very precise man" who "generally wore white buck-skin gloves, and disliked any stain upon them". He married a Quaker, Jane Greeves, of whom J N Richardson wrote "possibly because my visits to Sea Park may have generally been made in winter ... I always connect Mrs Owden with the idea of warmth - warm heart, warm welcome, warm house, warm hall, warm rooms". At some unascertained date, the entry in the Valuation book of 1836 was revised: "considerably improved with additions -

add 4/- in the pound for good situation and convenience to sea bathing ... £75." In the 1850s, the firm was then approaching the pinnacle of its prosperity, and Owden employed Thomas Jackson to double the size of his house. Copious drawings, all undated, survive; showing the house much as it now is, but for the Victorian tower, lightly sketched in in pencil. There is even a plan for a Turkish Bath, with divan, to be built in the detached stable block for Owden's "work people".

The surviving windows of the original house are still Georgian-glazed, fronted by a portico or veranda of four Tuscan columns. To the left and at right angles there is a long addendum, the ball-room, incorporating six segmental-headed windows and eight Ionic columns; on the other side, a canted bay with a portico of coupled Ionic columns; a Victorian segmental corner tower with triple windows using console brackets as dividers; and then a further seven bays round the corner facing south. There is a square five-storey lookout tower at the rear. It is only after these "modern improvements" had been completed that Owden bothered to buy the freehold from Lord Donegall for £4,000.

Owden's only child, and heiress, married another partner in the firm, Thomas Greer, and in 1867 father-in-law and son-in-law both gave their address as Seapark. Greer was MP for Carrickfergus from 1880 until 1885; his

McGregor Greer descendants continued to use Seapark as a summer residence until 1930. It then lay vacant for some time, but from 1938 till 1947 was the home of Sir George Clarke, formerly of Workman Clarke, shipbuilders. Thereafter, fallen on hard times, for many years an old people's home, then blocked up and in a poor way; but it is now in contemplation to demolish some of the accretions, restore chimneys and glazing bars, and make of it once more the charming house it must originally have been. And, since the decision to build on the site of Macedon, this is by far the most important coastal open space remaining in the seven mile stretch between Belfast and Carrickfergus; both seals and herons have been known to breed there.

Photograph: Courtesy of Dr Cecil Stewart.

Situation: 109, Shore Road, Carrickfergus; td, West Division; Parish and District Council, Carrickfergus; Grid ref. J 391 858.

References: House, gate-lodge, boat-house, and bathing-house all listed B1. Williamson, map, 1808; Atkinson, 'Ireland exhibited', 1823, II, p 83; Lewis, TD, 1837, I, p 273; J Boyle, OSM, 1840, Carrickfergus, as yet unpublished; VAL 1B/187, p 125, deeds, drawings and correspondence in D 2339, all in PRONI; Richardson, 'Reminiscences', 1911, p 49; C McClenaghan, 'Thomas Jackson', 1993, research report in QUB Library; 'Clergy of Connor', 1993, p 256; Rutherford, 'Carrickfergus', 1995, p 64.

Kilwaughter Castle (Ruins)

81. Designed before 1803 in his castellated style by John Nash for E Jones Agnew, Esq. (until he changed his name, Edward Agnew Jones) and his daughter, Miss Jones. This gentleman was a son of Valentine Jones of Belfast, a leading West India merchant, by his third marriage to Eleanor Agnew (only daughter of the 'Old Squire' of Kilwaughter, William Agnew), who, when he succeeded to the estate, took the name Agnew in compliance with his grandfather's will. Like his neighbour Henry Shaw of Ballygally, he was sympathetic to the United Irishmen, and helped many of them to escape to America. The family believed themselves to be descendants of Philip d'Agneaux, one of John de Courcy's 22 knights, though the egregious Frances Joseph Bigger took a different view: "Agnew is a very prevalent name, originally it was O'Gneeve, their ancestors were the hereditary bards of the Clan-a-boy O'Neills." (See also Hector McDonnell on Agnew/ O Gnimh). They owned nine-tenths of the 9800 acres in the parish, including the mountain known as Agnew's Hill, a corn mill, and a flax mill. Although it appears in Taylor and Skinner in 1778, the house is not unambiguously shown on Lendrick's map of 1780, but has been inserted in Williamson's revision of 1808, as Kilwaughter House.

A circular motte used to stand nearby. The oldest part of the castle is supposed to have been built either in 1566 or in 1662, according to the conflicting readings by James Boyle of the date "marked, in indented characters, nearly illegible, on a piece of old iron on a very old oak door covered with large nails, in the rear of the castle." Professor Jope preferred 1622, built by Patrick Agnew who married

Janet Shaw, sister of the builder of Ballygally Castle (20), in that same year; and considered it to have been a very similar early 17th-century castellated dwelling of Scottish type. In the Post-Chaise Companion of 1803 is the entry "Two miles on the Left of Larne, is Kilwater-House, the elegant seat of Mr. Agnew." "Killinaghter [sic] house, the seat and part of the extensive estate of Edward Jones Agnew, Esq, comprehends a fine castellated edifice of the modern architecture, and a beautiful and well planted demesne" observed Atkinson in 1817. In 1835, "The Castle is three storeys high and ornamented with six turrets, all built within the last 30 years, except one in the rear of the castle which is much older"; the small turret in front was, in 1840, said to be 15 years built; "the last turret ... and the oval [sic] window in front 10 years built." "Part of the roof is of prepared tar and sand and part is of lead" (no wonder the castle is today roofless).

"No regular style of architecture is adopted, but its appearance is very ornamental. It presents 2 fronts, stone-finished, with a very handsome octagon and circular tower at either end of the eastern front. The windows are beautifully ornamented and there are several smaller towers which give the building an appearance of grandeur" (Boyle, 1835). "The chief architect was Mr Nash, who built the houses of an entire street in London" (Regent Street). "Millar and Nelson of Belfast were also employed as architects ... The approach is through a fine stone gateway ... flanked by two octagonal towers." Very similar to Nash's West Grinstead Park in Sussex (now demolished). The demesne in 1835 contained 165 Irish acres of which 12 were lawn, 4 an artificial lake, and 6$^{1}/_{2}$ walled gardens;

the dovecote may have been the first in Ireland built for the use of ornamental, rather than purely edible, birds.

Jope remarks that Nash's corner turrets resemble those at Culzean; also that the sandstone window-sills are nicely carved in the manner of the O'Shea brothers. Generally, he comments: "The detail as a whole, except the window-sill carving, is poor and shoddy. Yet the grouping of the main masses of the design is impressive

and picturesque." The carving of the window-sills is almost unique (but see the entry for Glendaragh House, 190); certainly no other house known to be by Nash has this detail. Sniffy old Sir John Summerson, who so far as I know never saw Kilwaughter, remarked in 1980 "window sills were enriched with carvings of a primitive kind, supplied presumably by a local artist and probably never seen, still less approved, by Nash". Terence Davis, in 1960, was more generous: "The most curious exterior details were window-sill carvings in sandstone, carried out by a local craftsman of some skill and originality". For my part I think them charming: and cannot help wondering if there is a connection with the fact that John Millar's grandfather, who was owner of the Scrabo quarries, was also the principal Belfast merchant of marble and masonry.

Occupied by the army in 1940, unoccupied since then, and since 1951, a roofless ruin. It remains very impressive, high on its sloping hillside, despite the new farmhouse built very close by, and the incursions of agricultural debris. The interior of the great drum tower is now like an anatomical model of the internal organs of a building. Perhaps not quite beyond restoration, though it would require a person of wealth and courage. I have happy memories of the late Mariga Guinness trying to persuade the young John B McGuckian and his bride-to-be that he was such a one, and that the castle could make an ideal home for a young married couple!

Photographs: R J Welch, Ulster Museum W01/65/2; Michael O'Connell.
Situation: North of the road between the villages of Kilwaughter and Cairncastle; td, Kilwaughter; Parish, Kilwaughter; District Council, Larne; Grid ref. D 357 015.
References: Castle, gatehouse, screen and icehouse listed B1. Taylor and Skinner, 'Roads', 1778, p 14; Wilson, 'Post-chaise companion', 1803, p 37; Williamson, map, 1808; Atkinson, 'Ireland exhibited', 1823, II, p 133; J Boyle, OSM, 1835 and 1840, Antrim, III, pp 109, 117; Egerton and Bigger, 'Guide for tourists', 1906, p 10; PSAMNI, 1940, p 32; E M Jope, in UJA, 3rd series XIX, 1956, p 121; Bence-Jones, 'Burke's guide', 1978, p 177; Davis, 'John Nash', 1960, p 24, 1966, p 51; Summerson, 'John Nash', 1980, p 45; H McDonnell, in 'The Glynns', XII, 1984, p 25; Stewart, 'Summer soldiers', 1995, pp 98-9 and 136-9.

Holestone House, Doagh

82. In 1724, one Henry Owens married the daughter of William Gillilan of Holestone, from a family of Scots settlers. In 1703, John Gillilan had established the bleach works at Coggrey. The Owens family inherited the Gillilan property, and prospered. According to a map by Alex Stewart dated October 1768, John Owens already held the earlier house and 47 acres as a sub-tenant of John Gillilan, who then held under a lease of 1701 from the previous Lord Donegall. This was one of the freeholds bought from the embarrassed Donegall Estate. John Gillilan's 41-year lease of 594 acres, the whole townland of Holestone, fell in in 1824. The house was then "rebuilt and considerably enlarged in 1827" by James Owens, JP, DL. "Agreeably situated on the declivity of a considerable eminence in the townland of the same name: the house is a spacious and modern-looking two-storey edifice, presenting three stone-finished fronts. The offices, though not extensive, are suitable. There is a tolerable garden, and a small extent of tastefully laid out pleasure grounds" "In 1817 it was also a two-storey house, but not so large" (Boyle, 1839) Valued at £70 in 1860 - "good situation and well constructed".

The facade is a severe five-bay front of beautifully cut and laid ashlar (said to have been brought from Scotland), the openings (on this front only) idiosyncratically bevelled; a single-storey porch of paired Doric pilasters; and a two-storey semi-circular bay projecting at each end, with curved three-light windows lighting the drawing-room and dining-room inside. Georgian glazing bars are still complete upstairs only; the choice of red paint around the sashes is a little rustic for so urbane an exterior. There is a splendid semi-circular cobweb fanlight over the interior front door, echoed by another at the far end of the hall, on either side of which are two true and one false doorcases, which, like the cornice, oddly exhibit very correct guttae but not mutules. There is attractive Grecian plasterwork in the ceilings. Beyond the hall, a great square top-lit staircase, with an octagonal lantern unexpectedly carried on Gothick pendentives. Behind the staircase, what seems to have been the earlier farm-house, looking out on yard and rubble-stone buildings. A stone in the park records that 2,500 forest trees were planted there between 1791 and 1802 by William Owens. The park was for many years a great centre for hare coursing and the greyhound fancy; also red deer.

Whilst not in all respects characteristic, this looks like the work of William Farrell - though no documentary evidence has yet come to light. Its combination of austere exterior, richly-laid-out interior, generous scale, and superb south-facing site, makes it as delightful as it is unusual. After the death of the last male member of the Owens family his niece Jane Orr adopted the name Orr-Owens, and lived in Holestone until her death in 1919. The house was let or stood empty, until 1932, when it was sold to the late Captain W.G. Hamilton, in whose family it remains.

Photograph: Michael O'Connell. (See also colour-plate Va)
Situation: 23 Deerpark Road, Doagh; td, Holestone; Parish, Kilbride; District Council, Antrim; Grid ref. J 244 899.
Reference: Listed B1. Map October 1768, lease, 3 June 1783, D1824, VAL 2B/1/8B, all in PRONI; J Boyle, OSM, 1839, Antrim, XI, pp 138, 150; Cox, 'Kilbride', 1959, p 85; Young, 'Belfast and province of Ulster', 1909, p 230; Girvan, 'West Antrim', UAHS, 1970, p 20.

Lissue House, Lisburn

83. Built about 1807: Fagan, writing in 1837, says, "formerly the property of Robert Garrett Esq., who built the present house about 30 years ago, but from failure was never able to make the designed improvements. However, at a subsequent period he sold or mortgaged the place to a Major McCauley, who in 1830 sold his right of it to the present proprietor, Captain Crawford. Since the latter period the house was overhauled and several hundred pounds laid out on improvements". Not shown on Williamson's map of 1808.

"James Nicholson Richardson (1815-1899) spent his business career in Liverpool, but retired early, purchased Lissue, which he enlarged and beautified, and there for more than forty years devoted himself to country pursuits". Richardson employed Thomas Jackson about 1850 for his enlargement and beautification, and it is clear that many of the extensions at the rear and sides are his; but the very pleasant front, very Georgian in feeling, may well be earlier. Fagan describes it as "commodious, 2 storeys high and slated", standing on "a handsome eminence commanding a most delightful prospect of a wide extent of the counties of Antrim and Down": now, unfortunately, the Blaris radio mast and the roofs of modern factories.

My own guess is that the facade antedates Jackson. It is a fine, symmetrical, composition in yellow-painted stucco on an ashlar plinth, with a centred open porch recessed behind a doorcase of Ionic columns flanked by pilasters,

with a pulvinated entablature. The central section is of three bays; at each end there is a generous segmental bow with three windows, that in the centre wider than the others; all the windows are Georgian-glazed in quite a complex pattern of panes and dividers, varying with the heights and widths of the sashes. The slated roof is concealed behind a parapet.

The Richardsons lived on at Lissue until well into this century; it then passed through various hands before, in 1941, the then owner, Colonel Lindsay, offered it to the Belfast Hospital for Sick Children as a refuge from the air raids of that year. Later, in 1947, he gave house and demesne to the hospital as an outright gift. Until 1988, it was used principally as a convalescent home for children, and, inevitably, during this period many large and insensitive alterations were made. It has since then lain empty and deteriorating, but ruthless demolition of the accretions could still, perhaps, restore it to manageable proportions.

Photograph: Michael O'Connell.
Situation: 31 Ballinderry Road, Lisburn; at the end of an avenue, set back amidst trees; td, Teraghafeera or Lissue; Parish, Magheragall; District Council, Lisburn; Grid ref. J 229 646.
References: Listed B1. T Fagan, OSM, 1837, Antrim, II, pp 33, 34; 'The building news', 15 August 1890; Richardson, 'Reminiscences', [1911], p 60; C McClenaghan, 'Thomas Jackson', 1993, research report in QUB Library; 'Buildings at risk', UAHS, 1995, p 7.

Drumadarragh, Doagh

84. "Its situation, besides being low and disagreeable, is on the very edge of the public road. The house, though large, is by no means modern or neat in its appearance, nor is there a lawn or demesne attached to it. It is said that the original house was erected in 1641, rebuilt in 1742, and on coming into the possession of Mr Langtry again rebuilt in 1827 (by Patrick Allen, architect)" (Boyle, 1839). Lendrick shows both house and 'Bleach Yard' as the property of Patrick Allen in 1780; Williamson shows the house as the property of Mr Barklie in 1808, the ownership of the bleach green unchanged. Presumably, Mr Patrick Allen was his own architect. In the 1862 Valuation book, there is a note "a very large concern, but badly situated for a gentleman's residence; all in medium repair, £50".

In 1742, probably a fairly simple three-bay two-storey farm or mill house; Donegall Estate leases of a 700-acre holding, mill and bleach-greens were made to successive tenants for short terms, until in 1826 George Langtry obtained a lease for lives renewable for ever. In 1886, the Langtry interest was sold up through the Landed Estates Court, and in 1891 it was purchased by Sir Thomas Dixon and used by him only as an occasional residence. A considerable two-storey wing at the rear of the house, including the present rather splendid drawing-room, and bedrooms above, was added in 1903-5. It was requisitioned by the army in the second World War, and thereafter occupied, and eventually owned, by another branch of the Dixon family.

Externally, the house is now rather handsome, a long white facade set back (as Boyle remarked) only very slightly from the Drumadarragh Road amidst mature trees. There is a nice three-light doorcase with radial fanlight in the centre; the oculi in the ground floor are probably later; but those in the gables of the two-bay flanking extensions are presumably genuine, and so date from 1827. The quoins are of painted stone, the walls of white-painted roughcast. The interior is pleasant rather than distinguished. Window-sashes, fanlights, shutters and doors are all simple but evidently original. There are excellent ranges of stone outbuildings, and an outstandingly attractive garden, the creation of the late Lady Glentoran.

Photograph: Michael O'Connell.
Situation: At Dixon's Corner, off Drumadarragh Road, north of Doagh; td, Drumadarragh; Parish, Kilbride; District Council, Antrim; Grid ref. J 255 936.
References: Listed B1. Taylor and Skinner, 'Roads', 1778, p 269; Lendrick, map, 1780; Williamson, map, 1808; J Boyle, OSM, 1838, Antrim, XI, pp 138, 150; VAL 2B/1/8B in PRONI; Cox, 'Kilbride', 1959, p 81; Girvan, 'West Antrim', UAHS, 1970, p 20; Bence-Jones, 'Burke's guide', 1978, p 112.

ROMAN CEMENT

Plate I *(overleaf)*

    Leslie Hill,
Ballymoney (72)

Plate II

    a. St John's church,
Islandmagee (21)

    b. Dunderave,
Bushmills (91)

Plate III *(opposite)*

    a. Hillmount House,
Cullybackey (79)

    b. O'Hara Brook,
Ballymoney (74)

CUTSTONE

Plate IV *(opposite)*

    a. Beardiville Gate Lodge, Coleraine (195)

    b. Glenarm Castle (86)

Plate V

    a. Holestone House, Doagh (82)

    b. Stephenson Mausoleum, Kilbride (261)

CUTSTONE   Plate VI *(opposite)*   a. Gilbert's Dam, Aghagallon (239)

b. Drumnasole Gate Lodge, Carnlough (197)

Plate VII   a. St Joseph's church, Dunloy (66)

b. Garron Tower, Carnlough (90); note the disparity between the older, darker stone and the modern, lighter stonework to the left

Plate VIII *(overleaf)*   Drumnasole, Carnlough (88); a mixture of textures

Seymour Hill, Dunmurry

85. A very large, foursquare, Georgian house, possibly dating from 1789, according to Dean Barr; "Archibald Johnston's son Robert owned a bleach green at Seymour Hill and built Seymour Hill House. It was at this house that Robert Johnston's daughter was staying while her husband Henry Munro was being hanged for his part in the 1798 Rising." If this is the same as the Kilmakee bleach yard, then it does not appear on Taylor and Skinner's road maps of 1778, but does appear as the property of Robert Johnston on Lendrick's map of 1780. Dixon remarks, "its mid-Georgian features include a full, raised basement and a fine pedimented doorcase embracing a semi-circular fanlight" as well as "distinctive wide chimneys" (1983). Fagan says of it "... most delightfully situated ... The house is a spacious oblong building 2-storeys high and slated, besides garret and cellarage ... This was formerly the residence of Robert Johnson Esquire, who built the dwelling house and made various improvements on the demesne; but in 1822 the place, on which is situated an extensive bleach green, passed by purchase into the hands of [William Charley Esq], who since that period expended a very large sum of money on the dwelling house" (1837). For over a century, the seat of the Charley family, but after the death in 1944 of Captain A F Charley, the demesne was bought and the grounds developed by the NI Housing Trust, which converted the house into six flats. The house was vandalised, and there was a serious fire in 1986; however, it has been restored, again to provide six flats, by Belfast Improved Houses, to plans by Consarc, and was re-

opened by W R H Charley on 12th October 1990.

The house is roughcast, painted grey and cream; five bays wide, with heavy vermiculated double quoins, stone architraves, and wide eaves brackets, very likely dating from William Charley's refurbishments. The two giant chimney stacks topping the hipped roof have seven large chimney-pots each; this is odd, because old photographs clearly show that each stack should have eight pots, and they are as important to the composition as the stacks and pots, similarly arranged on the spine of the double cube, at Galgorm Castle (67). There are pie-crust dormers at the sides, slightly regrettable velux roof-lights to the front. The portico, with its broken pediment borne on coupled acanthus-leaf-capitalled columns, at the head of six stone steps, is very fine. The glass of the fanlight is inscribed 'Seymour Hill House. 1990. BIH'. The Georgian glazing has gone from all the windows. The plate glass, and the texture of the painted roughcast, somehow give this large building a slightly doll's-house air; it lacks the finesse and elegance it probably once had; but it is very imposing nonetheless.

Photograph: Michael O'Connell.
Situation: The avenue curves around the rear of the Housing Trust's Seymour Hill estate, to the south of the old main road from Belfast to Lisburn; td, Kilmakee; Parish, Derriaghy; District Council, Lisburn; Grid ref. J 293 679.
References: Listed B. Lendrick, map, 1780; T Fagan, OSM, 1837, Antrim, II, p 106; McCutcheon, 'Industrial archaeology', 1980, pl 107.2; Barr, 'Derriaghy', 1981, p liv; Proctor, 'Belfast scenery', edition of 1983, notes to plate XXII; 'Ulster architect', May/June 1991.

Glenarm Castle

86. As is right and proper, this is still the grandest mansion in the county from which the Earl of Antrim takes his title.

The original Castle of Glenarm was built by the Bysets in the mid-13th century on the opposite side of the river, but was broken down in 1597. In 1603, Sir Randal McDonnell started building the castle on the present site, making various additions up to his death in 1636. It was at this time that the inscribed stone, now incorporated in the Barbican, was placed over the entrance of the old castle: "With the leave of God this castle was built by Sir Randle McDonnel knight Erle of Antrim haveing to his wife Dame Aellis O'Nill in the yeare of our Lord God 1636." The first Earl had been bound by his grant from the Crown to erect a respectable residence in each of the four baronies comprising his estates: Dunluce Castle (18) was the most sizeable; there was "an elegant and substantial family residence" outside Ballycastle, Clare Park, on the site of the ancient Dunaynie; Clough Castle was still standing in the barony of Kilconway; but at Glenarm his "pleasant house" was burned in 1642 by the covenanters under Monro. For the next century it remained a gutted ruin, though the third Earl somehow managed to reside here in the latter years of the 17th century. By 1720 an L-shaped wing had been added; this later became the kitchen and domestic offices when the 18th-century house was built. Two simple doorcases with bolection mouldings, one of sandstone and one of wood, survive in the kitchen wing, still used for servants in the 19th-century rebuilding.

An inscribed stone announces: "Rebuilt by Alexander the Present Earl in the year 1756." It seems that, around this date, the body of the present house was built on the foundations of the Jacobean tower-house, to designs by Christopher Myers. In defending himself against scurrilous attacks in 1770, Myers asserts that he had been "invited from England by the Earl of Antrim to rebuild the Castle of Glanarm ... in which he acquitted himself with Reputation"; if so, it must have been almost his first architectural commission in Ireland; for in 1760 he told a Committee of the Irish House of Commons that he had been working at Ballycastle harbour since 1754. A native of Whitehaven, he was described on the same occasion by Thomas Omer, the canal engineer, as "a very knowing and experienced workman" in relation to "Works built in Water": which is not quite the same thing as an architect. Mr Ian Montgomery of PRONI has kindly drawn to my attention a power of attorney given by Andrew Brown of Ballycastle, mason, to Christopher Myers "of Glenarm" in May 1759, endorsed with Myers's own ornate signature in July of that year, so perhaps he managed to supervise simultaneously the work at Ballycastle and Glenarm, places not so very far apart. Further work seems to have been undertaken in the 1780s; Charles Abbott, passing through in September 1792, remarked on "an old house and ground belonging to the Antrim family, it is called Glenarm Castle but is a mere modern-looking house in a bad taste, shut up with walls & repaired in 1783". Two unsigned topographical paintings in the castle, and the print by Thomas Milton of 1793, show the Georgian house as a tall double-pile block, of nine bays, with tripartite windows, flanked by curving colonnades, each of ten columns, terminating in square two-storey pavilions with high pyramidal roofs; with a statue of Hercules "of esteemed Workmanship" (alas, gone missing) outside. The main block of the house is recognisably the same as that, now much altered, which still stands.

The 19th-century rebuilding was the work of Anne Katherine, Countess of Antrim in her own right, who succeeded in 1791, and married *en secondes noces* a Mr. Phelps, who changed his name to McDonnell, and to whom is attributed "the credit of improving tastefully and substantially" the family residence. The plans were exhibited at the Royal Academy in 1823 under the names both of Richard and William Morrison; in fact it appears that William was the author of the work, executed in 1824. The 18th-century house was barbarous to early 19th-century eyes; of it Hill says, "The castle is charmingly situated, but previously to Mr. McDonnell's time, its exterior had been disfigured by certain alterations, neither judiciously made, nor in good taste. He, however, had some portions altered and others rebuilt, until the whole structure has reassumed the character and appearance of a baronial castle of the fifteenth century ...... Lofty towers, terminating in cupolas and gilded vanes, occupy the angles of the building. The parapets are surmounted by gables decorated with carved pinnacles, and exhibiting various heraldic ornaments. The interior of the castle corresponds in every respect with its attractive and beautiful appearance outside."

And James Boyle, compiling his Ordnance Survey memoir for the parish in 1835, wrote: (the castle) "former-

ly consisted of a plain square building totally unadorned; the additions made to it are rather extensive; they are in the Elizabethan style of architecture and were executed by the Messrs Morrison of Dublin. Besides this the appearance of the castle was greatly improved by the addition of minarets at each of its angles, the cupolas and gilded vanes of which have a very beautiful effect rising above the groves of ancient oaks with which they are surrounded". After the completion of the rebuilding, the castle and gate lodges were valued at the staggering figure of £194.

The interior of the house presents little of historical interest, apart from the octagon bedroom, with good plasterwork including doves on the ceiling, plainly to Morrison's designs. The castle was gutted by fire in 1929, when rebuilding took place to designs by Imrie and Angell of London; a further fire in 1967 damaged the original servants' wing; this time the reconstruction was by Donald Insall. In 1929 the 'Gothick' windows on the ground floor were removed and plain rectangular ones substituted. Externally, this was a pity.

Basically, the castle remains a four square structure with an octagonal turret at each corner, topped by a domelet rather in the manner of the Tower of London. Very curiously, the corner turrets contain no accommodation, apart from two lavatories, but are otherwise of solid masonry filled with rubble. To this straightforward structure has been added a south-facing cutstone facade with detailing in the Gothick taste of the Regency period: 'Tudor' chimneys; Jacobean dripstones or label mouldings above the triple windows of the top floor, and the single windows of the first floor; coats of arms in the gables; and a porch with fretted strapwork, a pointed-segmental central arch, round-headed arches at the sides, borne on fluted Doric

columns - now glazed. The other facades are less imposing: the west front consists of two Dutch gables topped by quadruple chimneys: the north, or seaward, facade, is rendered, with windows unevenly spaced over five bays; the east front consists of a three-storey blackstone range, with pointed windows, an addition - though probably contemporary with the reconstruction of the castle as a whole. The interior is quite grand, comfortable rather than distinguished, largely ornamented by mural paintings and sculpted figures executed in the 1930s and 1940s by Angela, Countess of Antrim.

The Barbican (so-called, though not really correctly) was also the work of William Morrison of 1825, and bears an inscription - (in addition to that mentioned above, removed from the original castle) - "This Gateway was built and the Castle restored by Edmund McDonnell Esquire and his wife Anne Katherine, in her own right Countess of Antrim and Viscountess Dunluce A.D. 1825". It is the quintessence of Sir-Walter-Scott-antiquarianism, usefully furnished with portcullises and boiling-oil-holes. For the most part it is of random squared blackstone, with some galleting, and red sandstone dressings; the external buttresses on the river side have strange pink knobbly rustications. Nothing could be more dramatic and romantic.

There is a curtain wall along the north bank of the river, overhung by the branches of fine mature trees, designed to ensure the privacy of the gentry in the castle from the back windows of the village on the opposite bank. The work of the Morrisons is uncommonly well documented by elevations, and an attractive scrapbook of drawings and sketches compiled by Lady Louisa Kerr from 1835 onwards, all in the Public Record Office of Northern Ireland.

Photographs: Michael O'Connell. (See also colour-plate IVb and page 306). Drawing: PRONI.
Situation: Access to the demesne is through several gates on both sides of the Glenarm river; td, Glenarm Demesne; Parish, Glenarm; District Council, Larne; Grid ref. D 308 152.
References: Listed A, in conservation area. Letter from General Munro to the Earl of Argyll, 11 June 1642, in National Library of Scotland, Ms 3368 ff 1-3; Irish House of Commons journal, VI, 6 May 1760; 'Freeman's journal', 5-7 June, 1770; D 2977/3A/4/65/70E, VAL 2B/1/41A. p 128, and drawings and scrapbook, D 3560, all in PRONI; Taylor and Skinner, 'Roads', 1778, p 14; Charles Abbott, 'Tour through Ireland', 1792, Ms in PRO, London 30.9.23 - (for this quotation I am indebted to Dr C J Woods); Milton, 'Seats and demesnes of Ireland', pl XXI (p XLI); J Boyle, OSM, 1835, Antrim, IV, p 129; Hill, 'Macdonnells of Antrim', 1873, pp 188, 251, 370; Brett, 'Glens', UAHS, 1971, pp 11, 13; Angela Antrim, 'Antrim McDonnells', 1977, passim; 'Architecture of R and W V Morrison',1989, pp 99-102; Howley, 'Follies and garden buildings', 1993, p 93.

The Cottage, Lisanoure

87 (right). "In 1829 the present proprietor built the very tasteful and elegant cottage which is beautifully situated on the edge of the lake and at a short distance from the castle, and in this he resides ... The cottage presents two very elegant fronts, quite in the villa style ... It stands very near the edge of the lake with which it is almost on a level" (Boyle, 1835). In 1829, the Dublin architect J B Keane exhibited in the Royal Hibernian Academy, as exhibit No 261, a drawing entitled "Cottage Ornee, erected for George Macartney Esq. on the banks of Lough Gill, in his demesne, and contiguous to his seat Lisanoure Castle, Co. Antrim." Keane worked in the 'Elizabethan manor-house' style elsewhere in the north, near Belleek, and at Necarne, Irvinestown. Although he had at one time an extensive practice, his career seems to have gone into a decline - I have heard it suggested, due to money difficulties and a drink problem.

Girvan, however, considers that "the present building appears to be later", despite the fact that house and outbuildings exactly as at present appear on maps of 1832 and 1833. The present owner takes the view that the front four rooms of the house comprise the building on this site shown in the estate maps of 1772 and later; and it is not impossible that parts of the old were incorporated in the new. In the valuation of October 1833, Lissanore Cottage, measuring 60 feet by 38 feet, turf house, byre etc, 134 feet by 19 feet (evidently the return), and copious specified outbuildings, were together valued at £54.1.11; from which were deducted £10.1.11 because "cottage too small for a

gentleman of fortune" and £14.13.8 because of "too many offices for a cottage": the net value being £29.6.0. This value was not increased, but slightly reduced to £26.10.0 for (vacant) cottage and offices in 1859. On the basis of all this evidence, and given the welcome availability of funds on the death of Lady Macartney, and the extinguishing of her life interest in Lord Macartney's estate, in 1829, I think that both James Boyle's date and the attribution to Keane are almost certainly correct.

The buildings are for the most part one-and-a-half storey, irregularly disposed with differing gables, and dormers, chimneys, bargeboards and dripstones, the porch of stone, the rest of cream-painted stucco: Samuel Lewis calls it "an elegant cottage in the later English style, richly embellished, and forming a picturesque feature in the scenery of the vale". Projecting at the rear, what must be one of the longest and narrowest returns in Ireland, twelve bays long with eight dormers over; on each floor a long corridor serving a series of small rooms, probably originally offices or even parts of the farmyard. There is here a large cobbled area defined by blackstone coach-house and stabling, with an intriguing octagonal cutstone dovecote or gazebo, it is now impossible to be sure which, with inset ogee panels.

In front of the house are the lake and crannog, genuine or artificial, but probably the former. To the south, the remains of the formal gardens with rare azaleas planted by Lord Macartney, enormous yews which are thought to be far older, and a tremendous monkey-puzzler. To the

north, the ruins of the old castle built by Lord Macartney, partly in the Gothick and partly in the classical taste, rendered uninhabitable in 1847. "Its destruction on October 5th, 1847, was brought about in the following manner. A large number of invitations had been issued for a ball which was to be held during the night. About noon it occurred to the steward that a large quantity of gunpowder which had been stored in the vaults at the time of the Rebellion of 1798, or a few years later, by the local militia might have become damp, and ordered that one of the barrels should be removed and examined in one of the rooms. There was no fire in the room during the time, and it was generally believed that a spark must have been blown through the open window which ignited the gunpowder, and producing a most terrific explosion, wrecked the Castle, and Mrs Macartney was killed amid the ruins" (M'Cahan). The former offices, later farm-buildings, at the rear have now been well-restored for functions. These somewhat curious ranges of buildings seem to have dated, for the most part, from the 1780s.

The estate was acquired from the O'Hara's of Crebilly in 1733 by George Macartney, a member of the Irish Parliament for over 54 years; and passed in due course to his only grandson George, later envoy extraordinary to Catherine the Great, Chief Secretary for Ireland, President at Madras, Ambassador to China, Governor of the Cape of Good Hope, Earl in the Irish peerage and Baron in the British peerage, PC, FRS, and a Trustee of the British Museum; who died, childless, in 1806. His

nephew adopted the name Macartney as soon as he came of age, but only came into his full inheritance on the death of Lord Macartney's widow in 1828: so that expenditure on the cottage during the next couple of years would be understandable. The demesne remained in the family for another century, but was occupied by the US army in 1943-4; then, until 1946, used as prisoner-of-war camp for German submariners, the cottage constituting the officers' mess for the unit guarding them. The eccentric Travers Macartney, last heir, who taught me how to pan for gold in the head-waters of the river Bush when I was ten years old, died in 1943; his mother soon after; the whole estate was bought from her trustees that year, and from 1946 onwards was used by Mackies for the entertainment of overseas visitors, and as a winter shooting-lodge; it was not regularly inhabited until the present owners moved here in 1976.

Photograph: Michael O'Connell. (See also colour-plate XIIIa)
Situation: 11 Knockahollet Road, Loughguile; td, Castlequarter, formerly Lavin Lower; Parish, Loughgiel; District Council, Ballymoney; Grid ref. D 068 243.
References: Listed B. Maps and copy maps of 1760, 1785, 1788, 1802 and 1832 in house; maps of 1772, D 1062/2/4, pp 6, 7, 55, 55, T 1965/6/4, VAL 1B/1/146A, p 129, and 2B/1/37, p 84, all in PRONI; J Boyle, OSM, 1835, Antrim, IV, pp 62-3; Lewis, TD, 1837, II, p 315; Girvan, 'North Antrim', UAHS, 1972, p 48; 'Macartney of Lisanoure', 1983, passim; Stewart, 'RHA index of exhibitors', II, 1986, p 138; M'Cahan, 'Local histories',1988; Dean, 'Gate lodges', 1994, p 20; information from present owner.

Drumnasole, Carnlough

88. The original house belonged to the Donaldson family; here, in 1764, "the property included a good house, offices and garden." It appears in Taylor and Skinner and on the Lendrick map of 1780 as belonging to Francis Shaw. In 1808 the estate was sold by Francis Shaw of Ballyclare to Francis Turnly of Richmond Lodge, Knocknagoney (a returned nabob) for £7,400 - payable in gold! Turnly built first the school-house, now in ruins; by 1817, the Rev.

Richard Dobbs reports that, "in the rere of this house, and amongst some venerable trees, close to the site of an old house called Drumnasole, Mr. Turnly is building a most commodious and excellent house, 63 feet square, and four storeys high, including garrets and underground apartments." Atkinson, visiting in 1817, remarks that the "elegant and spacious edifice for his own private accommodation" was "too much retired from the public view, to correspond with that conspicuous scale of embellishment ...... best suited to the circumstances of this coast", but a map of 1823 as yet shows nothing but the schoolhouse.

By 1833, the house was still incomplete: the Valuation book of that year reports "Mr Turnly's house is a large extensive building not finished and without offices: nearly all the stucco work, ceiling, some plaistering and some flooring are yet to be completed." Size: 67 x 67 x 34 feet, excluding returns (it will be noticed that the foundations seem to have swelled up since 1817). Nevertheless, it was in Mr Turnly's occupation at least as early as 1826, possibly only as a summer residence, for some of his letters are from this address. In 1835, James Boyle described it as "a very capacious and extensive building, very neat and uniform in its appearance and beautifully situated ... the house, though it was commenced 25 years ago, is still far from finished internally and has already cost 7,000 pounds." "[insert addition: the house, which is a very fine one, though commenced 30 years ago, is still unfinished; it has already cost 10,000]".

In 1971, I suggested that probably the house was not finished until after 1835, the year when the youthful Charles Lanyon arrived in Co. Antrim, since the porch, the plaster ceiling in the long hall, and the stair-well roof-light, transmitted through two diminishing concentric circles, each with arboreal cast-iron balusters, looked to me very much like his work. However, having now read Turnly's correspondence with his agent in Cushendun, Archibald Hamilton, I have changed my mind. In the first place, Turnly (who never mentions Mr Lanyon, only Mr Bauld) disliked the line of Lanyon's new road across Glendun which, he thought, was adverse to his interests. Secondly, he was deeply versed in building skills; his letters show that he could set out a staircase, or calculate the fall of water required for a water-closet with purifier. I now think it likely that, though he may have obtained assistance from architect or pattern-book for the original design, he was mostly his own architect. By 1845 the house certainly seems to have been finished, for the Parliamentary Gazetteer calls it "the splendid recently erected mansion of F. Turnly Esq." This was in fact the year of his death - not here, but at Richmond Lodge. In 1854, the enthusiastic Doyle wrote - "In a sequestered dell, surrounded by perpendicular precipices, embosomed in the midst of thriving plantations of his own planting, Mr Turnly erected the elegant mansion of Drumnasole, - a little Tempè in itself".

The house is actually of two storeys, and attics, on basement, five bays wide and six deep, of basalt said to have been quarried from the hill behind, and rolled down to the site; with galleting and sandstone trim. The facade is a good deal less simple than it seems at first glance. There are six steps up to the front door, flanked by a curly balustrade of fat stone balusters, carried on a half-arch with a large roundel window on each side. The break-front doorcase has four Doric columns, side lights and cobweb fanlight; above this, a central window, and two (false) flanking windows; all the window-sills above and within the doorcase incorporating curious incised roundels. The main bay to each side is recessed; the corner bays have slim tall blind recesses, rectangular above and round-headed below. The windows in the main floor of the south front (only) drop down to floor level; they have all their glazing bars, as have the windows in the north front; otherwise, plate glass has been substituted in the lower sash of each window. The roof is hipped, with the dome to light the stairwell concealed in the central valley and behind this tall chimneys linked by a bell-turret. The yard, symmetrical returns, and whitewashed out-houses have been uncommonly little altered.

The estate remains, as it has been since 1808, in the ownership of the Turnly family.

Photographs: Michael O'Connell. (See also colour-plate VIII)

Situation: Inland from the coast road north of Carnlough; td, Drumnasole; Parish, Ardclinis; District Council, Larne; Grid ref. D 289 214.

References: Listed B. Taylor and Skinner, 'Roads', 1778, p 273, Lendrick, map, 1780; R S Dobbs, in Mason, 'Statistical account', III, 1819; Atkinson, 'Ireland exhibited', 1823, II, p 209; 1823 map, D543/6, VAL 1B 147B, in PRONI; J Chaytor, OSM, 1832, and J Boyle, 1835, Antrim, IV, pp 3, 6, 7; Turnly-Hamilton correspondence, 1825-1843, in Ulster Folk and Transport Museum; PG, I, 1845, p 52; Doyle, 'Tours in Ulster', 1854, p 216; Brett, 'Glens', UAHS, 1971, p 27; J Irvine, in 'The Glynns', II, 1974, p 48, and XI, 1983 p 20.

Cleggan Lodge, Aghafatten

89. The present building probably incorporates parts of the much earlier house named as Clagan on Taylor and Skinner's map of 1777, and shown as belonging to "O'Hara Esq". This was presumably the "Mr Brabstone O'Hara of Claggin" who successfully escaped from United Irishmen, when they discovered his hiding-place in Mr Wilson's house in Ballymena. Although the documentary evidence has almost all been destroyed, and although Atkinson mentions it as "Clagan, Ballymenagh, seat of Mrs O'Hara" in 1817, it appears that the present Cleggan was originally an eye-brow-thatched cottage orné, rather in the style of Nash, built by the bachelor Earl O'Neill, not long after the disastrous fire which destroyed Shane's Castle in 1816. Lieutenant Boteler in 1833 wrote, "In the townland of Cleggan is the hunting lodge of Earl O'Neill, who resides there but for a short time during the shooting season. It is built in the cottage ornée style and is prettily situated and surrounded by plantations of a considerable extent". A plan of the previous year survives, with a rather crude vignette of the house, unfortunately too foxed and faded for satisfactory reproduction, looking much as it now does apart from the thatch. In the 1836 valuation, the "Front of Cottage" was shown as measuring 76 feet long, by 21 feet deep, by 19 feet high, and was valued, along with the back quarters, "servants' apartments, and sportsman's dwelling." at a total of £39.9.6. In the same year, James Boyle wrote of this and the other gentlemen's seats of the Braid valley, a touch patronisingly, "They are all nice residences, and mostly modern, but there is nothing striking nor worthy of description in their appearance or architecture".

It was let to James Fisher of Barrow-in-Furness, the first to exploit the iron ore and bauxite deposits at Glenravel, in 1864; the lake below the house is still known as Fisher's Pond, though it seems to have been there before he came,

for it appears on the Ordnance Survey map of 1857. Cleggan was bought back by the 2nd Baron O'Neill in 1895 when the thatch was removed and the impressive double staircase inserted; additional rooms and gables were added in 1927; and the house was restored and re-roofed in 1978. Since then, in 1988, a large pavilion with cupola, providing a business room with enormous fireplace and shutters in the French manner, has been added to designs by Consarc Partnership and Robert McKinstry.

The house stands high on the wooded hillside looking south across the Braid valley to Slemish mountain: from below it seems to present a bewildering multitude of canted bays and dormers, one dormer surmounting each bay and a larger one in the centre: so that there are two facing south, two facing east, and three facing south-east. In fact, the underlying pattern is simpler than it seems: the large octagonal drawing-room at one end and the equivalent octagonal dining-room at the other are linked internally by the broad hallway containing the staircase, and externally by a rustic balcony carried on two octagonal columns. The walls are of whitened rough-cast; the windows are 24-pane casements; the roof is now of agreeable fish-scale slates. The upper bedrooms, with their dormers, have sloping cottagey ceilings. The house admirably combines the formal and the informal with the confidence characteristic of the Regency period.

Photograph: Michael O'Connell.
Situation: North of the main road from Ballymena to Carnlough; td, Longmore; Parish, Skerry; District Council, Ballymena; Grid ref. D 218 106.
References: Listed B. Taylor and Skinner, 'Roads,' 1778, p 21; Atkinson, 'Ireland exhibited', 1823, II, p 439; R Boteler, OSM, 1833, and J Boyle, 1835, Antrim, IV, pp 106, 111; VAL 1B/15B, p 18, in PRONI; Girvan, 'West Antrim', UAHS, 1970, p 32; Pierce and Coey, 'Taken for granted', 1984, p 118; Stewart, 'Summer soldiers', 1995, p 128.

Garron Tower, Carnlough

90. The former mansion consists of a considerable L-shaped range in black basalt, turning on an octagonal tower, with a square turret and Georgian glazing. The slightly later and lower range extends up to a gate-house at right angles. There are machicolations and crenellations, perhaps owing something to those of Burg Rheinstein, seat of the Archbishops of Trier. The group stands on a commanding cliff-top site, enclosed by battlements and adorned by cannon.

In 1970, the evidence available pointed to Lewis Vulliamy of London as the architect employed by Frances

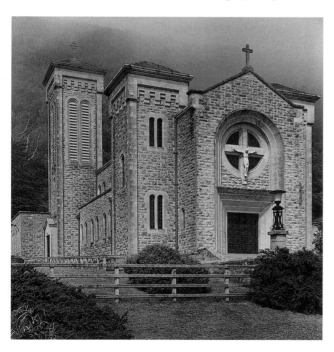

Anne Vane, daughter of the Countess of Antrim and wife of the Marquess of Londonderry, who laid the foundation stone in 1848. The main house was completed in 1850. Subsequent researches by the late Jimmy Irvine appeared to contradict this attribution: a letter of January 1849 from the builder, Charles Campbell of Newtownards, to the Marchioness, asserts "your ladyship has the specifications yourself for I require none, being the architect and director of the works myself." At this time, she had called in John Millar, architect, of Belfast, who had worked with Thomas Hopper on Gosford Castle twenty years earlier, to review the progress of the works. In a detailed letter dated 1st January 1849, he reported separately on the masonry ("generally forward"), the stone-cutting ("very backward"), joinery, plastering ("defective, very"), bell-hanging ("no preparation of any kind, this is preposterous"): and that "the word impossible having in a great measure become obsolete in our modern professional vocabulary", Mr Campbell could complete on time with "due energy under a more systematic arrangement". His offer of his own supervisory services was not taken up. There is no clear evidence that either Vulliamy or Millar had a hand in the original design; but, on the other hand, the design is more sophisticated than would be expected of a Newtownards builder. On a careful reading of the correspondence, and of Millar's three reports, it seems likely that Campbell was given an oil painting, a model, and various plans, all from an un-named source, and left to get on with the detailing and the interior arrangements as best he might. The researches of Paul Magill show that the gate lodge and porch were added in 1854; the Orchard House in 1856; the stables, designed by Charles Lanyon, in 1860; and the Dairy, designed by Vulliamy, in 1861.

After Lady Londonderry's death in 1865, the Tower was occupied only by servants until it was leased to Henry

MacNeill of Larne as a hotel in 1899. It was badly damaged by fire in 1914, and again in 1922, but on each occasion restored. During the second World War it was pressed into service as a refuge for the residents of Clifton House, Belfast. It was then bought by Bishop Mageean for conversion into a boarding-school, St McNissi's College: chapel, classroom blocks and other buildings were added, all to the designs of Patrick Gregory. In almost all respects the new work fits in admirably with the old, the chapel in particular being very successful, though it is perhaps a pity

that whilst the old buildings are of blackstone, the new ones are much lighter in colour.

Photographs: Michael O'Connell. (See also colour-plate VIIb)
Situation: Old Coast Road, Carnlough, just inland from the little harbour near the tip of Garron Point; td, Galboly Lower; Parish, Ardclinis; District Council, Larne; Grid ref. D 300 236.
References: Listed B. Hill, 'Macdonnells', 1873, p 371; family papers in Durham County Record Office and PRONI, D 2977/90; Brett, 'Glens', UAHS, 1971, pp 22-25; J Irvine, in 'The Glynns', IV, 1975, and V, 1976, p 29; Magill, 'Garron Tower', 1990, passim.

Dunderave, Bushmills

91. By far the grandest 19th-century house in north Antrim, just as Glenarm Castle (86) is the grandest 19th-century house in the southern half of the county. A fine example of the Italian palazzo style which had been pioneered by Charles Barry in London, first in the Travellers' Club and then in the Reform Club, and followed by Charles Lanyon in his reconstruction of the head office of the Belfast Bank, then, almost simultaneously with Dunderave, and Ballywalter Park. However, though an attribution to anyone other than Charles Lanyon seems inconceivable, I know of no firm documentary evidence that he was the architect: the plans and elevations in the house are unsigned and undated, and no correspondence whatever has so far surfaced.

Francis Macnaghten, younger son of Edmund Macnaghten of Beardiville (71), married his cousin Letitia Dunkin of Dunderave in 1787, and went to India to seek his fortune: in this he was highly successful, first as standing counsel to the East India Company, then as a Supreme Court Judge in Madras, then in Calcutta. In 1825 he

returned to Ireland, having inherited property in Co. Armagh, and purchased Roe Park, Limavady, where he lived for some years; and subsequently inherited Beardiville too. He was promoted from knight to baronet in 1836. Notwithstanding his prosperity, he appears by 1808 to have charmed his two Dunkin brothers-in-law into letting him have the Dunderave property "for a small price", and proceeded to build a house on it, known as "Bushmills House": the owner is shown by Lendrick in 1780 as William Dunkin Esq. but in Williamson's revision of 1808 as F McNaghten Esq.

On his death in 1843, his eldest son Edmund inherited the Dunderave property. He was already a very rich man: having been appointed, through his father's influence, to the post of Registrar of the Supreme Court in Calcutta at the age of 21. "The fees pertaining to this post were so large that during his first year's tenure they are said to have exceeded the salary of the Governor-General." He retired aged 24, having found it necessary to earn his living for only three years, and returned to live at Roe Park.

On his father's death, he set about demolishing Bushmills House and building a very much larger and grander house in its stead, on which work seems to have started in 1847.

Unlike Ballywalter, which is of three storeys, Dunderave is a large, nearly square, two-storey block with a hipped roof and an extra hat-like corrugated roof protecting the great central hall. The height of the chimney-stacks was cut down after one of them crashed through the roof in a gale. The details are of stonework, mostly sandstone, the flat parts of the walls finished in Roman cement. The entrance front is of six bays, with a thumping porch of Corinthian columns and pilasters; the north front is, basically, of four bays, the central two recessed but embracing a great ground floor bow, again with engaged Corinthian columns and pilasters, triple windows similarly framed on either side, and pediments above the outer upstairs windows; the garden front is, by comparison, austere, consisting of six bays without projection or recession, the only ornaments the quoins, the brackets at the eaves, the console brackets and architraves around the ground-floor windows, and the stone 'eyebrows' over the upstairs windows. The ground-floor quoins are vermiculated; the balconies have balustrades of pierced interlace ornament. Externally the house, grand as it is, is somewhat gloomy in appearance, partly because of the mixture of brown and grey colours, and the mixture of rough and smooth textures. But Girvan considers that "the whole exterior has an air of warmth and richness; its proportions are elegant and there is a pleasant interplay between smooth surfaces and well sculptured classical detailing."

Inside the front door, a barrel-vaulted entrance hall, like a tunnel, with classical bas-reliefs, leads to the main feature of the house, the great two-storey central hall, with arched galleries on all four sides, down-lighting from the round-headed windows under the supplemental roof, and a prominent interior cornice wide enough for children to run around. "The stairs are tucked away in a separate compartment" (Larmour). The detailing of the reception rooms is described by Girvan as "of great opulence". Certainly, the central hall with its marbling by Italian craftsmen is very splendid. The other rooms are spacious and imposing, partly no doubt to accommodate the large furniture brought from Roe Park, but the detailing is somewhat heavy and the habitability of the house restricted by its curious orientation on a very exposed site: which is the more surprising as the house was only designed for use in three months each year in the summer, yet always lacked such summery features as gardens and French windows, despite its 17 bedrooms.

As Rowan tactfully puts it, comparing Dunderave and Ballywalter, "which of the two houses is the better architectural composition must be a matter of personal preference for there can be no question that both are remarkable monuments of the Italianate taste of their day. Lanyon himself might not have been able to choose … "

Though it has passed through many vicissitudes since 1847, the house is still owned and occupied by descendants of its builder.

Photograph: Michael O'Connell. (See also colour-plate IIb). Drawing: courtesy of Sir Patrick Macnaghten.
Situation: 20 Dunderave Road, Bushmills; principal entrance off the main road from Bushmills to Ballycastle; td, Clogher North; Parish, Dunluce; District Council, Moyle; Grid ref. C 947 415.
References: Listed A. Lendrick map, 1780; Williamson map, 1808; Lewis, TD, 1837, I, p 234; drawings in the house; Macnaghten, 'Clan Macnachtan', 1951, passim; Girvan, 'North Antrim', UAHS, 1972, pp 24-26; Bence-Jones, 'Burke's guide', 1978, p 114; Pierce and Coey, 'Taken for granted', 1984, p 162; A Rowan, in 'Ballywalter Park', UAHS, 1985, pp 13-21; P Larmour, in 'Irish arts review', 1989-90, pp 204-5.

Abbeydene (formerly Lismara), Whiteabbey

92. A large, handsome, foursquare merchant prince's mansion of about 1850, of a fairly unusual golden sandstone, on the high bank east of Macedon Point, looking south over Belfast Lough.

The seaward facade has four single windows above, two very wide three-light curved bows below; the entrance front, a central triple window under a segmental pediment and two single windows above, a large enclosed portico with four Tuscan columns and round-headed windows below; the western front has another, this time false, portico, with four Tuscan columns. The detailing of the stonework of quoins, architraves, balusters, triglyphs and mutules is unfortunately much weather-worn. The roof is hipped; the chimney-stacks are surprisingly reticent, have they been cut down? The oversailing eaves are carried on numerous close-set brackets. Jackson's office or Lanyon's office? Not without hesitation, I vote for the former.

The house first appears on the 1858 Ordnance Survey map, and in the 1858 Street Directory, when the owner is shown as John Finlay, presumably the flax and tow merchant who carried on business at 7 Donegall Square East. In the 1870s, the seat of James Hind, described as "of the Belfast Banking Co"; in fact, he was never a director of the Bank, though his firm, John Hind and Co. owners of the Durham Street mill, were large shareholders in it until their failure in the depression in the linen industry of 1884; as a result of which the house seems to have lain empty for several years. From 1895 until 1915, it was the seat of Edward Robinson of Robinson & Cleaver's, and then of his widow; from 1916 the seat of Crawford McCullagh, a young man from Aghalee who had prospered in Belfast as merchant and property speculator - at one time, he was the largest individual ratepayer in the City, was elected Lord Mayor in 1914 and on 17 subsequent occasions, was knighted in 1915, and promoted to baronet in 1935. He died at Lismara in 1948; his son, the second Sir Crawford McCullagh, removed the name 'Lismara' to his new home in the grounds, and this house, renamed 'Abbeydene', became an old people's home, with the usual institutional alterations and additions: the additions now demolished. Its extensive wooded grounds are, at the time of writing, in the process of being built over by medium-density housing; the house, being listed, to be converted to three large flats.

Photograph: Michael O'Connell.
Situation: 385 Shore Road, Newtownabbey; td, White Abbey; Parish, Whitehouse; District Council, Newtownabbey; Grid ref. J 352 815.
References: Listed B1. OS map, 1858; Armstrong, 'Newtownabbey', [1979], pp 330, 331; Belfast street directories; Chambers, 'Faces of change' 1983, p 177; Ollerenshaw, 'Banking in 19th-century Ireland', 1987, p 168.

The Abbey, Whiteabbey

93. Built by Charles Lanyon about 1850 for Richard Davison, MP, on the site of a gentleman's cottage called Demyat owned by Davison's predecessor as MP, Samuel Getty; the Abbey first appears in the directories in 1852. On the death of Davison, Lanyon bought the house for his own use, and lived there until his death in 1889. Since Lanyon was elected to Parliament in 1866, the house was the home of three successive Members of Parliament.

A big Italianate house of stucco, two-storey on basement, the Abbey stands very foursquare on a bluff overlooking Belfast Lough. Each of the south and east-facing fronts has five tall rectangular windows, with console-bracketed hoods, on the principal floor, and five segmental-headed windows above. The western, or entrance, front has a projecting portico with Corinthian columns and pilasters; its symmetry is upset by an extra upstairs window, plainly not original. The stucco is enriched by heavily vermiculated quoins; the eaves are ornamented by one course of large dentils, one course of small dentils, and a course of crisply-moulded rings. The flat surfaces presently painted grey, the dressings terracotta. The original chimney-stacks appear to have been cut down and rather unworthily replaced. The bays at the rear, and the subsidiary segmental portico, now in poor order, appear to be later additions, dating from the conversion of the house to a hydropathic, subsequently a tuberculosis, then a general, hospital. It now serves as headquarters of the Loughside Unit of the Northern Health Board. Some good, if not outstanding, woodwork and plasterwork inside; but nearly a century of institutional life has inevitably subverted the original character of the great man's home.

Photograph: Michael O'Connell.
Situation: Originally off Station Road, now approached from Doagh Road, Newtownabbey; td, White Abbey; Parish, Whitehouse; District Council, Newtownabbey; Grid ref. J 349 823.
References: Listed B1. T McTear, 'Recollections', in UJA, 2nd series, V, 1899, p 167; Armstrong, 'Newtownabbey', [1979], pp 149, 232.

Ballygarvey, Ballymena

94. Built by Andrew Curell before 1859, very probably to designs by Thomas Jackson. The Curells had come to Ireland from the lowlands of Scotland in the 18th century; acquired Kildrum bleachworks; in 1814 rented additional works at Ballygarvey from William Gillilan; and bought both works and property in 1821. The house is shown on the Ordnance Survey map of 1861, and in the Valuation book of August 1859 is described as being of the highest quality, 49 feet by 38 feet by 24 feet high, with a wing nearly as large, valued at £46; with land worth £59, and beetling mills, bleach works, and 25 workers' houses, together valued at £170. Andrew Curell married late in life but fathered 11 children, to accommodate whom he found it necessary to add two later wings to the house, one of them now demolished. It is said that there was jealous rivalry between the Curells and their neighbours across the road, the Mortons; this house was deliberately named 'Ballygarvey' to annoy the Mortons whose older building was already named 'Ballygarvey House'.

Ballygarvey is a handsome painted stone and stucco house of ample dimensions, the main block three bays wide and two bays deep; the entrance through a central porch, its round-headed doorway flanked by polished marble colonettes, round-headed windows in the room over it, a generous carved cartouche above that. The roof, chimneys and chimney-pots are very much in the style employed by Thomas Jackson, with oversailing eaves carried on dentils alternating with paterae. Inside, there is a double arch, with a single central marble colonette, dividing the back hall from the staircase. There is some fine panelling, and some vigorous plasterwork. Four gate lodges, perhaps also by Jackson, were added in 1867.

Andrew Curell "did a large export trade with the Americas and the Philippines, being assisted therein by his relatives the Browns" (of Glencairn). "On Andrew's death his beautiful house and the works and property of Ballygarvey were sold" for £2,300 in 1906 to John Killen Wilson of Raceview Woollen Mills, in whose family it remained until 1981; since then it has been extensively restored and renovated by the present owners.

Photograph: Michael O'Connell.
Situation: 71 Ballygarvey Road, Ballymena; td, Ballygarvey; Parish, Kilconriola; District Council, Ballymena; Grid ref. D 124 061.
References: Listed B1. Title deeds 1793-1906, D2179/6, VAL 2B/1/66A, p 27 and VAL 12B/3/19A, pp 62, 63, all in PRONI; Bassett, 'Antrim', 1888, p 297; H C Lawlor, in 'Fibres and fabrics journal', October, 1941, p 8; Dean, 'Gate lodges', 1993, p 3; information from owners.

Springfield, Magheragall

95. A large and dignified two-storey mid-Victorian house, of white-painted stucco, amidst a rolling countryside; plain, spacious, a trifle austere: in every way appropriate to the needs of Joseph Richardson (one of my four great-grand-fathers), a wealthy Quaker linen merchant. Born in 1821, he was one of seven successful brothers, most of whom built houses for themselves in Co. Antrim or Co. Down. In his earlier years, he lived near Liverpool, and on his return about 1860 employed Thomas Jackson to design Springfield for him. "A born Chairman of Railways and other Companies, amongst others, the Co. Down Railway, the Northern Counties Railway, the Edenderry Spinning Co., The Island Spinning Co., etc, etc," he lived on until 1906, and himself had twelve children.

> "Where'er the red gold floweth
>> His coffers high to fill,
> His name is found, both sure and sound,
>> At back of banker's bill."

(Only a very small share of that red gold came my way, through my mother's marriage settlement).

The portico on the west front is restrained, sporting only four console brackets. There is a canted bay at the centre of the south front, looking out at Magheragall church over lawn and fields past two great trees, a cedar and a Wellingtonia. The windows are framed in plain architraves, segmental-headed above, square-headed and with hoods below, all with broad sashes of plate glass. The hipped roof is carried on a heavy cornice; all the original chimney-stacks and chimney-pots are there, and form an important ingredient in the overall gravitas of the design.

Between 1928, when Springfield passed out of the ownership of the Richardson family, and 1963, when it was bought by the present owner, it passed through the hands of a number of owners, all of whom dealt kindly with it. It is now almost certainly the last linen magnate's mansion on the Antrim slope of the Lagan valley still unspoiled, and in family occupation.

The earlier Springfield is still standing close by, a pleasant 18th-century cottage with Georgian glazing, single-storey to the front but with dormers to the rear. "The house was originally an ordinary farm house", but was rebuilt about 1780 by Edward Wakefield; Major Houghton acquired it in 1811, and made further improvements. It is now slated, and no longer answers to Atkinson's 1817 description of "the seat of Major Haughton ... a model of English neatness and beauty - the vermilion roof of Springfield Lodge, being happily combined with the snowy whiteness of its walls, and with the verdure of its lawns and plantations".

Photograph: Michael O'Connell.
Situation: 72, Ballinderry Road, Brookmount, Magheragall; td, Parish, Magheragall; District Council, Lisburn; Grid ref. J 218 655.
References: Listed B1. Atkinson, 'Ireland exhibited', 1823, II, p 21; T Fagan, OSM, 1837, Antrim, VII, pp 99, 100; 'Building news', 15 August 1890; Richardson, 'The Quakri at Grange', 1899, p 27 and 'Reminiscences', [1911], pp 80-83; H Dixon, in 'Proceedings & reports of BNHPS', 2nd series, IX, 1970/77; C McClenaghan, 'Thomas Jackson', 1993, research report in QUB Library; Pierce and Coey, 'Taken for granted', 1984, p 120.

Craigdun Castle, Craigs

96. A remarkable late Victorian mansion, having much in common with Belfast Castle of 1870, but a few years earlier: dated 1867 on the weathervane of an outbuilding. It was built by 'Long Eddie' (or 'Long Neddie') McNeill, so-called because he was 6 feet 7½ inches tall. "As a young man, Edmund had emigrated to Australia, where he ran a sheep ranch. After ten years in Australia he returned to Ireland for a holiday, intending to return, but in his absence his partner ... sold out and disappeared ... Edmund decided to stay at home and get married ... there is no doubt that he made a great success of his land agency business ... At first he carried on the business from Ballycastle, but finding that this was too far from his work he had a fine new house built at Craigs".

The house is said to have been built "close to the site of the ancient Craigs Castle, one of the three original 'Settlement Castles' built under grants from the Crown in the reign of James I. No ruins of the old castle remain" (1909). The site of the old castle, built by Houstons from Scotland, had been acquired by John McNeill of Parkmount; and Long Eddie laid out an attractive park of around 200 acres, and extensive walled gardens and hot-houses, with pretty little circular conical-capped turrets for game larder and apple-loft; of the gardens, little remains

save an exceptionally fine mature sycamore tree.

"The modern building is a mansion of black basalt, pointed with freestone, and is in the 'Scotch Baronial' style of architecture." Of this house, Girvan writes: "... in the Scottish baronial style, of coursed basalt with sandstone trim. Its main feature is a massive five-storied tower topped by bartizans. The rest of the house is triple-piled, three storeys high and its design gives a sense of irregularity, increased by asymmetrical placing of the bay windows. Splendid griffins and bogus olde beastes adorn the spouts on the front of the house ... The superb setting of the castle enhances its rather dull architecture". Whilst I cannot better Girvan's description, and agree with his tentative ascription to Lanyon, Lynn and Lanyon, I found this building far from dull. It seems to me to be a practice run for Belfast Castle, but in some ways preferable, because rather simpler and less cluttered; at this date, it could be the work either of W H Lynn or of John Lanyon, probably the former.

Internally, the house is notable more for the number of its rooms than for their size; though quite grand, they are by no means overwhelming in scale. There is not a great deal of internal ornament apart from a quatrefoil dado, and the fine central stair-case, the oak bannisters ornamented with strapwork, and the gallery of segmental arches on three sides of the stair-well.

The property was sold about 1912, for in 1913 Shaw describes it as "till recently the residence of Mr Edmund M'Neill"; probably Long Eddie, who died in 1915, was already ill, and his son Ronald (later Lord Cushendun) preferred to divide his time between Cushendun and London. The purchaser was John Percy Stott, son of a Ballymoney merchant; on his death in 1949 the property passed to his daughter, who had married a Commander Martin. In 1952, their only son died of polio, aged 15, whilst a schoolboy at Eton: and shortly thereafter his parents presented it for use as a holiday home for multiple sclerosis patients under the name 'Peter Stott Martin House'. The premises were not really suitable for institutional use - a hideous lift was installed in the courtyard, along with other unsuitable alterations; eventually the Health Board sold it, and in 1993 it was bought by the present owners who have brought it back into use as a private dwelling. Some of the original mahogany built-in cupboards, book-cases and such-like survived; despite its enormous size, it has turned out a surprisingly comfortable home, and appears to have taken on a new lease of life.

Photographs: Michael O'Connell.
Situation: 32 Dunminning Road, Craigs, Cullybackey; td, Craigs; Parish, Craigs, formerly Ahoghill; District Council, Ballymena; Grid ref. D 043 083.
References: Listed, house B+, gate-screen B1. Young, 'Belfast and province of Ulster', 1909, p 265; Shaw, 'Cullybackey', 1913, p 144; Girvan, 'West Antrim', UAHS, 1970, p 28; R McDonnell in 'The Glynns', I, 1973, p 21-24; Bence-Jones, 'Burke's guide', 1978, p 93; M McSparran, in 'The Glynns', XVI, 1988, pp 22-29.

Kintullagh (now St Louis Convent), Ballymena

97. A large, handsome, foursquare Jacobethan house of pinkish sandstone with ashlar dressings: of two-and-a-half storeys, with great curly gables, strapwork ornament over the windows, a very fine square portico (the stonework unfortunately painted), a tall square tower with an elongated-cupola roof, and a nice little conical-capped tower terminating the ground-floor facade. "A very satisfying design ... the interior is skilfully planned round a central pine staircase with an arcaded gallery ... The building is well-maintained and has been preserved without any alterations. A small L-shaped gatelodge with similar gables" (Girvan). The interior detailing is extremely fine - much pitch-pine panelling; the original over-doors, over-mantels, mantelpieces, and ornate ceiling roses; an extraordinary Doric screen, with columns *in antis*, in the front hall, made of solid pine tree-trunks: all in mint condition, in great contrast to the sorry mess the Cistercians have made of Portglenone House not so far away.

"All built about 1862 for William A Young and designed by Messrs Lanyon, Lynn and Lanyon, superseding ... the previous house on the site known as Hillhead, when it belonged to the Gihon family" (Dean). Dr William Young, who bought Galgorm Castle in 1851, had married Anne Gihon in 1823: his son William Alexander married another Miss Gihon, Margaret, and this was their wedding present from him. Their respective initials are to be seen incorporated in many of the embellishments, as also fleur-de-lys in compliment to the French origin of the Gihon family, a feature much appreciated by the nuns

whose order is also of French origin. Incidentally, Patrick Savage Young, son of John Young PC, in 1884 married Flora, youngest daughter of Sir Charles Lanyon.

Bence-Jones says "A Victorian Jacobean house, bearing a strong resemblance to Killashee, Co. Kildare, and to Tempo Manor, Co Fermanagh ... without doubt, the three houses are by the same hand". (Clotworthy House, 174, too?) On the basis of a tentative attribution of Tempo by Dixon and Rowan to Thomas Turner, both Williams and Bence-Jones attribute this house to him also; but Rowan has subsequently firmly attributed Tempo to "Sir Charles Lanyon in his most winsome Jacobethan Manorial style", and almost certainly Dean is right in attributing both this house and gate lodge to Lanyon. Kintullagh first appears in the 1870 Directory, not in that for 1865-6, so perhaps the house is slightly later than had been thought. After W A Young's death, in 1894, the house passed first to his widow, then to his unmarried daughters, Mary Anne and Edith, who seem to have fallen on hard times and left it in 1920. Thereafter the house passed jointly to Dr Edward Armstrong and his brother-in-law Mr Gilmore; the two couples shared the house amicably until they fell out in 1923 when the house was sold to the church and leased to the nuns as a school for young ladies. The first mass was said on 9th January 1924, the day after the sisters moved in.

In 1950, there were 24 nuns, running a school for 300 girls; in 1965 they acquired the freehold of the house and the area immediately surrounding it; since 1970, St Louis has been a co-educational grammar school, with primary school and nursery school attached, using more modern buildings in the grounds. Today, only two of the remaining eight nuns teach in the schools.

Photograph: Michael O'Connell.
Situation: Set back from Cullybackey Road, Ballymena; td, Carniny; Parish, and District Council, Ballymena; Grid ref. D 092 043.

References: Convent, lodge, gates and boundary wall all listed B. Street directories; Burke, Landed gentry of Ireland, 1958; Girvan, 'Antrim & Ballymena', UAHS, 1969, p 19; H Dixon and A Rowan, in 'Country life', 1973, pp 1495-6; Dixon, 'Introduction', 1975, p 60; Bence-Jones, 'Burke's guide', 1978, p 177; Pierce and Coey, 'Taken for granted', 1984, p 45; Dean, 'Gate lodges', 1994, p 18; Williams, 'Architecture in Ireland', 1994, p 2; information from Mrs J B Bryson and from the sisters.

Ballynacree House, Ballymoney

98. Originally, the first of the 17th-century seats of the Moore family. In April, 1861, "Ballynacrea House, Co. Antrim, the property of Marcus Gage, Esq, is being re-built on the site of the old mansion. The design is Italian. The facade presents a frontage of 107 feet, with handsome Ionic portico, campanile," ? "etc. The eaves all round the house project 2 feet, with deep carved trusses under, and moulded panels between. The principal floor contains drawing and dining rooms, each 28 feet by 18 feet 6 inches and 13 feet 6 inches high ... The hall and principal stairs are 14 feet wide; the library, 20 by 18 feet. House-keeper's room and store-room, butler's pantry, cloak room, water-closet, back stairs, pantries, muniment room and wine cellars are also added. The kitchen, servants' hall, culinary apartments and servants' bedrooms are contained in the wings of the old courtyard. The bed-room floor contains 9 bed rooms, with bath rooms and water closets etc; this storey is 12 feet high. The portico, moulded base, plinth, and belt courses, with decorations of windows, chimney cappings, etc. are ... of Scotch sandstone. The works are being carried out from the designs of Mr Fitzgibbon Louch, CE, architect, of Londonderry".

An extremely large and ambitious mansion, the main block two-storey, five bays wide and four deep, with segmental-pedimented windows flanking an imposing tetrastyle Ionic portico: the triple central window above the entrance recessed, the support for the roof being here provided by four heavy wooden brackets. Originally red-brick with Scottish sandstone dressings, but the brick has been pebble-dashed. Very heavy and ornate palmetto-capitalled screen in the front hall; imposing double staircase; much louche detail. Good trees, fine situation, extensive outbuildings; derelict Gothick gate lodge and fine curly iron gatepillars. For some time the house lay empty whilst in the ownership of Desmond Fulton, who built himself a far smaller house on the land. In 1994, bought by Robert Dunlop, champion motor-cycle racer, who started work on its restoration, but was obliged by a racing accident to re-sell to the present owner in 1995.

Photograph: Michael O'Connell.
Situation: Glenstall Road, Ballymoney; td, Ballynacree More; Parish, District Council, Ballymoney; Grid ref. C 911 246.
References: Listed B1. 'Dublin builder', 15 April 1861, p 486; Girvan, 'North Antrim', UAHS, 1973, p 45; Dean, 'Gate lodges', 1994, p 3.

Castle House, Lisburn

99. A large and imposing mansion, built in 1880 for the town's landlord, Sir Richard Wallace, owner of the Wallace Collection in London, "to redeem a promise made in 1845 by the 4th Marquess of Hertford to his tenantry ... to build a house in Lisburn". Sir Richard had succeeded to the Hertford estates in Lisburn, worth £50,000 a year, in 1872, after "long and costly litigation with Sir Hamilton Seymour"; he may have been a son of an ex-ballet dancer, Maria Fagniani, who had married the 3rd Marquess in 1798; or he may have been the son of "a Scotch girl of humble birth", Agnes Wallace, afterwards Jackson, "a kind of *fille du régiment* of the 10th hussars." In youth, he was known as Dick Jackson. However that may be, he only resided in Castle House "for a very short time, a few months in all". In his latter years he became a recluse, and died in Paris in 1890. His heir, Sir John Murray Scott ('Seery' to Victoria Sackville-West), "although he visited Lisburn on several occasions, never resided in Castle House, the valuable contents of which were removed to London. The Castle House was acquired from the Murray Scott Trustees by Lisburn Urban Council in 1914 for £2,000 for the purpose of forming a technical school" (A S Moore). There were fine fireplaces, tapestries, clocks and furnishings; which did not form part of the gift to the nation, but were otherwise distributed or sold: my grandfather, Alfred Brett, remembered being taken to see them.

Architect unknown, but probably William McHenry CE, who acted as surveyor to the Wallace estate, and certainly designed the almost contemporaneous court-house (sadly, demolished); not, as Hugh Dixon believed, by T B Ambler, who may have remodelled Hertford House in London for Sir Richard. The builders were James Vernon and Sons, and "all the work in connection with it was done by residents in the County Antrim". Externally, a fairly plain symmetrical red-brick building in a late-classical (or Queen Anne?) style; hipped mansard roof with round-headed dormers tucked behind cornice and balustrade; quoins; tall Georgian-glazed windows, triple above the porch, with eyebrows and architraves of stone; pedimented aedicules framing the ground-floor windows; tetrastyle Doric portico.

Inside, astonishingly grand: a central hall with gallery all round carried on richly-carved pine console brackets, and eight large doors and doorcases opening off it, but not symmetrically disposed. A very splendid staircase at one end, opening off the hall; on the back or garden front, a particularly fine saloon with a great bow at the centre of the rear facade. The arrangement is almost as grand as Lanyon's at Ballywalter or Dunderave (91).

Photograph: Michael O'Connell.
Situation: 35 Castle Street, Lisburn; td, Lisnagarvey; Parish and District Council, Lisburn; Grid ref. J 269 644.
References: Listed B; in conservation area. [Greene], 'History of Lisburn and neighbourhood', 1906, p 25; A S Moore, in 'Lady of the house', 1917, reprinted in 'Lisburn standard', copy in James Carson scrapbook in Linen Hall Library; photographs by W A Green, WAG 868, 869, 874, in Ulster Folk Museum; Camblin, 'Town in Ulster', 1951, pl 48; Brett and Dunleath, 'Lisburn', UAHS, 1969, p 10; J F Burns, in 'Lisburn Historical Society journal', III, 1980, pp 8-22; H Dixon, in 'Lisburn Historical Society journal', IV, 1982, p 7.

CHAPTER FOUR

CLERGY HOUSES

The former Glebe House, Billy (104), and outbuildings. Photograph: Michael O'Connell

CLERGY HOUSES

Maurice Craig has written, of the glebe-houses of the (formerly established) Church of Ireland, "the characteristic glebe-house is a two-storey three-bay house with a basement, a hipped roof and either two stacks or a single stack, well set about with trees and with a yard at the back. They set the tone for many another decent-sized and comfortable house ... For the most part the glebe-houses have been sold off by the church authorities and are now in the hands of lay occupants, and for the most part they are of suitable size for modern needs: they have thus tended to survive ... for the most part they are very simple, very appropriate, and very well built."[1]

As previously recorded, in 1792 Dr Beaufort noted only 10 glebe-houses, to serve 41 churches in 73 parishes, in the whole of County Antrim.[2] Between 1809 and 1832 the Board of First Fruits in Dublin effected a major improvement, building some 18 new rectories, at the rate of roughly one a year. Unfortunately, all its records were destroyed in the Four Courts. But J A Pilson[3] and Samuel Lewis[4] seem to have had access to records now lost to us, and between them, provide what must be a fairly complete list: 1809, Finvoy (102), and Ramoan; 1810, Billy (104); 1812, Dunluce (105); 1813, Kilwaughter; 1814, Carnmoney; 1815, Ahoghill (106); 1816, Dunaghy; 1818, Glenavy; 1820, Connor; 1822, Kilconriola; 1824, Larne, and Killead; 1825, Aghalee (107), and Derrykeighan; 1826, Ballymoney (108); 1831, Newtowncrommelin. John Bowden, the Board's architect in Dublin, was probably responsible for most of the basic designs, but there were many local variations.

Most of these buildings were provided by the parishes with the aid of grants, or loans, or a mixture of the two, from the Board. But in some cases, clergymen of wealthy family - or with wealthy wives - laid out their own money on building. One example is Portglenone House, built by Bishop Alexander of Down and Connor (later of Meath), nephew of the first Lord Caledon, probably about 1810 (as reported by Dr O'Laverty)[5] rather than 1823 (as reported by James Boyle),[6] and subsequently lived in by his son the Rev. Robert Alexander, rector of this exceptionally rich parish, with an income of £11,000 a year. An exceedingly grand and handsome mansion, incorporating pink marble columns brought back from Rome by Frederick Hervey, Fourth Earl of Bristol and Bishop of Derry (known as "the

Earl-bishop") to Ballyscullion, it is still standing, but unhappily quite ruined by unsuitable and unsympathetic alterations both to house and surroundings, and so is not here recorded. On the other hand, Ballinderry glebe-house (113), built in 1846 by the Hon. and Rev. W S Blackwood, younger son of the third Lord Dufferin, far too large for most other clergymen, is now in lay ownership and in excellent condition.

So far as I am aware, the Presbyterian church has never had any general fund, corresponding to the Board of First Fruits, for the central provision either of churches or of manses; it was up to each congregation to provide its own. Since Presbyterian congregations were uncommonly fissiparous in the first half of the 19th century, this could cause problems, and it is not surprising to find, here again, that comparatively well-off ministers, or those who had married comparatively well-off wives, set about providing themselves with residences of their own. This procedure, however, gave rise to difficulties on the death of a minister; the widow was hardly likely to wish to relinquish to her husband's successor the home which had been paid for out of her own dowry. For much of the last century, many ministers must have lived, not in manses as such, but in lodgings, or in dwellings (sometimes quite modest) rented from members of the congregation.

Likewise, it was not until well into the second half of the 19th century that it became commonplace for parish priests to be provided with presbyteries of their own; most must have lived in rented accommodation. By degrees, as new Roman Catholic churches went up, it became the custom to accompany them with solid and durable presbyteries, usually foursquare buildings of stucco, or of red brick, sometimes polychrome. Few of these, however, are of much architectural interest; the money of the faithful mostly went into the beautification of the churches, rather than the comforts of the pastors: as many would consider right and proper.

References: 1. Craig, 'Classic Irish houses', 1976, pp 38-9. 2. Beaufort, 'Memoir of a map', 1792, p 110. 3. Pilson, 'Annals of Co Antrim', in his 'History of Belfast', 1846, passim. 4. Lewis, TD, 1837, 1840, 1847, passim. 5. O'Laverty, 'Down and Connor', III, 1884, p 367. 6. J Boyle, OSM, 1835, Antrim, VIII, p 12.

Mount Druid, Ballintoy

100. The vestry minute-book for the parish contains the following uncommonly useful entry: "There was 40 acres granted by Alexander Thomas Stewart Esq. of Acton to Revd. Robert Trail and his successors, Rectors of Ballintoy, in perpetuity, for a glebe, in the townland of Magherabuy on the 9th of August 1788. Rent £25.5.0. In May 1789 Mr Trail began to build a Glebe House and got possession of it on the 14th November 1791 - changing the name of the place from Magherabuy to Mount Druid, on account of the Druid's Temple now standing on the Glebe. 7 May 1792. Robert Trail, Rector." In fact, this is one of the best documented buildings in the county: "An excellent Glebe House lately built by Mr Traill, the incumbent" (Beaufort). "Mount Druid, the residence of the Reverend Mr Traill, the rector of the parish, is the only gentleman's seat in the parish ... The house is substantial, roomy, and 3-storeys high, and commands a fine view of the sea and Scottish Coast. There is no planting about the house" (Boyle). "A handsome mansion deriving its name from the Druidical relic on the hill above it" (Lewis). "1791: Ballintoy glebe-house erected on a glebe of 40 acres" (Pilson). Unfortunately, despite this wealth of documentation, there is nothing to say what builder, mason, carpenter or architect was involved: no payments appear in the vestry book since Mr Traill evidently paid for the house out of his own pocket. It is possible, but pure conjecture, that Henry Wynn, carpenter, of Dervock was employed here, as he was certainly employed twenty years later at the rebuilding of the parish church (38). The lack of evidence is the more regrettable if Glendun Lodge (154) and Rockport (155), both at Cushendun, are taken to be

by the same hand. According to Boyd, "The rectory-house had, through the failure of one of the gables, to be rebuilt, involving heavy expense on his successor, Rev. Henry Carter".

A remarkable house, on an extraordinarily prominent (and exposed) hillside, looking out due north across the North Channel to the cliffs of Oa on Islay. The house is of two storeys, on a generous basement, with tiny attic windows in the gables; in principle, 7 bays wide, with generous canted bays facing north - but the central face of each bay is blank - as Girvan says, "giving a very bleak effect, not inappropriate to the inhospitable position". Between the bays, a tall round-headed window lights the upper part of the staircase, an oculus above and below. The remaining windows are 15-pane Georgian-glazed. There are six chimney-pots on each stack: the doorcase in the square porch in the entrance front facing south is modern. All in very good order.

The Rev. Traill, son of the Rev. Robert Traill of Forfarshire, was rector of Ballintoy for 65 years, from 1777 until his death at Mount Druid aged 87 in 1842. He was no mean character; I have heard it said that every time a baby was born in the parish, whatever its parents' denomination, he sent his coachman and carriage to bring it to him to be christened. Boyd has another, perhaps more charitable, version of this story: "He spent the last ten years of his ministry in bed at Mount Druid. The only part of the duty he could perform was christening infants, and many a Ballintoy parishioner used to boast 'I was christened in the oul' rector's bed'".

In 1817 Atkinson was greatly impressed by the success

of his authoritarian regime: "Without any other physician than this priest, these good people have contrived to spin out their lives to the age of 80, 100 and even 110 years; and without a single lawyer ... How is it that they have lived so long without priests, lawyers and physicians, we beg them to explain ... for undoubtedly it is an anomaly in the history of Europe - indeed the record of this parish ought to be placed in the museums of that quarter of the world, as a philosophical curiosity."!

Photograph: Michael O' Connell.
Situation: 2 Ballinlea Road, Ballintoy; td, Magheraboy; Parish, Ballintoy; District Council, Moyle; Grid ref. D 034 442.
References: Listed, B1. Vestry minute-book in the care of the Rector; D A Beaufort, 'Tour', 1807, p 23; Ms 4033 in TCD Library; Williamson, map, 1808; Atkinson, 'Ireland exhibited', 1823, II, p 226-8; J Boyle, OSM, 1835, Antrim, IX, p 15; Lewis, TD, 1837, I, p 119; Pilson, 'History of Belfast', 1846, p 147; Girvan, 'North Antrim', UAHS, 1972, p 32; H A Boyd, in 'Northern Constitution', 8 April 1978.

Farmhill, Carrickfergus

101. Rather a handsome stucco house on the slope of the Knockagh hill beside Woodburn Glen; of about 1795: probably enlarged at various dates: "old house, and new house", together valued at £18.16.9 in 1836.

"Farm Hill, the residence of Stewart Dunn Esq., is pleasantly situated ... It is a small but neat residence situated in a lawn of about 6 acres which is trimly planted"; and: "Farm Hill is of the cottage form and is situated near the Knockagh on the Woodburn Road. Part of it is a 2-storey house and part 1-storey. It was built about 45 years ago by the Rev. John Savage, a Presbyterian minister. Ten years ago the present proprietor Stewart Dunn purchased it" (Boyle, 1838). John Savage, aged 26, was ordained at Carrickfergus in 1783, and died at Farmhill in 1822.

An L-shaped house, 2 storey, 3 bays deep, each section framed in pilasters. There is a central portico with Tuscan columns: the front door-step, a slab of slate nicely inscribed "In the morning Hope, in the evening Peace", apparently commissioned about 1970 by the then owner,

Jack Ross, from Robert Hart of Carnmoney, stonemason. It is said to have been at one time a rectory; to have been occupied by the army during the 1939-45 war; and to have been bought by Mr Ross, an ebullient small builder, thereafter. It was acquired from his estate by the present owners in 1975. An agreeable ground plan of the house and grounds which they found in the attics is unfortunately undated and unsigned, as well as being much faded, but gives an idea of the layout of the place in the middle years of the 19th century.

Photograph: Michael O' Connell.
Situation: 116, Upper Woodburn Road, Carrickfergus; td, Middle Division; Parish, and District Council, Carrickfergus; Grid ref. J 389 88.
References: Not listed; not in conservation area. OS map, 1832; VAL 1B/187, p 127, in PRONI; J Boyle, OSM, 1839-40, Carrickfergus, as yet unpublished; Ms Presbyterian Fasti in Linen Hall Library; map in house; information from owner.

Finvoy Lodge (formerly The Glebe), Finvoy

102. "There was no glebe-house in Finvoy till very lately ... in 1809 a glebe of 10 acres of land was procured from Mrs Strettel of Dublin, and Sampson Moore, Esq., upon moderate terms: upon this a house and offices were built by the writer of this account, which cost £760, and which are considered as handsome and well-finished, as any buildings belonging to the church in this country."

"The Glebe, the residence of the Reverend Richard Waddy, perpetual curate of the parish, is situated in the Glebe townland, about 1 and ¹/₂ mile south of the church. The house is plain and 2-storey high, and was erected in 1809 by the Board of First Fruits at a cost of 760 pounds" (Boyle). Lewis said in 1837 that there was no glebe house, but corrected himself in the edition of 1847: "The glebe house was built in 1810, at a cost of £500, of which £450 was a gift, and £50 a loan, from the Board of First Fruits".

Prominently sited on a hill-top, this rather handsome house stands on a basement, now well lit by two quadrant-shaped areas flanking the six steps up to the front door: so that, from near at hand, it seems to be of three storeys not two. The porch has the remains of pilasters. The front is of three bays, the (later) return another three bays. The house was valued at only £7.2.0 in 1834, before the addition of this return. The windows are Georgian-glazed, the walls are of well-painted stucco with strongly emphasised quoins - double quoins where the old house and the extension meet; a round-headed window at the side lights the staircase. There are four emphatic chimney-stacks.

It does not seem to be remembered when the church sold this building : there is a slightly later house, also with a glebe-like look though now a residential home, just opposite the church. The present owners, whose restoration work is nearing completion, acquired the house from a Mr Henderson in 1978; before that, it belonged to a Mr Hale.

Photograph: Michael O' Connell.
Situation: 211 Finvoy Road; td, Glebe; Parish, Finvoy; District Council, Ballymoney; Grid ref. C 958 167.
References: Not listed. Rev. J Grier, curate, in Mason, 'Statistical account', I, 1814, p 393; OS map, 1833; VAL 1B/158B, p 75, in PRONI; J Boyle, OSM, Antrim, 1835, VIII, p 71; Lewis, TD, 1837, I, p 631; 1847, I, p 618; information from owners.

Craigmore, Aghagallon

103. Whilst never, strictly speaking, a clergy dwelling, this is a remarkable bastion of Methodism: the clump comprises a little chapel of 1845, a long double house, extensive ranges of outbuildings, an elegant square brick mill chimney, and a sort of baroque two-storey blackstone stable (now garage) with bell-turret and clock, formerly accommodating four stands and two loose-boxes.

This was for several generations the home of the Shillingtons, a Methodist family, still prominent in Northern Ireland, which came to Ireland from Herefordshire around 1675. The house to the left, with semi-circular fanlight, was originally probably a single-storey cottage, later "riz and slated"; the house to the right, with segmental fanlight, was added somewhat later as a dower-house, beneath the same roofline: so the white-washed facade ends up with six triple windows above, four below (those on the left-hand house being apparently modern replacements, those on the right-hand house perhaps original), plus two doorcases with fanlights and sidelights, that to the right being the later and the more ornate.

Fagan, in 1838, reports - "the Methodists have class meetings weekly at different farmhouses throughout the parish. Mr. Henry Shillington of Ballymacilrany, a farmer, is the principal class leader". Hand-loom weaving was also extensively carried on in the district, and this seems to have been an important collection point. Moreover, it appears that Shillington actually manufactured linen here. "Weaving of linen, cotton, and cambric is carried on to a wide extent by the small farmers and cottier class residing in this parish. Cambric weavers particularly are more numerous here than in any of the parishes before

described. There are some diaper weavers also here. These trades are in great measure the support and comfort of those who pursue them, particularly the cottier class." The chapel stands just beside the house: roughcast, with quoins, originally white-washed, it has round-headed Georgian-glazed windows on either side of the (later) porch, and in one side wall.

In 1835, Henry Shillington's house, offices, and kiln were classified 1B and valued at £5.4.9; by 1859, the house of Henry Shillington senior had been reclassified 1A - "a nice house" and revalued at £9.10.0, whilst the new house of Henry Shillington junior, next door, was valued at £22.0.0; and the adjacent "Wesley Chapel", though exempt, was valued at £8.

Having prospered greatly, the Shillingtons removed to Belfast in 1902, when they gave the house to the Belfast Central Mission for an orphanage, and the land was by degrees sold off. The orphanage closed in 1937; a local farmer, James Martin, bought the place for a mere £400; his son resold about 1948; the present owners have been in occupation since 1951.

The history - social, agricultural, commercial, manufacturing and religious - of this unusual group would well repay study in much greater depth.

Photographs: Michael O' Connell.
Situation: 18 and 20, Hollow Road, Aghagallon; td, Ballymacilrany; Parish, Aghagallon; District Council, Craigavon; Grid ref. J 118 661.
References: Not listed. T Fagan, OSM, 1838, Antrim, VII, p 21; VAL 1B/165A, p 20, and VAL 2B/1/54, in PRONI; information from B Mackey, Lisburn Museum.

Glebe House, Billy

104. "The glebe-house was built in 1810 by the Rev. J Babington, vicar, aided by a gift of £350 and a loan of £450 from The Board of First Fruits" (Lewis). "Billy Glebe, the residence of the Rev. Archdeacon Creery, rector of the parish: the house consists of a basement and 2 upper storeys, and is situated close to the parish church. There is a small confined lawn with a few trees" (Boyle). In 1833, occupied by Archdeacon Stuart, valued in category 1A at a total of £17.4.7; in 1858, described as "house small, but in good repair," reduced to £15, in the occupation of Archdeacon James Smith. A handsome old 2¹/₂ storey-on-basement house, with central bow containing the entrance, at a curious midway point between basement level and ground floor level, and staircase: a fine pair of doorcases leading to drawing room and dining room on a kind of plinth beyond the front door. The windows all Georgian-glazed; roughcast walls painted a pale grey with white trim; two large chimney stacks at the gable-ends; all well restored and in very good order.

Between the house and the church (1815, cost £1200), the remains of another much more modest building, possibly outbuildings, but perhaps the earlier rectory of the much older church here: small-paned windows, rubble walls and a heavy stone outside staircase leading to the upper floor (see page 119). There is also a splendid antique hand-pump. Sold by the Church to its present owner c. 1988.

Photographs: Michael O' Connell.
Situation: 5, Old Cabragh Road, Billy, Bushmills; td, Glebe; Parish, Billy; District Council, Moyle; Grid ref. C 957 383.
References: Listed B. J Boyle, OSM, 1835, Antrim, V, p 46; VAL 1B/138, p 81, and VAL 2B/1/25A, p 66, in PRONI; Lewis, TD, 1837, I, p 206; Pilson, 'History of Belfast' , 1846, p 153; Girvan, 'North Antrim', UAHS, 1972, p 28; Pierce and Coey, 'Taken for granted' , 1984, p 115.

Dunluce (Old) Rectory, Bushmills

105. "The glebe, a very neat and comfortable residence of the Reverend James Morewood, rector of the parish, is situated near the church. The house is roomy, 2-storey, well built and kept in the nicest order. It was erected in 1814 by the Board of First Fruits. Mr Morewood has since expended 700 pounds in improving and enlarging it, 500 pounds of that sum he obtained as a gift and 200 pounds as a loan from the Board. There is a neat little lawn and some planting in front of the house" (Boyle). Pilson says in 1812; so does Lewis.

"The glebe house was built by a gift of £400 and a loan of £300 from the late Board of First Fruits, in 1812" (Lewis). Apparently built (or rebuilt) by the Rev. Charles McDaniel Stewart, vicar of Dunluce from 1804 to 1826: he named it apparently after the Stewart property of Rockfield, Co. Roscommon. A rather plain two-storey over basement cement-rendered house, now five bays wide but originally probably only three; Georgian-glazed with six-over-three-pane windows upstairs, long nine-over-six-pane windows below; later porch with fanlight and reeded pilasters; the chimney-stacks at the ends of the original roof, leaving the gable of the extension looking rather bare. Sold by the Church of Ireland to the present owner in 1986, when a new bungalow was built for the rector on part of the "neat lawn".

Photograph: Michael O' Connell.
Situation: Priestland Road, Bushmills; td, Glebe; Parish, Dunluce; District Council, Moyle; Grid ref. C 938 405.
References: Listed B1; outside conservation area. J Boyle, OSM, 1835, Antrim, V, p 110; Lewis, TD, 1837, I, p 585: Pilson, 'History of Belfast', 1846, p 154; Stewart, 'Three hundred years in Innishowen', 1929, p 307; Boyd, 'Dunluce parish', 1937, p XIV.

The Glebe, Ahoghill

106. Built in 1815, "at a cost of £1600, defrayed by the Board of First Fruits" (Pilson). "The glebe-house was built by a gift of £100 and a loan of £1500 from the late Board of First Fruits in 1815; the glebe comprises 138¹/2 acres" (Lewis, 1837). "The residence of Revd. George Kirkpatrick, Curate of the parish, is a roomy comfortable and modern 2-storey house, situated in the Glebe townland. The view from it is extensive and there is some young planting about the house" (Boyle, 1835). Boyle also reports that the parish was then, before Portglenone and Craigs were hived off, the largest in the county. In 1834, there were within it 985 Episcopalians, 12,918 Presbyterians, 4,120 Roman Catholics, 767 Moravians, and 955 other Dissenters. The rector, at Portglenone, received tithes of no less than £11,000 a year; "the curate has the Glebe House (in which he resides) and 40 acres of the glebe ... for his support",

plus a salary of £69.4s.9¹/2d. Notwithstanding his modest emoluments, the curate was provided with the most lavish wine-cellar, with the greatest number of bins, I have ever seen. In 1859, the occupier being Rev. Alfred S Lee, the valuation of house, offices and gate-lodge was increased from £20 to £30.

A very strange house indeed, now with no proper front, if indeed it ever had one: the original front door was removed and a porch built in the early 19th century; but the front door then inserted is now a lavatory, and the entrance is through a curious modern addendum at the opposite side of the porch. Girvan describes it as "an attractive double pile, two-storey house; harled, with entrance in the gabled facade". But this is flattery; and the house has been considerably altered, not for the better, since he wrote. It has now brown-painted quoins and walls painted a surprisingly bright yellow; it is really of two tall storeys, plus attics, and large basement: the valleys of the roof have been filled in; there is an astonishing cliff-like vertical four-storey drop into the back yard. The glazing-barred windows are strangely disposed both on the front facing south-east, and on the north-west front facing the walled stable-yard. The best features of the house are interior, rather than exterior: especially the charming, almost spiral double staircase, lit by a tall round-headed window on the first landing, and a very pretty rose window on the landing above.

Bought from the church after 1945, and thereafter, until 1969, the home of Lord O' Neill of the Maine, formerly Captain Terence O'Neill, and his wife Jean who was

a distinguished gardener; considerable mementos of her handiwork survive, though the house is now concealed from the road by a thick screen of woodland. Most of the alterations made after his day by Mr Samuel Getty who lived here from 1970 until 1985.

Photograph: Michael O' Connell.
Situation: 55 Glebe Road, Ahoghill; td, Glebe; Parish, Ahoghill; District Council, Ballymena; Grid ref. J 049 997.
References: Not listed. J Boyle, OSM, 1835, Antrim, VIII, pp 12, 16; Lewis, TD, 1837, I, p 24; PG, I, 1845, p 26; Pilson, 'History of Belfast', 1846, p 155; VAL 2B/1/68 in PRONI; Girvan, 'Antrim & Ballymena', UAHS, 1969, p 29.

The Rectory, Aghalee

107. Dating from 1826, an excellent example of the classic Irish late-Georgian clergy-house of this period: and, for once, still used for the purpose for which it was built.

"The house was completed 1826, cost of building and other appendages £687 ... a very neat commodious house and eligibly situated for a gentleman's residence ... the house is nearly a square building 2-storeys high and slated, with good offices ... the garden is neatly laid off" (Fagan 1838). "1826: the glebe-house of Aghalee, Aghanless, or Soldierstown erected, on a glebe of thirteen acres, valued at £12.8.6 per annum" (1846). The glebe-house and out-buildings valued at £14.1.6 in 1834, at £16 in 1859, on both occasions occupied by Rev. Robert Hill.

Set back in a good garden, with mature trees and a satisfying carriage-sweep served by two stone gateways, a two-storey-on-basement three-bay roughcast house with a hipped roof and three proportionable chimney-stacks. The wooden doorcase, with radial fanlight and side-lights, stands at the head of five broad steps.

Photograph: Michael O' Connell.
Situation: Soldierstown Road, Aghalee; td, Killough; Parish, Aghalee; District Council, Lisburn; Grid ref. J 133 637.
References: Listed B1. Lewis, TD, 1837, I, p 16; T Fagan, OSM, 1838, Antrim, VIII, p 31; Pilson, 'History of Belfast' , 1846, p 159; VAL 1B/166, p 12, and VAL 2B/1/58B, p 79, in PRONI.

The Rectory, Ballymoney

108. A rather out-of-the ordinary foursquare rectory, according to Lewis built at a cost of £2278, of which £1384 was a loan from the Board of First Fruits in 1826, though it looks a good deal later: this time built not of stone or of stucco but of uncommonly pleasing variegated red bricks, with stone string-course and porch: Georgian-glazed to the front, and the side facing the church, four Victorian-glazed windows at the rear: surprisingly, four bays to the back, three bays to the front; all two-storey, with a lower service wing at the side. The roof is hipped, with very wide over-sailing eaves and two chimney stacks in the middle. Inside, tall rooms, a good staircase in the late-Georgian tradition, and some 1840'ish plasterwork; all the original fireplaces have unfortunately been replaced. Valued at £40.6.4, in category 1A, in 1844, when in the occupation of the Rev. Dean Greene.

Of the ground-floor-front windows, no less than three - the two tall windows flanking the porch, and one of the two in the west wall - are false; that is to say, bricked-up, plastered, and painted black behind the sashes, which are nonetheless glazed and complete, externally most deceptive. This has given rise to the legend that they were blocked up to avoid liability to window-tax. This seems highly unlikely, for window-tax was never as great a problem in Ireland as in England. When it was first introduced as a war-time measure in 1799, over a century after the tax's introduction in England, the first seven windows of every dwelling were exempt in Ireland, as against the first six in England. The tax appears to have fallen most heavily on shopkeepers, clerks, and members of the newly emerging lower middle class; it is unlikely to have had any effect on the design of an expensive rectory such as this. In any case, Section 3 of the 1799 Act imposed a fine of £20, and the pay-

ment of double duty, on any person who should, for the purpose of evading the duty, conceal any window; and a Notice of the Excise Commissioners, published in 1818, required that, to avoid liability, "Windows or Lights shall be stopped up with the like materials as the wall or roof is composed of", which does not here seem to be the case. It seems more probable that a later occupier found the north- and west-facing rooms too cold and draughty, and, along with other alterations made in the mid-19th century, turned the house round so as to make better use of the south-facing rooms. The tax was abolished, both in England and in Ireland, in 1851, after unsuccessful

attempts to secure its repeal earlier at the end of the Napoleonic wars on grounds of public health.

Photographs: Michael O'Connell.
Situation: Off Queen Street, Ballymoney; td, Glebe; Parish and District Council, Ballymoney; Grid ref. C 948 258.
References: Listed B, with tentative attribution to Thomas Jackson, which cannot be right; outside conservation area. Irish Statutes, 1799, cap XV; BNL, 12 August, 1818; Hansard 'Parliamentary debates', XL, 5 May 1819, col 134; 'The Irishman', 28 December 1821, 19 April 1822, D 120/1, VAL 1B/142/C, pp 103, 119, all in PRONI; OS map, 1830; Lewis, TD, 1847, I, p 144; Hamilton, 'Ballymoney', 1957, p 94; Pierce and Coey, 'Taken for granted', 1984, p 115; N Jackson, in 'Construction history', 1992, pp 55-67.

109. Quite close to the road but completely hidden by its trees, a very pleasant, and quite unspoiled, late-Georgian house: 3-bay, 2 storeys and attic windows in the gables, roughcast painted grey, original Georgian glazing complete; radial fanlight at the front door, mouth-organ fanlight at the back door. The chimney-stacks have been rebuilt using squared stone blocks, and there is much stonework in the unusual sunken garden at the front of the house and in the banks of the avenue leading to the farm outbuildings.

According to James Boyle, writing his fair sheets between July and November 1839, "Revd John Stuart is 9 years in the parish and is the first Orthodox minister. His income is 75 pounds per annum, regium donum Irish, and 58 pounds 16 s per annum; collection in the meeting house amounts to about 30 pounds per annum. His hearers consist of 360 families, making 1,714 individuals ... his residence is in a good 2-storey house, slated, about 100 perches above the village. It was built in 1839 at his own expense."

However, it may be earlier, for both house and plantings appear to be shown on the Ordnance Survey map of 1832. Mr Stuart was ordained into Ballycarry on 3rd April 1832, aged 33, at a time of passionate schism, and served there as minister for 49 years, dying "at his residence, Temple Corran, in 1880." "The wave of popular excitement which spread over the province broke in its strength over Ballycarry. The Minister of the congregation, the Rev Mr Glendy, had joined the Arian party, while some members of the Session warmly espoused the evangelical cause. One of them seized the communion vessels, and crying "Whoever is on the Lord's side, follow me," left the old ancestral meeting house to form, with others, a new congregation, of which Mr Stuart was the first minister ... Sectarian feeling ran so high in the neighbourhood at the time, that on the night of his ordination a musket-shot was fired into his

Templecorran House, Ballycarry

sitting-room; but fortunately he had a little before retired to rest, and so escaped." In 1861, still occupied by Mr Stuart, the house was valued at £15.10.0, in category 1A.

The house passed from Mr Stuart to Gordons; then to a Miss Adrain; then, some 70 years ago, to the family who still own and occupy it.

Photograph: Michael O'Connell.
Situation: 47, Manse Road, Ballycarry; td, North West Ballycarry; Parish, Templecorran; District Council, Larne; Grid ref. J 440 941.
References: Listed B. OS map, 1832; J Boyle, OSM, 1839, Antrim, X, p 129; VAL 2B/1/16, p 28, in PRONI; Ms Presbyterian Fasti in Linen Hall Library; 'Presbyterian churchman', 1880, pp 76-78.

Boulderstone House, Templepatrick

110. A handsome south-facing Georgian house, tucked away behind the parish church which it embraces between its front and back drives. The church was built in 1827, this vicarage or glebe-house five years later. Valued at a modest £13, classified 1A, in 1835. "The residence of Rev. Hammond Dawson, the curate of the parish, is situated immediately adjoining the eastern side of Templepatrick. It is a neat and modern-looking two-storey house erected in 1832. Mr Dawson rents it with ten acres of land from Lord Templeton", and: "Mr McCartney the Vicar of the parish receives from it £400 tithes and the curate Mr Dawson has £69 per year" (1836).

Although the church and parsonage were built by Lord Templeton, the presentment rested with Lord Donegall, who chose first George Macartney, Vicar of Antrim, then his son Rev. Arthur Chichester Macartney (who had fought as an artillery officer both at the battle of Antrim, and in the Napoleonic Wars): the latter was Vicar of Templepatrick from 1813, and of Belfast also from 1820, until his death in 1843. In winter, he lived in Belfast; in summer, at New Lodge (137), just up the road at Muckamore; and for most of this time, the episcopalian needs of this very Presbyterian parish were served by Mr Dawson, a younger son of the Castledawson family, who, however, did not pursue his career in the church. A subsequent Vicar, Mr Adair, seems to have preferred to live in his family home nearby at Loughanmore; so the glebe-house was let out to a succession of tenants by the Templetons, who finally disposed of it early in the 20th century.

There is a tradition that the free standing building now used as a garage was built as a court-room: if so, it must have housed the manor court of Ballylinney, whose seat was in Templepatrick.

"Near the pound on the farm of the Rev. Hammond Dawson" an enormous boulder known locally as "the Boulderstone", and formerly as "The Gray Stone", is said to have been at some date a place of burial; it is also said to have formerly stood upright; but in 1978 Brian Williams of the Archaeological Survey described it as "undoubtedly a glacial erratic". It is unclear whether the house is named for this stone, or from the thick rubble walls, now harled, of which it is built.

The entrance front is half-heartedly castellated, asymmetrical, and incorporates a half-round Gothick-glazed window and a straightforward fanlight over the front door. The garden front is much more elegant - basically of three bays, but with a wide two-storey bow with triple windows above and below, divided externally by curious cylindrical columns with square blocks at top and bottom; internally, by nicely proportioned and reeded columns. There have been various extensions, including a Victorian canted bay and a modern conservatory. The garden is attractive and contains trees evidently of considerable antiquity, though in 1838 "There are no trees about it, nor ornamental grounds of any extent".

Early in this century, the house seems to have been a girls' school, with bars on all the windows, whether to keep the girls in, or the boys out. The last incumbent to live there seems to have been a Mr Deacon (curate from 1865, vicar from 1874 to 1893). Since then, the property has passed through several hands to the present owners.

Photograph: Michael O'Connell.
Situation: Set back off Antrim Road, Templepatrick; td, Parish, Templepatrick; District Council, Antrim; Grid ref. J 227 855.
References: Not listed. J Boyle and J Bleakly, OSM, 1836, 1838, Templepatrick, as yet unpublished; VAL 1B/129/A, p 17, in PRONI; M H F Collis, in UJA, 2nd series, III, 1897, p 91; 'Clergy of Connor', 1993; information from Rev. Moore.

Carncairn Lodge (formerly Glencairn House), Broughshane

111. According to H C Lawlor, the Brown family "was seated in the mid 17th century at Kenbally, a mile or so north west of Broughshane ... the family later built the fine old Georgian house of Glencairn lying east of Broughshane. Here in 1715, was born William Brown" who "apparently developed the [linen] business left him by his father and, some time after the death of John White of Whitehall in 1760, leased the Whites' bleachworks there." Some parts of Glencairn may be incorporated in the present house, or its U-shaped outbuildings at the rear.

It is now an almost square, slightly boxy, five-bay, two-storey house, the walls cream-painted roughcast, with wide over-sailing eaves and a hipped roof topped by a pair of modern chimney-stacks containing seven chimneys. The windows are Georgian-glazed, 3-over-3-pane sashes upstairs, 6-over-6-pane sashes below. The doorcase and fanlight are neither circular nor segmental, on the contrary, they are ever-so-slightly pointed: possibly hinting at an ecclesiastical connection.

In fact, the house in its present form was built by the Rev. William Crawford, curate from 1815 and rector of Skerry from 1825 until 1869. In 1799, following the rising of the United Irishmen, the last of the Browns to live here had emigrated to America, and Glencairn passed into the ownership of the O'Neills of Shane's Castle, along with Tullymore House (whose boundaries march with those of Glencairn). They are reputed to have used it as a shooting lodge, but in 1829 the rector, who came of a wealthy

Belfast merchant family, married Miss Armanilla Wilson of Ballycastle and set about rebuilding the house under lease from the O'Neills. By 10 April 1833 Mr Crawford was certainly in occupation, for a certificate of that date states that, within the previous 12 months, he had planted a total of over 14,000 trees on the 63 acres he had leased from Lord O'Neill; and Lieutenant Boteler, writing in the same year, says that he "has built an extensive house in Carnkeine townland". Two years later, James Boyle lists amongst the gentlemen's seats of Skerry "Glencairn in the townland of Carnkeeran, the residence of the Rev. William Crawford." Mr Crawford lived on until 1881, his second wife died in 1882, and his son William Crawford junior, a Belfast stockbroker, seems to have gone bankrupt in that same year. In 1883, William Cathcart is shown as occupier in the valuation list - "a farmer's house" - in whose family it remained until 1934. Since then it has belonged to the Reade family.

Just when and why the name of the house was changed from Glencairn House to Carncairn Lodge does not seem to be known.

Photograph: Michael O' Connell.
Situation: 40, Carnlough Road, Broughshane; td, Carnkeeran; Parish, Skerry; District Council, Ballymena; Grid ref. D 165 073.
References: Listed B1. VAL 1B 15A and B, TI809/252, VAL 2B/1/4C, VAL 12B/3/7A, all in PRONI; R Boteler, OSM, 1833, and J Boyle, 1835, Antrim, IV, pp 107, 111; H C Lawlor, in 'Fibres and fabrics journal', September 1941, p 5; Girvan, 'West Antrim' , UAHS, 1970, p 30.

Ballyhamage House, Doagh

112. This bizarre house has an appropriately bizarre history to account for its strange lop-sided appearance.

James Boyle of the Ordnance Survey did not approve of the Rev. George H Johnston, the rector from 1814 to 1864, nor of this house, Mr Johnston's private property: "A small and by no means neat-looking two-storey house, the occasional residence" of the rector: "there is a trifling lawn attached to it". This survives as a harled and whitewashed five-bay two-storey farmhouse of the better sort, perhaps late 18th-century, with heavy grey-painted architraves round the windows. Elsewhere, Boyle reprobated the absenteeism of Mr Johnston, a clergyman of private means who had married his cousin, Lady Anne Maria Annesley, and who preferred to live in his far grander house at Ballywillwill near Castlewellan. He had some excuse, for Kilbride was a very Presbyterian parish where members of the Church of Ireland were few, and tithes were bitterly resented and ill to collect. The only church was at Donegore and out of repair, and there was no rectory.

Mr Johnston decided in 1853 to give his bishop a nice surprise by building a new church, at his own expense, next door. This is a taller building of squared basalt, with granite dressings, and round-headed windows above and below: incongruous, but not of itself unpleasing. Having completed it, he invited Bishop Mant to consecrate it, but the bishop was furious, and refused first because he had not been consulted, and second because there was a direct communication through the wall into the house next door!

It was licensed for use only as a chapel of ease. In 1862, the valuer noted "A very odd-looking concern - part like a factory. Was let at £75" but valued the buildings at £35.

On Mr Johnston's death, aged 90, his successor, nephew and curate, Mr Young, built the new church outside Doagh; and on his death, the house, church, church furnishings and 21 acres of land were sold by auction. Since then, the house has been owned in turn by the Clements and Catherwood families, by whom by degrees, the intended church has been well and truly laicised. The "church" has been divided horizontally: the lower part of chancel and nave are now a roomy drawing-room; the vestry is a bar; most astonishing, the upper part of the building now accommodates a charming octangular bedroom with ornate ceiling and some strange combinations of curves and angles, and a lesser bedroom.

A further addition to the side of the church houses an indoor swimming-pool, and two of the polychrome geometrical stained glass windows designed for the church have been reinstalled so as to protect the privacy of the swimmers. Windows and doorcases have been much altered; but some fine original features survive.

Photograph: Michael O' Connell.
Situation: 43, Burn Road, Doagh; td, Ballyhamage; Parish, Doagh; District Council, Newtownabbey; Grid ref. J 254 890.
References: Not listed. J Boyle, OSM, 1839, Antrim, XI, p 139; VAL 2B/1/8B, p 2, in PRONI; Cox, 'Kilbride', 1959, p 15; Girvan, 'West Antrim', UAHS, 1970, p 18.

The Glebe, Upper Ballinderry

113. "Until the year 1846 there was no glebe house in the parish; but about that time, during the incumbency of the Hon. and Rev. W S Blackwood, the present glebe-house, which is one of the most commodious in the diocese, was built on 8 acres of glebe land" (1886). Mr Blackwood was a younger son of the third Baron Dufferin and Clandeboye, and could no doubt apply private means to the cost of building a better-than-ordinary glebe house. No longer so used: bought about 1940 by R H Gibson, an architect of some distinction, trained by and later in partnership with Henry Seaver, who had designed the War Memorial Hall at Ballinderry (224) fifteen years earlier. Acquired from him by the present owners in 1989.

An exceptionally grand rectory - it could well be a deanery, or a bishop's palace - two-storey on (invisible) basement, probably by Thomas Turner, who was working in the office of Charles Lanyon, the diocesan architect, at this date; and who employed the same rather unusual ornament, a vertical recessed panel containing overlapping discs or paterae, in his Northern Bank in Derry twenty years later. Rather surprisingly, described as "very neat but not large" by the valuer in 1861, who valued it at £33

and classified it 1A. No other records seem to survive in any of the usual places. Of cream-painted stucco with a hipped oversailing roof carried on twinned brackets; two chimney-stacks close together. The entrance, south-facing, is through a large square porch with the panels of overlapping paterae above vermiculated quoins. The west front has a triple window in a curved bay - the sashes themselves are prettily curved - and another triple window with console brackets to the morning-room beyond. The east front, of three bays, is plain. There are three-storey offices in the return at the rear. Internally, the detailing is fine, though Mr Gibson appears to have made some changes, especially to the very successful arrangements for rooflighting to landing and mezzanine.

Photograph: Michael O'Connell.
Situation: At No. 126 Lower Ballinderry Road, Upper Ballinderry; td, Brackenhill; Parish, Ballinderry; District Council, Lisburn; Grid ref. J 169 671.
References: Listed B. Ewart, 'Down & Connor & Dromore', 1886, p 61; account of R H Gibson, in IB, 29 August 1931, p 753; Pierce and Coey, 'Taken for granted', 1984, p 120.

Old Manse, Portrush

114. A comfortable-looking blackstone building with very strong cream-painted quoins, label mouldings, chimney-stacks, and curly Dutch gables with knops: and corner porch. A panel in the porch parapet is incised with the date, 1850. The adjacent church was apparently designed in 1843-4 by John Williamson, a builder-architect who was also a member of the congregation. The energetic minister, Rev. Jonathan Simpson, collected around £600 in America to pay for the manse. However, Mr Simpson had by then fallen out with Williamson over the bill for the church; the dispute was eventually submitted to the arbitration of an un-named "Belfast architect who was surveyor to the Town Council". Might this have been Charles Lanyon, the County Surveyor to the Grand Jury? Might Mr Simpson then have asked him to draw plans for the manse? Although not very subtle, the manse is somewhat reminiscent of the work of Lanyon in his Jacobethan mood; and the conjecture is an attractive one.

The building was enlarged about 1860. No longer used as a manse, now the Old Manse Guest House.

Photograph: Michael O' Connell.
Situation: Main Street, Portrush; td, Port Rush; Parish, Ballywillin; District Council, Coleraine; Grid ref. C 858 406.
References: Listed B. Simpson, 'Annals of my life' , 1895, p 248; Girvan, 'North Antrim', UAHS, 1972, pp 9, 10; Mullin, 'Presbytery of Coleraine', 1979, pp 149, 150.

Old Rectory, Glenarm

115. A large and handsome yellow-painted mid Victorian stuccoed building, in a vaguely Jacobethan style, beautifully sited on a steep slope so as to look across and down the glen. 1858, restored as a private house by Hector McDonnell MCMXC (datestone over front door). Probably built without benefit of architect by the Antrim estate workmen who had learned their trade at Glenarm Castle working under the Morrisons. In 1859, the residence of the Rev. Hugh Waddell, in category 1A, "would set for £21" per annum, valued at £19.5.0. An earlier rectory must have stood on the same site, for on 1st September 1835, John Barrow "took up his quarters at the abode of the Rev. Ross Jebb", the rector; "the parsonage-house with the glebe-land stands beautifully at the head of the valley, in one of the most lovely situations imaginable, commanding a complete view of the town, the castle and its demesne, and the sea. In looking down from this elevated spot, the castle is seen apparently embosomed in the wood at the bottom of the glen, and forms a striking and

picturesque object which, with the blue expanse of sea beyond it, and a distant view of the coast of Scotland, when the sky is clear, presents a picture which the most fastidious cannot, I think, but admire". The house is new, the views remain equally striking.

A two-storey house, the upper windows part-dormers, all the windows round-headed irregularly arranged singly, in pairs, or in threes, mostly with dripstones above. Internally, drawing room with coved corners, and in this and other rooms a number of elements derived from other houses - including Mount Panther, Clandeboye, and the Saltbox near Ballycastle - incorporated in the course of the restoration. Studio in the outbuildings in the rear.

Photograph: Michael O' Connell.
Situation: Munie Road, Glenarm; td, Glenarm Demesne; Parish, Glenarm; District Council, Larne; Grid ref. D 297 133.
References: Not listed. Datestone; records in library of RCB; Barrow, 'Tour round Ireland', 1836, p 57; VAL 2B/1/41A, p 130, in PRONI.

CHAPTER FIVE

MIDDLING-SIZED HOUSES

As Maurice Craig remarks, "the 'big house' of Irish traditional ways is not always very large: the term denotes the fact that it was the house of a substantial, and usually resident, landowner, rather than its mere size. As well as these 'big houses' there were and are considerable numbers of houses, built or lived in by minor gentry or prosperous farmers, or by manufacturers and traders, or occupied as dower houses, agent's houses or as glebe houses".[1] It is of this category (glebe-houses apart) that I treat in this chapter.

In County Antrim, many of these middling houses are associated with water-powered mills - often beetling-mills, sometimes corn-mills - and so it is not surprising that they are most frequent in the valleys of the Bann, Bush, Lagan, Main, Straid, Kells Water, Six Mile Water, and numerous lesser rivers or rivulets. But there is no great difference between the houses of mill-owners and the houses of strong farmers, except, perhaps, for a tendency towards hipped roofs at the gentry end of the scale, a tendency towards gabled roofs at the other end. Over a period of a century and a half, from around 1720 to around 1870, there is remarkably little change in house-forms, materials, and building methods. This makes it exceptionally hard to date these buildings with confidence. Documentary evidence is all too rare, and not always either wholly reliable, or altogether free from ambiguity.

The people of Antrim are in many ways a conservative race, and certainly, until quite recently, very conservative regarding the forms and structures of their houses. There is a close relationship between the houses of this county and those across the narrow sea in lowland Scotland: as Maurice Craig says, "It has been shown that Irish designers used the plates of William Adam the elder ... but houses in Scotland, and their counterparts in Ireland, resemble each other much more than either of them resembles the Adam plates. Irish buildings of the period not only are solid; they have also, and very markedly, the appearance of solidity; climate, geology, economics and temperament were to ensure that this would hold good right down to the frontiers of the vernacular manner, and beyond."[2]

Very few, if any, of these houses were built with benefit of architect, though pattern-books may very occasionally have been consulted. It is remarkable that, despite considerable efforts, I have been unable to discover the name of the architect, or even builder, of a single one of the houses described in this chapter before the closing years of the 19th century. The names of a few mysterious individuals described as "architect" do, it is true, turn up in deeds or lists of residents for quite small towns; there were apparently four in Ballymena so early as in 1835; but I know of no instance in which a particular building can be attributed with any confidence to one of them. As the Ordnance Survey Memoir-writers put it in 1834, "Though a good many wealthy people reside in or near the town of Ballymena ... the style of country house in the neighbourhood is small, snug and boxy"[3] - in contrast to some of the ostentatious palaces now to be seen in this vicinity!

Probably most of these houses were the work of experienced builders, employing skilled craftsmen - bricklayer, stonemason, joiner, slater, cabinet-maker even - as requisite. But plainly some people just set to and built their own houses with their own hands. One uncommonly well-documented example is the Cairn, Aghalee (180), whose builder, Robert Best, left a meticulous account of the cost of all the materials he used between May, 1853 and September, 1855. Another and more unusual example is the last house in the chapter, the house at Ballintoy (186) built for himself by the eccentric "professor" Newton Penprase.

Appearances can be very deceptive. Most people have an image of the traditional Irish farmhouse and cottage as being harled or roughcast, and then trimly white-washed; whilst the big houses of the gentry were of cut stone. The evidence, however, seems to point the other way. In 1812, Wakefield writes of the "neat white-washed houses belonging to opulent manufacturers and merchants of Belfast" along the "whole northern shore of Belfast Lough".[4] According to the Ordnance Survey Memoirs, many great houses - including Castle Dobbs (70), Castle Upton (68) and Shane's Castle - were whitewashed even in the late 1830s; whilst old photographs show that farmhouses, mill buildings and cottages were often of unwhitened fieldstones: though, as Alan Gailey points out, the availability of limestone must also have affected the distribution of white-washed buildings.[5] To quote Dr Craig once more, "The vast majority of Irish houses, like most other Irish buildings down to the middle of the 19th century, are built of rubble stone, the walls varying in thickness from two feet upwards according to the size of the building ... A fair amount of brick is used in rear-arches, linings, and of course vaulting; but brick as a substantive building material is rare, except in the coastal towns, before the 19th century."[6] Roman cement, sometimes tinted, seems to have come into occasional use during the first three decades of the 19th century; smooth rendering, and especially the horrible cement renders, only in the last years of the century; and it is only in the second half of the 20th century that it has (mercifully) become usual to paint over cement render as though it had been the smooth creamy stucco of the Regency.

These middling-sized houses constitute the greatest wealth of the county's built environment. Too few of them enjoy the protection of statutory listing. Too many of them have been spoiled by injudicious 'improvements' - picture windows, pebble-dash, concrete tiles, plastic doors, and so on. But there are grounds for hope: a surprising number of the new houses going up in the county are respectable imitations of the traditional ones. Indeed, when ivy has embosomed them, forest trees have grown, and the gardens have matured, it will scarcely be possible to distinguish them from the originals without going to the back to look at the plumbing. Whilst purists do not care for reproduction work, imitation remains the sincerest form of flattery; so, perhaps the genuine older houses are themselves coming to be more valued by a younger generation.

References: 1. Craig, 'Classic Irish houses', 1976, p 3. 2. Craig, op cit, p 24. 3. J Boyle, OSM, 1835, Antrim, VIII, pp 110, 121. 4. Wakefield, 'Account of Ireland', 1812, I, p 13. 5. Gailey, 'Rural houses', 1984, p 62. 6. Craig, op cit, p 15.

Doorcase, Dunore House, Aldergrove (181). Photograph: Michael O'Connell

Crookedstone, Aldergrove

116. At the end of a singularly long lane, its farmland embracing the little Dunore river, overlooking the flats running down to Lough Neagh, a remarkable survival: a two-storey five-bay still-thatched whitewashed farmhouse of 1699 (the date clearly inscribed on the front wall). Built by Patrick Cunningham; and still owned and occupied (after one interregnum) by his descendants. Glazing bars are not original; oak beams and planks survive internally; the kitchen is much as it must always have been; the addition of 1966 is not unduly obtrusive.

"The Cunninghams were settled at Crooked Stone near Antrim in the middle of the seventeenth century. Thomas Cunningham (will dated 1727) had a son Samuel who succeeded him, and by his wife Mary Thompson had ... two sons. The younger, William, inherited Lisnafillan from his wife's family, and of his four sons, Samuel Cunningham succeeded his father there, and built the works and the original house at Fenaghy; John built the bleachworks at Dunoein; David ran the bleachworks at Glarryford, and was also a partner with William in the Dromona bleach green" (Lawlor). Samuel Cunningham took a lease of lands at Crookedstone, already occupied by him, in 1739; and in 1769 John Cunningham took a lease of "the Mill of Crooked Stone commonly known as Nial Ogue's Mill" with six acres Irish, the mill dam, "and all the stripes lying up the water", with the kilns "and all other houses belonging to the said premises". The family has had extensive commercial interests, in the West Indies as well as in Ireland, in printing, newspapers and stock-broking as well as textiles, and remains a prominent and influential one in the county.

Photograph: Michael O'Connell.
Situation: Crookedstone, Ballyarnott Road, Aldergrove; td, Crookedstone; Parish, Killead; District Council, Antrim; Grid ref. J 157 822.
References: Listed B+/Q. Family records in possession of owner; D 1824/B/1/3/3/1, B/1/2/2/7, in PRONI; H C Lawlor, in 'Fibres and fabrics journal', September 1941, p 6; Girvan, 'West Antrim', UAHS, 1970, p 10; Pierce and Coey, 'Taken for granted', 1984, p 122.

Park View (formerly Mansion Farm, formerly Mill Hill), Crumlin

117. A handsome two-storey three-bay farmhouse, slated and whitewashed but ivy-clad, with wide 16-pane Georgian windows, slim 'lamb's tongue' glazing-bars, and a rectangular 'mouth-organ' fanlight.

Said to date from 1756. A lease for lives renewable for ever was accorded to one Thomas Wilson on 8 January 1738; "the Mansion Farm" was sold, most unusually in fee simple, through the Landed Estates Court in 1856 - "estate of Thomas Wilson and John Wilson" - as "a good and substantial slated dwelling house with out-offices in tolerable repair". But James, then Thomas, Wilson was shown as occupier between 1835 and 1860: and John, then Thomas Wilson in 1862: valuation category 1B. The same family has owned the farm since 1935.

Photograph: Michael O'Connell.
Situation: 21 Antrim Road, formerly Dublin Road, Crumlin; td, Dungonnell; Parish, Killead; District Council, Antrim; Grid ref. J 149 819.
References: Listed B. VAL 1B/164B, p 150, VAL 2B/1/53B, p 1, in PRONI; Landed Estate Court particulars, 1856, in possession of owner.

Ballylough House, Bushmills

118. The castle at the rear, of which only a fragment remains, was probably a seat of the MacQuillans, then of the O'Kanes. By 1641, Archibald Stewart of Ballintoy was owner of a house here. The present house was probably built by his grandson Alexander Stewart, factor to the Antrim estates, between the date of his appointment, 1720, and the date when he and his employer fell out, 1740. In the latter year, it is recorded that valuations were inspected "at Mr Stewart's office, Ballylough", and in December 1740 or January 1741, "Mr Stewart asserted that ∴ Lord Antrim had ordered his servants to seize and carry off an iron chest from Ballylough House, which contained almost all the papers relating to the management of the estate". Mr Stewart died in the following year, 1742, after "defending himself successfully at law against all the accusations of Lord Antrim". In 1789, the estate was sold by Alexander Stewart to Archdeacon Traill, for £4,300 (one of the witnesses was my forbear John Brett, solicitor, of Downpatrick); in 1792 the Archdeacon bought in the fee simple for another £340.

The house passed to the Archdeacon's son William: "Ballylough, the residence of William Traill Esquire, situated in the townland of Ballyloughmore ... the house, which is comfortable, and suited to the residence of a gentleman's family, consists of a basement and 2 upper storeys, and is prettily situated on a rising ground in a little valley. An old castle, or rather part of the ruins of one, stands near the house. There is an excellent garden and hot-house. The demesne, though not extensive, is well laid out with a good deal of young planting" (Boyle). In 1846, or perhaps earlier, William Traill removed to Dublin, and for the next twenty years the place was rented to Captain

James Hannay, late of Bath, who paid £168 per annum for the "mansion house, other gardener's and herd's house and 2 porters' lodges thereunto belonging", plus 75 acres of demesne, the bog, the avenue and the plantations. Captain Hannay was the grandfather of 'George A Birmingham', the novelist. On William Traill's death in 1875, he was succeeded by my energetic great-grandfather Dr Anthony Traill, described by Camac in 1908 as "one of our best-known public men, having always had the courage of his convictions". As Provost of Trinity College, Dublin, he provoked the undying hatred of Professor Mahaffey, and the witticism, on hearing of what was to be the Provost's last illness, "nothing trivial, I hope?"

The north-facing house is of two storeys and attic, on a substantial basement, of rubble stone encased in rendering, part creeper-covered, at one time (but no longer) yellow-washed. The front is of three bays, with triple win-

dows; the attractive castellated quadrant walls are inscribed 'AT, 1815'; it is thought that the Archdeacon added a wing at the back, and raised the roof, at about the same date. There is a most agreeable segmental bow-window in the south-facing room at the rear. The Tuscan doorcase, at the head of 7 steps, was rather unhappily removed in 1930 from its central position; in the process, it lost its pediment; at some earlier date, it had also lost the 'mouth-organ' fanlight which served to align the top of the door with the main window lintels on either side. (My grandmother never forgave this alteration, and from 1930 until her death in 1965, refused to pass over the threshold.) Internally, there is pleasant plasterwork, but the spiral staircase, tucked away just inside the original front door, is a disappointment.

The great avenue of beech trees had to be felled in 1942; the drum gate lodge on Riverside Road is in the last stages of disintegration, but the lodge on Castlecat Road is in good order and merrily painted. Ballylough is still in the ownership of Archdeacon Traill's descendants.

Photographs: Michael O'Connell; photo of c 1920 per Richard Traill.
Situation: 12 Riverside Road, Bushmills; td, Ballylough More; Parish, Billy; District Council, Moyle; Grid ref. C 948 376.
References: Listed B. Taylor and Skinner, 'Roads', 1778, p 272; Lendrick, map, 1780; J'Boyle, OSM, 1835, and T Fagan, 1839, Antrim, V, pp 45, 46, 70, 71; VAL 1B/138, p 85, VAL 2B/1/25A, p 53, and title deeds in D 4081/1/1, all in PRONI; Hill, 'Macdonnells of Antrim', 1873, p 67; Hill, 'Stewarts of Ballintoy', 1865, pp 51, 52; Camac, 'Derrykeighan parish', 1908, p 68; Young, 'Belfast and province of Ulster', 1909, p 270; Macnaghten, 'Clan Macnachtan', 1951, p 87; Girvan, 'North Antrim', UAHS, 1972, p 28; Bence-Jones, 'Burke's guide', 1978, p 24.

Milltown House, Derriaghy

119. "A commodious, oblong house, slated and 2-storey high, the seat of the Reverend Thomas Thompson, vicar of Derryaghy ... it is a neat situation." Datestone in the front wall inscribed RMM 1747. "This is said to be the date at which the house was rebuilt and that it was originally built before the rebellion of 1688. However, it was newly roofed and slated in 1828, and in 1836 about £180 spent on repairing it and the appendages annexed to it" (Fagan, 1838). It was the old vicarage until Mr Thompson died there in 1858.

I have been able to find no record of the owner(s) of the initials RMM, the last two letters being divided by a carved heart. A very pleasant two-storey house, of five bays plus two, all windows Georgian-glazed, the doorcase having sidelights and a radial fanlight; now rendered, with dripstones, and painted grey; four rendered brick chimney stacks. There are attic windows in the gables. The paired wooden banisters are particularly fine. Tucked away out of sight in an old garden amidst mature trees. Formerly known as Milltown Lodge.

Photograph: Michael O'Connell.
Situation: 35 Derriaghy Road, Lisburn; td, Parish, Derriaghy; District Council, Lisburn; Grid ref. J 267 679.
References: Listed B1. T Fagan, OSM, 1837, Antrim, II, pp 105, 106; Barr, 'Derriaghy', 1974, pp 41, 42.

Fleming Hall, Dunloy

120. An attractive early Georgian two-storey five-bay house, an original three bays and two possibly added later, situated inconspicuously on a hillside. Apparently originally a property of Lord Antrim, who settled in this vicinity the family of an impecunious kinsman, Colonel Christopher Fleming, 22nd Baron Slane, a Jacobite who had followed King James into France, much later procured a pardon from Queen Anne, and died in Dublin in 1726. He had been brought up a Roman Catholic in Paris; sat in the 'Patriot Parliament' of 1689 in Dublin; fought on the losing side at both the Boyne and Aughrim; was taken prisoner, attainted, his peerage forfeited, and exiled, when he served first in the French, then the Portuguese army. He had returned to England, and conformed to the Church of England, before 1706.

He was succeeded by a nephew, William, whose son Christopher on 5 January 1747 obtained a long lease from Lord Antrim of the 'four quarterlands of Anticur', and who seems to have been the first Fleming of Fleming Hall. However, he too was at that date "a papist or a person that had not performed all the requisites prescribed by Parliament for persons conforming from the popish to the protestant religion"; so by a legal fiction his Dublin glovemaker, William Hemming, obtained judgement for the premises, but secretly declared that he held them in trust for Christopher Fleming; who having conformed, and the glove-maker having died in the meantime, obtained a conveyance of Fleming Hall in 1762 from William's brother John Hemming, Peruke-maker. In 1771, Christopher Fleming leased part of the land to Sir George Macartney, dying at Fleming Hall that same year; both he and his father were buried with their McDonnell cousins at Bonamargy. "His daughter, Mary-de-Fleming, married an humble person named Felix O'Connor" - this house is shown by Lendrick in 1780 as the seat of Mr O'Connor - "and at his death she was obliged to give up the house in Anticur". The property then passed to Sarah Fleming, who in 1789 became the second (and much younger) wife of James Leslie, builder of Leslie Hill (72), and it was offered for sale by her trustees, subject to a life interest for "my dear sister Jane Thompson otherwise Flemming". It was unsold for some time, but seems in the end to have been bought by a Mr Richards, who in turn sold to one Samuel Wallace of Kirkhills, Ballymoney, before 1836, when the house was valued at £7.0.6: after subtracting a sum "deduct for being unsuitable for a farm-house". To our eyes, the house seems modest enough; but ordinary farmhouses must then have been more modest still; the valuers of 1836 must have considered it a nobleman's mansion.

O'Laverty, in 1887, remarks "in the last century, the last Lord Slane resided in the townland of Anticur, where his mansion may still be seen in tolerable good order, being tenanted by one Wallace, a farmer". Samuel Wallace became eccentric in his old age, but is remembered for causing a 'dumb' beggar-woman to speak up, loud and clear, by dropping a hot coal down the back of her neck. He was succeeded by John Wallace JP, a notable breeder of cattle who dominated the Presbyterian minister and elders of Dunloy for many years. The family still owns the property, though occupying a modern bungalow, and letting the old house.

The house, which is rendered with smooth stucco dressings, is largely masked by a mixture of ivy and creep-

ers. The photograph, taken on 1st April, 1870, constitutes interesting evidence that random rubble walls were not always coated by the original builders in roughcast or render, or even whitewashed. In fact, Fleming Hall seems to have been rendered only around 1900, evidently to conceal the quite drastic alterations to the windows made at that time. The body of the original house is only one room deep, but there are earlier two-storey outbuildings at the rear, including an interesting and little altered kitchen with internal screen wall.

Photograph: Michael O'Connell; photographs of 1870 and of around 1900, courtesy of Mrs Filor.
Situation: 61 Anticur Road, Dunloy; td, Anticur; Parish, Finvoy; District Council, Ballymoney; Grid ref. D 037 181.
References: Listed B1. Taylor and Skinner, 'Roads', 1778, p 270; Lendrick, map, 1780; D639/3-7, D2052/11, D1974, VAL 1B/62, p 51, VAL 2B/1/50B, all in PRONI; O'Laverty, 'Down and Connor', IV, 1887, p 60; Hill, 'Stewarts of Ballintoy', 1865, p 12; 'Complete peerage', XII, pt 1, 1953, p 19 et seq; 'Burke's Irish family records', 1976, p 719; S A Blair, in 'Coleraine Tribune', 20 March 1985; Blair, 'In the midst of the village', 1991, p 65; information and old photographs from the owner and his aunt, Mrs Filor.

Ballydivity House, Ballymoney

121. "Ballydivity ... comprehends a good family edifice, and 120 acres of a demesne tolerably well wooded ... a place pretty well sheltered by surrounding trees, and of a somewhat ancient respectability, though standing upon a lowly site" (Atkinson). "Ballydivity, the seat of Stewart Moore Esquire, is situated in the townland of the same name and on the road from Dervock to Bushmills. The house is not modern, but it is roomy, comfortable, 2-storey and suited to the residence of a gentleman's family. It is perfectly plain in its architecture. The lawn and demesne are of tolerable extent" (Boyle).

An austere, modest, but attractive house, believed to have been built by James Moore, linen draper, a relation of the Moore family of Moore Lodge (129), between 1737, when he obtained a grant from Lord Antrim, and his death in 1748 aged 86. His grandson, James Moore also, shown as the owner in Lendrick's map of 1780, died in 1788, aged 35, leaving no male issue; but, so Thomas Camac's grandmother told him, three illegitimate daughters to whom he gave a good education, by a woman named Maxwell; "one of them died, another fell from her carriage in Dublin and was killed, the third one, to which her father left Bellisle, married a man named Campbell." In consequence, the Ballydivity estate passed to his nephew James Stewart, a descendant of a Jacobite family which had removed to Ireland after Culloden: who took the name of Stewart Moore. In 1798, the house was sacked by the United Irishmen, and the family had to take refuge first in Coleraine, then with friends at Blackheath.

On their return, early in the 19th century, substantial rebuilding appears to have taken place, and the house was improved and enlarged: also turned around to face south. By 1833, it was put in Category 1B, and valued at "say £40 for all": as also in 1859.

Externally, it is a very plain 3-bay house, 2-storey-on-basement with attic windows in the gables, plastered in grey cement render with large modern brick chimney-stacks (rebuilt 1934) at the gables; all the windows are Georgian-glazed, a couple of them at the rear with Gothick details. There is a good doorcase with sidelights and pretty rectangular fanlight: an excellent staircase with a double curl to the bannister-rail, culminating in a splendid geometrical cage for confining children to the attics. An alcove was added to the drawing room in 1910; the house was done up in 1959 when the present generation of the Stewart Moore family moved in; otherwise, it is little altered and quite unspoiled. Fortunately, ambitious plans by Henry Seaver, prepared in 1911, were never executed.

Photograph: Michael O'Connell.

Situation: Castlecat Road, Ballymoney; td, Ballydivity; Parish, Derrykeighan; District Council, Moyle; Grid ref. C 957 363.

References: Listed B+. Lendrick, map, 1780; Atkinson, 'Ireland in the nineteenth century', 1833, pp 202-3; J Boyle, OSM, 1835, Antrim, V, p 84; VAL 1B/139B p 25, VAL 2B/1/32 p 45, in PRONI; Camac, 'Derrykeighan parish', 1908, pp 51-52 and unpublished ms notes in T 1177/14 in PRONI; Girvan 'North Antrim', UAHS 1972, p 35.

Ballinderry House, Lower Ballinderry

122. A pleasing five-bay two-storey house, with a single-bay extension, of cream-washed stucco, with slated roof and four chimney-stacks. All the windows are Georgian-glazed, nine-pane upstairs, twelve-pane downstairs. The present porch is unexciting, but unexpectedly conceals an internal doorcase, with fanlight and side-lights, perhaps that of the original house; on the whole it seems likely that the datestone of 1827 represents the date of an enlargement or modernisation, rather than that of the building's original construction, but it is difficult to be sure. It is said that, on 5th July 1771, John Wesley preached through an end window to a large congregation in the adjacent paddock; how far the present house is one and the same may be open to some debate, but certainly it is very Georgian in character and retains many peculiar features of internal detailing which cannot be much later: alcoves, overmantels, fan-carved shutters, brass fingerplates, even curtain-poles; and, especially, the niche in the internal wall by which the curl at the foot of the bannister-rail is specially accommodated.

This house belonged to a Captain Nelson in John Wesley's day; although he is not mentioned in Wesley's journal. But it must have been a largeish house, for "a specimen of the society, consisting of about 50 members, I had in the house where I dined ... an earnest, simple-hearted people". Edward Nelson Esq. is shown as occupier both in 1837 and in 1859. Subsequently it belonged, in succession, to McKeown, Gracey, and Higginson; and has been in the ownership of the latter family since 1930.

It is exceptionally well-loved and cared-for: it sits on a slight hill above the village, amidst trees, flowers, and white-painted memorabilia of every kind.

Photograph: Michael O'Connell.
Situation: 23 Lower Ballinderry Road, Lower Ballinderry; td, Parish, Ballinderry; District Council, Lisburn; Grid ref. J 131 674.
References: Listed B1. Wesley, 'Journal', Friday, 5 July 1771; datestone of 1827; VAL 1B/167, p 109, VAL 2B/1/58B, p 21, in PRONI.

Willowdale, Dunmurry

123. An astonishing survival in a secret world of its own, a wooded triangle lying concealed on the one side from the M1 motorway and on the other from the Seymour Hill Housing estate close to the point where, amidst splendid mature trees, the Derriaghy River flows into the Lagan.

The house, a five-bay two-storeyed Georgian farmhouse, is thought to date from about 1750, antedating both the nearby canal and the Charley's bleachworks. Its thick stone walls are covered in whitened roughcast, masked in a mixture of climbers and creepers, the quoins, window-surrounds and door-surround of red sandstone painted black, unfortunately completely obliterating the date said once to have been painted on the keystone above the fanlight. The roof is slated between chimney-stacks at the gable-ends. There is a two-storey return at the rear, the windows here smaller than those (not very much larger) at the front: only one window retains sashes and horizontal glazing bars in the manner of the 1830s, the rest have been not very happily modernised. There are extensive byres, stables, tack-rooms and haylofts, very little altered from their original agricultural character. The trees on the lawn running down to the river altogether conceal the house from passers-by on the towpath on the opposite bank; they include weeping ash, acacia, chestnuts, and both English and Irish yews.

For some reason, possibly because of an entail, the house and farm, though for many years occupied by tenants, were not bought out under the Land Acts. From 1939 until 1950 one George Graham lived here; before that a Mr Burrowes who was unhappily drowned in the river Lagan. At some period, the house must have been occupied by members of the Charley family, who sold to the present owner in 1952.

Photograph: Michael O'Connell.
Situation: Down a long avenue off Ballybog Road, Dunmurry; td, Kilmakee; Parish, Derriaghy; District Council, Lisburn; Grid ref. J 294 678.
References: Listed B. OS map, 1837; information from owner, and from W R H Charley.

Lagan Lodge, Lambeg

124. "Lagan Lodge, the seat of Robert Willson, Esquire, is situated on the old or lower road leading from Lisburn to Belfast and contiguous to the village of Lambeg. It is an oblong building, 2-storeys high and slated, with good office houses attached ... The house is spacious and situated on an eminence commanding a fine prospect ... It was built by some of the Wolfenden family about 100 years ago and remained in their possession up to a late period" (Fagan, 1837). The Wolfendens were manufacturers at Lambeg of best quality woollen blankets: in 1787, Dr D A Beaufort wrote in his Journal, "here at Lambeg are made the finest blankets in Ireland or England". "It was occupied up to recently by Mrs Robinson and her daughter" (Marshall, 1933); bought by a Mrs Black in 1965, from whom the present owners of No 29 bought in 1979, and carried out extensive, and necessary, restoration.

Now divided into two houses: so that No 29 is a two-and-a-half storey house, with Georgian glazing, and a great half-round three-storey stair-case annexe at the rear; while No 27 has only one bay on each storey under the same roof, but a substantial single-storey addition. There are the remains of fine columnar balusters, and elegant niches on either side of the window, in each storey of the splendid staircase tower. The timber construction and detailing would seem to support an early date, perhaps in parts even 17th-century.

Oral tradition has it that this originally formed part of a row of cottages attached to the mill, known as 'Primrose Cottage'; that the extra storey, attics, and staircase tower were added for the benefit of an in-coming mill manager; and that the resulting house was vertically divided when one of the two sisters who owned it married a gentleman uncongenial to the other. It is also said that, at one time, this was an inn used by travellers on the road which ran at (what is now) the back of the house.

Photograph: Michael O'Connell.

Situation: 27/29 Church Hill, Lambeg; td, Lambeg North; Parish, Lambeg; District Council, Lisburn; Grid ref. J 283 666.

References: Listed B1. D A Beaufort, Ms Journal, 1787, III, p 52, in TCD Library; T Fagan, OSM, 1837, Antrim, II, p 137; Marshall, 'Parish of Lambeg', 1933, pp 39, 116; Pierce and Coey, 'Taken for granted', 1984, p 120.

Ballybollen House, Ahoghill

125. In appearance, a classic five-bay two-storey late Georgian farmhouse of the better kind, with rectangular recessed doorcase (now missing its once-attractive geometrical fanlight), glazing bars, white-painted walls, and a chimney-stack at each end of the roof; formerly thatched, slated since a fire at the turn of the last century. In fact, this seems a late 18th- or early 19th-century addition to a much earlier house at right angles behind it: of which the ground floor dates probably from the 17th century, the upper storey about the middle of the 18th century. The house used to be surrounded by fine cedars of Lebanon, and three great beech trees known as 'the three sisters', but all these have expired from old age, though the surroundings are still attractive; there are extensive black-stone out-buildings with a fine stone archway; and there is a rath in the fields belonging to the house.

Shane Brian O'Neill granted Ballybollen to his son Shane in 1606; Henry O'Neill was in possession in 1647; Ambrose O'Neill of Ballybollen was "a solicitor of great practice in the early 18th century". His daughter Bridget married Daniel O'Rorke of Drumahaire, Co. Sligo, who claimed direct descent, via 37 generations, from the Princes of Breffni. Shown as the seat of Ambrose O'Rourke on Lendrick's map of 1780. In 1783, Mary O'Neill of Brecart and Bridget O'Rorke (née O'Neill) released their interests in the house in favour of Ambrose O'Rorke of Ballybollen, gentleman, except for a life interest reserved by his mother in "the Appartments in said Dwelling House now in her immediate occupation". In 1835, Ballybollen was "the seat of Ambrose O'Rourke Esquire" who, by 1856, was JP, DL, and High Sheriff of the County. His younger brothers were Alexander and Daniel, both solicitors, the former founder of the still-extant firm of O'Rorke, McDonald and Tweed. The family was very much a legal one, for "Adam Dickey of Hollybrook about 1840 married Miss O'Rorke of Ballybollan; their son was the late Edward O'Rorke Dickey of Belfast of the firm of Cunningham and Dickey, Solicitors" (Lawlor).

In the Valuation book of 1869, Ambrose O'Rorke was shown as holding 97 acres of arable land worth £65.15.0, and 109 acres of bog worth a mere 15/-; but the house was valued at only £9, later increased to £14. This Ambrose , "a very big man whose voice could be heard in the next townland", died in 1884, his widow in 1914.

"For many years, the house was occupied only at week-ends", when Mr Howard O'Rorke (who lived first at Greenisland, then at Holywood) "brought house-parties of his friends", who included Francis Joseph Bigger the antiquarian and Squire Bumper Jones of Moneyglass. Howard O'Rorke died in 1902; his only son, Lieutenant Daniel O'Rorke, was killed in action in France in 1918. The place was then sold by William E O'Rorke, a Dublin barrister, who had inherited, to Matthew Getty of Cullybackey, whose family lived here until 1946; since when, it has been occupied by four generations of the Johnson family.

Photograph: Michael O'Connell.
Situation: Clooney Road, Ahoghill; td, Ballybollen; Parish, Ahoghill; District Council, Ballymena; Grid ref. J 045 973.
References: Listed B. Lendrick map, 1780; Deed of Release, 1783, LPC 971, and VAL 2B/1/68, I, p 10, both in PRONI; OS map, 1832; J Boyle, OSM, 1835, Antrim, VIII, p 12; Lewis, TD, 1837, I, p 24; O'Laverty, 'Down and Connor', III, 1884, pp 389, 390; 'Belfast Telegraph', 24 December 1932; H C Lawlor, in 'Fibres and fabrics journal', November 1941, p 9; information from owners.

Breckenhill, Ballyclare

126. Tucked inconspicuously away in a cleft of the rather bleak hillsides, with marvellous views southwards over the Tildarg dam to the Cave Hill. The initials 'IG' and the date 1755, very neatly incised in a fieldstone in the barn wall, appear to be those of "James Gilliland of Waterhead or Bracken Hill. This place shortly after" (1780) "passed to James Owens of Tildarg, a cousin of the Holestone family, but it seems to have fallen into the possession or tenancy of the Allens after 1820 in which year James Owens's sudden death is recorded in the local press" (Lawlor). In a family deed of 1809, it was recorded that James Owens of Brackenhill, Esq, nephew of William Owens of Holestone, was entitled both to Brackenhill Farm and Brackenhill Bleach Green, both in the townland of Tildarg. The Allens belong to the same clan that built Lisconnan (139) and Springmount (78).

"The residence of John Allen, Esq.. The house, though old, is rather spacious and modern, and is prettily situated in the midst of some planting in a retired district" (Boyle).

The house itself was, until quite recently, single-storey over basement, with attic windows in the gables only; but a good fanlight and doorcase at the top of a flight of six fine granite steps. Five-bay - now two-storey - on basement, the walls roughcast and painted grey. There is reeding in the pilasters inside the front door. It seems that one Sam Todd and his forebears farmed here for several generations, until the place fell into dereliction; it was rescued by its present owners in 1989, when very extensive restoration was called for, and the opportunity was taken to raise the house a storey when re-roofing it. The result is a little bulkier than the original long low house hugging the hillside; but it retains much individual character.

Photograph: Michael O'Connell.
Situation: 45 Breckenhill Road, Ballyclare; td, Tildarg; Parish, Rashee; District Council, Newtownabbey; Grid ref. J 241 955.
References: Not listed. D1824/B/1/1/10/1 in PRONI; J Boyle, OSM, 1835, Antrim, XII, p 136; H C Lawlor, in 'Fibres and fabrics journal', January, 1942.

Lemnalary House, Carnlough

127. A tall stone house, two storeys and attics on a high battered basement, built by one John McCollum some time not long after 1737, in front of the site of an earlier house of the 1630s. Hugh McCollum is shown as owner on the Lendrick map of 1780. It is of fieldstone, formerly peeping through the render but now, rather unhappily, completely obscured by grey roughcast, as also are the brick lintels and chimneys; the south-west wall was formerly slate-hung. Five bays wide, with original glazing pattern entire, and a hooped rectangular fanlight over the door. Dressed stone copings at the eaves, and a flight of seven stone steps up to the front door.

Home from 1964 until his death of Jimmy Irvine, local historian, who admirably disentangled the complicated ownership history of the house in 'The Glynns' of 1984 and 1985. It transpires that John McCollum's son Hugh, 1726-1793, had an illegitimate son by his housekeeper, the much younger Jane Matthews; the son, Randal, died in the West Indies, perhaps of fever, perhaps not; in 1797 she married a young officer, Lt Peter Matthewson of the Reay

Fencibles, a Highland regiment which had been part of the garrison of Belfast just before the 1798 rising, but died in 1802; in 1806 Matthewson remarried, a much younger woman, and lived on in Lemnalary until it fell into disrepair and, in 1830, he took his family to Bay Lodge. In 1833 the house was "old and dilapidated and scarcely habitable"; in 1835, "unoccupied and almost in ruins". The Rogers family eventually moved into part as caretakers: bought the freehold from the White estate under the Land Acts: and the last of them sold to the Irvines in 1964. The house is now rendered unwelcoming by a prominent satellite dish attached to the front wall, and by cages full of terriers in the yard at the rear.

Photograph: 1970, before alterations, NI Tourist Board.
Situation: Old Coast Road, Carnlough; td, Lemnalary; Parish, Ardclinis; District Council, Larne; Grid ref. D 287 195.
References: Listed B+. Taylor and Skinner, 'Roads', 1778, p 273; Lendrick, map, 1780; J Boyle, OSM, 1835, Antrim, IV, p 7; Brett, 'Glens', UAHS, 1971, p 20; J Irvine, in 'The Glynns', XII, 1984, p 5, XIII, 1985, p 5.

Wheyburn (or Weyburn) House, Ballygally

128. A most attractive stone two-storey house, hidden away at the end of a long lane, looking eastwards to the Maidens. Said to have been built for, and the home of, the Rev. John Lewson, ordained at Cairncastle in 1738, who married a Miss Shaw of Ballygally Castle (20); retired in 1793; and died in 1803. Oral tradition has it that this is the original house, but it may have been rebuilt (or at any rate refaced) after Mr Lewson's death. A map by P Magee of 1833 shows the house and farm of 61 acres as belonging to Mr Campbell Wilson. In the Valuation book of 1834, the name of Campbell Wilson Esq. has been struck out, and the name of David McN Beatty substituted: the house, in category 1B, valued at £23.13.11, less a reduction "for distance from market, situation, etc" to £18.19.2. In 1863, when the house was valued at £18, the name of Mr Beatty was in its turn struck out, and the name of John Tweed substituted. The present owners acquired the property from the last of the Tweeds in 1935.

The house is of coursed basalt, part rendered, of two storeys on basement, three bays wide; the very finely detailed doorcase, with radial fanlight and geometrical sidelights, and the window above it, are contained in an arched recess. There are quoins both at the outer corners and at the arris of the recess. Georgian glazing bars survive in the downstairs, but not the upstairs, windows. The south gable is slate-hung; angle-cut slates serve as chimney-pots, as at O'Hara Brook (74) and Seaport Lodge (73), the only other houses I have noted as still retaining this ancient singularity. Internally, the rooms are tall and well-proportioned, there is a staircase with stair-rail of mahogany cut across the grain, and generally the house is uncommonly close to its original state. The same goes for the range of outbuildings at the rear.

Photograph: Michael O'Connell.

Situation: Down a long lane off Wheyburn Road, Ballygally; td, Ballygalley; Parish, Carncastle; District Council, Larne; Grid ref. D 365 075.

References: Listed B1. OS map, 1834; VAL 1B/150, p 78, VAL 12B/7/4A, p 15, in PRONI; map of 1833 and information collected by the late J Irvine of Lemnalary, in possession of owners.

Moore Lodge, Finvoy

129. On a marvellous site, high above but close to the River Bann, "certainly one of the prettiest and most retired spots in this country" (1814). An attractive two-storey house whose facade is very Georgian in character, with broad curved triple windows in each of its two-storey bows, central doorcase with triple window above, and single attic dormer above that in the middle of the pitched roof. The doorcase, and one window at the side of the house, have attractive Gothick lattice ironwork of around 1845: there is a square porch probably of about the same period. An extension to the right, one room above another, incorporates a stone dated 1759; the three-gabled extension to the rear was added in 1901. The date of the main block of the house is more problematical, and Lieutenant Alexander of the Ordnance Survey is not much help: "The house, though rather modern in its appearance, has been built for some time"! ("the seat of George Moore Esq., the house, which is 2-storey and in very nice order ... commands a fine view of the river"). Pierce and Coey accept 1759 as the date of the main house as well as the extension, and may well be right.

It seems that Benjamin Galland, who was High Sheriff in 1702, resided in a mansion house at the Vow, probably thatched, on this site; by a conveyance of 1717 the property passed for £500 into the ownership of William Moore, apparently to the annoyance of the family of the former owners, who on Sunday morning the 29th June 1729, according to vivid depositions of which transcripts survive, "with a great number of men with guns and bayonets, marching in great fury towards the said house of Vow" ... "carrying a Pott with hot burning sluggs" fired two volleys which "set said house aflame of fire that with great difficulty the said Moore's servants escaped with their lives; and that said house of Vow together with" ... "beds & hangings, tables & chairs, meal & butter, cheese and several other goods" ... "was in a short time consumed to ashes".

However, it must be doubted whether any of the present house, as opposed to the outbuildings, dates back before this fire; even the heavy, old-fashioned staircase, delightful as it is, looks to me as if it is from the first half of the 18th century: or at any rate the lower section of it, for it is surprising to find it continuing grandly right up to the, quite modest, pair of attic rooms under the roof. Interestingly, there are lugged architraves to the doorcases upstairs but not downstairs. The house stands on an (invisible) basement. There is a pleasing 19th-century dovecote at the corner of the lawn.

The estate has remained almost continuously in the ownership of members of the Moore family, with one break, since the early 18th century, though it was let to one James Smith at the time of the 1859 valuation, which remarks "too old, too many offices - house and offices too large for the present occupier - settle at £17". The present owner's great-grandfather was an eminent physician; his grandfather, William Moore KC, MP, MA, JP, DL, was an exceedingly active Unionist politician whose reward it was to be Lord Chief Justice of Northern Ireland from 1925 to 1937, created a baronet in 1932. The house had fallen into disrepair by the time of its sale in 1982, but was extensively restored in the ensuing years, and bought back by the present owner in 1986.

Culmore, Rasharkin

130. A fine house, set on a wooded knoll overlooking the River Bann, at the end of a very long lane. Lieutenant R Alexander, writing in September 1831, described it as "the residence of James William Armstrong Esquire: it is a plain modern house with nothing about it worthy of notice". Although very much late-Georgian in style, the interior detailing has a Regency flavour: the house might be tentatively dated to around 1820, but its resemblance to Moore Lodge (129), so short a distance downstream, would suggest a considerably earlier date. In 1836 it was valued at £23.6.11, but £3.6.11 was knocked off because of the "dead approach and want of meetings about place and neighbours". In 1859, when James William Armstrong was still the occupier, the buildings were valued at £17. The Armstrongs originated in Co. Meath; another branch of the same family is at Dean's Hill, Armagh. In 1921, on the death of Captain Alexander Moore Armstrong, who had been appointed in 1897 as agent of the Mercers' Company of London, the house was bought by the grandfather of the present owner.

It is of five bays, two storeys, white-painted roughcast, with hipped roof; the slightly unfortunate square modern porch, with window above, is flanked on each side by a full-height bow with two (not three) tall Georgian-glazed windows on each floor. These bows contain woodwork of splendid quality - not just the curved sashes and glazing-bars (window-sills too) but also the play of double curves, with reeding in the pilasters, and fan reeding at the angles. There are in fact quite sizeable attics, but they are invisible from outside, lit only by roof-lights, and were probably originally reached by ladder; the staircase has been rather clumsily extended at some date in such a way that it cuts right across the tall round-headed rear window designed to light the first floor landing. Return and farmyard at the rear.

Photograph: Michael O'Connell.
Situation: At 54 Bann Road, near Kilrea, but on the Rasharkin side of the river; td, Culmore; Parish, Finvoy; District Council, Ballymoney; Grid ref. C 934 143.
References: Listed B1. R Alexander, OSM, 1831, Antrim, VIII, p 71; VAL 1B/162, p 181, VAL 2B/1/50A, p 49, in PRONI; Girvan, 'North Antrim', 1972, p 51; Dean, 'Gate lodges', 1994, p 9.

◁

Photograph: Michael O'Connell.
Situation: Vow Road, Finvoy; td, Moore Lodge; Parish, Finvoy; District Council, Ballymoney; Grid ref. C 931 178.
References: Listed B+. Copy presentments 1729-30 in Groves collection, T808/14896, family papers in D 1066/6 and D 2171, VAL 1B/158B, p 79, VAL 2B/1/47B, p 125, and G J records, all in PRONI; Taylor and Skinner, 'Roads', 1778, p 18; Lendrick, map, 1780; Wilson, 'Post-chaise companion', 1803, p 71; R Alexander, OSM, 1831, Antrim, VIII, pp 67, 71; Rev. James Grier, in Mason, 'Statistical account', I, 1814, p 381; Young, 'Belfast and province of Ulster', 1909, pp 238, 431; 'Weekly Irish Times', 29 June 1940; Girvan, 'North Antrim', 1973, p 50; Pierce and Coey, 'Taken for granted', 1984, p 114.

Limepark, Armoy

131. "Lime Park" is shown as the residence of the Revd Mr Clarke in Taylor and Skinner's Road Book of 1778; and was still shown as "the seat of the Revd. Mr Clarke" in Wilson's Post-Chaise Companion of 1803, though Alexander Clark, vicar of Loughgiel, had died in 1792, and described himself in his will as "late of Limepark". Lime Park has been added in Williamson's revision of 1808 of Lendrick's map of 1780. In 1834, the house was tenanted by one Patrick McAlice, being described as "too near road and rather good for a farm house"; 49 feet long by 26½ feet deep by 17 feet high, valued (after deductions) at £8.6.0; very soon after, the occupier was James Craig, who died in 1898 aged 83 - said to have been originally a hard-working herdsman from Scotland. By 1859, he had improved both land and house: held 140 acres, plus bog and limestone quarries, from the Macartney estate, the house itself by now described as "well situate" being valued at £15. By 1878, the value of the quarries had risen to £15, and that of the house to £20. The family prospered: his grandson, James Alexander Craig, conducted a famous international ploughing match on the farm in 1959, commemorated by a curious 'cairn of peace' by the front gate, and died in 1963. In 1984, when grants for farm modernisation became available, the house was fairly mercilessly modernised, the back half of the double-cube being demolished, and the last of the Craigs emigrated: the house was bought from them in 1992 by the present owners.

Externally, it remains a Georgian farm-house, dating from around 1760, of considerable charm: two-storey, five-bay, cream-washed, and very well painted. There is a segmental fanlight at the inner front door, enclosed within a (not unpleasing) later square porch, with simplified acroteria at the corners. The stone outbuildings are extremely fine and extensive, and include a blacksmith's forge in working order.

Photograph: Michael O'Connell. (See also colour-plate XIIIb)

Situation: 37 Drones Road, Armoy; td, Moyaver Upper; Parish, Armoy; District Council, Moyle; Grid ref. D 067 316.

References: Listed B1. Taylor and Skinner, 'Roads', 1778, p 20; Williamson, map, 1808; 'Clergy of Connor', 1993, p 262; Lendrick, map, 1780; Wilson, 'Post-chaise companion', 1803, p 58; gravestones in Armoy Presbyterian churchyard; VAL 1B/141, p 21, VAL 2B/1/37, p 19, VAL 12B/4/1A, p 41, all in PRONI; Girvan, 'North Antrim', UAHS, 1973, p 37; information from owner, and from Mr Acheson of Turnarobert.

Clady House, Dunadry

132. A fine, big, 18th-century house, probably built by Hugh Swann, who died in 1848 aged 95, two-storey plus basement and attics, on a marvellous site beside the Clady Water (with its own, restored, white-painted foot-bridge) amidst magnificent mature trees. Probably, but not quite certainly, the same as the house shown by Lendrick in his map of 1780. The front has been stuccoed at a somewhat later date, and the main facade, facing north-east, now has slightly heavy pediments on the ground-floor windows, quoins, dripstones, and dentils. Three triple windows above, below two, all Georgian-glazed, flanking a fine doorcase with fanlight and side-lights at the top of four stone steps. Plain pitched roof; an attic window in each gable; at the rear, overlooking handsome outbuildings, a very tall round-headed window lighting the staircase.

Inside, there is attractive and rather unusual plaster-work; reeding in the doorcases and in the dividers of the three-light windows; pleasant stairs, and nice curly mahogany bannisters. After the death of Hugh Swann's widow, the property was bought by William Cinnamond, and remained in his family until 1900, when the family fell upon hard times, and, being unable to repay a mortgage of £600, his grandson Thomas Hall Cinnamond shot his mother and then himself. Since then, it has had a number of more fortunate owners; and retains the feeling of an uncommonly light, airy and pleasant house.

Photograph: Michael O'Connell.
Situation: 18 Shanoguestown Road, Dunadry; td, Shanoguestown; Parish, Templepatrick; District Council, Antrim; Grid ref. J 195 844.
References: Listed B1. Lendrick, map, 1780; Bassett, 'Antrim', 1888, p 147; H C Lawlor, in 'Fibres and fabrics journal', July 1942, p 172; Girvan, 'West Antrim', UAHS, 1970, p 12.

Hollybrook House, Randalstown

133. In 1778, the seat of - Dicky, Esq. (Taylor and Skinner); Holly Brook has been added by Williamson in his 1808 revision of Lendrick's map, seat of Adam Dickey; in 1817, the seat of J and H Dickey, Esqrs (Atkinson). A fine five-bay two-storey house, with three round-headed dormers, apparently original; roughcast, Georgian-glazed; the porch possibly later, with Greek key pattern ornament on the lintel and a glazing-pattern similar to that seen at Glendun Lodge (154) and Rockport (155). A good curly staircase. It may be that the somewhat lower two-storey return, running parallel to and just above the River Main, is the earlier house on the site, probably an O'Neill farm-house, and that the bigger house facing downstream is a somewhat later addition. In 1833, "Hollybrook is the seat of Mrs McManus, a respectable tenant on the Randalstown estate, one of those properties of the Earl O'Neill we have already mentioned ... It comprehends a neat family edifice, and 10 Irish acres of demesne ... a pretty rural residence." The draft Ordnance Survey Memoir of May 1835 shows "Hollybrook: unoccupied". Later, it looks as if Adam Dickey, proprietor of the mill, lived in the lower house, and Colonel Kennedy lived in the upper house, as both are shown as resident at Hollybrook in the 1846 Directory. "John Dickey, reputed to have been the first linen merchant to erect a power-driven bleach-green in Ireland, married Martha Hill of Hillmount, Cullybackey," (79) "left a large family, and by 1780 his descendants of his name were represented by no less than five firms actively engaged in the staple trade ... but the family became extinct in the male line, with one

exception: Adam Dickey of Hollybrook about 1840 married Miss O'Rorke of Ballybollan:" (125) "their son was the late Edward O'Rorke Dickey of Belfast, solicitor" (Lawlor). Lt Colonel Arthur Kennedy, who had served in the 18th Hussars with Wellington throughout the Peninsular War, lived and on 15 September 1855 died there, aged 74. For many years thereafter, it belonged to the Webb family. Since then, it has passed through the hands of a number of owners.

According to Lewis, "The spinning of cotton and weaving of calico were extensively carried on at Randalstown, there are excellent sites for bleach-greens and beetling engines at Hollybrook and a considerable quantity of linen is woven in various parts of the parish." However, rather surprisingly, Hollybrook is not mentioned in the lengthy Ordnance Survey Memoir for the parish of Drummaul; though Boyle remarks that "in the year 1818, the great weekly linen market, which for a long time had been almost the sole support of Randalstown, began to decline" in favour of Ballymena.

Photograph: Michael O'Connell.
Situation: Up a long lane, at 1 Magheralane Road, Randalstown; td, Magheralane; Parish, Drummaul; District Council, Antrim; Grid ref. J 084 925.
References: Listed B1. Taylor and Skinner, 'Roads', 1778, p 17; Williamson, map, 1808; Atkinson, 'Ireland exhibited', 1823, II p 443; Atkinson, 'Ireland in the nineteenth century', 1833, pp 185-186; Lewis, TD, 1837, I, p 518; J Boyle, OSM, 1837, and G W Hemans, 1835, Antrim, VI, pp 41, 81; Slater, 'Directory' 1846, p 524; H C Lawlor, in 'Fibres and fabrics journal', November 1941, p 9; Girvan, 'West Antrim', UAHS, 1970, p 21.

Islandreagh House, Dunadry

134. Said to be of late 17th-century date, probably built by the owners of the mill on the Six Mile Water close by. But the position here is exceptionally confusing: as H C Lawlor remarked in 1942, "the mills shown on Lendrick's map were close together and it is now very difficult to say exactly which is which". The position is complicated still further by the fact that there are two buildings today known as "Islandreagh House", one in Islandreagh Road, and this one in Islandreagh Drive. Lawlor thought this house and mill were owned by James Luke from 1778 until his death in 1813, which is confirmed by Lendrick's attribution of Islandreagh Bleachworks in 1780 to "Mr Luke", unchanged in Williamson's revision of 1808. James Beck, in a letter of 1944, cites an advertisement of 1768 in the Belfast News-letter referring to the bleach green here of James and John Luke; and another of 1 May 1812 in which James Swan offers the premises for sale. Atkinson says that, in 1817, it was the seat of James Stuan Esq - presumably a mistranscription of 'Swan'. Hamond, basing his analysis largely on the Valuation books, thinks that the bleachworks was owned by John Swan in 1808; then by John and William Ferguson; then by Robert Benson; then rented by the Arthur family; since 1877, by the McClure family.

Internally not much changed, though externally there is little to betray its antiquity; new windows, chimneys and porch combine with pebble-dashed walls to belittle the interest of the house, which is nonetheless considerable. Of four wide bays, and two storeys, plus a return added around 1888 by Samuel McClure using the bricks salvaged from the demolition of the former owners' home in Donegall Square, Belfast, to make way for Robinson & Cleaver's emporium. It is surrounded by splendid old trees, tucked away in a near-secret terrain between river and railway cutting, approachable only by a fine stone viaduct over the railway line.

Photograph: Michael O'Connell.
Situation: Off Islandreagh Drive, Dunadry; td, Islandreagh; Parish, Grange of Nilteen; District Council, Antrim; Grid ref. J 192 849.
References: Not listed. Lendrick map, 1780; Atkinson, 'Ireland exhibited', 1823, II, p 443; Bassett, 'Antrim', 1888, p 148; H C Lawlor, in 'Fibres and fabrics journal', March 1942, p 68; notes by F W Hamond in MBR; letters and deeds in possession of owner.

Glen Oak, Crumlin

135. This may or may not be the original mill-owner's house shown on the Lendrick map of 1780, which belonged to the adjacent flour-mills built in 1765 by Rowley Heyland. Atkinson, visiting in 1817, says that this and the nearby Ben Neagh "comprehend two respectable edifices, with suitable offices, extensive flour and corn mills," and "240 Conyngham acres of demesne, 140 of which are attached to Glen Oak, the seat of James McCawley, Esq., and 80 acres to that of Ben Neagh, the new and handsomely circumstanced villa of his son, Mr Robert McCawley. These seats, together with the village of Crumlin, may be considered as distinguished features of improvement on the estate of Colonel Pakenham, or Colonel Heyland, we know not which." In 1837, Lewis remarks that the mills had passed to the firm of Robert Macaulay & Son; both he and James Boyle show the house as belonging to Robert Macaulay Esq. but Boyle describes the house as "of modern construction and appearance". Also writing in 1837(?), James Boyle says, in his Ordnance Survey memoir of the parish of Camlin, "The origin of Crumlin is of modern date and has been caused by the erection of the very extensive, well-known flour and corn mills of the Messrs MacAulay, at which period Crumlin consisted solely of a public house and a smith's forge. The mills alluded to are situated on the opposite bank of the Crumlin water, and in the parish of Killead ... the Messrs MacAulay have their mills in this parish insured for £3000, and those in the adjoining parish for £19,000" - a staggering figure for that period.

Attractive as it is, it is very close to the industrial site, and when Girvan wrote in 1970 it was "now deserted and being fast over-run by dry rot". Happily, rescue has arrived in the person of Raymond Mairs, architect, whose restoration work is well advanced. The house is T-shaped: the cross-bar on the T is five bays wide, tall rooms with long architraved and Georgian-glazed windows on either side of a round-headed doorcase with radial fanlight and curly plaster ornament above the door. At each end, a generous bow containing two large windows. The original upper floor with five windows has been replaced by a considerably lower roof with three dormer windows. The shank of the T may well be earlier, and comprises a fairly simple house of nine bays and two storeys, incorporating the staircase.

Photograph: Michael O'Connell.
Situation: Milltown, Crumlin; td, Crosshill; Parish, Killead; District Council, Antrim; Grid ref. J 157 765.
References: Listed B. Perhaps shown on Lendrick, map, 1780; Atkinson, 'Ireland exhibited', 1823, II, p 177; Lewis TD, 1837, I, p 439, II, p 133; J Boyle, OSM, 1838, Camlin and Glenavy, as yet unpublished, and in OSM, 1837(?), Antrim, VII, pp 65, 69; Girvan, 'West Antrim', 1970, p 9.

Fisherwick Lodge, Doagh

136. A hunting lodge built (or re-built) by the extravagant 2nd Marquess of Donegall in the middle of an extensive walled deerpark containing nearly all of six townlands and dating from, perhaps, a century earlier than the house. The Ordnance Survey Memoir dates it to 1805: "an elegant and uniform structure in the Cottage style, forming with the offices a spacious quadrangular enclosure. It contains a regular suite of handsome apartments, and is constructed and finished in the most modern style" (1838). One of the houses added by James Williamson in his 1808 revision of Lendrick's map of 1780. 1805 seems right, too, for in 1804 Lord Donegall for once laid his hands on some ready cash; and in January 1806, "after the contents of the house in Belfast had been seized" by his creditors "the Donegalls took refuge for a time at Fisherwick Lodge" which, that year, was alleged to contain "a great quantity of splendid and valuable furniture". In 1807, Dr Beaufort wrote "close to Doagh on the North Mr May has lately built a very neat large cottage and dressed the grounds about it"; which Dr Maguire explains neatly: "Donegall was being hotly pursued by his English creditors about then, and such people usually found that when they got close to his property, it turned out not to be his any longer, but Edward May's" - Lord Donegall's shrewd and grasping brother-in-law. In 1812, Dubourdieu described the house as "very handsome". It "was substantially altered and enlarged at some point in the early-19th century, with extensive stabling, kennels for hounds, and improvements to the grounds (including the construction of an artificial lake)."

There is a handsome central pedimented doorcase, with fluted wooden columns, pilasters, and lofty radial fanlight, leading into a splendid hallway with coved ceiling, original fireplace, and pretty shallow plasterwork of fans, feathers, and sprays of leaves (see colour-plate IXa). All the main rooms in this front south wing have coved ceilings; behind them, an internal corridor, lit by skylights, runs round the whole square. Basically, the house is single-storey, though there are servants' attics in parts of the roofspace. The external doorway to the west wing is contained beneath a gable in a double-recessed arch with fanlight, and the subsidiary hallway has a particularly charming stucco bouquet for ceiling rose. The old wine-cellars were, as one would expect, capacious. There are extensive stone outbuildings and stables, some with pointed upper windows, now all incorporated into a working farmyard.

Since its sale by the Donegall family about 1847, the house has belonged in turn to members of the Molyneux, Hagan, and (since 1940) Patton families. It was at some date divided into two, the main house, of nine bays, facing south, the other, of five bays, facing west; but these are currently occupied by different generations of the same family, and remain in the same ownership.

Notwithstanding his financial difficulties, in 1815 Lord Donegall was instrumental in the formation of "the celebrated hunt club known as the Antrim Hunt"; and "the very extensive hotel" in Doagh "was soon after enlarged ... it contained a large and handsome club-room and spacious accommodation, besides stabling for 70 horses ... on the decline of the Donegall family, caused by their embarrassments, the club began to dwindle and was finally broken up in 1835. Now" (1838) "the spacious hotel" originally built in 1799, "is nothing more than an alehouse".

Photograph: Ulster Museum, courtesy Dr W A Maguire.
Situation: Off Main Street, Doagh; td, Doagh; Parish, Grange of Doagh; District Council, Newtownabbey; Grid ref. J 263 898.
References: Listed B1. D A Beaufort, 'Tour', 1807, Ms 4033 in TCD Library, p 36; Williamson, map, 1808; Dubourdieu, 'Antrim', 1812, p 472; J Boyle, OSM, 1839, J R Ward, 1835, and J Bleakly, 1847-9, Antrim, XI, pp 69, 85, 92; Cox, 'Kilbride', 1959, p 83; Maguire, 'Living like a lord', 1984, pp 29, 32, 38, and private information from him.

New Lodge and Ballybrophy House, Muckamore

137. These two houses, facing in opposite directions but linked by two large and attractive ranges of stone out-buildings, cannot well be discussed separately, although they have in recent years become separated, and the larger house has been renamed.

Girvan, followed by the listers, and by Pierce and Coey, seems to have assumed that the larger house, No 26 New Lodge Road (now called Ballybrophy House, formerly called New Lodge) is one of those shown on the Lendrick map of 1780, and that the smaller house, No 28 (now called New Lodge) was 'originally for staff'. I do not think this can be right. The smaller house is much too roomy and well detailed to be just servants' quarters; the larger house looks, at first glance, to date from around 1845 (but see below). I cannot pin down any of the houses shown by Lendrick as representing New Lodge.

In 1838, Boyle wrote of "New Lodge, the summer residence of Rev. Arthur MacCartney, Vicar of Belfast" as "two storeys high, a small but neat and modern-looking residence." Mr Macartney, a former captain of artillery who had served in the Peninsular War, was Vicar from 1820 until his death in 1843. My guess is that he lived in the smaller house, and that the larger house was added by the Chaine family after his death. This seems to be confirmed by the Ordnance Survey map of 1833; also by the Valuation books. On Mr Macartney's

death, the house was bought by James Chaine, but leased to one Charles Creery; in 1859 it was noted "main house not large, but spacious returns and very fine out-offices."

The smaller house is well shown in a faded photograph of about 1890, built of squared blackstone, flanked on each side by an ashlar archway, one pedimented and flanked by blind arrow-slits, one not, with elaborate Regency glazing; it was for many years occupied by the Clarke family of Islandbawn, who unfortunately inserted plate-glass windows in the sashes, and pebble-dashed the front. The interior is surprisingly spacious, with good plasterwork and windowcases, the hall and stairs lit by a central dome. The very extensive stone coach yards, stabling and walled gardens at the rear are now, happily, full of

well-cared-for coaches, carts, traps, and carriage-horses to match.

The 1880 Valuation book shows two substantial houses in the townland, one worth £54 and one worth £60, both in the ownership of James Chaine, but both apparently occupied by members of the Dawson family: it is impossible to distinguish from the entries which is which.

The larger house, which seems not to appear in the 1862 Valuation book and is presumably, therefore, later, is of white-painted stucco, two-storey and five-bay, with a half-hipped roof and yellow-brick chimney-stacks set rather close together. There is a simple porch with Tuscan columns but no pediment. At one end, there is a canted bay, at the other, a fine big conservatory; at the rear, an extensive range of blackstone out-offices with brick dressings, running back to the stables behind, in the same style and apparently of the same date as those of the smaller house. The glazing-pattern throughout - as also in the

front of the smaller house, in the old photograph - is extravagantly complex, with 12 panes in each of the lower sashes, 25 in each of the upper ones, and no less than 28 in the front door. Some of the outer panes are of stained glass, those in the front door - patterned in red and gold - being strikingly attractive. The newel post is in the Victorian taste, though the style of the staircase itself is more conservative. A handsome house, with good trees and garden.

Photographs: Michael O'Connell; old photograph, c 1890, courtesy of Mr William Knipe.
Situation: Nos 26 and 28 New Lodge Road, Muckamore; td, Islandbane; Parish, Muckamore; District Council, Antrim; Grid ref. J 183 857.
References: Ballybrophy House, Listed B1; outbuildings of New Lodge B1. OS maps 1833, 1857; VAL 1B/63, VAL 2B/1/52, VAL 12B/1/1A and D, in PRONI; J Boyle, OSM, 1838, Muckamore, as yet unpublished; Girvan, 'West Antrim', UAHS, 1970, p 13; Pierce and Coey, 'Taken for granted', 1984, p 121.

Ballybogey House, Dervock

138. An attractive two-storey three-bay house, roughcast but creeper-covered, with triple round-headed windows with Victorian-pattern glazing-bars; whereas the segmental headed doorcase retains its 'Gothick' fanlight. The front rooms contain plasterwork in the style of 1840; there is a curious internal doorway with radial fanlight in the hall, arousing the suspicion that somehow the hall, front rooms and facade were later additions, perhaps about 1840, to a smaller, older and earlier house behind.

This theory may not stand up to close examination, but is supported by the evidence that the house was built by the Macnaghten family as part of the Benvarden property (77). Bartholomew Macnaghten, younger brother of John who was hanged in 1761, certainly lived at that period in Ballybogey. It was shown as property of Catherine Macnaghten, though vacant, in 1859, but in 1864 belonged to Captain R J Montgomery: house and offices valued at £10.11.8 in 1859, £23 in 1864, so if a new front was erected, it was probably between those dates. It was used by the Montgomerys as dower house, or residence for their agent, until 1964; and bought by the present owner in 1966.

Photograph: Michael O'Connell.
Situation: 93 Benvardin Road, Ballybogey; td, Ballybogy; Parish, Dunluce; District Council, Ballymoney; Grid ref. C 923 325.
References: Listed B. VAL 1B/140, p 83, VAL 12B/4/5A, p 88, in PRONI; Macnaghten, 'Clan Macnachtan', 1951, p 82; Girvan, 'North Antrim', UAHS, 1973, pp 21, 22.

Lisconnan House, Dervock

139. "Lisconnan, the seat of Dr Samuel Allen, Esq: ... the house is 2-storey, there is a tolerable garden and orchard and some planting which almost conceals the house. The situation is peaceful and retired" (Boyle). "The property and residence of Dr Samuel Allen - over the wild heath, and the river Bush, the plantations of Leslie Hill and Benvardin are seen lending a small proportion of their influence to rescue the scene from absolute inanity"! (Atkinson).

The lands of Lisconnan were bought in 1778 by Samuel Allen, of Allen's Brook near Larne, a successful linen merchant who previously lived at Bellisle, married a Miss Higginson, and was High Sheriff in 1790 (see also Springmount, 78, for this family). The house seems to have been built about that date, though it does not appear on Lendrick's map of 1780; it may or may not be the house shown as 'Liscollin' on Williamson's revision of 1808. In the valuation of 1833, the dwelling was classified 1A and, with its outbuildings valued at £24 reduced to £16; "offices inconvenient, and a want [of] neatness and convenience altogether". In 1859, the occupier shown as Henry Ellis Allen, and the value reduced to £14. The last of the family to live at Lisconnan died in 1977, since when the house has changed hands more than once.

An extremely attractive H-shaped group of buildings, the central section (with staircase) the oldest and constituting a double cube at right angles to the 7-bay block to the front, now all 2-storey but until 1880 only partly so; and to the servants' wing at the rear. The porch, added about 1900, contains a very plain wide segmental fanlight, and is surmounted by a Venetian window; on either side six tall windows, all Georgian-glazed. The walls are of cream-washed roughcast; it is a pity that the four cement-rendered chimney stacks have not been coloured to match. Internally, there is much excellent detailing, particularly reeded doorcases, shutters, and dummy doors; the Venetian window is much better detailed inside than out; hall, drawing-room, dining-room, and a charming coved-ceilinged room upstairs, are all well proportioned and well detailed.

Photograph: Michael O'Connell.
Situation: Lisconnan Road, Dervock; td, Lisconnan; Parish, Derrykeighan; District Council, Ballymoney; Grid ref. C 955 321.
References: Listed B. Williamson, map, 1808; Atkinson, 'Ireland in the nineteenth century', 1833, p 204; J Boyle, OSM, 1835, Antrim, V, p 84; Lewis, TD, 1837, I, p 454; VAL 1B/139A, p 77, VAL 2B/1/32, p 1, D 2134/1/1, print of 1850, and T734(15), all in PRONI; Camac, 'Derrykeighan parish', 1908, p 61; Girvan, 'North Antrim', UAHS, 1973, p 35; Bence-Jones, 'Burke's guide', 1978, p 185.

Coldagh, Ballymoney

140. On a narrow strip of ground between the Ballymoney river and the road from Ballymoney to Balnamore, a modest but pleasant small Georgian house, just across the river from O'Hara Brook (74). The main part of the house is two-storey, four-bay, rendered but creeper-covered, with quoins, pitched roof, and three chimney stacks. There is a stone, rather oddly placed below one of the upstairs windows at the rear, inscribed 'W C June 1801'; this may record the date when the original single-storey house was raised a storey and slated; it is unlikely that it represents the date when Coldagh was first built, probably around 1775. The front door was originally in the gable, facing the road, but was moved into the extension (formerly stable with loft over) before the second World War; the 'fanlight' dates from 1950. The windows are of various sizes and patterns: a round-headed one, with Gothick cusps, is said to have been brought from Leslie Hill (72), though it is difficult to see from what part of that house it could have been taken. There is a pleasing cobbled yard, with a range of unspoiled outbuildings.

"In giving specimens of the seats in this neighbourhood, we must not overlook a neat cottage beauty ... the property of a Mr Cramsie, the proprietor of a weekly mercantile journal in Belfast". Here Mr Atkinson, visiting it in 1832, got quite carried away: "although it stands on a lowly site, closely approximating with the road ... it presented such marks of taste in its arrangement, and such charms of solitude for the man of contemplative habits, as irresistibly impelled us to enter and review it. We found it standing on a demesne of about 40 acres, situated on a bank of the Ballymoney river, over which it commands an interesting view of the splendid demesne of O'Harabrook on the distant shore" ... "These cottage beauties" etc etc etc "force the philanthropist to cry out, in the language of Penn to Cortes ... 'Here is a sight for an angel to behold!'" (In case the reader has doubts whether William Penn and Hernando Cortes ever in fact met, Atkinson helpfully footnotes a reference to Lyttelton's Dialogues of the Dead).

In 1833, the dwelling was valued at £7.17.0; and an adjacent flax mill, "built by Mr Crampsie himself", at £10, though "the miller says this mill could not be worth more than £15 per year". Alex Cramsie was still the occupier in 1859, under lease from the Hon. Mrs Campbell, when the house was valued at £6.10.0 and the flax mill again at £10. Despite its earlier occupancy by Mr Cramsie, and the possible ownership implied by the initials inscribed on the datestone, it is said to have passed with the O'Hara Brook property to the Cramsies in 1889; in 1888, it was the residence of one Robert Parkhill; then in this century it was bought by Senator Leslie, whose daughter Audrey, married to one Maitland Titterton, is said to have brought the window from Leslie Hill, moved the front door, and lived here until 1937. Since then, the house has remained in the occupation of the same family despite a change of ownership.

Photograph: Michael O'Connell.
Situation: 36 Balnamore Road, Ballymoney; td, Coldagh; Parish, District Council, Ballymoney; Grid ref. C 928 248.
References: Listed B1. Atkinson, 'Ireland in the nineteenth century', 1833, p 194; VAL 1B/142A, p 148, VAL 2B/1/35A, p 32, in PRONI; Girvan, 'North Antrim', 1973, p 45.

Burleigh Hill House, Carrickfergus

141. Added by Williamson in his 1808 revision of Lendrick's map of 1780. Built "about 1793 by the late George Burleigh Esq. of Burleigh-Hill", who was admitted a burgess of Carrickfergus on 12th September 1799, sheriff in 1818, and who died in 1822 aged 78, leaving no child to inherit the place. "John Robinson, his nephew, succeeded him 16 years ago and still resides in it" (1838). "The house is a spacious and modern-looking residence two storeys high and having a wing at each side. It is situated in a handsome lawn of about 36 acres. There is a good garden and the offices are of a suitable extent" (1838). House, north wing, south wing, basement and offices, all particularised in detail, were together valued at

£44.15.0 in 1836. Now, an attractive stone farmhouse, roughcast, looking south down the hillside over Carrickfergus. The main house is of two storeys on basement, and five bays; to each side there is a slightly lower wing; in turn, each wing is flanked by a stone wall, and a pair of exceptionally fine square gate-posts with tall pyramidal tops. Glazing bars are complete in the upper windows of the main block only. There is a pleasant and slightly unusual fanlight above the pilastered front door, reached by a set of seven stone steps.

The subsidiary wing to the east, of random basalt with some galleting visible under the rendering, is said to have been built with stones from the ruins of the ancient Carnrassa (or Carnrawsie) church in the field at the rear; if so, this wing must have been built in 1827, for until that year most of the walls of this church were still standing. The deeds are said to have been destroyed in Dublin; it has been in the ownership of the present family since 1963.

Photographs: Michael O'Connell; Jim McCall.
Situation: Up a long lane from Middle Road, Carrickfergus; td, Middle Division; Parish, District Council, Carrickfergus; Grid ref. J 398 901.
References: Listed B1. Williamson, map, 1808; M'Skimin, 'Carrickfergus, 1811, pp 116, 158; James O'Kane, map of 1821, in Robinson, 'Carrickfergus'; D 1489, VAL 1B/187, p 133, in PRONI; J Boyle and S M'Skimin, OSM, 1839-40, Carrickfergus, as yet unpublished; O'Laverty, 'Down and Connor', III, 1884, p 72; Rutherford, 'Carrickfergus', 1995, p 60.

Drumnagessan House, Dunseverick

142. A large, imposing, but slightly clumsy-looking three-bay two-storey house with basement and attics. The entrance front has a sandstone pediment at the attic, cut-stone string-courses, and a large square double-sided porch, with a flight of eight curving steps and a quadrant wall at either side. The back - if it is really the back - is of three bays, with two oculus windows and four chimneys. There are upstands at the gable ends as though the building might once have been thatched: but, against this, there are fine cut-stone eaves-courses. Glazing bars complete. Girvan reported the building, in 1974, as "sadly dilapidated": in 1976, it was cement-plastered all over - the 'front' having formerly been, apparently, of random blackstone, the 'back' of ashlar - no doubt much to the benefit of its weatherliness, if somewhat to the detriment of the appearance of what must once have been really rather a grand house.

Boyd says firmly "Major William Stewart" (born in 1779, later a Major in the 30th Regiment) "built Drumnagesson House, and was followed there by his son James ... James Stewart sometimes referred to as 'the last of the Stewarts', was the second and last generation of the younger branch of the Stewarts of Ballintoy to live at Drumnagesson." His "eight children all emigrated to Canada when they grew up. Their father was said to have been improvident in his ways, with the result that the eight children were followed to Canada by their parents after Drumnagesson House was sold."

Major Stewart's daughter Jane married Dr John Dunlop, of Straidkillen, who seems to have been the purchaser. But Camac gives a different account: he mentions one Alexander McAuley KC, author of a book on pensions, "late of Drumnagessan and then of the city of Dublin", as taking other lands, under lease, from Lord Antrim in 1735. At some period not specified by Thomas Camac, Archibald Dunlop, grandson of Bryce Dunlop, a Scottish settler from Arran, married Rose, daughter of Alexander McAuley "with whom he obtained Drumnagessan".

In 1817, John Dunlop obtained from Lord Caledon a renewal of a lease from McAuley to his father of 1762. The house and farm were bought from the Caledon estate in the following year by Archdeacon Traill of Ballylough, subject to the interest of the Dunlop family. Occupied by Major Stewart in 1835, when dwelling and offices were valued at only £3.18.0; and by John Dunlop, MD, in 1859, when house, offices and gate lodge were valued at

£27; so there must have been substantial building work between those dates.

The house and farm were occupied by a quarrelsome family, the Forgies, from 1896 to 1916; after the death of Provost Traill, this property was bought under the Land Acts by the then tenant, William McCurdy of Bushmills; by whom it was sold to the present owner's grandfather, Patrick Kane, in the early 1930s.

Photographs: Michael O'Connell.
Situation: 31 Drumnagee Road, Dunseverick; td, Drumnagessan; Parish, Ballintoy; District Council, Moyle; Grid ref. C 993 419.
References: Listed B. OS map, 1832; VAL 1B/131, p 96, VAL 2B/1/24A, 1859, and deeds in D 4081/1/1 and /2/8, all in PRONI; Camac, 'Derrykeighan parish', [1908], p 56; Girvan, 'North Antrim', UAHS, 1972, p 32; H A Boyd, in 'Northern Constitution', 22 July 1978; Pierce and Coey, 'Taken for granted', 1984, p 116.

Clontarriff House, Upper Ballinderry

143. A very decent late-Georgian three-bay two-storey farmhouse of the better kind, roughcast and whitewashed, with a segmental-headed fanlight and side-lights, and windows Georgian-glazed. Nice stone outbuildings, and a blackstone return with red brick dressings to its Georgian-glazed windows. This seems to have been in 1837 the home of John Taylor, classified 1B, and valued at £6.17.0; in 1859, that of Sarah Jane Taylor, presumably his widow or daughter, classification 1B+ and the valuation increased to £10, despite the note "offices not good".

Recently very thoroughly restored after many years of neglect at the hands of an elderly bachelor owner; a pity about the new-looking redbrick chimney-stacks; it would not be hard to roughcast and whiten them.

Photograph: Michael O'Connell.
Situation: Clontariff Road, Upper Ballinderry; td, Cluntirriff; Parish, Ballinderry; District Council, Lisburn; Grid ref. J 157 667.
References: Listed B2. OS map, 1833; VAL 1B/167, p 106, VAL 2B/1/55A, p 41, in PRONI.

Prospect House, Carrickfergus

144. First mentioned in 1767, but usually thought to have been built a few years earlier by Alderman Henry Ellis, mayor of Carrickfergus in 1737, 1754-6, and 1773. However, James Boyle of the Ordnance Survey, writing with the assistance of Samuel M'Skimin, is quite definite that the present house ("a handsome and modern-looking residence" ...... "a two- storey house with 2 sexagons in front") was "erected about the year 1800, by the late Henry Clements Ellis Esq" by whom, according to Atkinson, it was still occupied in 1817. This later date may be confirmed by its insertion in Williamson's revision of 1808 of Lendrick's map of 1780. Valued at £76.14.0 in 1836, the name of John Vance as occupier having been at some later date struck out, and the name of John Borthwick substituted.

However this may be, it is a fine upstanding two-storey-on-basement foursquare late-Georgian house, looking south over the town, built of squared basalt blocks with some galleting. Between two full-height canted bays a flight of nine steps sweeps up to a grand Doric doorcase and fanlight, with a pretty iron balcony above, complete with lamp-holders, and Palladian window. The original glazing-pattern survives upstairs, but not downstairs where rather clumsy Victorian casements have been inserted. The attics are lit by oculi in the gables. The interior retains some good woodwork. Now a restaurant, hemmed in by post-war housing, and not very sympathetically painted, it remains impressive in its island of trees and greenery.

Photograph: Michael O'Connell.
Situation: Woodburn Road, Carrickfergus; td, Middle Division; Parish and District Council, Carrickfergus; Grid ref. J 402 882.
References: Listed A; outside conservation area. Williamson, map, 1808; VAL 1B/187, p 132, D 811/77, D 671/D3/8/5A & 6, all in PRONI; M'Skimin, 'Carrickfergus', 1811, p 53; Atkinson, 'Ireland exhibited', 1823, II, p 446; Campbell and Crowther, 'Carrickfergus', UAHS, 1978, p 32; Pierce and Coey, 'Taken for granted', 1984, p 37.

The Steeple, Antrim

145. "The Steeple, the residence of George Jackson Clark Esq. JP, is cheerfully situated on a gentle swell three quarters of a mile north of the town of Antrim. It takes its name from the ancient round tower" (4). "The dwelling house which is spacious and modern presents rather a handsome appearance. It is two storeys high and was erected by the late Mr Clark in 1827" (Boyle, 1838). J Fleming Tait of the Ordnance Survey, however, considered: "There is nothing extraordinary in its style of architecture. It is a large and rather handsome building." There must have been an earlier house, as it is unambiguously shown on almost exactly the same site in the 1783 edition of Taylor and Skinner, as also Lendrick's and Williamson's maps. It remained in the ownership of the Clark family for a century, and was sold in 1927 to Mr Fawcett. Now the District Council offices, well cared for, the stucco nicely painted in pale green and white, two segmental bows framing a Tuscan portico with a nice pair of ornamental cannon; substantial cornice and modillions; roof and chimneys all in good order. The front hall is outstandingly fine, with a screen of three fluted Doric columns, surmounted by triglyphs and metopes expressed with exemplary crispness, leading to a curving staircase with brass balusters and a mahogany hand-rail terminating in a spectacular curlicue. Otherwise, ornamental plasterwork and detailing have mostly had to give way to the exigencies of bureaucracy; but still, this is an all-too-rare example of a dwelling house adapted to office use without detriment to its external appearance.

Photograph: Michael O'Connell.

Situation: Steeple Road, Antrim; td, Steeple; Parish and District Council, Antrim; Grid ref. J 156 878.

References: Listed B+. Taylor and Skinner, 'Roads', 1783, p 280; Lendrick, map, 1780; Williamson, map, 1808; J Boyle, OSM, 1838, and M M Kertland, 1835, Antrim, XI, pp 21, 50; Young, 'Belfast and province of Ulster', 1903, p 284; Girvan, 'Antrim & Ballymena', UAHS, 1978, p 264; Smyth, 'Antrim', 1984, p 83.

Gracehill House, Stranocum

146. Standing in the midst of good parkland, at the end of the long straight downhill Bregagh Road flanked by great beech trees - presumably, the front avenue before the Land Acts. James Stuart, born in 1743, son of the Rev. Irwin Stuart, built and settled at Gracehill, naming it after his wife Grace Lynd of Stewartstown, probably soon after inheriting on his father's death in 1772. It is clearly shown - "Gracehill - Stewart Esq" - on Taylor and Skinner's map of 1778. Valued in 1833 at £28.13.2, but the "offices badly arranged and inconvenient"; a sketch of their arrangement in the Valuation book. "The residence of Henry Irwin Stuart, treasurer of the county ... the house is rather old, but comfortable" (Boyle, 1835). In 1859, occupied by Mrs Mary Stuart, the valuation increased to £45; soon after, her name struck out, that of the Hon. Chichester Skeffington substituted as lessee from Representatives of General James C Stuart, and the valuation further increased to £50.

Evidently originally a double-pile house facing north-east; to which a new front, facing south-west, was added before 1811. The facade has a central doorcase with Tuscan columns, and an unusually shallow fanlight, at the head of a flight of seven steps with a curved retaining wall; above this, a tall round-headed window; above this, the most austere of pediments. There are two 12-paned Georgian-glazed windows on each floor and on each side. It is only gradually that the eye realises, uneasily, that the

two halves are not symmetrical; nor are the chimney-stacks on the roof. The quoins, of smooth render, are original at the corners of the house, but evidently not so the very large ones around the front door. The walls are of white-painted roughcast. The basement has openings only to west and rear; the west front has a pleasant semi-circular bow of uncertain date; the east front, two large triple windows.

On the death of James Stewart's son, Major-General James Stewart CB, in 1859, the house passed to Thomas S Irwin, whose mother was the General's youngest sister Caroline. In 1872 James Stewart Irwin was the owner; the house was bought about 1955 by Major Windsor, who had married a Chichester of Galgorm; bought from him by the present owner in 1971. The house is still his private residence, but the extensive outbuildings have been converted into a golf club-house in 1994 to sympathetic designs by Caroline Dickson.

Photograph: Michael O'Connell.
Situation: Gracehill Road, Stranocum; td, Gracehill; Parish, Derry-keighan, District Council, Ballymoney; Grid ref. D 029 335.
References: Listed B1. Taylor and Skinner, 'Roads', 1778, p 272; J Boyle, OSM, 1835, Antrim V, p 84; Lewis, TD, 1837, I, p 453; VAL 1B/139A, p 60, VAL 2B/1/32 p 31, in PRONI; Young, 'Three hundred years of Innishowen', 1929, pp 305-6 and 313; Camac, 'Derrykeighan parish', 1908, p 69; Girvan, 'North Antrim', UAHS, 1973, p 35.

Moylena, Muckamore

147. On a splendid site, tucked into a bluff above the Six Mile Water - though cut off from it by the railway - a confusing house of several different dates and materials, on several levels, with paths criss-crossing the wooded hillside behind at even more levels.

The property was originally known as Moylinny, and leased by the Massereene estate to Lewis Reford, linen draper, in 1733. It is shown as the property of Miss Reford on Lendrick's map of 1780. "This snug lodge and tolerably extensive farm is held under the Massereene family, by Mr Joseph Reford, of the firm of Steen and Reford, proprietors of a bleach yard on the river Clady ... it has also the advantage of a glen, which if properly planted, would shed a pleasing and picturesque influence upon the neighbouring lands" (Atkinson, visiting in 1817). Later, on the failure of the Refords, acquired by the Chaine family of Ballycraigy: and evidently much enlarged. M M Kertland of the Ordnance Survey, writing before April 1835, asserts roundly that Moylinny Cottage was built in the year 1832; James Boyle, in 1838, says only "Moylinny Cottage, the residence of William Chaine Esq. Junior, is beautifully situated ... in the townland of Moylinny and on the bank overhanging the romantic glen of that name." Subsequently occupied by Major Torrens, a director of the railway company, who found it convenient to open a

wicket-gate from his garden onto the line so that he could stop a train when he wished to board it. After sundry lettings, the place was finally bought by a Mr Frederick in 1960; and by the present owners in 1994.

The entrance, with nice fanlight and geometrical sidelights, is tucked under over-sailing eaves between two broad canted bays. For the rest, the house is part one-storey, part two-storey, part three-storey: part coursed basalt, part rubbed bricks. It is a complicated house, with many stairs, and some of the grandest rooms at the top of them. It seems likely that the back part is the oldest, each successive addition having been added to the front. There are many pretty details of plasterwork, shutters, pilasters and interior fanlights. The Georgian glazing-pattern is complete except in the 19th-century dormer windows at the front.

Photograph: Michael O'Connell.
Situation: 81 Belfast Road, Muckamore; td, Moylinny; Parish, District Council, Antrim; Grid ref. J 166 857.
References: Listed B1. Lendrick, map, 1780; Atkinson, 'Ireland exhibited', 1823, II, p 148; Memorial of Conveyance, 13 October 1823, Joseph Reford to William Chaine; J Boyle, OSM, 1838, and M M Kertland, 1835, Antrim, XI, pp 21, 50; Girvan, 'Antrim & Ballymena', UAHS, 1969, p 13.

Turnarobert House, Armoy

148. In 1835, "Turnarobert, the residence of the Revd Stevenson Hunter, is situated in the townland of the same name and close to the Glebe. The house is 2-storeys high. There is a tolerable garden and some planting about the house ... Mr Hunter is rector of Loughguile parish" (Boyle).

A very plain, pleasant, five-bay two-storey and attics late-Georgian house without frills, apart from a nice radial fanlight: the walls encased in limestone dry-dash; Georgian-glazed throughout although, oddly, only the lower sashes are made to open. Reputed to have been built by one Hugh Clark, a member of the Clark family of Upperlands, between 1790 and 1800 - the latter on the evidence of maps no longer available; but this is another of the houses added by James Williamson in his revision of 1808 of Lendrick's map of 1780. Atkinson confirms that Henry Clarke Esq. was resident in the house in 1817. In the yard, an earlier building, which may be the 17th-century house of Walter Kennedy, who in 1620 inherited his father's house of "Twornyrobert".

The 1834 valuation shows it as a 2½ storey house valued at £21.15.7, but "too near neighbours for which we deduct £1.12.7"; by 1859, the accommodation comprised "parlour and dining-room, small room behind, 4 bedrooms, 2 garrets, kitchen and small room" but the value had fallen to £18. After Mr Hunter came the Rev. Francis Dobbs, then in quick succession Robert Smyth, John Mullin, and Hugh Gamble: great-uncle of the present owner.

Photograph: Michael O'Connell.
Situation: 185 Glenshesk Road, Armoy; td, Turnarobert; Parish, Armoy; District Council, Moyle; Grid ref. D 075 332.
References: Listed B. Williamson, map, 1808; Atkinson, 'Ireland exhibited', 1823, II, p 448; OS map, 1833; VAL 1B/130, p 94, VAL 2B/1/23A p 46, VAL 12B/2/1A, p 69, all in PRONI; J Boyle, OSM, 1835, Antrim, IX, p 4; Hill, 'Macdonnells of Antrim', 1873, p 64; Hill 'Stewarts of Ballintoy', 1865, p 14; Girvan, 'North Antrim', UAHS, 1972, p 37.

Photographs: Keith Gilmour; Alan Turkington.
Situation: 73 Shankbridge Road, Kells; td, Kildrum; Parish, Connor; District Council, Ballymena; Grid ref. J 131 974.
References: Listed B1. Lendrick, map, 1780; Atkinson, 'Ireland exhibited',

1823, II, p 201; VAL 1A/1/38, p 32, VAL 2B/1/2B, p 29, VAL 12B/3/18A, p 106, in PRONI; J Boyle, OSM, 1835, Antrim, VI, p 21; Girvan, 'West Antrim', UAHS, 1970, p 30; J Kenny, in 'The Glynns', XXII, 1994, p 34.

Kildrum House, Kells

149. A two-storey five-bay Georgian mill-owner's or gentleman-farmer's house, with very tall 12-pane windows upstairs and down, and round-headed windows in the gables lighting the attics, and at the rear, lighting the staircase. The front door has a good segmental-headed doorcase with cobweb fanlight, Greek-key pattern architrave,

and Tuscan columns. At the time of writing, undergoing major repairs and restoration.

Lendrick, in his map of 1780, shows a house named Kildrum, and a 'Bleach Yard' belonging to Mr Mat. Maxwell. It is recorded that Cahill O'Hara, who died in 1640, resided at Kildrum under lease from the Chichesters; it may be this older house that is shown on the map. Girvan thought it might be the present house: but I think this one must date from the age of elegance between 1790 and 1810: the glazing bars are the slimmest I have ever seen (most of the panes are the original glass), and the cross-grained mahogany banister-rail and its terminal curlicue are equally elegant. There is delicate plasterwork in the central hall and stairwell. The house nestles comfortably between a wide lawn with ancient yew-tree, and the (later) stone outbuildings of the farmyard.

Apart from Atkinson, no tradition seems to survive as to its early owners. He writes of Kildrum - "This is a trading establishment of considerable extent (on the Mount Cashel estate) the property of Jesse Millar Esq" (see also Valley Cottage, 212), "and combines with its trade a farm of 100 Irish acres of a stiff clayey soil, in high heart" (1817). He then enumerates the mills on the Kells Water: concluding with the mills of Kildrum, and their production of bleached, brown, and black linen. Boyle, in 1835, interestingly enumerates Kildrum, "residence of Jesse Millar Esquire," amongst the "Gentlemen's Seats". The valuation of 1837 categorises the house 1B, and values it at £28.10.0; by 1861, it was occupied by Mary Miller, presumably his widow, then by Jesse Miller (junior); at some date between 1870 and 1879, both house and bleaching mill passed to John Ross. The house, with 60 acres, was bought by the father of the present owner in the mid-1960s, having previously been the home of the dowager Lady Dunleath.

New Lodge, Kells

150. A late-Georgian house, said to date from about 1805; but perhaps a little later, since it is not shown on Williamson's map of 1808. Atkinson says that in 1817 it was the seat of John Baily, Esq. but may be referring to the other New Lodge at Muckamore (137). In 1836 it was classified 1A, in the occupation of George Boyle, and valued at £16.3.6; in 1860 "a large house but has a neglected appearance, offices not kept in good repair either," occupied by William Boyle, then William Boal. By 1867, in the occupation of Thomas Fry: from 1876 until his death in 1900, occupied by Rev. Thomas Eaton, and thereafter by his widow Matilda Anne: this was a tenancy of a private house, not a manse. By 1892 it was described as "very old house in bad repair", the valuation reduced to £10.

The buildings are T-shaped, the older part at the rear having been substantially rebuilt in recent years. The front block, with an exceptionally fine recessed doorcase, is of two storeys on basement, five bays, Georgian glazing pattern intact (though the sashes are modern replacements), the walls of rubble encased in rendering, with quoins and architraves in the manner of the 1840s. The doorcase is notable for the barley-sugar fluting of the curiously-carved wooden columns dividing the geometrical sidelights from the door itself; the fanlight itself is good, but plain. The front part of the house has recently undergone thorough restoration as a result of an outbreak of dry rot.

Photograph: Michael O'Connell.
Situation: 55 Shankbridge Road, Kells, just by the turn of the Shank Bridge; td, Carnaghts; Parish, Connor; District Council, Ballymena; Grid ref. J 127 982.
References: Listed B1. OS map, 1837; VAL 1B/12, p 39, VAL 2B/1/2A, p 57, VAL 12B/3/18A, p 56, 12B/3/18B, p 78, 12B/3/18C, p 75, Wills and administrations, 1900, all in PRONI; Atkinson, 'Ireland exhibited', 1823, II, p 445; Pierce and Coey, 'Taken for granted', 1984, p 119.

Greenfield House, Kells

151. "Greenfield, the seat of Mr William Johnston, a respectable bleacher on the Mount Cashel estate, comprehends a very neat lodge in the villa style, 75 acres of demesne, and machinery in the above department which finish, on an average, of brown and white linens, about 20,000 pieces annually" (Atkinson, visiting in 1817). A handsome 5-bay 2-storey and attics double-pile house with quoins. The front windows have had plate glass inserted, but the side windows retain their Georgian glazing: excellent fanlight with geometrical sidelights. The house is encased in Roman cement with mature and magnificent magnolias trained up it; clipped back each year when the flowering season is over, they almost conceal the facade when the foliage is at its most luxuriant.

It seems that Girvan accidentally confused this with Templemoyle House close by. It is exceptionally difficult to trace and disentangle the frequently changing ownership of the mills and mill-owners' houses in Kells and the adjoining townlands. It seems likely that Templemoyle, though now much altered, was earlier than Greenfield; both would seem to date from the early 19th century. Templemoyle is one of the houses inserted by Williamson in his 1808 revision of Lendrick's map of 1780, but Greenfield is not shown in either. The Ordnance Survey

Memoir of 1835 (describing it as a "modern and comfortable 2-storey residence") says that this was then occupied by - Maxwell. In the 1837 valuation it seems to be the house in category 1B, measuring 47 feet by 28 by 22, valued at £33.17.9, and occupied by William Charles Johnston. In 1861, its value has dropped to £25; occupier, Robert Brown. In the next thirty years, it was occupied by Thomas McGill, Hugh Wallace, and Robert J Calvert. In 1888, Arthur & Co. bleachers dyers and finishers, occupied Greenfield Mill, but possibly not Greenfield House, which at some time passed into the ownership of the branch of the Dinsmore family which ran the "Old Green Woollen Mills". The last of this branch sold the house in 1954.

Photograph: Michael O'Connell.
Situation: 9 Greenfield Road, Kells; td, Kells; Parish, Connor; District Council, Ballymena; Grid ref. J 144 973.
References: Listed B1. Atkinson, 'Ireland exhibited, 1823, II, pp 147, 447, J Boyle, OSM, 1835, Antrim, VI, p 21; VAL 1B/12, pp 16, 38, VAL 2B/1/2B, pp 34, 36, VAL 12B/3/18A, pp 93, 95, in PRONI; Bassett, 'Antrim', 1888, pp 322-4; Girvan, 'Antrim & Ballymena', UAHS, 1969, p 32; Pierce and Coey, 'Taken for granted', 1984, p 119; Dean, 'Gate lodges', 1994, p 16.

Saint Catherine's, Carrickfergus

152. A white-painted and roughcast house of 1805, built by William D Burleigh Esquire (who also had a seat nearby called "Pausilypo" in 1811) on the site of an older house. The main front of five bays, two-storey on basement; six red sandstone steps up to a very charming, somewhat later, porch, perhaps of about 1815, an amusing construct like a small greenhouse built of tall Georgian-glazed windows - but its foundations have drooped, so it is probably not contemporary with the main building. At the south end of the house, looking out over Carrickfergus and Belfast Lough, a broad semi-circular bay with three windows on the ground and first floors, but only one (not in the centre) in the basement. Black-painted window-surrounds, white painted sashes with Georgian glazing-pattern. Hipped roof with three chimney-stacks.

In 1817, according to Atkinson, the residence of William Stewart Esq. Described in 1839-40 as "the plain but neat residence of the late Colonel Walsh", "there is an excellent garden and good offices". Occupied by Hill Woods in 1836, and described as "all in bad repair", and: "St Catharine's is a plain, 2-storey house, slated. It was built about 35 years ago by William Burleigh Esq. He was succeeded by William Stuart Esq, 14 years ago, Colonel Walsh is now 4 years in it. Now to be let" (1838). It has since had many occupants and owners; possibly because of problems of water supply. The present owner has lived here since 1956.

Photograph: Michael O'Connell.
Situation: 12 Redbrae Road, Carrickfergus; td, Middle Division; Parish, District Council, Carrickfergus; Grid ref. J 407 900.
References: Listed B1. M'Skimin, 'Carrickfergus', 1811, p 116; James O'Kane, map of 1821 in Robinson, 'Carrickfergus'; Atkinson, 'Ireland exhibited', 1823, II, p 446; VAL 1B/187, p 143, in PRONI; J Boyle & S M'Skimin, OSM, 1839-40, Carrickfergus, as yet unpublished.

▷

Photograph: Michael O'Connell.
Situation: 131 Dunminning Road, Glarryford; td, Dunminning; Parish, Craigs, formerly Ahoghill; District Council, Ballymena; Grid ref. D 050 106.
References: Listed B1. Atkinson, 'Ireland exhibited', 1823, II, p 201; J Boyle, OSM, 1835, Antrim, VIII, p 130; Lease of 24 Oct 1798, James Caulfield and John Staples to John Birnie, D 1902/8/4, VAL 1B/1/162, p 35, VAL 2B/1/50B, p 60, in PRONI; Shaw, 'Cullybackey', 1913, pp 146-7; H C Lawlor, in 'Fibres and fabrics journal', September 1941, p 5; Girvan, 'West Antrim', UAHS, 1970, p 33; information from Mr James Fenton.

Dunminning, Glarryford

153. In October 1798, one John Birnie took a series of renewable leases of land at Dunminning from the Caulfield estate, with a view to laying out mill-house, bleach greens and linen mill, under the recent legislation for the encouragement of the Irish linen industry.

In about 1817, "Dunminning stands on the River Maine, which issues from a bog on the Countess of Antrim's estate, of which this residence is a respectable and useful feature - It is the seat of Thomas M Birnie, Esq. and comprehends a handsome modern edifice, on a lawn pleasingly elevated and imbosomed in hills; 100 acres of demesne and farm lands, and a valuable establishment in the bleaching department, in which 15,000 pieces of linens are annually finished, besides double that number in a brown state, under the firm of Birnie and Conyngham" (Atkinson). And, in 1835: "Dunminning, the residence of Thomas Birnie, Esquire, is a neat, modern and commodious dwelling, prettily situated ... near the Main river, the banks of which for more than a mile are beautifully varied and clothed with a thriving plantation of fir, larch, and some ash and beech, the property of Mr Birnie. There is a handsome lawn and numerous and extensive walks in the plantings". And: "Two beetling mills on the Main river are the property of Thomas Birnie Esquire". In the following year, "dwelling, bleaching concern, beetling mill and offices" were together valued at £53.6.0.

This is a fine example of a large late-Georgian mill-owner's house. Ostensibly five-bay and two-storey, with attic windows peeping out of the gables, in fact it stands above a large basement of which the front openings and

area have been filled in. There are massive chimney-stacks serving thirteen hearths; the front door, up three steps, has a nice broad fanlight with side-lights and reeded pilasters. The original window sashes have gone, but have been replaced by reasonably unobtrusive substitutes. The walls are roughcast and white painted. There are extensive stone outbuildings. The situation is enchanting.

At some time soon after 1836, Thomas Birnie - a very wealthy man - emigrated to America, selling the whole place to "the Doctor-Linen-Merchant John Patrick MD of Ballymena" (Lawlor), a descendant of a Scottish family of settlers. For many years the Patricks likewise prospered there, acquiring much surrounding property. In 1862 the house, with "basement story all through", was valued at £16.16.0, with a note "Two sides of a square of Farm House just built. Proprietor "(John Patrick)" intends take down the thatched offices and completing of square", presumably the yard at the rear. "The lands of Dunminning, the most beautiful part of the wide territory formerly owned by the Earl of Mount Cashell. The estate, which has belonged to the Patrick family for generations, is well wooded ... The Maine ... flows out and in among the woods in a most delightful way" (Shaw, 1913). Brigadier John Patrick of Dunminning (the fourth) was MP for Mid-Antrim from 1937 to 1945; but in 1952 the house, with various 19th-century additions, had fallen into decay. It was then sold by John Patrick of Dunminning (fifth and last) to a Mr Maybin, who demolished the accretions and restored the house, selling it again in 1964 to a Mr McQuigg of Ballymoney: who in turn sold to the Fenton family in 1985: who again restored it in 1989.

Glendun Lodge, Cushendun

154. A five-bay two-storey house with a square two-bay extension at the right-hand end of the facade; looking up the glen, not down at the sea, at the end of an avenue of fine trees. Not shown on the White estate map of 1812; evidently built some time in the course of the next twenty years. It seems likely that this, rather than the less attractive Glenmona, was, after Rockport (155), the second building venture in the district of General O'Neill; a conjecture supported by the survival of a panel carved with the O'Neill crest in the dining-room chimneypiece. It seems that Glendun Lodge is the same as "Glens Cottage,

the summer residence of Major James Higginson, a roomy 2-storey house ... within half a mile of the sea", with "some planting about it", described by Boyle in 1835. It was valued at £11.2.0 in 1834, and at £22 in 1860, between which dates its ownership passed from Major Higginson to Richard C Dobbs.

Certainly, the distinctive glazing-pattern both of the wide eight-pane sashes, and of the front door and doorcase side-lights, are almost identical with that of Rockport. Although the roof is this time pitched not hipped, and there are no canted bays, the similarity is striking and is, surely, evidence of the hand of a single progenitor - be he owner, architect, or builder.

The house was the home of "Conway Edward Dobbs, late of Glendun Lodge, Esquire" whose will was proved in 1870 by Conway Edward Dobbs, of 41 Leeson Street, Dublin, Esquire, barrister-at-law, his sole executor: effects under £2000. It was then for many years occupied by Daniel McNeill, Lord Cushendun's uncle, a retired captain in the Indian army, 6 feet 6 inches high, and a notable character; and from his death in 1902 until her own death, aged 98, in 1959, by his redoubtable daughter, known throughout the Glens as "Miss Ada". Thereafter it passed to Mrs Patricia English, a descendant of the Whites of White Hall (76). Well restored after a fire in 1979.

Photographs: Michael O'Connell.
Situation: 65 Cushleake Road, Cushendun; td, Cushendun; Parish, Culfeightrin, District Council, Moyle; Grid ref. D 236 330.
References: Listed B; in conservation area. VAL 1B/1/27B, p 104, in PRONI; OS map 1833; J Boyle, OSM, 1835, Antrim, IX, p 45; White estate map, 1841, D543/7, in PRONI; Brett, 'Glens of Antrim', UAHS, 1971, p 40; Ronald McNeill, 'Antrim and the McNeills', typescript in Linen Hall Library, 1933; Pierce and Coey, 'Taken for granted', 1984, p 115; Rutherford, 'Carrickfergus', 1995, p 72; information per Malachi McSparran; family papers in PRONI and with title deeds.

Rockport, Cushendun

155. The handsome white-painted house can be dated with some exactitude to 1813; for it does not appear on William Martin's very careful map of 1811-12; but Anne Plumptre, who visited in the summer of 1814, wrote - (Cushendun) "is an excellent part of the country for game; on which account Lord O'Neill, the proprietor of Shane's Castle", (in fact, his younger brother; see below) "has built a little shooting-box very near the shore, whither in the season he often comes to shoot". It stands between Castle Carra and the sea. Tradition has it that the great Shane O'Neill was treacherously murdered here by the retainers of Sorley Boy McDonnell, in the course of a banquet, in 1567: "The reception he got from them, after having been for some time in their company, was to mangle him nimbly". "An earthen mound covered with shrubs is said to mark the place where ... Shane was mortally wounded, and running for a short distance fell dead near Castle Carra" (M'Cahan). However, the sober Dr McNeill points out that the killing of O'Neill took place "in his camp; there is no mention of a castle".

In 1789, the 'Castle Park' belonged to the heirs of Hugh McCollum; in 1811, it formed part of the estate of John White (of White Hall, 76); all of the townlands of Castle Park and Cushendun thereafter passed into the possession of Edmund Alexander McNeill, a local gentleman who chose to spend most of his life in Jersey. According to the Memoirs of his grandson, Lord Cushendun, "a great friend of my grandfather at Cushendun was the last Lord O'Neill of the old creation. He had a mania for building, and, having taken a great fancy to the neighbourhood, he built two houses there, one after the other, on my grandfather's property of which he took a lease, namely Rockport and Glenmona Lodge."

It is curious, however, that no such lease seems ever to have been recorded in the Registry of Deeds; few people would build substantial houses without the security of

tenure of a lease for at least 21 years. The first Viscount had been killed at the Battle of Antrim in 1798; the second died, unmarried, in 1841; the title then passed to his brother, General O'Neill, until both expired in 1855. John Barrow, on 2nd September 1835, "proceeded in a car towards Cushendun, in order to deliver the letter of introduction given to me by Lord O'Neill to his brother the General, who resides at that place ... a clear rivulet ran gurgling down to the sea, close to which the General's house is situated; so close, indeed, that when sitting in the drawing-room, which is on the ground-floor, no object

meets the eye but the waves of the sea, with which the ear is also greeted pretty loudly. The house, in fact, stands upon a rock projecting into the water. The General received me with marked civility..."

According to Boyle, in 1835, the house - "the summer residence of Major-General O'Neill MP" - "is a modern two-storey edifice, and very commodious". It was valued, on 9th August 1834, at £20.13.0. of which £2 was added "for vicinity to sea, being a good situation for sea bathing"; compared with £11.2.0 for Glendun Lodge: soon after, the name of General O'Neill was struck out, and that of Matilda Kearns substituted. Her name in turn was struck out in 1868, when Nicholas Crommelin moved here from 'The Caves', the house being then valued at £38. In 1873, Joseph Richardson of Springfield (95) took the house for four years as a place of refuge "while the maids were spring-cleaning Springfield" (oral tradition from my grandmother). Thereafter it was home to the Higginson family of Springmount (78) from 1874 until the 1930s.

The south front faces across the beach to the village, and consists of three canted bays, set in a zigzag under the wide eaves, leaving triangular recesses in between: five 16-pane windows on the ground floor, three more, and two oculi, in the upper floor. The entrance front, of four bays,

has wide Georgian-glazed windows and a pleasant geometrical glazing pattern in the doorcase in the recessed porch. Probably the work of the same architect or skilled builder as Glendun Lodge (154), perhaps also Glenmona and Mount Druid (100).

The house now belongs to the National Trust, and has recently been extensively restored by its lessee. Other lessees and summer tenants have been numerous; the best-known was Nesta Higginson, whose *nom-de-plume* was Moira O'Neill, many of whose poems about the locality were set to music for drawing-room performance before the days of radio and TV.

Photographs: Michael O'Connell. Map of 1841, D543/8, in PRONI.
Situation: Reached down a lane from the Torr Road; td, Castle Park; Parish, Culfeightrin; District Council, Moyle; Grid ref. D 250 334.
References: Listed B+; in conservation area. D543/3, 5, 8, VAL 1B/1/133, 1B/1/135, p 154, VAL 2B/1/27B, p 93, VAL 12B/2/8A, p 7, all in PRONI; Plumptre, 'Residence in Ireland', 1817, p 112; OS map, 1833; J Boyle, OSM, 1835, Antrim, IX, p 45; Barrow, 'Tour round Ireland', 1836, pp 61, 62; M'Cahan, 'Local histories', 1988; Ronald McNeill, 'Antrim and the McNeills', typescript in Linen Hall Library, 1933; Brett, 'Glens', UAHS, 1971, p 40; T McNeill, 'Stone castles of North Antrim', in UJA, 3rd series, 1983, p 46.

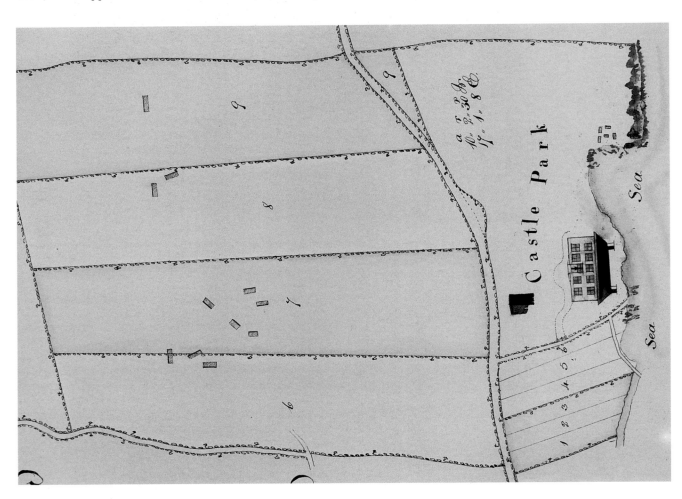

Photograph: Michael O'Connell.
Situation: 1-3 White Park Road, Ballycastle; td, Drumawillin; Parish, Ramoan; District Council, Moyle; Grid ref. D 103 393.
References: Not listed; outside conservation area. 'Faulkner's Dublin Journal', No 1179, 29 Oct to 1 Nov 1737; 'Abstract of the proceedings of the Incorporated Society', Dublin, 1733-1737, and 'A continuation' 1737-8; Taylor and Skinner, 'Roads', 1778, pp 20, 273; T C Robe, OSM, 1831, Antrim, IX, p 91; VAL 1B/135, p 106, VAL 2B/1/28A, p 76, LRI/266/2/A/11 and B, 1881, all in PRONI; Akenson, 'Irish education experiment', 1970, pp 30-36; documents in possession of of owner.

Drumawillin House, Ballycastle

156. Originally the seat of the Boyd family, before the building of the Manor House (now gone) in either 1739 or 1743; granted by Hugh Boyd with 20 acres of land to 'The Incorporated Society for Promoting the Protestant Religion in Ireland'. In 1737, Faulkner's Dublin Journal reported that the Society's Charter School at Ballycastle in the County of Antrim was expected to be "compleated about Michaelmas, and fit to receive its Complement of Children": adding that the Society's "Undertaker for Buildings, and who drew the Plans for the Charter Schools," was no less than "Mr Castle," that is, the distinguished Dublin architect now best known as Richard Cassels. Plans and elevations, in a severely classical style with Diocletian windows, annexed to the 1738 Abstract of the Society's proceedings may well be by Cassels; but the present building bears little, if any, relationship to them. The 1738 minutes record of Ballycastle - "house finished except some inside work." It is shown as "Charter School" on Taylor and Skinner's map of 1778.

The charter schools, incorporated in 1733, received warm support from the Irish Parliament, which, in 1747, made them "the first parliamentary grant to elementary education in the history of the United Kingdom". But it appears that, unhappily, "the charter-schools system was ultra-fanatic - it was formed for the purpose of fanaticising the country - it out-churched the church: it was determined to educate outright into protestantism, and carry the nation by a coup-de-main". The first Report of the Irish Commissioners of Education in 1825 gave the charter schools "a thorough official roasting." And, in the aftermath of Catholic Emancipation, public funding was withdrawn. So, in 1831, Lieutenant Robe writes "Near the Parish church there is a charter school where 60 female children used to be maintained and educated until the age

of 14 when they were bound apprentices to such persons of good character as might require their services. Government having lately decided that no more parliamentary grants should be made for these schools, except for such children as were at them at the time, this establishment will of course soon be at an end." And in 1834, the "old Charter School, belonging to the Incorporated Society" comprised a dwelling measuring 78 feet by 21 feet by 18 feet, with stable, barn, byre etc, and old infirmary, together valued at £13.3.6 - "too large and inconvenient, for which we deduct 5/- in the £:" occupied first by Walter Nugent, subsequently by Lady Honora Boyd, who was still in residence in 1859, when the house was described as 1½ storey, the valuation having increased to £17.10.0.

In 1881 the Society granted a 31-year lease of the place with 33 acres to one William Hayes, "Gentleman Farmer," at a rent of £55 per annum; and in 1908 agreed to sell him the freehold. It seems that the rent was used to augment the endowment of the Church of Ireland parish school in Ramoan. In 1952, the father of the present owner bought Drumawillin from Gardener Hayes.

The frontage to the road gives the appearance of a quite modest cream-painted 3-bay 2-storey farmhouse, with a rectangular doorcase, and plastic windows. To the left, gable-on to the road, what looks like an early-Victorian villa, with ornamental barge-boards. Beyond that, looking out over the town of Ballycastle to Fair Head, the charming Gothick schoolhouse, quite unspoiled, with a pointed door, flanked by slit windows, at the top of three stone steps, more frilly barge-boards, and a fine pair of chimney-stacks near the middle of the roof: clearly not a design by Cassels, but most probably the schoolmaster's residence, of some date between 1790 and 1830.

Collin House, Glenwhirry

157. A pleasant two-storey five-bay roughcast traditional house of three dates: the right-hand part, three bays wide, of 1763 (datestone); another two bays, the windows more widely spaced, added probably before 1830; and a return at the rear. The fanlight and glazing bars are modern, but the house succeeds in retaining much character, inside and out.

There are indications that this was the shooting lodge or rustic retreat of merchants or minor gentry, not just a working farm: there is parkland, there is a garden, the farmyard is at some remove from the house: though the Ordnance Survey writers assert that there is no gentleman's seat at Glenwhirry. It is reputed to have belonged first to the Gillilan family (Atkinson records it as the seat of John Gilleland Esq. in 1817); and from around 1830, to the Allens, with whom in his youth the poet Sir Samuel Ferguson, whose grandmother was Ellen Gillilan, spent

his holidays. "He said that at Glenwhirry he received impressions of nature and romance which influenced all his habits of thought and sentiment in after life", according to S A Blair. In 1836, Collin House was valued at £17.5.4: probably John Allen, whose family also owned Breckenhill (126) nearby, had enlarged it, for only part of the house appears on the 1832 Ordnance Survey map. Since 1896, the house and farm have belonged to the Crawford family.

Photograph: Michael O'Connell.
Situation: 74 Collin Road, Glenwhirry; td, Tildarg; Parish, Rashee; District Council, Ballymena; Grid ref. J 227 982.
References: Not listed. Datestone, '1763, JBP'; Atkinson, 'Ireland exhibited', 1823, II, p 439; OS map, 1832; J Boyle, T C Hannyngton, OSM, 1835-6, Antrim, XII, pp 76, 79; VAL 1B/111, in PRONI; Ferguson, 'Sir Samuel Ferguson', 1896, I, p 24; Blair, 'Co. Antrim characters', 1993, pp 86, 87.

Brecart Lodge, Toome

158. A two-storey rendered house, recently completely restored and renovated, on a marvellous site overlooking the Lower Bann between Lough Neagh and Lough Beg, the bank bound together for almost a quarter of a mile by enormous old lime-trees, planted close together.

It is, however, a puzzle to know whether this is "Brecart Tower, the residence of Captain Daniel O'Neill. It was in 1818 the house was commenced and almost every year since that time additions have been built to it by Captain O'Neill. Previous to the above date it was a thatched cottage"; or "Brecart Cottage, situated on the north-east side of the Bann in the townland of Brecart near the Tower. The house was erected, about 50 years ago by John O'Neill Esq, who was succeeded by Mr Samuel Finiston ... The planting consists of all sorts of forest trees of Irish growth, about 7 acres" - (both descriptions by J Bleakly, July 1837). The puzzle is compounded by the fact that the present, faintly Elizabethan-revival, buildings look as if they date from around 1835; and the valuation of 1839 reports house, office, gate-lodge and 32 acres occupied by Mr Francis M Cox: "house valued at £19, add for situation £6.10.0, and good finish ... £1.10.0": total, £27 for buildings and £33 for "good arable pasture and meadow".

The principal front is of three bays, the two corbelled and gabled wings advancing, with Georgian-glazed windows under label mouldings; a central porch with a castellated parapet, concealing a nice internal fanlight and sidelights; at the back of the hall a good staircase, lit by a tall round-headed Georgian-glazed window. Extensive out-buildings around a yard at the rear. There is a surprising, later, gate-lodge, now derelict, with Puginesque bargeboards, perhaps to a design by James Sands.

The actor, Richard Todd, spent much of his childhood here with his step-grandfather, S R Hunter, and has written a charming account of the house in the first volume of his autobiography. He describes Brecart as "a long, low L-shaped house of Queen Anne origin, the outside rendered over and painted greyish-white ... its longest elevation was only one room deep, the rooms leading off a lengthy, shadowy corridor on both ground and first floors ... Beyond the lawn lay a strip of grassland bordered by a beautiful line of fifty lime trees, and then the river ... Brecart had been built on the site of a priory or some such religious foundation that had been sequestrated after the Reformation. The story went that, before his charge was seized, the abbot or prior had drowned himself in the well in the courtyard and had pronounced a curse on the place to the effect that whatever family should inhabit Brecart would end in degradation and ruin." Unhappily, his own mother drowned herself in the river in 1937, and he has never returned.

Photograph: Michael O'Connell.

Situation: 34 Roguery Road, Toome; td, Brecart; Parish, Duneane; District Council, Antrim; Grid ref. H 995 918.

References: Listed B1. J Bleakly, OSM, 1837, Antrim, VI, pp 116, 117; VAL 2B/1/72B, p 35, in PRONI; O'Laverty, 'Down and Connor', III, 1884, p 349; Dean, 'Gate lodges', 1994, p 6; Todd, 'Caught in the act', 1986, pp 19-29, 32; notes by D Crawley in HMB.

Union Lodge, Toome

159. A two-storey three-bay house of blackstone with red-brick dressings, covered in clipped ivy. The windows have eight panes in each sash: there is an unusual porch, painted red, and geometrical front door of three circles one above another - a close copy of the original door shown in a Green photograph.

In 1837, "Union Hall is the residence of Mr Robert Davison. The house is 2-storey high, slated, and was commenced in 1834 and finished in 1837, and cost £1,000. It is situated near the corn mill in Ballymatuskerty, on Lord O'Neill's estate. The above appropriate name was given to it by the proprietor Mr Davison, as it was from the benefit of the Union linen Mr Davison made his money." But by the time of the valuation and perambulation of

December 1839, the house was occupied by one Jacob Green. The entry in the Valuation book contains comments in three different hands: the first, "this house would be worth £15 to £20, but as occupied only by a small farmer I have kept the value lower"; the second, "a small farmer holding 78 acres statute is a large farmer here"; the third, perhaps rather later, "Gentleman's residence, well finished". In the event, the valuation was raised from £13 to £16.

There are extensive farm outbuildings, like the house itself in excellent condition, at the rear. Up a wooded lane opposite, the remains of another house built with textile money, "Cotton Bank, the residence of Mrs McMullan, built about 24 years ago" (1837); occupied in 1817 by Mr James McMullan.

Photographs: Michael O'Connell; W A Green, Ulster Folk Museum WAG 1739.
Situation: 21 Ballymatoskerty Road, Toome; td, Ballymatoskerty; Parish, Duneane; District Council, Antrim; Grid ref. J 017 923.
References: Listed B1. Atkinson, 'Ireland exhibited', 1823, II, p 440; J Boyle, OSM, 1837, Antrim, VI, p 114; VAL 2B/1/72B, p 23, in PRONI.

Laurel Vale, Aghalee

160. A very pleasing three-bay two-storey late Georgian house of about 1830, of grey random rubble, with an uncommonly congenial patina, set off by red-painted brick relieving arches over the openings. All five windows in the facade are Georgian-glazed; the wide doorcase has a very good segmental fanlight; door and side-lights, both in a nice scumbled finish. The roof is of slate with a grey chimney-stack at each gable. There is a three bay two-storey return.

In 1834, Mrs Anne Thompson lived here, the house being classified B+ and valued at £10.10.0. "Mr Samuel Thompson has on the north side of, and contiguous to the old church of Aghalee, a very neat 2-storey and slated house lately built by his parents. To it is attached good office houses and well-enclosed yards ... The aforesaid buildings and other improvements surrounding the old church give the place altogether a beautiful appearance" (Fagan, 1838). Mr Thompson sold to one Robert Joseph Lewis, from whom the present owner bought the farm in 1948.

The garden is framed, on the right-hand side by greenhouse and the survivor of a pair of very fine monkey puzzlers, on the left-hand side by extensive white-washed and glazing-barred outbuildings: it has splendid geometrical box edgings. Opposite the back door, under a spreading damson tree, a dog-house and two duck-houses are built into a whitewashed stone wall; all three just at present untenanted.

Photograph: Michael O'Connell.
Situation: 15 Ballinderry Road, Aghalee; td, and Parish, Aghalee; District Council, Lisburn; Grid ref. J 128 656.
References: Listed B. OS map, 1832; VAL 1B/166, p 19, in PRONI; T Fagan, OSM, 1838, Antrim, VII, p 32; information from owner.

Crew Mount, Glenavy

161. A three-bay two-storey white-washed rubble late-Georgian farmhouse, in the traditional style: the outbuildings including a quite unspoiled cobbled yard, and lofts with stone exterior staircase. There is a curving screen wall, and a stone arch giving access to the yard, gable, return and back door. The front has a Georgian glazing-pattern of smaller square windows above, deeper windows below, all set in heavy black-painted architraves with unusual lugs above the sill level at the bottom. The door-case has rectangular fanlight and side lights divided by slim geometrical bars in the manner fashionable about 1840. There are three yellow-brick chimney-stacks unevenly spaced on the ridge of the slated roof; that over-looking the yard bears the date 1908, which may refer to the date when the house was raised a storey.

Crew Hill, close by, where the Ordnance Surveyors established a triangulation point near the ancient boulder, is a place of great antiquity and, it would seem, importance: 'The Spreading Tree of the Hill', referred to in the Annals of the Four Masters, was where the ancient Kings of Ulidia were inaugurated. There, Dr O'Laverty reports,

Brian Boru encamped in 1005 AD, and was supplied with 1200 beeves, 1200 hogs, and 1200 wethers; for which he bestowed 1200 horses, besides gold, silver, and clothing. Mr Warner thinks the low mound behind the house may well mark one of the sacred places of the Hill of the Tree.

Henry Moore built himself a new house in 1837, valued, however, at only £3.5.6. This may or may not be the house, valued at £9 in 1860, occupied in that year by Isaac McKinstry McNeice, the only house in the townland of so high a value. In the ownership of the present family since 1945; previously, one of the farms in the district owned by the Ballance family, whose most distinguished representative emigrated to New Zealand.

Photograph: Michael O'Connell.
Situation: 15 Carnkilly Road, Glenavy; td, Crew; Parish, Glenavy; District Council, Lisburn; Grid ref. J 165 712.
References: Listed B2. OS map, 1832; VAL 1B/167, p 67, VAL 2B/1/58A, p 60, in PRONI; O'Laverty, 'Down and Connor', II, 1880, pp 294-6; R B Warner, in 'Lisburn Historical Society journal', VIII, 1991, p 40; Totten, 'Gleanings from Glenavy parish', [1980], p 30.

Moore Fort, Ballymoney

162. Hidden away amidst mature woodland, an attractive late-Georgian house which, for once, can be dated with accuracy: Atkinson wrote in 1833 of visiting the previous year "Moorefort ... a new house (to which splendid approaches with corresponding plantations were talked of) was then in progress of erection ... when the improvements already contemplated have been completed, Moorefort will be a seat of considerable respectability". Two years later, James McGann wrote "Moorefort, the seat of James Moore Esquire ... is large and has a good appearance. There is a large garden on the north of the house walled all round ... The general appearance of the place is naked at present, but the planting is very young..."

Samuel Lewis, in 1837, surprisingly remarks " ... at Moore Fort, about 3 miles distant" (from Ballymoney) "is a very extensive distillery belonging to James Moore, Esq., in which from 50,000 to 60,000 gallons of whiskey are annually made: there is also a mill for spinning flax, and a very extensive flour-mill." This sorts oddly with the tradition that there was a room used for Quaker meetings: the solution is to be found in the Valuation book of 1860: the "old distillery", valued at £15, "is going to ruin, all the machinery taken away, of no value as it stands at present," but "Mr Moore uses a loft in this for preaching in and for no other purposes."

Of five bays and two storeys, stuccoed and with quoins,

Georgian-glazed windows complete, long return and a big yard at the rear, it does not quite live up to first impressions. The front wall is carried up higher than usual to the eaves to allow space for large attic rooms, lit by windows in the gables; but this sets the proportions astray. There is a most curious canted porch, with fanlight and outer doorway at each side, leading to an internal doorway with a very wide radial fanlight and Gothic glazing bars in double doors and sidelights. The principal rooms have very heavy floral cornices and centre-pieces, mostly with the original lurid Victorian polychrome paintwork; the kitchen ceiling has no less than 78 hooks for hanging things from. The staircase and bannisters are pleasing, with a peculiar curly turn at the first landing, and a kind of semi-circular kink at the attic landing.

The house appears to have remained in the ownership of one or other branch of the Moore family until bought by a Mr Henry, who died in 1995.

Photograph: Michael O'Connell.
Situation: 39 Glenstall Road, Ballymoney; td, Drumaheglis; Parish, and District Council, Ballymoney; Grid ref. C 907 256.
References: Listed B. Atkinson, 'Ireland in the nineteenth century', 1833, p 193; J McGann, OSM, 1835, Antrim, V, p 9; Lewis, TD, 1837, I, p 150; VAL 2B/1/35A, p 41, in PRONI; Girvan, 'North Antrim', UAHS, 1972, p 45.

Ballyhibistock (or Ballyhivistock) House, Ballymoney

163. Built by Charles George Stuart, son of a Co. Antrim clergyman, who fought in the 88th Regiment (the Connaught Rangers) in the Peninsular War, after which he returned to his father's home at Dunluce rectory. "After his father's death in 1826 he settled at Ballyhivistock, which he built, planted, and improved, and became agent for several important estates in north Antrim. He lived for some time in the old rectory at Derrykeighan, while Ballyhivistock was being built. The house was planned for himself, and his sister Eliza alone, as he had at that time no intention of getting married." However, in 1846 he married a daughter of the rector of Billy, by whom he had eight sons and two daughters: so that the house had to be enlarged in the 1850s to accommodate them all. In the 1833 valuation, "Charles George Stewart Esq" is shown as the occupier of a cottage in category 2C, 57 feet 6 inches long but only 9 feet six inches high, valued with offices and cart-shed at a mere £4.15.9: but a pencil note indicates that rebuilding is in hand: and by 1859 he is shown as occupier of a house in category 1A, measuring 35 feet by 35 feet by 19 feet high, and valued at £28. His sons William and Leslie in turn followed him there, the former having spent most of his life in Canada, the latter in Australia.

Two-storey, on cellar, three-bay, of white-painted stucco, no quoins but an interesting pattern of recessions in the walls and surrounds to the upstairs windows; hipped roof with (modern) central roof-light; wide eaves on paired wooden brackets. Unfortunately, the condition of the house had greatly deteriorated by 1956 when it was acquired by the present owner from Leslie Stewart; alterations resulting from dry rot included the removal of chimney-stacks and the insertion of plastic windows. The front door is quite plain, contained in a not very happy modern porch. Nevertheless, the house, in its setting of well-matured trees and gardens, has a certain presence which survives its indignities.

Photograph: Michael O'Connell.
Situation: 147 Castlecatt Road, Ballymoney; td, Ballyhibistock Lower; Parish, Derrykeighan; District Council, Ballymoney; Grid ref. C 957 344.
References: Not listed. VAL 1B/139/B, p 28, VAL 2B/1/32, p 48, in PRONI; Camac, 'Derrykeighan parish', [1908], p 55; Young 'Three hundred years of Innishowen', 1929, pp 308-311; Girvan, 'North Antrim', UAHS, 1972, p 35.

Moyarget Lodge, Armoy

164. Externally, an austere and box-like house, two-storey and three bay, with oversailing hipped roof on brackets, glazing bars complete; very plain rectangular doorcase; walls covered in cement render and quite devoid of detail or ornament. Internally, a cheerful and comfortable house, but with no features of especial distinction.

Moyarget was built between 1835 and 1842 by John Stewart Moore, a younger son of the Ballydivity (121) family who went to India in 1826, rose to become a Lieutenant Colonel in the army of the East India Company, and returned, not very much richer, about 1834. He seems to have lived in a much smaller house at Moyarget whilst this one was a-building. In 1852, he married Elizabeth Dunlop of Drumnagessan (142), by whom he had six daughters.

After his death, the place passed to his spinster daughter Elizabeth - "Cousin Bess" - who lived from 1857 until 1947: she was a popular lady who actively farmed the property herself. On her death, it passed to the sons of her youngest sister, who had married Francis Turnly Gage in 1890; from them it was bought back in 1947 as a home for James Stewart Moore on his retirement from the Royal Navy, and subsequently, in 1971, was acquired by his younger brother Hume when James moved into Ballydivity.

Photograph: Michael O'Connell.
Situation: 98 Moyarget Road, Armoy; td, Moyarget Upper; Parish, Ramoan; District Council, Moyle; Grid ref. D 072 381.
References: Not listed. Letters from John Stewart Moore in possession of present owners; family tradition.

Larchfield, Kilraghts

165. Since the house does not appear on the first Ordnance Survey maps, nor in the Memoirs, it must be later than 1835; but it looks earlier, a fine big four-square mill-owner's house in the late-Georgian rectory tradition. Perhaps about 1840? Said to have been built by, or for, a Mr Hugh Moore; in the valuation of 1861 the occupier was James Dawson but the owner Hugh Moore; the house was valued at £28, the flax mill and offices at £16; no other building in the townland was valued at more than £5, save the covenanters' meeting house at £8.

A three-bay two-storeyed house, Georgian-glazed, walls roughcast, quoins, architraves and stringcourse of smooth stucco, centred on a very pleasing doorcase with nice fan-light and curlicues in the side-lights. The wide oversailing eaves of the hipped roof, with its two chimney stacks, are most attractive. At the rear, a half-round-headed window lights the landing of the disappointingly meagre staircase.

Bought by Finlay from Moore; by Stewart from Finlay; and, in 1924 by Andrew Sayers from Stewart: and still owned and occupied by his descendants.

Photograph: Michael O'Connell.
Situation: 176 Kilraghts Road, Kilraghts; td, and Parish, Kilraghts; District Council, Ballymoney; Grid ref. D 015 262.
References: Listed B1. VAL 12B/4/18A, in PRONI; Girvan, 'North Antrim', UAHS, 1972, p 47.

Kilcoan House, Islandmagee

166. A four-bay two-storey late Georgian house, with a four-bay single-storey extension, white painted roughcast walls, Georgian glazing complete, a nice radial fanlight in the round-headed doorcase. In 1840, James Boyle reported that there were in Islandmagee parish 487 houses, of which 31 were of two storeys, all the latter (with two or three exceptions) "of comparatively modern erection, and of neat and modern appearance." There was no two-storey house in this townland in 1834, only a largeish cottage, 10 feet high, valued at £8.2.0., belonging to a Mrs Gordon. Between that year and 1860, probably earlier rather than later, Arthur Hill built a new 2-storey house, measuring 15 yards by 7 yards, and classified 1A, which

was valued at £11.7.6, in the latter year. He was followed by William B Hill; the value of the dwelling fell gradually to £8.10.0 in 1878, presumably through decay or neglect. Purchased by the present owner in 1986 from a descendant of Arthur Hill, and well restored since then, the red ensign flies at the flagpole all year round in memory of his father, an Islandmagee seafarer drowned in the 'European Gateway' at Harwich.

Photograph: Michael O'Connell.
Situation: 16 Millbay Road, Islandmagee; td, Kilcoan More; Parish, Islandmagee; District Council, Larne; Grid ref. J 458 993.
References: Listed B. VAL 1B/118, p 116, VAL 12B/7/12A, p 68, in PRONI; J Boyle, OSM, 1840, Antrim, III, p 35.

Woodbank, Whiteabbey

167. Built on a bluff, the seaward facade, with a central canted bay, looking east over Belfast Lough towards Grey Point; the entrance facade, with a handsome fluted Doric porch, facing more or less south; the western facade has a semi-circular bay with two windows. Most of the latter retain their Georgian glazing bars save in the ground floor of the canted bay. Of two and a half storeys, with a nice (but evidently not the original) staircase.

Said to date from 1810, on the site of, and possibly still incorporating, a much earlier house; if so, greatly altered over the years. Disconcertingly, James Boyle, writing in 1839, says "Woodbank is the residence of the Rev. Robert W Bland [and] is of the Grecian and Elizabethan style. Built 1837, 2-storeys high, with 3 acres of ornamental ground and planting. Thomas Jackson Belfast, architect." Can this be the same house? Has there been some transposition of names? The present house does not present any 'Elizabethan' characteristics, and only the porch seems 'Grecian'.

Thomas McTear, born in 1800, says that, in his boyhood, "Abbeylands was then occupied by - Haslet, who sold it, about 1803, to the late Hugh McCalmont ......; Woodbank adjoins, then the residence of - Hill; next to it was Abbeyville, the residence of Maxwell Lepper, who

sold it to the widow of Thomas Sinclaire, who left it to her nephew, the late Rev. R W Bland of St. George's Church, and is now occupied by his son, General Bland, RE" Perhaps it was Abbeyville, not Woodbank, that was Elizabethan. Abbeyville was knocked down to make way for the late-Victorian convent. Both houses were for many years occupied by members of the Bland family. In August 1910, Miss Lilian Bland became the first Irish aviatrix, flying her home-made plane at Randalstown: "There was no petrol tank, so we used a whiskey bottle and fed fuel into the engine with my aunt's large ear trumpet." In 1923 sold to Mr Crookshank KC; the art historian Anne Crookshank spent her childhood here.

The house is of white-painted (not lately) stucco; it has chimney stacks placed close together on a hipped roof; ample outbuildings; mature trees; and a steeply sloping garden running down to a private slipway.

Photograph: Michael O'Connell.
Situation: 451 Shore Road, Newtownabbey; td, White Abbey; Parish, Carnmoney; District Council, Newtownabbey; Grid ref. J 355 819.
References: Listed B2. OS map, 1833; J Boyle, OSM, 1839, Antrim, I, p 84; interview with Miss Bland, 'Sunday Express', 18 April 1965; Thomas McTear, in UJA, 2nd series, V, 1899, p 165.

Loughside (formerly Copeland View), Greenisland

168. An intriguing house (or pair of houses, it is not quite clear which. On the face of it, two semi-detached houses formerly with a connecting door upstairs, perhaps designed to allow the owner to make summer lettings of half his home to Victorian commuters). According to the Parliamentary Gazetteer of 1845, along this shore "Villas, cottages and miscellaneous lodgings for the accommodation of sea-bathers, are numerous and in great request". Facing south over Belfast Lough, close to the high tide mark, but shielded from northerly gales and public view by a high bank, and a clump of fine mature trees.

The house first appears, substantially in its present form, on the Ordnance Survey revised map of 1857. The name was changed between 1870 and 1877. It was occupied from 1880 until his death in 1899 by Professor James Cuming, Professor of Medicine at Queen's University, the first alumnus to be appointed to a chair, and the only Roman Catholic on the academic staff throughout his 34 years of office: educated in Dublin, Paris and Vienna, as well as at Queen's, he was an admirer of Horace and inventor of the celebrated Cuming's dyspepsia powders. It was apparently he who tacked onto the west-facing gable a splendid Victorian cast-iron conservatory, with ratchets for ventilation, fat heating pipes, and fruiting vine, all still

in working order; and at the other end of the house a fine music-room - still so used. The Professor's third hobby, that of siting statuary in trees, is commemorated by a plaster skull embedded in a tree close to the house. After Cuming's death, the house was occupied by Tom Sterling, JP, confectioner, "with branches all over the city"; the drawing-room and music-room, as they were in 1909, were illustrated in 'Belfast and the Province of Ulster', to show off his "collection of antiques, furniture and silver, etc ... unequalled in the north of Ireland".

A plain, white-painted, block, with blue trim, of six bays, the pitched roof bearing three chimney stacks with nice black pots; the upper windows now glazed with plate-glass, but many of the others Georgian-glazed; a long enclosed veranda has at some later date been added. The drawing-room of 53B still has the fireplace visible in one of the photographs of 1909.

Now two semi-detached houses.

Photograph: Michael O'Connell.
Situation: 53A and 53B Shore Road, Greenisland; td, West Division; Parish, and District Council, Carrickfergus; Grid ref. J 379 847.
References: Not listed. PG, I, 1845, p 324; Bassett, 'Antrim', 1888, p 163; Young, 'Belfast and province of Ulster', 1909, pp 182, 184, 228, 454; Moody and Beckett, 'Queen's', 1959, I, pp 175,176, II, p 606.

Glenochty House, Glarryford

169. A 19th-century farmhouse in the Georgian tradition, on a hillside looking out east over Glarryford and its valley. Evidently originally of three bays, with two similar bays added; 8-pane sashes upstairs and down, the lower windows both taller and wider than those above, in stucco architraves, the walls rendered or roughcast; simple pilastered doorcase with modern door; lower three-bay extension with 3 over 6-pane sashes; three chimney stacks surmounting the ridge.

In 1836, this seems to have been the home of James Smith, though then only 12 feet high, valued at £6.19.4: "too near neighbours, for which, and exposure, we deduct £1"; "large farm and wealthy". By 1861, it was occupied by Francis Dysart of Portglenone, who leased it from George Gray; and was a two-storey house with return. In 1870, "house rebuilt": but valued at only £6; still in the occupancy of Francis Dysart, who died in 1912 aged 76. His son Matthew died in 1942, and Matthew's widow in 1962. The Dysarts had sold to one Thomas Gordon in 1920; the present owners bought from the Gordons in 1990.

Photograph: Michael O'Connell.
Situation: 28 Duneany Road, Glarryford; td, Duneany; Parish, Rasharkin; District Council, Ballymena; Grid ref. D 035 134.
References: Not listed. VAL 1B/162, p 195, VAL 2B/1/50B, p 56, VAL 12B/3/15A, p 36, in PRONI; gravestone in Killymurris 2nd Presbyterian churchyard; information from Mr Ernest Dysart and Mr John Ross.

Ollar Lodge, Ballyclare

170. Set back from the road near the heart of Ballyclare, behind a nicely-laid-out garden with a large weeping ash at its centre, a very pleasant range of white-painted rough-cast two-storey houses under a single roof, with a central doorcase with fanlight and side-lights, the dressings round the openings painted black. Evidently early 19th-century; named from the former name of the river. The main house occupied for many years by Christie Beggs, a solicitor, who hung Chinese lanterns on his tree to celebrate the coronation of King Edward VII in 1902, to great effect. The separate upper room used at various dates as a Unitarian meeting house, a schoolroom, and a court-house.

There are 10 bays in all, unevenly spaced, but this terrace is of sufficient merit to be treated as a single entity. Despite the facts that some doors and windows have been blocked up, plastic doors and windows inserted elsewhere, the original roof replaced by asbestos tiles, and the chimney stacks rebuilt, the group somehow manages, just, to transcend all the inappropriate alterations; and still great-ly lightens and enhances the character of a rather pedestrian town centre.

"In addition to the beautiful big weeping ash which still stands in the centre of the garden today, there were two fine overhanging trees, one growing at each corner of the grounds, their wide branches stretching far out towards the roadway. There on hot summer days the ancients of the village would foregather under their shady branches to enjoy their smoke and afternoon gossip. They would lie, pipes between their teeth, arms folded, backs against the wall and with feet outstretched on the 'cassie', a look of contentment on every face, and all at peace with the whole world" (Grange).

Photograph: Michael O'Connell.
Situation: 10-14 Main Street, Ballyclare; td, and Parish, Ballyclare; District Council, Newtownabbey; Grid ref. J 288 912.
References: Not listed. Armstrong, 'Newtownabbey', [1979], p 178; extracts per Jack McKinney from R T Grange, mss.

Glenhurst, Muckamore

171 (left). Evidently built about 1845 (on the evidence of the glazing-pattern): or perhaps a little earlier? A two-storey five-bay house (with extensions at either end), with Tudor window-heads and label mouldings: the pretty glazing lifts it out of the ordinary: there are 26 panes of glass in each pointed upper sash, 19 in each lower one. Pierce and Coey call it "an attractive Regency Gothic house". Formerly a mill manager's house for the Chaine family's Muckamore Mill, it was purchased by the present owners, as sitting tenants, from the Liquidator of the York Street Flax Spinning Company in 1958: an uncommonly shrewd buy. Unfortunately, the original chimneys have been dispensed with, and their substitutes are unworthy. The site, on a ledge above the Six Mile Water, is magnificently romantic.

Photograph: Michael O'Connell.
Situation: 29 Oldstone Road, Muckamore; td, and Parish, Muckamore; District Council, Antrim; Grid ref. J 166 854.
References: Listed B. Girvan, 'Antrim & Ballymena', UAHS, 1969, pp 11, 13; Pierce and Coey, 'Taken for granted', 1984, p 121.

Oatland Cottage, Upper Ballinderrry

172. The original cottage was probably built between 1810 and 1820: it must have been very handsome, with its exceptionally fine and spidery fanlight and sidelights, framed between four delicate Ionic columns; the walls are of coursed blackstone with extensive galleting; the window surrounds are of red brick, painted; the Georgian glazing-pattern still complete, downstairs. A curiously exotic porch, which appears in photographs of the cottage before the upper floor was built, added at some date in the mid-19th century. This was the home of Mr Thomas Walkington, owner of extensive corn mills, and of his descendants who are said to have been successful investors in banks and railways, and to have grown rich. The Valuation books for Upper and Lower Ballinderry are exceptionally hard to interpret, especially as the family owned more than one property in each, but this is probably the house, in Category 1A, valued at £14.7.5 in 1837, and at £32 in 1862.

In 1903, Mrs Octavia Walkington, second and much younger wife of Mr Samuel Walkington, decided that the house should be enlarged and modernised, and brought in the Belfast architect William Fennell, at this time engaged in the restoration of Ballinderry Middle Church (25), to add another storey to the front of the house: which he did, in a sort of Norman manner: with the surprising result that all the upper windows to the front have casements and shutters, in striking contrast to the Georgian glazing bars in the sashed windows below. The mixture is one seldom found elsewhere, save in the Channel Islands, where Victor Hugo remarked on the differing characteristics of 'French' windows and English 'guillotine' sashes. The result is nevertheless rather charming; the frilly brackets at the eaves, the strapwork, the paintwork, are all nicely executed. In consequence of this somewhat bizarre transmogrification, never in fact completed internally, the house has a distinctly androgynous air - masculine below, feminine above; and the unfounded rumour has gained currency that the addition was the work of an imported French architect. The rest of the family, it is recalled, did not think Aunt Octavia's alterations to be much for the better.

There is a very fine monkey-puzzler in the lawn in front of the house. The last of the Walkingtons sold to the present owner in 1950.

Photograph: Michael O'Connell.
Situation: 6 Lower Ballinderry Road, Upper Ballinderry; td, Ballyscolly; Parish, Ballinderry; District Council, Lisburn; Grid ref. J 162 673.
References: Not listed. Not referred to specifically in the 1830 OSM, but clearly shown on the OS map of 1832; VAL 1B/167, p 92, VAL 2B/1/55A, p 59, in PRONI; information from Hugh Kirk, Kathleen Gleave, and Sally MacIntyre, née Walkington.

Glenravel House, Cargan

173. Concealed behind an inscrutable belt of trees, a fine house, part early-Victorian, part of this century, but hard to be sure which is which; with views of woodland, lake, and mountains. Built by John Benn, the landlord of Glenravel, probably in 1842, to take advantage of the building in that year of the new road from Ballymena to Cushendall, in place of Binvore Cottage, further up the hill, his previous home.

John Benn's sons, George and Edward, tried to build up at Cargan a new industry distilling whiskey from potatoes, but (despite persuasive letters to members of the Government, coolly rebuffed) this venture was closed down by the excise authorities. George Benn lived here a retired life for more than thirty years, and it was here that he wrote the greater part of his two-volume History of Belfast. In 1876, the house was evidently let to John Fisher, the Cargan mineral developer; valued at £25 in 1860, £30 in 1864, so additions would seem to have been made between those dates. On George Benn's death in 1882 (he left £1000 to the Belfast Charitable Society to provide a special dinner for the residents of Clifton House every Christmas and Easter), Glenravel was bought at auction by his brother-in-law, Professor Hodges, a man of inquiring mind who set up here his own private experimental agricultural station where he carried out research into flax, manures and silage. After his death in 1899, and that of his elder son killed at the Somme, the house was inhabited by his younger son, Captain Jack Hodges, a champion boxer, golfer, and drinker, who lived on there with his first and second wives until his death in 1970. Acquired by the present owner in 1974 from Captain Hodges's sister, Betty Gardiner.

The early-Victorian house (really, delayed-Georgian) survives in the very nice segmental headed doorcase, with ornate fan borne on two pairs of thin Ionic engaged columns; the charmingly proportioned lobby at the head of the main staircase; and the glazing bars, intact (or replaced) in almost all the windows. The walls are now roughcast and painted white, there have been numerous additions and alterations over the years, and the house has been re-roofed in brown tiles. (The slates were removed - it is said that they sufficed to slate 17 lesser houses in Glenravel! - and replaced by bright red tiles, by which Captain Hodges had been attracted during the first World War; but these proved unsuited to the climate, and the house had to be re-roofed again about 1970). Much, including a Queen Anne style dormer, does not look original. Nevertheless, as at the not wholly dissimilar Cleggan Lodge (89), the original character of the house is still discernible.

Photograph: Michael O'Connell.
Situation: 151 Glenravel Road, Cargan; td, Craigdunloof; Parish, Dunaghy; District Council, Ballymena; Grid ref. D 163 172.
References: Not listed. Datestone in stable yard; Benn papers, D 3113, VAL 2B/1/46A, p 18, and VAL 12B/3/22A, p 12, all in PRONI; Hamond, 'Industrial heritage', 1991, p 19; 'Glenravel', 1993, pp 32-48.

Clotworthy House, Antrim

174. Built about 1840 as carriage houses and stabling for Antrim Castle; now an Arts Centre. In 1838 James Boyle of the Ordnance Survey had written that "the offices, a little to the north of the castle ... are suitable as to size but in other respects unworthy of notice and in bad repair". This new range first appears on an unsigned map of "Antrim Demesne and Massereene Park" of 1844. In 1860, Charles Henry O'Neill referred to "the new stables - a handsome block of buildings enclosing a square yard - presenting a castellated front to the river and the Castle. The entrance to the stables is by an arched gateway, surmounted by a handsome clock" (now missing) "... The entire of this building ... is a picturesque object, and adds

considerably to the beauty of the landscape."

It consists of a very grand gateway, with square Tudoresque cupola turrets of an unusual design, and the family arms with the motto erroneously carved - "per augusta" instead of "per angusta ad augusta". There is a screen wall at each side, then a two-storey range with a fancy pinnacle at the summit of each gable under which are over-large portrait heads of a jocose kind flanking each central lancet. At the rear of the paved courtyard, a light monopitch-roofed passage links the two sets of buildings facing each other; one for looseboxes, with hayloft and tackroom above, the other coach-houses with wide 4-centred segmental arches. The entire range is of lighter-

coloured-than-usual Antrim basalt, with ashlar dressings. It has been suggested that it might be by Sir Richard Morrison, but the experts on his work decline to entertain this possibility. Girvan has suggested that it has features in common with buildings of the early 1840s by Charles Lanyon such as Ballymena Court House (220), and the Deaf and Dumb Institution in Belfast, but there seems to be no written evidence, and any such attribution must be fairly conjectural. Neither the cupolas, nor the rather vulgar gargoyles, seem characteristic of Lanyon. The building for some reason seems to have been known as Clotworthy House for many years; but, sometimes, as 'Castle Farm'.

When Antrim Castle itself burned to the ground on 28th October 1922, during a ball, six months after the destruction of Shane's Castle by the IRA and possibly also

with their connivance although it was never proven, the family installed fireplaces and chimneys in the carriage-house range of Clotworthy House and used it as their home until the death, in the house, of the 12th Viscount Massereene in 1956. It was occupied for 12 years as home of Canon Collins and his family; ultimately, in 1992, sensitively restored and converted to an Arts Centre by the Antrim Borough Council to designs by Caroline Dickson.

Photographs: Bryan Routledge, Antrim Borough Council; Michael O'Connell.

Situation: Off the road from Antrim to Randalstown; td, Town Parks; Parish and District Council, Antrim; Grid ref. J 145 869.

References: Listed B1. J Boyle, OSM, 1838, Antrim, XI, p 11; map, 1844, at Chilham; O'Neill, 'Antrim Castle', 1860, p 32; Girvan, 'Antrim & Ballymena', UAHS, 1969, pp 7, 8, and private correspondence; Smyth, 'Antrim', 1984, passim.

Drumadoon House, Cloughmills

175. Very close to the road, a foursquare two-storeyed hipped-roof house of squared basalt blocks with mellow red-brick dressings; windows all Georgian-glazed, stucco porch with semi-pilasters; and a very large stable yard built round a quadrangle at the rear. The front is three bays wide, the long side facing the busy road five bays. A familiar and cheering sight to travellers northbound to Ballycastle or Ballymoney.

Tradition has it that this was an 18th-century coaching or posting inn, but the buildings are not described in the first Valuation books, nor shown on the first Ordnance Survey map of 1833; although an inn is marked at approximately this point, but on the other side of the road, in Taylor and Skinner's 1778 Road Book, more or less where Logan's emporium now stands. The outbuildings may be earlier, but the present house seems to date from about 1845. In the valuation of 1859, almost the whole townland belonged to Alexander Murray; the largest house and offices, valued at £14.10.0, were in the occupation of Mrs Mary Murray, who "holds from her son"; there was also a petty sessions house, exempt from rates, probably in the outbuildings. By 1880, Alexander Murray, Esq. was described as "of Chester": who leased "the messuage or mansion House of Drumadoan" and 110 acres in that year to Hugh Carson, farmer, who had apparently lived there since 1876 and had by 1880 acquired Ulster tenant right. Hugh Carson was called on to covenant expressly to reside in the house and make it his usual place of residence. In due course he bought out under the Land Acts, and left the place first to his wife for life, then to his unmarried daughter Tilly, from whom the property was bought (with difficulty, and the help of his in-laws) by her brother William: whose son sold it in 1936 to a Mr Kennedy, in whose family the property remains.

Photograph: Michael O'Connell.
Situation: 236 Frocess Road, Cloughmills; td, Drumadoon; Parish, Killagan; District Council, Ballymoney; Grid ref. D 052 186.
References: Listed B2. Taylor and Skinner, 'Roads', 1778, p 270; VAL 2B/1/48, in PRONI; OS map, 1857; lease of 2 September 1880, A Murray to H Carson, and other family papers in possession of owner.

Rockstown House, Finvoy

176. An unusual three-bay two-storey hipped-roof house, two bays deep, then continuing under the same roof as a series of farm buildings with lofts over. White roughcast, black quoins, architraves and string-course; good square central doorcase with reeding and roundels. A single red-brick chimney-stack at the apex of the pyramidal roof. The Rosnashane property belonged to Samson Moore, gent, in 1774, but early in the 19th century passed out of the ownership of the Moore family.

The evidence of the Ordnance Survey maps and the Valuation books is confusing. It seems that one William Anderson, son of one Sir James Anderson, built a larger and grander house at Rosnashane next door about 1855 - now replaced by a modern redbrick farmhouse. In 1857, "House, offices, and gate lodge" were valued at £30; this figure included "a new house and good offices", but not "a new flax mill not worked" which was not valued. By 1870, however, the flax mill was disused: "scutching machinery removed and sold 2 years since. Used now as lumber house and condemned to be pulled down". William Anderson died in 1873. Rockstown, so named on the 1857 Ordnance Survey map, may have been either the mill house or the mill manager's house for Rosnashane: but it seems probable that it was, with 32 acres of land, Lot 6 in the auction of 1908, "the extensive slated building thereon which can easily be converted into a dwelling-house and offices". The place was bought, at the auction or not long after, by Thomas Hart of the Vow, whose only

son died young; but in whose family it remains. The sale took place on the death of William Anderson's elder daughter and sole legatee, Wilhelmina Mary Jane Learmont Anderson, who on her marriage to Francis Macauley of Coleraine made him adopt her surname, at the same time reserving by the marriage contract her separate property - she was in 1885 "possessed of considerable real and personal estate and is also engaged in extensive business as a farmer and owner lessee and keeper of thoroughbreds and other sires and stock." An exceedingly doggy and horsey lady, whose husband seems just to have disappeared (his address was unknown in 1900), she was placed in her coffin to await burial and "a rubber tube is inserted to let out Gaseous Smells - it is inserted up the chimney". Mr Porter of Coleraine, who tells us this, also reports that he has counted and described "the complete list of 13 dogs, 9 of which were in the house", to each of whom 4/- a week for life had been left in her will; he adds, "I don't think they could palm off any young dogs - likely to live longer - in place of the above".

Photograph: Michael O'Connell.

Situation: 30 Rosnashane Road, Finvoy; td, Rosnashane; Parish, Finvoy; District Council, Ballymoney; Grid ref. C 945 167.

References: Not listed. OS map, 1857; VAL 2B/1/47B, VAL 12B/4/25A, p 21, and D 1550/74, all in PRONI; information from family of present owner.

Craig's House, Parkgate

177. Since the mid-18th century at least, this farm has belonged to the Ellison family; and it still does. The older and lower range at the rear may well date from the early 18th or even 17th century. The front part was added by James Ellison, born in 1810, in the mid-19th century.

In 1836, when John "Allison" (sic) was the tenant, the house and offices were valued at £8.8.0; in 1860, at £14, with a note against "£7 (Struck out)" - "offices are slated and good - £7 is an absurd valuation for such a concern"! The value remained unaltered at £14 at least until 1881; so the new front would seem to have been added between 1836 and 1860.

Two-storey, three-bay, with half-hipped roof and central pair of chimney stacks, it is of coursed random black-stone, relieved by ashlar Gibbsian architraves around the Georgian-glazed windows upstairs and down: the very fine central doorway has a pair of fluted Doric columns, Greek key pattern in the entablature and a rectangular fan-light above with geometrical glazing bars in the manner of about 1845. The gables are roughcast; that to the garden has a good round headed window.

Photograph: Michael O'Connell.
Situation: 59 Grange Road, Parkgate; td, Cromy and Taggartsland; Parish, Donegore; District Council, Antrim; Grid ref. J 229 883.
References: Listed B+. VAL 1B/18, VAL 2B/1/8B, 17A, 17B, in PRONI; Girvan, 'West Antrim', UAHS, 1970, p 18; information from owner.

Dromore House, Glarryford

178. An unusually attractive mid-19th-century venture in the late Georgian style: a handsome two storey three-bay house, with stucco strip quoins: the most conspicuous feature being the five extra-large Georgian-glazed windows, with eight panes in each sash; and the central doorcase, enclosing the wide fanlight between tapering pylons in the Egyptian taste: the chimneys set close together on the ridge of the unhipped roof. The original blackstone has now been covered in white dry-dash. The windows would have suggested a much earlier date; but the house cannot be earlier than 1862, so its builder must have had old-fashioned tastes.

On 1 November 1861 Thomas Greg of Ballymenoch (who had acquired the townland of Dromore from the Mount Cashel estate) leased the farm and previous farmhouse for 31 years to Rev. John Wilson, of Killymurris

Presbyterian church, subject to a covenant within 5 years to expend not less than £500 on the erection of a new dwelling. Known as the manse, it did not however belong to the church; it was paid for with Mrs Wilson's money; on the minister's death in 1884 the house and farm passed to her, on her death in 1916 to her family. In 1932 it was bought by a farmer named Robert Paul, and on his death in 1942 it was bought by the father of the present owner. It is now part residence, part solicitor's office.

Photograph: Michael O'Connell.
Situation: 174 Dunminning Road, Glarryford; td, Dromore; Parish, Rasharkin; District Council, Ballymena; Grid ref. D 053 118.
References: Listed B. Basset, 'Antrim', 1888, p 157; deeds in possession of owner.

Dundermot House, Glarryford

179. This seems to incorporate the "neat looking little house, two storeys high, lately erected by Mr Andrew Boyd, on the lands of Dundermot, near the Danish fort, almost opposite to the Glaireford bridge" described by Shaw Mason's correspondent, Rev. William Mayne, in 1814. It seems that Mr Boyd died soon after, for in 1818, an advertisement appeared - "To be set, the Farm of Dundermont ... has upon it a very good house, which was the residence of the late Mr Andrew Boyd, & is well supplied with Turbary. It is favourably situated on the Mail Coach Road from Ballymena to Ballymoney". The present house, one of considerable individuality and character, appears to date from about 1850, but may well incorporate a good deal of the older one. It is L-shaped, the south-facing front two-storey and three-bay, stuccoed, with a pilastered doorcase and tall windows with glazing-pattern of the period; beneath it, a very extensive range of cellars, communicating directly both with house and farmyard The return contains the chimneys, set close together on the ridge. Looking west to Dundermot Motte (8), a two-storey canted bay-window, with a round-headed attic window in the gable; looking east, a tall landing window with 26 panes, incorporating coloured glass.

Some of the blackstone stables and out-buildings have been converted to form an attractive music-room suite. It is reported that Jessie Adams, the hymn-writer, was inspired to write the hymn 'I felt the winds of God' whilst standing in the draught from the drawing-room bay window! The place has belonged in turn to members of the Morrow and Johnston families, from whom the present owners bought in 1991.

Photograph: Michael O'Connell.
Situation: Station Road, Glarryford; td, Dundermot; Parish, Grange of Dundermot; District Council, Ballymena; Grid ref. D 063 134.
References: Not listed. Mason, 'Statistical account', I, 1814, p 247; BNL, 12-19 November, 1818; J Boyle, OSM, 1835, Antrim, IV, p 31; information from owners.

The Cairn, Aghalee

180. One Robert Best came here as a tenant farmer in 1804, and accorded himself a Christmas present of a sundial, signed and dated: "Robt Best His Dial Dec 25 1804". Fifty years later, he had prospered enough (from potatoes ?) to build the present five-bay, two-storey house between 1853 and 1855. Of brickwork, roughcast, with Georgian glazing and internal shutters throughout, it has a wide segmental-arched doorcase and fanlight with architraves to the lower windows. The roof is half-hipped and slated. There are fine old outbuildings, now in some disarray, of which one is reputed to have been the earlier farmhouse before conversion to lowlier purposes.

This house is remarkable not merely for the fact that its ownership remains in the family of its builder; but because he prepared, and passed down, a meticulous record "what it took to build a dwelling house in Ballycairn for Robert Best". It starts off, in May 1853, with 37 tons of coals for moulding and burning 100,000 bricks at 5/6 per 1000: "total cost of burning and making bricks, £55:12:4." It lists the quantities and prices of all the materials and labour employed, from nails to marble fireplaces; and comes to a total of £619.13.9, with the note "there is none of the Horse work included in this save the drawing of the lough sand ... This 28th September 1855 Robert Best".

The return was added in 1907. The house is well sited amidst good trees.

Photograph: Michael O'Connell.
Situation: 14 Brankinstown Road, Aghalee; td, Ballymacilrany; Parish, Aghalee; District Council, Craigavon; Grid ref. J 113 649.
References: Listed B1. Documents in possession of owners.

Dunore House, Aldergrove

181. An extraordinary mid-Victorian house, in a fairly unscholarly Egyptian style, plonked down in the rural landscape: the date 1870 incised in a projecting stone in the reveal of the back landing window: the corn mill belonging to the site allowed to fall into ruins by 1880. Reputed to have been built by a Colonel McCance: possibly John McCance of the Royal North Down Militia (though he was not promoted Lieutenant Colonel until 1885) who was a grandson of John McCance MP of Suffolk, and died at Knocknagoney in 1922 aged 79; so this house could have been built at the time of his marriage. However, neither he nor it appear in the Directories. The valuation records confirm the date - "new house" is entered both in the Valuation book and the map for 1870 - but the rated occupiers are shown as David McCance (1870); Edward Nicholas (1871); Henry Hall (1872); Robert Irvine (1873); James McCance (1874); and John McCance only from 1881, when he appears to have bought out the freehold; all of which is puzzling in the extreme. Between 1920 and 1927 the home of Dr Irwin, minister of Killead Presbyterian church, whose views on Home Rule did not accord with those of his congregation; a close personal friend of Mr De Valera, ultimately obliged to accept a call to Scotland. During, and after, the second World War, used as official residence for the officer commanding Aldergrove military aerodrome.

The house is very generously proportioned, inside and out: of horizontally channelled Tardree granite, except for the sandstone carvings, of two rather sinister Pharaohs, and two Nubians with thick ear-rings and lips (see page 139); one has some doubts whether the Egyptian hieroglyphics incised on their chests are likely to prove significant: other hieroglyphs are said to have been erased. Gordon Wheeler takes the view that, since all four heads have the sacred serpent, the unbearded figures wearing ear-rings are not Nubians, but Mrs Pharaohs; and finds all four friendly rather than sinister. Could this be the work of the Fitzpatrick brothers, who carved the, not wholly dissimilar, figures of the continents on the McCausland's building in Belfast in 1868?

Internally, the hall and staircase are particularly handsome; the pattern of the balusters is most individual, and terminates with the head of a toothed serpent - which might constitute a craftsman's signature. The front and back windows all have large Victorian sashes; but, strangely, the side windows are casements.

The building is agreeably set back behind a stream and ponds; the new farmhouse and farm buildings at the side in no way detract from the picture.

The Dean's House, Whitehead

182. A fine example of a marine villa, original garden intact, built as "Seaview House" in (or, though not shown on the 1858 Ordnance Survey map, perhaps a little before) 1860 by James Wright, harbour-master of the White Harbour and manager of the Whitehead quarries belonging to D S Ker, MP; sold in 1862 to the Dean of Connor, Very Rev. G Bull, and renamed in 1924. In the Valuation book for 1861, the house has two entries: the first has the name of James Wright ("lives at Knocknagulliagh") struck out, and the name of Very Reverend George Bull, Dean, substituted - "ho and offices in progress; painting not finished but will be worth £25 a year"; the second entry shows three-storey-and-basement house, offices and gate lodge together valued at £75.

A three-bay-wide, three-bay-deep, two-storey-on-basement house of well-painted stucco, with heavy architraves to door and window openings, a segmental-arched geometrical fanlight, hipped roof, and prominent chimney stacks set close together. When built it stood in open country, commanding a splendid view of the entrance to Belfast Lough; it turns its back on the Edwardian and later buildings of York Avenue.

Photograph: Michael O'Connell.
Situation: 6A York Avenue, Whitehead; td, White Head; Parish, Templecorran; District Council, Carrickfergus; Grid ref. J 475 915.
References: Not listed; in conservation area. VAL 2B/1/16, pp 48, 58, in PRONI; OS map, 1858.

◁

Photograph: Michael O'Connell.
Situation: Crookedstone Road (off main Airport Road); td, Crookedstone; Parish, Killead; District Council, Antrim; Grid ref. J 159 816.

References: Listed B1. VAL 12B/9B,C, VAL 12D/1/55A, in PRONI; Girvan, 'West Antrim, UAHS, 1970, p 10; information from the owner, from W R H Charley, and from Rev. Derek Weir.

Magherintemple (formerly Churchfield) House, Ballycastle

183. Originally quite a modest house, to which an addition in an austere Scottish Baronial style was added around 1874: making something of a mongrel. The farm originally belonged to the Stewarts of Ballintoy, who leased it to the Rev. Michael Harrison, rector of Culfeightrin; his son Hugh married Mary Casement, daughter of Hugh Casement of Bessvale, Ballinderry (187). Fagan, in 1838, says that "a large portion of the walls" of the old Culfeightrin church nearby "was carried off to a modern building in its neighbourhood by the late Hugh Harrison, who is said to have subsequently experienced much distress and calamity in family and effects." The implication is, clearly, that this was the result of his impiety. On his early death in 1786, his widow, with ten children to support, found herself unable to pay the rent: in 1790 her father acquired the lease and then sold it to her brother Roger, a prosperous Ballymena solicitor, who seems never to have lived there, though several of his many sons did so, including Robert, whilst curate of the parish, possibly Thomas, as reported by Lewis, and ultimately John. This last was a medical doctor who did not need to practise as his first wife was a Miss Newcomen of the Dublin banking family, his second wife a Miss Miller, daughter of a wealthy Ballycastle merchant.

In 1834, the house was classified 1A, but valued at only £11.15.0. In 1835, "the house is 2-storey, plain and prettily situated". It was John Casement who added the Victorian house, with datestone and his initials above the drawing-room window. It is a very Scots, very plain, very porridgy composition, executed in Ballyvoy stone, somewhat grim except for the lavish crowsteps, finials and

chimney stacks: not a turret or bartizan in sight. The gate-lodge is in the same style, and dates from 1874 also. The new house interferes with the layout of the old: there is good reeded ornament in the Georgian house, much fancy pine detailing in the Victorian one. Between 1851 and 1879, Churchfield House was valued, with its outbuildings, at £25; in 1878 it was shown as "rebuilding", and in the following year, not surprisingly, the valuation rocketed to £60.

No clear evidence as to the name of the architect appears to survive. The family believes the house was the handiwork of John Lanyon. Dean tentatively attributes the gate lodge to S P Close. Williams just says "the architect remains unknown." Could it have been a Scottish architect, working in a simplified version of the style pioneered by David Bryce and William Burn?

John Casement, no doubt under the influence of his second wife, inscribed over the front door "In all thy ways acknowledge Him and He shall direct thy paths"; and took the pledge. Some of the next generation took to seafaring : the fate of another son, Sir Roger Casement, is well known. The house still remains in the ownership of the family.

Photograph: Michael O'Connell.
Situation: 51 Churchfield Road, Ballycastle; td, Churchfield; Parish, Culfeightrin; District Council, Moyle; Grid ref. D 145 396.
References: Listed B1. J Boyle, OSM, 1835, and T Fagan, 1838, Antrim, IX, pp 45 70; Lewis, TD, 1837, I, p 441; VAL 1B/135, pp 53, 144, VAL 12B/2/11A, p 6, 11B, p 8, in PRONI; Dean, 'Gate lodges', 1994, p 21; Williams, 'Architecture in Ireland', 1994, p 2; information from Patrick Casement.

STUCCO

Plate IX

   a. Entrance Hall,
Fisherwick Lodge,
Doagh (136)

   b. Dining-room,
Castle Upton,
Templepatrick (68)

FIELDSTONES   Plate X   a. Old Congregation Presbyterian church, Randalstown, from the rear (34)
GREENERY   b. Londonderry Arms, Carnlough (231)

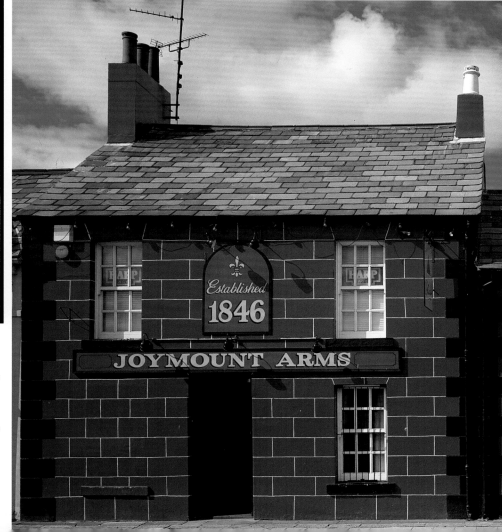

STONE and STUCCO

Plate XI

    a. Dolmen and Druid's Cottage, Ballylumford,
Islandmagee (3)

PAINTED IRONWORK

    b. John Carey's garden gate at Rarity Cottage,
Duneane (264)

PAINTED STUCCO

    c. Joymount Arms, Carrickfergus (233)

THATCH   Plate XII *(opposite)*   a. Dunminning Cottage, Glarryford (191)

                                                  b. Clady Cottage, Dunadry (189)

CREAM WASH or PAINT   Plate XIII   a. The Cottage, Lisanoure, Loughgiel (87)

                                                  b. Limepark, Armoy (131)

WHITE PAINT
or WHITEWASH

Plate XIV

   a. Parish church,
Ballintoy (38)

   b. Bendhu,
Ballintoy (186)

Plate XV *(opposite)*

   a. Seaport Lodge,
Portballintrae (73)

   b. Causeway School,
The Aird (223)

CUTSTONE

Plate XVI *(overleaf)*

   Chaine Memorial,
Larne (265)

Seabank Hall, Portrush

184. An extremely large, muscular, four-storey-and-dormers stucco house, 5 bays wide, in a sort of Queen Anne revival style (the listers say Italianate). Somewhat pyramidal in form, with a square central porch with Ionic engaged pilasters, and a two-storey bow to each side, all topped by balustrades: the central window above the porch with a segmental pediment: the windows above that with their heads supported by curiously patterned brackets: the windows above that framed in plain architraves: ending up with a hipped roof on a modillion cornice, three dormers, and two strong stone chimney stacks: all windows Georgian-glazed, surprisingly, given the magnificent view out over the east strand, but very satisfactory. Well restored in 1989, and well repainted in 1995.

One John Hetherington took a 99-year lease from the Antrim Estate in 1888 of a large block of land, extending from Bath Terrace backwards to the shops at Nos 2 to 12 Main Street. He seems to have built this enormous board-ing house about 1890, along with two slightly earlier neighbours; in that year house, yard, conservatories and garden (alongside) were valued at the very large sum of £40. In the estate office ledgers, it is first shown as being occupied by lodgers; in 1915, owned by a Miss Emily Fitzpatrick and known as Seabank Private Hotel.

Rumoured to have been built by the Earl of Antrim for his own summer use, but the rumour appears to be unfounded. For many years used as a students' hostel: today, a residential home for the elderly. The eagles at the entrance gates, recorded by Girvan, have flown away.

Photograph: Michael O'Connell.
Situation: 13 Bath Terrace, Portrush; td, Ballywillin; Parish, and District Council, Coleraine; Grid ref. C 859 408.
References: Listed B1. VAL 12B/6/2/E, VAL 12B/4/22A, p 75, D 2977/25/50 and D 2977/3B/30, all in PRONI; Girvan, 'North Antrim', UAHS, 1972, pp 12, 13.

Brooklands, Dunmurry

185. An interesting and very individual Arts-and-Crafts house in the so-called 'Cotswold' style, built for his own occupation by the architect Percy Morgan Jury (of Blackwood and Jury) in 1909. It was then "in the depth of the country, beautiful trees and meadows all around, and even a view of the Mournes" (Nancy Jury). Of brick, roughcast, with smaller-than-usual greenish Cumberland slates; highly romantic detailing. Jacobean windows with artificial stone transoms and mullions and numerous leaded lights; twelve enormously tall octagonal Jacobean chimney stacks (or pots, it is hard to be sure); and numerous gables, "which steepen pitch at the apexes, where the ridge-tiles tilt exotically upwards" (Millar). The various tilted peaks and apexes give the impression that this was designed by Arthur Rackham as home for a witch or a wizard. Built into the north-facing facade above the entrance in 1928, a two-light medieval blank window, brought from Athenry, Co. Galway, where Jury was build-

ing a new branch of the Ulster Bank; and a carved panel with the date 1909 and the architect's initials.

The original garden was of considerable interest, and some parts of it survive; but both it, and the views of the house, are now spoiled by intrusive Leylandii, presumably planted to hide the encroachments of suburban villadom at Brooklands Grange next door, and of Poleglass housing estate just up the hill. Percy Jury died in 1945; from 1949 until 1972 it was the home of Alan Rogers and his family; then of a Mr Donnelly until 1984; now used as the Radha Krishna Temple of the Hari Krishna sect. Generally, rather down at heel, and in need of care and attention.

Photograph: Michael O'Connell.
Situation: 140 Upper Dunmurry Lane, Lisburn; td, Ballycullo; Parish, Derriaghy; District Council, Lisburn; Grid ref. J 271 693.
References: Listed B1. 'Belfast Telegraph', 30 Aug 1977; letter from Nancy Jury to Belinda Jupp of 7 December 1989 in MBR; P R Millar, RIBA dissertation, 1993, in MBR.

Bendhu, Ballintoy

186. Even the listers categorise this as "an eccentric and highly original house", built with his own hands by Newton Penprase, a Cornishman, born in 1888, son of an interior decorator, who at the age of 23 was appointed to a teaching post at Belfast College of Art. He began work in 1936 and, despite his retirement in 1953, persevered with it until an accident to his hands prevented him from carrying out any further work. It was his intention that the house should be "all of concrete": to quote the exhibition catalogue of 1977, "The building shows how he interpreted this intention, for part is reinforced concrete, which has been cast in situ using shuttering, part has been built from several varieties of concrete bricks and blocks many of which have been made individually as required, and there are, too, many different surface textures, frequently applied with a hand trowel. It is no exaggeration of Pen's when he tells you that his house was built out of a bucket." After his death in 1978, it was bought by Richard McCullogh, who plastered the exterior, and rendered the house habitable after a fashion; in 1993, it was bought and (more or less) completed by its present owners.

On an exceptionally dramatic site, its strange prickly silhouette and primitive-seeming structure of cubes, squares and rectangles are still pretty disconcerting, though less so since the exterior has been very well painted in a subtle mixture of white and cream (inspired by the interior of Ballintoy parish church, 38, close by, perhaps?).

There are some surprising details; home-sculpted horse and bull, rising from the waves above the front door: "bird-table, garden pool, and cliff-face stairway" included in the listing; Zodiac ceiling in the bedroom though, alas, "Prometheus stealing flame from Heaven" has disappeared; and innumerable idiosyncratic domestic details, some of them worthy of Heath Robinson, or of Dr Strabismus (whom God preserve) of Utrecht.

This is what most people probably think of as 'modern' architecture. For over fifty years it lay, raw and incomplete, and probably - on that prominent site - turned more Ulster people against contemporary architecture than any other building. Yet its origins are indeterminate; its author seems never to have left Ireland after 1911; it belongs in no style or school; its fidgety detailing would have appalled the members of the Bauhaus school. As the effusive comment in the official list puts it, "a uniquely sculpturesque product of a highly individual and creative artistic personality."

Photograph: Michael O'Connell. (See also colour-plate XIVb)
Situation: 40 Harbour Road, Ballintoy; td, Ballintoy Demesne; Parish, Ballintoy; District Council, Moyle; Grid ref. D 039 454.
References: Listed B1 (!). P Larmour, 'Bendhu House', in 'Big A', III, 1973; Johnston, 'All his own work', Catalogue, Arts Council exhibition, 1977; A Cowser, in 'Perspective', May/June 1995, pp 20-23.

CHAPTER SIX

SMALL HOUSES
AND COTTAGES

The smaller the dwelling, the less there may seem to tell of it: but the rural cottages of Northern Ireland have received more detailed study than any other category of building. Much energy has been devoted to mapping the areas where the gable-hearth is most common, those where the central hearth is paramount; and to studying the constructional details of different categories of cruck, and other, roof. A little surprisingly Alan Gailey tells us that hipped-roof thatched cottages are of the older, indigenous, Irish ancestry, whilst gable-ended thatched cottages are of English plantation descent.[1]

As he also remarks, despite the evident contrasts between the rustic and the more polished, "reality is a continuum of buildings between those representing the extremes of the formal and the vernacular".[2] At the former end, there is to be found in County Antrim a group of delightful, sophisticated, delayed-Georgian cottages from the mid 19th century: mostly of one-and-a-half storeys, that is, the principal rooms with windows to front and back on the ground floor only, bed-rooms with attic windows in the gables only or, less often, dormers,and (unlike similar cottages farther south) no basement.[3]

Another, and often most attractive class of small dwelling is the gate-lodge; these have been very thoroughly surveyed by J A K Dean, who discusses no less than 374 gate-lodges in County Antrim alone (including how-ever Belfast); so I have confined myself to a very few examples.[4]

Of the small thatched cottages which, in my youth, were scattered all over the County Antrim countryside - there were 30,000 in Northern Ireland in the 1950s[5] - only a handful survive, and those mostly in use as slightly self-conscious holiday or weekend cottages. There are still a few of the slightly larger English-style thatched farmsteads in the Lagan valley and near the shores of Lough Neagh; but not many. The best-known of the 18th-century cottages, the elliptical so-called Dean Swift's house at Kilroot, was burned down in ambiguous circumstances in 1959, and no other quite like it survives in the county. The caves, with door- and window-openings in their built-up front walls, at Red Bay, have not been occupied in living memory. The primitive one-roomed cabin has now quite disappeared. These tiny living-spaces, barely enough for one straitened human, are now represented instead by caravans of the smallest kind, by a few inter-war sea-side holiday shacks (one of which I illustrate), and by sheltered dwellings designed for old people.

References: 1. Gailey, 'Rural houses', 1984, p 67. 2. Gailey, op cit, p 4. 3. Craig, 'Classic Irish houses', 1976 p 33. 4. Dean, 'Gate lodges', UAHS, 1994. 5. P Robinson, in 'Perspective', July/August 1993, p 50.

The so-called Dean Swift's cottage at Kilroot, now disappeared. Photograph: WJ Welch, Ulster Museum W01/93/9

Bessvale, Upper Ballinderry

187. Almost certainly late 17th-century: an unusual example of a thatched and whitewashed farmhouse on a sloping site, apparently single-storey, but in fact two-and-a-half storey.

The facade is of five bays, with a plain farm front door in the centre, flax-thatched roof, and chimneys at the gable ends; the four windows Georgian-glazed, with triangular insets above the internal panelling of the windowcases. There is an attic window in each gable: the timbers of the roof are fully exposed, and appear to have been either altered, or re-used. There is a central staircase leading down from the front hall to the kitchen and living-room below. The two-storey Georgian-glazed return is somewhat later.

In 1837 it belonged to John Hill, valued at £13.0.5, and described as "very neat"; in 1862, valued at £12, it passed to Robert Hill. Hugh Casement, ancestor of the Casement family of North Antrim (183), lived here in the mid-18th century; the Higginsons of Springmount (78) also lived in Bessvale at a later date. The farmhouse has belonged to the family of the present owner since about 1900.

Photograph: Michael O'Connell.
Situation: Down a lane at 63 Ballinderry Road, Lisburn; td, Money-crumog; Parish, Ballinderry; District Council, Lisburn; Grid ref. J 179 663.
References: Listed B1/Q. OS map, 1830; VAL 1B/167 p 89, VAL 2B/1/55A, p 67, VAL 12B/8/1A, p 43, in PRONI; Pierce and Coey, 'Taken for granted', 1984, pp 82; 85, 86.

Rock Cottage, Toome

188. A whitewashed and thatched cottage orné perched, amidst a clump of trees, on the Rock high above the road from Moneyglass to Toome. The main part one-and-a-half storey, with a tiny window in the gable; a somewhat later addition at the rear, two-storey, slated; two chimney stacks set rather close together on the ridge of the flax-straw thatch. The front windows glazed in the pattern of around 1840; but in the gable facing east, an extraordinary octagonal window, glazed in an elaborate geometrical pattern, strongly reminiscent of those shown in the elevation of the nearby but now disappeared 'Raymond Cottage', built by Henrietta Frances O'Neill, wife of the Hon. John O'Neill, about 1777, and shown in a water-colour by John Johnstone reproduced in 'Lost Demesnes'.

This must surely be the "Cottage at Brecart ... on the north-east side of the Bann in the townland of Brecart, near Brecart Tower ... erected about 50 years ago by John O'Neill Esq... the present proprietor is Mr. Samuel Finiston" (Boyle). If so, the cottage dates from about 1785; and the window may well be a cousin of those at the Raymond Cottage. In 1839, occupied by Daniel McKeown, with 16 acres, held from the Rev. Chichester O'Neill; valued at £2.10.0, at some unspecified date increased to £4; still a very modest valuation.

Acquired in 1932 by the present owner, Mr Owen McMeel, a third-generation master stone mason, from Master O'Grady; the extension added by members of the Devlin family at an earlier date. Restored by Mr McMeel some 25 years ago, and now in excellent trim.

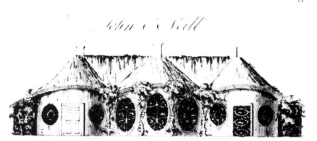

Photographs: Michael O'Connell. Water-colour: John Johnstone, c. 1810.
Situation: 40 Roguery Road, Toome; td, Brecart; Parish, Duneane; District Council, Antrim; Grid ref. H 998 916.
References: Listed B1/Q. OS map, 1830; J Boyle, OSM, 1837, Antrim, VI, p 117; VAL 2B/1/72B, p 36, in PRONI; Malins and Knight of Glin, 'Lost demesnes', 1976, pp 82-83.

Clady Cottage, Dunadry

189. An unusually sophisticated thatched gentleman's cottage, (a genuine *gentilhommière*), of uncertain date, but probably of about 1780. Of coursed basalt with galleting and brick trim: two 16-pane nearly-square windows flanking a doorcase with very pretty sidelights and fanlight. The thatched roof is half-hipped, and conceals an upper storey with windows in the gable-ends.

This seems to be the thatched house, one-storey with attic, occupied by John Watt and valued at £10 "including interest on new buildings" in 1862. Originally much more modest, but enlarged by successive owners, who raised the roof by half a storey and removed the chimneys to their present position. The garden was laid out by John Cowan, who came from Scotland about 1880, and whose successors sold to the Webb family in 1958, when renovation and additions (at the rear) were handled with reasonable tact. The house is set in an attractive garden with fine mature trees, and constituted for many years the very fitting seat of the first Chairman of the Historic Buildings Council for Northern Ireland, the late Charles Kinahan.

Photograph: Michael O'Connell. (See also colour-plate XIIb)
Situation: Clady Road, Muckamore; td, Straid Ballymorris; Parish, Templepatrick; District Council, Antrim; Grid ref. J 196 844.
References: Listed B+. VAL 2B/1/11, p 5, in PRONI; Girvan, 'West Antrim', UAHS, 1970, pp 13, 27; Dixon, 'Introduction', 1975, p 43; Pierce and Coey, 'Taken for granted', 1984, p 66.

Glendaragh, Crumlin

190. A late-Georgian gentleman's cottage: not shown in Lendrick's map of 1780, but one of the new houses - "Glendaragh Cottage" - inserted by James Williamson in his revision of 1808. Shaw Mason's correspondent, the

Rev. Edward Cupples, remarks in 1816 "Crumlin is held immediately under Lt Colonel Heyland, whose elegant seat of Glendaragh is contiguous to it". James Boyle, writing in 1835, says it is the seat of John Moore Esq; "quite in the cottage style, one storey, in the exterior nothing ornamented or striking but the interior admirably constructed. Vestibule, hall, corridors and doors of the Gothic style, the windows of the dining and sitting rooms beautifully stained. Built by the late Col. Heyland about 1805". John Moore seems to have been only a tenant. Also in 1835, the house, classified 1A, was valued at the large sum of £60.0.9 - "add 10% for good situation, deduct 1/6 per £ for large amount". In 1837, Lewis described it as "the beautiful cottage and highly embellished grounds of Glendarragh, the seat of Col Heyland, through which flows the river Crumlin." In 1862, it was unoccupied, and in poor shape, but "all repairing now": "Mr Pakenham is repairing all these houses, not yet near finished". By 1909 it belonged to Col C E McClintock, the then land agent at Langford Lodge, and, after his death, was acquired in 1922 by the Aldworth family to whom it still belongs.

Originally the house appears to have been built in four ranges around a square central courtyard; a convincing reconstruction of the original ground plan has been prepared by J A K Dean; but nearly half was demolished due to dry rot in the 1950s, leaving an L-shaped single-storey house on a basement (invisible from the front), and with bedrooms inserted in the attics. The whole front is covered by a luxuriant two-foot-thick growth of greenery. A nice quadruple doorcase, and four windows with X pattern glazing bars, lurk behind the vegetation; the front faces of the window-sills are delicately carved, as at Kilwaughter Castle (81). Internally, the X pattern is reversed so as to produce diamond-shapes in door and shutter panels -

until, that is, the house turns Gothick at the entrance to a large and handsome drawing-room, one wall a great curved bow, with harps in the cornice-plaster and elegant reeding in doorcase, recess, and mantelpiece. The stained glass, however, has not survived. A small house of uncommon charm, many details of which I should attribute, I hope without dangerous over-confidence, to the unconventional Belfast architect John Millar.

Photographs: Michael O'Connell.
Situation: 10 Crumlin Road, Crumlin; td, Crosshill; Parish, Killead; District Council, Antrim; Grid ref. J 148 768.
References: Listed B. Williamson, map, 1808; Mason, 'Statistical account', II, 1816, p 231; J Boyle, OSM, 1835, as yet unpublished; VAL 1B/164C, VAL 2B/1/53B, in PRONI; Lewis, TD, 1837, I, p 439, II p 133; Young, 'Belfast and province of Ulster', 1909, p 213; Girvan, 'West Antrim', UAHS, 1970, p 9.

Dunminning Cottage, Glarryford

191. A tiny, delightful, thatched cottage with gothic door and window-openings, just beside Dunminning Bridge over the River Main. Because of the hipped roof and the shaping of the thatch, it seems deceptively un-rectangular. The roof is topped by a modern red brick chimney with one red pot; it is rather a pity the chimney was not, like the walls, rendered and white-washed. There is "an unusual roof window peering out from the thatch at the rear".

This cottage comes as a very pleasant surprise round a sudden corner, the more so as it seems to be of genuine antiquity - it appears on the Ordnance Survey map of 1832. It is said to have been built to house the toll-keeper of Dunminning bridge; when responsibility for the bridge was assumed by the Grand Jury, the house was bought by the Patricks of Dunminning as a residence for their gardener, and a matching pointed doorway was opened in the demesne wall immediately opposite his cottage. For many years occupied by Joe McDowell who was exceptionally adept at fishing the immediately adjoining river.

Photograph: Michael O'Connell. (See also colour-plate XIIa)
Situation: 147 Ballywatermoy Road, Dunminning; td, Dunminning; Parish, Craigs; District Council, Ballymena; Grid ref. D 050 109.
References: Listed B1/Q. OS map, 1832; Girvan, 'West Antrim', UAHS, 1970, p 28; Pierce and Coey, 'Taken for granted', 1984, pp 63, 64; information from Mr James Fenton and Mr J W Frazer.

40 Port Road, Islandmagee

192 (right). A classic little thatched and whitewashed fisherman's cottage, in a green field not far from high tide mark, at a point where two converging channels have been cleared through the rock-strewn shoreline. A cottage appears on this site on the first Ordnance Survey map of 1834. It is not possible to identify it in the first Valuation book, but it seems to be the "house and garden, 1 rood and 10 perches", land valued at 8/- and buildings at 12/- which are listed in the later Valuation books under reference 17C. If so, the occupier during the 1860s was Jane McKay; during most of the 1870s, Joseph Hay; from 1897 to 1919, Mrs Annie McGowan; at other periods, the cottage seems to have changed occupiers with uncommon frequency - perhaps because of its exceedingly exposed position. It has a little rectangular chimney at each gable-end, with no chimney-pots; upstands at the gable to protect the ends of the thatch; small windows, a hall-door, and an appropriately nautical flagstaff - for is not Islandmagee by tradition the home of seafaring men?

Photograph: Michael O'Connell.
Situation: 40 Port Road, Cloghfin, Islandmagee; td, Cloghfin; Parish, Islandmagee; District Council, Larne; Grid ref. J 484 943.
References: Listed B. OS map, 1834; Griffith Valuation of Co Antrim, 1861, p 104; VAL 12B/7/12A, B, C, D and E, in PRONI.

Legatirriff House, Ballinderry

193. A four-bay two-storey thatched farmhouse, rendered, with three windows upstairs (each of six panes) and three downstairs (each of twelve panes) and off-central doorway. Four chimney stacks, no chimney-pots. The roughcast used to be whitewashed but no longer. Nevertheless, an attractive small Georgian farm-house in good order and well-cared for.

This seems to be the house, classified 1A in 1837, val-ued at £8.10.0, belonging to "Mark Peel's heirs"; in 1859 classified 1B, the value reduced to £5.10.0, now belonging to another Mark Peel.

Photograph: Michael O'Connell.
Situation: 17 Lough Road, Ballinderry; td, Legatirriff; Parish, Ballinderry; District Council, Lisburn; Grid ref. J 152 695.
References: Listed B1/Q. VAL 1B/167, p 73, 2B/1/55A, p 20, in PRONI; OS map, 1832; Pierce and Coey, 'Taken for granted', 1984, p 119.

Glenbank, Glenshesk

194. "About 3 miles south-east of Ballycastle is Glen bank, the seat of John Cuppage Esq."(Atkinson, 1817). "Glenbank, the residence of Mrs Cuppage, is about 4 miles from Ballycastle, up the Glenshesk river. Being quite among the mountains the scenery is of a wild character and, though not sufficiently so to entitle it to the appellation of romantic scenery, it possesses considerable beauty. The house is small, 1-storey high and is seated on the edge of the road. It is very neat and tasteful in its appearance" (Boyle).

The house has been extended and added to over the years - four dormers have been built, and the roof raised over the left-hand range - but the tall Georgian windows of the dining-room and drawing-room (the latter a finely-proportioned room with a high ceiling and good cornice) still mark out the original house, perhaps of around 1800, judging by the elegant reeding in the arch of the hallway: very likely built by John Cuppage. Not shown on Lendrick's map of 1780, but inserted by Williamson in his revision of 1808. In the 1833 valuation, classified 1A, though described as "Far from road, remote, not a pleasant situation." "It was the late Mr Adam Cuppage who planted the trees around Glenbank in 1846" (M'Cahan). In 1859, the one-and-a-half storey house, measuring 24 yards wide by 7 yards deep, owned by Adam Cuppage in

fee, was valued at £20. The porch is modern; the original Georgian sashes have been replaced; but the white-painted house on the hillside, tucked away behind a fringe of trees, retains its essential character.

On the death of Adam Cuppage, without issue, in 1879, the house passed to his nephew, Dr Dunlop, coroner for North Antrim: presumably one and the same as the John Dunlop MD, who was living at Drumnagessan (142) in 1859; the owner in 1908 was his son Dr John Bryce Dunlop. The present owner, who carried out extensive renovations in 1977, bought the place in 1942 from the widow of a Major Creery, who, and whose predecessor Major Wright, both of the Indian Army, suffering from the cold climate, made various alterations with a view to rendering the house less draughty.

Photograph: Michael O'Connell.
Situation: 18 Glenbank Road, Glenshesk, Ballycastle; td, Aghaleck; Parish, Ramoan; District Council, Moyle; Grid ref. D 125 352.
References: Not listed. Williamson, map, 1808; Atkinson, 'Ireland exhibited', 1823, II, p 230; T C Robe, OSM, 1831, and J Boyle, 1835, Antrim, IX, pp 90, 96; VAL 1B/135, p 112, VAL 2B/1/2BA, p 16, in PRONI; Camac, 'Derrykeighan parish', [1908], p 72; M'Cahan, 'Local histories', 1988; information from owners.

Beardiville Gate Lodge, Coleraine

195. The most enjoyable gate lodge in the county: "a delightfully naive composition . . . like a country cousin of the gateway to Coleraine Market" (Girvan); "delightfully naive Classical composition in basalt rubble dressed in granite" (Dean). The latter, speculatively but rather plausibly, attributes it to Richard Elsam, a quarrelsome English architect described by H M Colvin as "a self-conscious seeker after ingeniously geometrical plans clothed either in neo-classical or picturesque Gothic dress", who fled from his English clients, set up practice in Londonderry at some time between 1805 and 1808, and published there his The Gentleman and Builders Assistant, before removing to Dublin; he returned to England in 1820, was involved in litigation over his design for Dover gaol, and thereafter disappeared from sight.

Howley, who thinks the gate lodge contemporary with Beardiville House (71) and so mid 18th-century, comments: "This is a very simple building with just enough Palladian refinement to make it stand out and provide a dignified and notable point of entrance, even with the slightly clumsy way in which the hipped roofs of the wings are designed. It provides a divided living area similar to the Rathfarnham lodge, but somehow its lack of pomp andgrandeur makes this more acceptable".

The lodge has two rooms, one on either side of the pedimented archway, the Diocletian windows now blocked up with causeway basalt. "Chimney flues carried over the archway to emerge magically from the central ridge" (Dean). Flanked by curving walls, tall and low, the latter topped by causeway stones, set at an angle to the crossroads: all very geometrical and pleasing to the eye.

Photograph: Michael O'Connell. (See also colour-plate IVa)
Situation: At the cross-roads between Ballyhome Road and the main road from Bushmills to Coleraine; td, Beardiville; Parish, Ballywillin; District Council, Coleraine; Grid ref. C 902 369.
References: Listed B (surely too low a grading?). Girvan, 'North Antrim', UAHS, 1972, pp 3, 15; Colvin, 'Dictionary', 1978, pp 292-3; Howley, 'Follies and garden buildings', 1993, p 88; Dean, 'Gate lodges', UAHS, 1994, p 4.

Randalstown Gate Lodge, Shane's Castle

196. Dean says "The *pièce de résistance* of the estate and the most impressive entrance complex in the Province ... a vast Tudor Revival fantasy of flamboyant castellated outline ... all in coursed basalt rubble dressed in contrasting granite": suggests "c 1848; architect probably James Sands"; and adds, "again seems to show James Sands' dependence upon pattern books, showing as it does similarities with Francis Goodwin's entrance to Markree Castle, Co. Sligo, published in his 'Rural Architecture', 1835". There is evidence that Sands was working at Shane's Castle in 1841 and in 1847. The demesne wall seems to have been built in 1844-5, possibly as a Famine relief scheme: it is hard to tell whether this gateway is to be regarded as the final flourish of the wall, or as a later companion piece to the railway viaduct of 1855; or is it to be interpreted as a declaration that, if the Skeffingtons and Massereenes looked to Antrim as their base, the O'Neills looked rather to Randalstown?

By the mid-century, every nobleman needed a barbican or castellated gateway. In County Antrim, the earliest was perhaps that provided for Kilwaughter Castle (81), in 1810, probably to the design of John Nash; now demolished. The next was the gateway to Antrim Castle, usually dated 1818 and attributed to John Bowden: but, to the best of my knowledge, the sole evidence for Bowden's involvement is a letter of that year from him to Colonel Skeffington, with a sketch of the gatehouse in the margin. On a close reading, however, it is clear that Bowden was volunteering suggestions - not in the event adopted - for the improvement of another man's work; whose, we do not know. "I like much your entrance it is admirably executed ... I beg to suggest an addition to your gatehouse it really wants it ..." Then comes William Vitruvius Morrison's well-documented Barbican (86) at Glenarm, of 1824.

Next, Edmund Blore's gateway of about 1837 to Castle Upton (68). And finally, the impressive Randalstown gate, with its curving quadrant walls, corbelled bartizans, coats of arms, octagonal chimney pots, octagonal tower, and enormous mock-portcullis.

The great railway viaduct nearby (249) "built in 1855 by William Dargan to designs by Charles Lanyon", clearly interrupted the previous access arrangements through theRandalstown drive; my own guess is that the new gateway was built as part of the associated accommodation works, designed to reconcile the third Viscount O'Neill to the disruption and intrusion involved. (In fact, he seems to have died before the works were completed.) This would appear to raise the alternative possible attribution of the gateway to Charles Lanyon, rather than to James Sands, for whom this seems rather a late date. It may or may not be significant that Lanyon was employed by Viscount O'Neill's heir, the Rev. William Chichester, six years before he was created Baron O'Neill, to build the new Shane's Castle in 1862; but the new house, though fine, was suitably non-baronial, rather plain, lacked battlements and bartizans, and bore no discernible resemblance to the Randalstown Lodge. So that is not much help.

In the absence of documents there can be no certainty, but it does seem to me likely that viaduct and gateway, both of coursed blackstone, are from the same hand. The dwelling element in the composition is minimal; the group now seems so over-theatrical as to be slightly ridiculous, especially as it is now cut off (save for an underpass) from the demesne proper by the elevated Motorway. Nevertheless, as Dean remarks, it remains perhaps the most impressive entrance complex in the province - after the Barbican at Glenarm?

Drumnasole Gate Lodge, Carnlough

197. A particularly nice little 'Picturesque' lodge on the main coast road between Carnlough and Garron Point, with uncommonly fine curly ironwork railings and piers, bargeboards and finials. Mostly of blackstone with limestone dressings and quoins: the central chimney stack in polychrome brick.

Dean dates this c 1860, but does not venture even on a conjectural attribution. This seems to be an almost unique example of a building venture by the generation following Francis Turnly, original builder of Drumnasole (88); but no documentation whatever appears to survive.

Photograph: Michael O'Connell. (See also colour-plate VIb)
Situation: on coast road between Carnlough and Garron Point; td, Burnside; Parish, Ardclinis; District Council, Larne; Grid ref. D 197 212.
References: Listed B. Dean, 'Gate lodges', UAHS, 1994, p 10.

◁

Photograph: Michael O'Connell.
Situation: off the old main road from Antrim to Randalstown; td, Shane's Castle Parks; Parish, Duneane; District Council, Antrim; Grid ref. J 083 903.

References: Listed A as "Ballygrooby Lodge, c 1840". D 3244/E/5/19, 40, 41, and T 2519/1996, in PRONI; Bence-Jones, 'Burke's guide', 1978, p 257; Girvan, 'Antrim & Ballymena', UAHS, 1969, p 27; Dean, 'Gate lodges', UAHS, 1994, pp 27, 28.

16 Charlotte Street, Ballymoney

198. A pleasing if plain three-storey three-bay Georgian town house, of squared blackstone, with quoins, and brick dressings round the openings, all well painted in two shades of grey; Georgian glazing bars (white-painted) all complete, and a simple radial fanlight in the low doorway. A tall chimney stack, without pots, surmounts each gable.

James McGann of the Ordnance Survey, writing so late as 1835, says "The town contains about 430 houses ... the greater part of the houses are built of stone, the general height being 2-storeys, and there is very little uniformity in their appearance. There are very few of the houses in the main street which have gateways attached to them or any entrances in their rear, and the consequence is that cows, horses etc have to pass to their stables either through the halls or kitchens of such houses ... Many new houses have been recently built and are now building, mostly on the upper and lower ends of the town. They are principally of brick and are slated. The greater number now building are 3-storeys high,but some of them are only 1-storey."

There was certainly a house on this site, in what was then called Pyper Row, shown on the map of 1734, reproduced in the conservation area booklet, but it seems more likely that the booklet is right in dating the present house to the early 19th century: perhaps about 1820? But it is almost impossible to date a house of this kind without documentary evidence.

Photograph: Michael O'Connell.
Situation: 16 Charlotte Street, Ballymoney; td, Town Parks; Parish, District Council, Ballymoney; Grid ref. C 947 257.
References: Listed B; in conservation area. OS map, 1832; J McGann, OSM, 1835, Antrim, V, p 9; Girvan, 'North Antrim', UAHS, 1973, p 40; conservation area booklet, 1994; sale particulars, Lockhart, estate agent, 1995.

7 - 10 Main Street, Glenoe

199. In June 1840, James Boyle vividly described Glenoe: "Few hamlets of similar extent possess as great attractions as to position, but few more irregularly constructed. It consists almost exclusively of one little main street, which straggles for 190 yards up the steep declivity in an extremely crooked direction. Its dwellings, 17 in number, are of a very humble description and are in most instances in bad repair. Not more than 4 are to be found together, the others straggling at irregular intervals. 2 only possess a second floor, 10 are slated and 7 are roofed with thatch. All are built of stone and lime. They are neither neat nor cleanly in their appearance, nor substantial nor comfortable in their construction. Few of them are roughcast or whitened". Despite all this, he considered Glenoe "a pretty little hamlet" (in contrast to the nearby village of Raloo, of which he wrote: "It would be difficult to find a parallel for Raloo as to filth and slovenliness"!) And he drew particular attention to "a very pretty ornamental cottage, the property of Miss McClaverty of Glynn", which had been "until 1834 celebrated for the taste of its construction and the beauty of its situation ... the scene of numerous Pic Nic parties from the neighbouring towns": which, however, had been demolished to provide the site for Charles Lanyon's little church (52). The village, and its glen (now owned by the National Trust), were much visited in the 19th and 20th centuries by lovers of the picturesque, and many picture postcards survive.

Not so, unfortunately, most of the houses; two have been replaced by very brash and inappropriate 'modern' homes; and a flourishing ice-cream factory, Maud's, fills the heart of the village, which still has no shop, post office, or pub. Of the four remaining cottages, No 7 remains privately rented; Nos 8 and 9 have been combined into a single house; they and No 10 (at one time a pub) having been completely restored in 1992-3 by Hearth Revolving Fund. Nos 7 to 10, if not amongst those described by Boyle, cannot be much later than 1840.

Photograph: Michael O'Connell.
Situation: Main Street, Glenoe; td, Ballywillin; Parish, Raloo; District Council, Larne; Grid ref. J 394 967.
References: Listed B1. J Boyle, OSM, 1835, and 1840, Antrim, XII, pp 83, 89, 90, 124-5; 'HEARTH review', 1994, p 47.

Lisheegan Cottage, Finvoy

200. A pretty little gentleman's cottage apparently of about 1830 with just one great big Georgian-glazed window on each side of the central porch, topped by a dormer-pediment containing a slightly-pointed Gothick-glazed window, and attic windows in the gable-ends. Quoins and window dressings are of smooth stucco, the remainder rendered but unpainted. Three chimneys, with one chimney-pot each, asymmetrically disposed on the roof-top. Well restored in 1984.

In 1834, the dwelling was apparently single-storey, belonging to Mrs Moore of Moore Lodge (129), and perhaps providing a modest dower house, valued at £6.19.0;

by 1859 it was described as a "slated house of two stories", occupied by John Thompson, the dispensary doctor, as tenant of the Misses Moore. For many years occupied by the Young family, one of whom is said to have acted as the local money-lender; acquired from them by the present owners in 1982.

Photograph: Michael O'Connell.
Situation: 17 Lisheegan Lane, Finvoy; td, Lisheegan; Parish, Finvoy; District Council, Ballymoney; Grid ref. C 938 158.
References: Listed B1. OS map, 1833; VAL 1B/1/158B, p 77, VAL 2B/1/47B, p 123, in PRONI.

The Wheelrow, Muckamore

201. Three pairs of semi-detached ornamental two-storey cottages set back a little from the roadside: perhaps of about 1830, an adjunct of the Chaine property at Ballycraigy and mill at Muckamore. In 1862, described as "neat workman's cottages, all held from William Chaine", and valued at £2 each. Now in differing ownership, and it shows, with varying paintwork, door-and-window detailing, chimney-pots and garages; the value of the group would be enhanced if the owners could collaborate in a more co-ordinated scheme.

The central pair are smaller than the others, which have each three tall triangular gables, with ornate fretwork bargeboards, roundels,and wooden finials; 16-pane sash windows set in pointed-arch recesses on the ground floor, and Gothick doors and doorcases; red and yellow brick chimneys with prominent chimney-pots. Known as "the Wheelrow" by reason of the pierced roundels at the gable-ends.

Photograph: Michael O'Connell.
Situation: On the main road from Templepatrick to Antrim; Nos. 163-5 (and 167-9, and 171-3) Belfast Road, Muckamore; td, Islandbane; Parish, Grange of Muckamore; District Council, Antrim; Grid ref. J 186 853.
References: Listed B. OS map, 1832; VAL 2B/1/52, pp 55, 56 in PRONI; Girvan, 'Antrim & Ballymena', UAHS, 1969, p 13.

Gill's Almshouses, Ellis Street, Carrickfergus

202. Six houses (or "three double houses") first opened for pensioners on 23rd October 1820, built under the 1760 will of Alderman Henry Gill. He was a wealthy bachelor storekeeper to the Castle garrison who left "£10 each per annum and also houses and gardens to 14 aged men, decayed in their circumstances" provided that they were not "inclined or given to idleness, or Drunkenness, ... and that they were remarkable for their inoffensiveness."

These one-and-a-half storey houses, with their sharply-pointed gables at right angles to the street-line, are reminiscent of Dublin King Billies; and were thought by the UAHS listers in 1978 to be the original almshouses built in 1766; but it is clear from the Trustees' minute book that this was not so. In 1820 these houses cost £290.14.9½ including all extras, plus ten guineas to Archibald Wilson "for his trouble in furnishing a specification and superintending the work". Restored in 1904, and again in 1980 by the James Butcher Housing Association; the smooth render below, and rougher harling above, both presently painted a slightly surprising light green.

Photograph: Michael O'Connell.
Situation: 32-36 Ellis Street, Carrickfergus; td, Middle Division; Parish and District Council, Carrickfergus; Grid ref. J 405 880.
References: Listed B1; outside conservation area. M'Skimin, 'Carrickfergus', 1811, pp 50, 150, 151; Gill's Charity, Minute book, 1820, folios 208-210, in Carrickfergus Town Hall; Campbell and Crowther, 'Carrickfergus', UAHS, 1978, p 30.

Gill's Almshouses, Governor's Place, Carrickfergus

203. Additional almshouses, built under the will of Henry Gill, to replace the original charity houses of 1766 in Essex Street, which were reported in 1839 by George Parkhill, architect, so decayed as to be "not worth laying out money on". Datestone, 1842; to designs by Charles Lanyon, then county surveyor, in the attractive Tudor revival style characteristic of his work at this period. However, his original plans of 1839 were not accepted as they stood: in 1841, the Trustees resolved "that Mr Lanyon be requested to alter his Plan so as to give the additional accommodation of a loft to each house over the kitchen and room, with a step-ladder up to each". A symmetrical front of five bays, the second and fourth set back; an upper dormer at each end, a strong central doorcase with segmental arch, hood moulding, and cabbagey bosses. The steeply pitched roof is topped by twin square chimney stacks set diagonally to the ridge. The black-painted quoins, bosses and finials,

and the mouldings surrounding doors and windows, stand out in contrast to the white-painted walls. Originally of brick, but this was already giving trouble by 1850, and in 1851 the Trustees agreed to take proposals for "stone finishing with cement and painting". Well restored by the James Butcher Housing Association as old people's dwellings in 1980: an attractive group on a prominent site: though perhaps a little overcrowded by the modern additions, in themselves remarkably sensitively designed, crammed onto the site at the rear.

Photograph: Michael O'Connell.
Situation: 11-13 Governor's Place, Carrickfergus; td, Parish and District Council, Carrickfergus; Grid ref. J 411 873.
References: Listed B1; in conservation area. M'Skimin, 'Carrickfergus', 1811, pp 170-1; Gill's Charity, Minute book, 1839-1851, folios 222-235, in Carrickfergus Town Hall; Campbell and Crowther, 'Carrickfergus', UAHS, 1978, p 24.

Sheils's Almshouses, Carrickfergus

204 (left). An attractive series of thirty two-storey houses and a superintendent's house with tower. The original twenty-one houses, Nos. 7 to 27, were built in 1868 to designs by Lynn & Lanyon; Nos. 28 to 31 in 1901 to a complementary design by Young & Mackenzie; and the final block, Nos. 1 to 6, in 1915, to a slightly different design by R M Close.

Charles Sheils, who died in 1861, was a philanthropist much in advance of most of his contemporaries. He left £90,000 to provide housing for the needy in Armagh, Dungannon, Killough, Stillorgan and Carrickfergus. Each group of houses was to be managed by a local committee of four members of the Church of Ireland, four of the Roman Catholic Church, and four of the Presbyterian Church: the rules stated that "no religious disputes of any description will be tolerated". Each house was to have a separate entrance, to be of nearly Parker-Morris dimensions, and to have two sleeping-rooms. In one respect, however, the layout departs from present-day practice:

instead of facing inwards onto a court, close or quad, the buildings face outwards in a rather un-neighbourly way.

The tower-house, with clock, for the superintendent, has a pointed-arch doorway, enclosing a cusped arch, the space between inscribed in gilt letters on red with the words 'Charles Sheils' Institution 1868'. The tower is frilly with wooden pentices, chamfers, gablets, and downspouts: probably the work of John Lanyon, it seems too fussy to be that of his father, too cheerfully unscholarly to be that of W H Lynn. The houses, originally of red brick, are now stuccoed, the roofs are covered in bands of plain and of fish-scale slates. Altogether, a considerable ornament to the town.

Photograph: Michael O'Connell.
Situation: 48 Larne Road, Carrickfergus; td, North East Division; Parish, District Council, Carrickfergus; Grid ref. J 425 883.
References: Listed B1. Campbell and Crowther, 'Carrickfergus', UAHS, 1978, p 36; extensive unsigned notes in MBR.

Farmhouse, Ballybracken

205. An attractive farmhouse and outbuildings set into the hillside above the valley dividing Tardree Mountain from Drumadarragh Hill, of rubble-stone roughcast and at some date lime-washed; 3-bay 2-storey house and out-buildings: the new front door, despite its mouth-organ fan-light, and the regrettable plastic windows very recently installed, are not entirely appropriate, but fairly accept-able from a distance.

Perhaps of about 1820 or 1830? Bought by the present owner's family in 1937 from Miss Agnes Barkley; inside, on the wall, an admirable map of the property of Mr Samuel Barkley prepared in 1884 by one Martin Sumner, architect, of Ballymena.

Photograph: Michael O'Connell.
Situation: Numbered at the gate 96, Ballybracken Road, Doagh; td, Loon-burn; Parish, Doagh; District Council, Antrim; Grid ref. J 226 945.
References: Listed B (but as 91 Ballybracken Road); OS map 1833.

Ballyloughan House, Ballymena

206. Just where town meets farmland, a very pleasant group: the "neat" house evidently of about 1845, or perhaps a bit earlier; five-bay, one-and-a-half storey, stuccoed and painted rust-colour, with quoins, dormers, copious chimneys, and a nice hood at the porch carried on console brackets. Two Georgian-glazed windows in the eaves, topped by pretty trellis-pattern bargeboards. Excellent, and in appearance somewhat older, outbuildings asymmetrically disposed around an oddly shaped but most attractive farmyard. Evidently built by a Mr Wilson,

whose widow Mrs Margaret Wilson lived on until in the 1868 revaluation the name of John Beaumont appears as occupier: valued at £8. Mature trees, and the remains of an ornamental garden: the house approached up a one-sided avenue of trees.

Photograph: Michael O'Connell.
Situation: 101 Grove Road, Ballymena; td, Ballyloughan; Parish, Kilconriola; District Council, Ballymena; Grid ref. D 098 053.
References: Listed B. OS map, 1833; VAL 2B/1/64A, p 45, VAL 12B/3/5A, p 51, in PRONI.

Laurel Hill, Aghalee

207 (left). Set in a nice garden, approached by a magnificent avenue of mature chestnuts and lime trees of several different varieties, a modest but pleasing long low blackstone house, with brick dressings, five bays, one-and-a-half storey, of about 1835. The slated roof is half-hipped; the upstairs windows are in the gables; there are two prominent chimney-stacks (presumably later) of yellow brick. The large windows are Georgian-glazed: the front door is half-concealed by a rustic trellis-work porch.

Forming an L-shape, the long single-storey return, formerly thatched, but now tiled, must be the original farmhouse. This seems to have been the single-storey house, classified 1B and valued at £5 occupied in 1837 by Thomas Walkington, subsequently by William John Turtle, who was still there in 1859, when it was classified 2B+, revalued at £12, and described as "very neat cottage

with good approach". This may well have been the "Mr John Turtle, grocer and haberdasher, who is also extensive in the grain trade" who occupied a "handsome seat and lofty corn store ... erected by Mr John Heastie, merchant, within the last 25 years" at the west end of the village of Aghalee, in 1838: or, perhaps, his son. It was acquired from the Turtle family about 1890 by the present owner's grandfather: who married a Beckett from the next farm, so that (as it happened) the two farms became one: and so remain.

Photograph: Michael O'Connell.
Situation: 17 Chapel Road, Aghalee; td, Moygarriff; Parish, Aghalee; District Council, Lisburn; Grid ref. J 148 655.
References: Listed B. T Fagan, OSM, 1838, Antrim, VII, p 33; VAL 1B/167, p 105, VAL 2B/1/55A, p 4, in PRONI; OS map, 1857.

Duneoin, Cullybackey

208. The house appears on the Ordnance Survey map of 1832. In 1835, "Dunoyne, the residence of John Cunningham, Esquire, is a pretty cottage situated in the townland of Dunminning"(Boyle). "He must have been an ingenious and forceful entrepreneur, because he created at Duneoin an industrial site of considerable technical significance. It all depended upon the gathering together of two small streams of water rising in the hinterland of the mill and supplemented by a large reservoir with a stone breast situated on the ridge between the Maine and the Bann catchments, and about four miles distant from the mill site. This water was carefully led down to a series of dams at the premises and operated three 'falls' one after the other to drive the bleachworks machinery ... one of the three dams still exists"(J W Frazer). "The motive power ... is drawn from two streams known as the Limnarrick, famous for the purity of its water, and the Carclinty. The water is collected in four large dams, one of which covers an area of about 12 acres" (Shaw).

In 1861, the "neat cottage", held by John Patrick under lease for ever, was separately valued at £8.6.10; by 1888, "Duneoin Green" was "a comfortable private residence, which Mr. [John] McIlroy occupies. It was built by Mr John Cunningham, and has a handsomely-planted lawn and pretty gardens ... About 200 acres of land belong to the property ... Duneoin Green, ... was established over 80 years ago, by Mr John Cunningham [who] was succeeded by his son William, and after him the Green passed through various hands. Mr Thomas Giffen, Mr Joseph

Magill, and Mr John Wood, each had it for a short time. Mr McIlroy bought it from Mr Wood, in 1884" (Bassett). John Cunningham, a descendant of Thomas Cunningham of Crookedstone (116), "built or purchased the bleach works at Duneoin on the Maine river near Glarryford: in this he was succeeded by his son William who apparently died without issue. Duneoin then passed through the hands successively of Thomas Giffen, John Woods and John McIlroy. In recent years it has been converted into a flax processing works by Mr Malcolm Patrick, MP, of the Dunminning family, its present owner" (Lawlor).

A handsome two-and-a-half storey 5-bay early-19th century house: eight steps up to the front door, and with radial fanlight, sidelights, and reeding, above an extensive basement - the windows not the originals but reasonably unobtrusive; white-painted walls; attic windows in the gables; ten hearths. For many years owned by Malcolm Patrick, younger brother of Brigadier Patrick of Dunminning (153), sold by his heirs to William Fenton in 1962, and restored by Mr Fenton's grandson Paul in 1990.

Photograph: Michael O'Connell.

Situation: 107 Duneoin Road, Cullybackey; td, Dunminning; Parish, Craigs, formerly Rasharkin; District Council, Ballymena; Grid ref. D 046 103.

References: Listed B. OS map, 1832; J Boyle, OSM, 1835, Antrim, VIII, p 130; VAL 1B/1/162, p 35, 1836, VAL 2B/1/50B, p 8A, in PRONI; Bassett, 'Antrim', 1888, pp 155-6; Shaw, 'Cullybackey', 1913, p 148; H C Lawlor, in 'Fibres and fabrics journal', September 1941, p 6; information from Mr James Fenton, and from Mr J W Frazer.

Droagh Cottage, Drains Bay

209. A one-and-a-half storey cream-painted stucco cottage, perhaps of around 1820, with later additions to the rear; between the coast road and the shore, Georgian-glazed throughout. The pilastered porch is flanked by a single window on each side; the upper rooms, surprisingly lofty, have their windows in the gables. There is one return which seems to be original, and another, incorporating a splendid first-floor drawing-room with ornate ceiling-rose and canted bay window looking out over the North Channel, continues irregularly round the corner giving seven bays to seaward. The upper storey (including this window) was added in 1867 to designs by William Hastings, of Belfast, for Sir Edward Coey; originally the extension contained one large bedroom, now drawing-room, three smaller bedrooms, and a lavatory. A complicated house of great character, noted on the first Ordnance Survey map of 1834 though in the Valuation book of 1834 the highest-valued house in the townland is that of Saul Hunter, at £5.4.8. Probably, this is the house

valued at £12 shown in the valuations from 1861 onwards as in the occupation of one John Caldwell.

Originally part of the far-flung Antrim estates - leased by them in 1738 to Robert Allan - it belonged to the Coey family until 1927, then provided a holiday home for a Mrs Beatrice Kirk and her Armstrong relations. On her death in 1936, it passed to William Chaine; following his death in 1938, Droagh was sold to a Mr Pollock for £1750 at the same time that Cairndhu was sold to Sir Thomas Dixon. Since then the property has had eight owners, and is once again for sale at the date of writing.

Photograph: Michael O'Connell.
Situation: 175 Coast Road, Drains Bay; td, Droagh; Parish, Carncastle; District Council, Ballymena; Grid ref. D 387 065.
References: Not listed. OS map, 1834; VAL 1B/150 p 67, VAL 2B/1/44A p 13, VAL 12B/7/4A p 57, T2325/3, drawings by W Hastings in D 1977/37/2/1, all in PRONI; title deeds in possession of owners.

Ardvernis, Galgorm

210. A 19th-century stucco gentleman's cottage, said to date from 1839, just too late for inclusion in the first Ordnance Survey maps or memoirs, and to have been built by the then owners of Fenaghy: approached up a long curving avenue flanked on one side only by mature beech trees, formerly part of the Fenaghy property. The front is simplicity itself: a broad 16-paned window, set in a formal architrave with a simple hood moulding above, on either side of a central doorcase, with nice fan and side-lights. Attic windows in the gables; a chimney stack at each end of the roof-ridge; later extension at the rear. Adam Dickey of Lowtown "lived in the old Georgian house Ardvernis, near the works"; but it seems the Dickeys were in the end "unfortunate in trade". Samuel Cunningham, of Lisnafillan and Fenaghy, seems next to have owned Ardvernis. His only son died in 1850, unmarried; his sisters Catherine and Jane "lived to the respective ages of 86 and 94, and ... were locally known as 'the rich old Miss Cunninghams' ". The mill having been sold to the

Youngs, and probably the house with it; in 1872, the Misses Catherine and Jane Cuningham (so spelled) took a lease of Ardvernis from John Young, and bought in the freehold in 1887. The Cuningham Memorial Church in Cullybackey was built by Miss Jane on her sister's death, at a cost of £5,500, in memory of their mother; and on Miss Jane's death, the property passed to a distant relative, a Mr Dickie, who sold it to Col Chichester and his wife Hilda (*née* Young) of Galgorm Castle who planned to live there in their retirement. The house was rented in the meanwhile to a succession of tenants; it had deteriorated greatly when, in 1967, the Chichesters changed their plans and sold it to the present owners.

Photograph: Michael O'Connell.
Situation: 120 Fenaghy Road, Galgorm, Ballymena; td, Galgorm Parks; Parish, Kilconriola; District Council, Ballymena; Grid ref. D 068 044.
References: Listed B2. Bassett, 'Antrim', 1888, p 125; H C Lawlor, in 'Fibres and fabrics journal', October 1941, p 8.

Killagan Cottage, Cloughmills

211. Three Huey brothers are said to have come over from Scotland about 1800; here they made their home, and here their descendants still reside. There may well have been an earlier house on the site; Taylor and Skinner show 'Killagan, - Moore Esq' on approximately this site.

A one-and-a-half storey stucco gentleman's cottage, said to have been built in 1841 on the occasion of the marriage of James Huey to a Miss Wallace of Broughanore, Ballycastle. By 1859, Mrs Mary Huey was living here - house valued at £6, beetling mill at £20, cornmill and kiln at £7.10.0; by 1866 "this beetling & flax mill are let at £30 free of all taxes". Two eight-over-eight-pane sashed windows flanking a good doorcase with pilasters and pretty segmental fanlight: heavy quoins, and complicated architraves round the windows. There is a tradition that Killagan Cottage was either designed, or built, by the same individual as designed (or built) Larchfield (165) at very much the same date. The double pile at the rear added by the present owner's grandfather, when various internal alterations were made. Nicely painted, in an attractive setting, with a stream running through a little valley away from the main road; - the group originally comprised house; trees; bridge; farmyard; cornmill; flax mill; and bleach green, of which the three last are now gone.

Photograph: Michael O'Connell.
Situation: 49 Ballinaloob Road, Cloughmills; td, Drumadarragh; Parish, Dunaghy; District Council, Ballymoney; Grid ref. D 045 212.
References: Listed B1. Taylor and Skinner, 'Roads', 1778, p 270; VAL 2B/1/48, p 9, VAL 12B/4/15A, p 32, in PRONI; Girvan, 'North Antrim', UAHS, 1973, p 51.

Valley Cottage, Crevilly Valley

212. A charming, modest house, roughcast with stucco trim, very well painted and cared for, set amidst magnificent trees: evidently built in three sections. It has characteristics in common both with Ardvernis (210), and with Killagan Cottage (211); it would not surprise me if all three were the work of the same architect or builder.

Evidently a mill-owner's house built by Jesse Miller, formerly of Kildrum (149), owner of the extensive beetling mills on the Kells Water nearby, probably around 1850; described in the Valuation book of 1859 as "A very neat cottage, well built and finished, and in excellent repair - offices all good": valued at £20. The mills had been operated in 1836 by David Miller and William Miller, but were then much less extensive; they were held under lease for ever of 1818 from the Mount Cashel estate. Jesse Miller seems to have died around 1870, when the house and mills were taken over by the Kirk family; Bassett shows William Kirk as occupier in 1888; then, in 1893, taken over by Arthur Loughlin or Lachlan. The present owner bought in 1982 from the family of one Jack McAllister, a greyhound-racing gambling man, who is said himself to have

bought the place out of one day's winnings.

The main block is one-and-a-half storey, three bays wide, a tall Georgian-glazed window on each side of a box-like porch, a single flattened-Gothick window in a peak above the porch; pilasters painted a very pale pink contrasting nicely with the cream of the walls. The two-storey return to the left with windows upstairs and down Georgian glazed, and the fine single-storey canted bay to the right, with three tall Georgian-glazed windows, containing dining room and drawing-room, were added by the present owner in 1982 to designs of Joe Kerr, architect, of Ballymena. All concerned deserve credit for a most sensitive and successful restoration and enlargement: a pity, though, to allow so very obtrusive a tv aerial to spoil it.

Photograph: Michael O'Connell.
Situation: 15 Valley Road, Carnaghts, Ballymena; td, Crevilly Valley; Parish, Connor; District Council, Ballymena; Grid ref. J 111 973.
References: Not listed. VAL 1B/12, p 9, VAL 2B/1/2A, p 42, VAL 12B/3/18A, B, C, and D 1991/614/2, p 22, all in PRONI; Bassett, 'Antrim', 1888, pp 289, 307.

Audley Lodge, and Audley Cottage, Ballymena

213. A pair of almost (but not quite) identical pretty stucco Regency-style cottages, one on either side of Fountain Place. Both appear to date from about 1840, though oral history has it that Audley Cottage came first, then Audley Lodge, then Audley Terrace next door, all named after the Adair family's London house in South Audley Street. The Cottage is said to have been at one time the home of Lord Waveney, formerly Sir Shafto Adair, presumably before the erection in 1870 of Ballymena Castle. Each is single-storey, with a dormer - that of Audley Lodge somewhat taller than that of its neighbour - over the central arched doorcase, each has nice segmental fanlight and Ionic columns; on either side another large window with 10 panes in each sash; quoins; and wide over-sailing eaves carried on wooden brackets. The side elevation of each has two more windows at ground level, one in the dormer. Audley Lodge, very freshly and trimly painted white, has a single-storey three-bay extension of 1923, formerly doctor's surgery, and a better garden with stone curtilage wall and three trees.

Dr Armstrong records that his grandfather, who owned a farm up Glenwhirry, bought the house so that his wife could live in it, his children could go to the town schools, and his cattle could take advantage of the field at the back on their way to and from market!

Photograph: Michael O'Connell.
Situation: Audley Lodge, Nos. 29/31, Audley Cottage, No. 33, Ballymoney Road, Ballymena; td, Town Parks; Parish, Kilconriola; District Council, Ballymena; Grid ref. D 105 035.
References: Audley Lodge, listed B; Audley Cottage, listed B1. OS map, 1857; Girvan, 'Antrim & Ballymena', UAHS, 1969, p 19; Pierce and Coey, 'Taken for granted', 1984, p 64; information in MBR, and from Dr S T Armstrong.

The Square, and Maud Cottages, Cushendun

214. Ronald McNeill, later Lord Cushendun, married Maud Bolitho of Penzance, Cornwall in 1884; in 1910, on the death of his mother, they made their Irish home in Glenmona, "a neat modern bathing lodge" perhaps built by General O'Neill (see Rockport, 155), and later enlarged by Michael Harrison. Ronald McNeill, son of 'Long Eddie McNeill' of Craigdun Castle (96), was a lawyer, journalist, and Conservative politician who subscribed numerous articles to the 11th edition of the Encyclopaedia

Britannica, lived mostly in London, but valued his Irish connections. At once they commissioned the youthful Clough Williams Ellis, an architect then fashionable amongst rising politicians, to make improvements, both to the house and the village, in a slate-and-whitewash style intended to combine an Irish with a Cornish flavour.

The Square was built in 1912; a public hall and club were designed, but not built, in the same year; a gate lodge in 1913; Glenmona was rebuilt in 1923, after being burned

in the Troubles of 1921, to Clough Williams Ellis's designs; Maud Cottages were built in 1926; and McAlister's shop in 1932, though it seems not now to be quite in accordance with the drawings (the pillars have gone, if, indeed, they were ever executed).

The Square comprises seven houses set around three sides of an enclosed garden, with mansard slated roofs and shutters; Maud Cottages comprise a terrace of five houses, the upper storey slate-hung, a central bow, and recessed arcading; all of two storeys, white-painted, and Georgian-glazed. These are wholly successful examples of sensitive in filling, a model for later generations to follow. Unfortunately, Glenmona itself was rebuilt in a rather more pompous and ornate style, not displeasing but not quite in keeping with its site.

All in the ownership of the National Trust since 1954.

Photographs: Michael O'Connell; Jim McCall.
Situation: On the landward and seaward sides respectively of, but in each case set back from, Cushendun main street; td, Cushendun; Parish, Layde; District Council, Moyle; Grid ref. D 247-8 325.

References: Listed B; in conservation area. Plans, elevations and sketches in RIBA Library, Portman Square, RAN 32/F/8, 9, 10, 11, 12; Brett, 'Glens', UAHS, 1970, pp 42, 43; Gallagher and Rogers, 'Castle, coast and cottage', 1986; pp 35-37.

Tin Shack, Brown's Bay

215. Three bays wide and two bays deep, of red-painted corrugated iron, with a hipped roof of patchwork bituminous cloth of different colours, the crudest of holiday bungalows: yet still not quite forgetting its classical ancestry: its proportions, and the rudimentary pseudo-pediment at the porch, alike attest its descent. This seems to have been one of five 'summer houses' at Brown's Bay which were first valued in 1924; this one, property of Sandy McKay, valued at 15/-. It appears that either he or his brother Billy was, or both were, roadmen, and that they built it themselves.

Very large numbers of simple chalets such as this were built around the coastline of County Antrim between the wars by those who, in times of recession, could not otherwise afford holidays; many of them, despite their primitive amenities, were pressed into full-time use in the aftermath of the 1941 air raids on Belfast. Most have either disintegrated, or been up-graded; but numbers survive, particularly around Whitehead and Islandmagee, where they are within reasonably easy reach of the city.

Photograph: Michael O'Connell.
Situation: Brown's Bay, Islandmagee; td, Ballycronan Beg; Parish, Islandmagee; District Council, Larne; Grid ref. D 434 027.
References: Not listed. VAL 12B/7/12 E, F, in PRONI; local information.

CHAPTER SEVEN

PUBLIC BUILDINGS, COMMERCIAL, ETC.

This chapter is, unavoidably, something of an omnium gatherum. Nevertheless, only a limited number of categories of building is here represented. I found it necessary to reject, firmly, the temptation to include representative samples of every kind of building, for my broad principles of selection would have been undermined had I started to burden this chapter with buildings I found neither likeable nor interesting. So, the chapter contains no town hall or municipal building; no poor-house; no hospital; no prison; only one police station; only two, untypical, school buildings; only one bank; only a handful of shops; and no office block at all.

I am uncomfortable about the dearth of buildings, apart from bridges, of the early years of the industrial revolution. The pioneering work of Rodney Green,[1] of W A McCutcheon,[2] and of Fred Hamond,[3] have between them thrown much light on the industrial archaeology of the county. Corn and grist mills go back to the 17th century; by degrees, there grew up on the river banks scutching mills, tuck mills, wash mills, beetling mills (very numerous) and eventually spinning mills, weaving factories and dyeworks; not to mention paper mills, spade mills, sawmills, and bleach greens. One would have expected to find many well-preserved relics from such a wealth. But, in fact, many have been pulled down, their stones, slates and timbers cannibalised for newer buildings; many others stand roofless displaying, at best, the romance of ruin: whilst, if still in use, the mill buildings which survive have been subjected to so many alterations as to render them unrecognisable. And industrial buildings are not always attractive or architecturally significant: as McCutcheon

puts it, "technological content ... may upgrade an inoffensive or singularly unattractive building to the premier rank, worthy of every effort to retain and restore."[4] Whatever their intrinsic historical interest, I have not found it possible to include the Carrickfergus gasworks, or Patterson's spade mill, in my personal anthology; and the comparatively unaltered older sections of the Barbours' great thread mill at Hilden (242) will have to stand for its kind.

In sectors other than water-power, the material available is variable. There seem not, in the past, to have been many wind-mills in County Antrim; I know of no surviving stump; surprising in a hilly county exposed to many coastal winds. There is a considerable volume of literature on the Irish railways, but not much of it relates to station architecture. There is not a great deal on light-houses; less on bridges; less still on coastguard stations. My own monograph of 1973 on court houses and market houses[5], though long out of print, seems still the only work on the subject. I know of no serious work dealing with inns, hotels, public houses and spirit grocers; nor shops, as opposed to shop-fronts; nor the wealth of local meeting-rooms - orange halls, hibernian halls, masonic halls, church halls, war memorial halls - with which the north of Ireland is so liberally supplied. Information about power stations is exceptionally difficult to find. Some interesting subjects here, perhaps, for post-graduate research?

References: 1. Green, 'Lagan valley', 1949. 2. McCutcheon, 'Industrial archaeology', 1980. 3. Hamond, 'Antrim coast & glens', 1991. 4. McCutcheon, op cit, p 357. 5. Brett, 'Court houses and market houses', UAHS, 1973.

Details from Hilden thread mill (242). Photographs: Michael O'Connell

Court House, Antrim

216. This court house, built by the Grand Jury in 1726, is the oldest still standing in the province, and one of the finest. "It is an ornament to the town, though the inhabitants do not seem to think so" (J F Tait, 1835). It is of stone and stucco, free-standing on an open site at the head of the High Street. The ground floor is arcaded : originally the arches served to provide a covered market; then they became "a temporary bridewell for confining drunkards, rioters, and prisoners under trial"; then a public library; then, the petty sessions offices. The Parliamentary Gazetteer of 1845 was scathing: "The market house in the centre of the street is, at least in its uses, a sort of medley of public buildings ...... The bridewell of the town, though serving for a considerable circumjacent country, is a wretched little cluster of filthy barbarous cells, under the Market-House ...... An iron railing encloses it from the thoroughfare; a narrow space between this and the cell doors is an apology for an airing-yard, and serves for both males and females; the cell for male prisoners is both day-room and night-room, and has two deal bedsteads, the one over the other; a small cell for drunkards adjoins, and holds fast for 48 hours each convicted drunkard who cannot pay the adjudged fine; and the cell for females, situated at the other end, corresponds in every respect with the general character of the establishment. We could copy from the Report before us some other dismal features of the place, but are driven to forbearance by sheer disgust." Access to the court-room upstairs is by a double flight of steps in the west front, leading up to a large and rich Doric doorcase with segmental pediment, comparable in quality

to those at Gill Hall (demolished) and at Moira Parish Church, both in County Down.

Each of the longer sides is of nine bays, with five arches in the centre, and two bays at each end quoined and breaking forward. The 15-pane upper window-sashes are framed in architraves and wide sills. The hipped roof has very wide wooden eaves above a prominent dentilled cornice, much admired by the classicist C R Cockerell when he paid a visit in 1823, though he added "the dripping of the eaves is excessively inconvenient". The little octagonal lantern or cupola was added by Lord Ferrard in 1817.

Despite years of neglect, and some bomb-damage, the court house is presently well-painted and cared-for: the grilles on the arches below, the Venetian blinds above, and the various security precautions are no more conspicuous than they need to be. Now disused, its original furnishings long since lost. It is to be hoped that the future of this excellent building may not have been jeopardised by the completion of the not-very-pleasing new yellow-brick court complex nearby.

Photograph: Michael O'Connell.
Situation: High Street, Antrim; td, Town Parks; Parish, District Council, Antrim; Grid ref. J 148 867.
References: Listed A; in conservation area. D207/15/26, and GJ presentments, in PRONI; Cockerell, Diary, 24 October 1823, in RIBA Library; J Boyle, OSM, 1838, and J F Tait, 1835, Antrim, XI, pp 9, 48; Lewis, TD, II, 1837, p 38; PG, I, 1845, p 45; Girvan, 'Antrim & Ballymena', UAHS, 1969, p 8; Brett, 'Court houses and market houses', UAHS, 1973, p 25; Dixon, 'Introduction', UAHS, 1975, pp 33, 34.

Market House, Dervock

217. A sadly derelict little building, but still with a certain presence, despite its rather unappetising surroundings and a curious naive war memorial painting on an adjacent wall. Originally "a very handsome two-storey building of random stone with cut-stone dressings, its two public fronts - and even the octagonal cupola - have been mercilessly pebble-dashed. The main front is quoined and has the remains of a gable pediment; below this a tall central recessed arch framing two windows, one above another, in a single architrave. The symmetry of the pediment has been spoiled by a water-tank perched on the roof-line" (Brett).

Built in 1805 by a Mr Peacock for Lord Macartney, of Lisanoure Castle, as part of an endeavour to foster the linen trade of the district. In March of that year, the Rev. George Macartney wrote "he could not have enclosed the fair hill until Peacock had finished the market house ... [it] is all slated except a small part near the belfry, he intends for ornament to make it four feet higher than the contract". Three weeks later, "The market house is slated, the steeple and spire finished all to putting on the Vane and

Gilding the Ball under it - the workmen are ceiling and plastering the inside and preparing deals for flooring". The building actually opened, and the first market there was held, in December 1805 when "it blew a hurricane, with heavy showers of snow and hail": which must have been trying for the "forty very genteel people" who attended an "elegant Ball and Supper in the Market Hall the night before, and did not part till 7 am." Two years later, in 1807, Beaufort remarked on the "handsome Market House with a steeple and a small spire, having a very neat ball room over it, built by Lord Macartney".

In January 1860, described as the property of George Macartney Esq, in fee, and valued at £16.5.0, but marked down to £12 with the note "deduct from the whole 2/3rds for finish": which does not seem to make arithmetical sense: and is the more curious as the building is categorised 1A. In 1973, but no longer, used as a co-op shop; now a small part of it is occupied by the owner of the adjoining flat-roofed dwelling, the rest, unhappily, vacant, and deteriorating fast.

Market House (now Library), Randalstown

218. Of 1831; a two-storey five-bay building of brown squared basalt, topped by a central cupola and two chimney stacks, and with two lower wings. "A plain substantially built edifice ... surmounted by a wooden cupola on which is elevated a gilt vane. The underfloor is used as a market for the sale of and for the storage of grain ... Two apartments on this floor are fitted up for the purposes of a dispensary. The upper floor is used as a court in which petty sessions, manor courts, courts leet etc are held. This market house was erected in 1831 at an expense of £500, of which Lord O'Neill contributed £100" (1838).

Today, "library and information point"; in reasonable condition, though it is overshadowed by the radio mast of the police station next door, as well as by an excess of poles and wires. A set of new chimney pots would do as much for it as a set of new dentures for an old man with only one tooth. The clock has stopped. Other bomb damage, resulting from the proximity of the RUC barracks, has been pretty well made good.

Photograph: Michael O'Connell.
Situation: 34 New Street, Randalstown; td, Ballygrooby; Parish, Drummaul; District Council, Antrim; Grid ref. J 082 902.
References: Listed B1. Lewis, TD, 1837, II, p 484; J Boyle, OSM, 1838, Antrim, VI, p 43; Girvan, 'Antrim & Ballymena', UAHS, 1969, p 24; Brett, 'Court houses and market houses', UAHS, 1973, p 34.

◁

Photograph: Michael O'Connell.
Situation: At the cross-roads by the bridge, Main Street, Dervock; td, Ballyratahan Upper; Parish, Derrykeighan; District Council, Ballymoney; Grid ref. C 977 318.
References: Not listed. Macartney papers, D 572/1B/76, 77, 79, 113, D 588/2, D 662/1, and VAL 2B/1/33, all in PRONI; D A Beaufort, Journal, 27 October 1807, Ms 4033 in TCD Library, p 16; Brett, 'Court houses and market houses', UAHS, 1973, p 32; Girvan, 'North Antrim', UAHS, 1973, p 34; 'Macartney of Lisanoure', 1983, p 302; 'Buildings at risk', II, 1995, p 12.

Court House, Ballymoney

219. Completed in 1838, at a cost of £1,125, plus £40 for the bench and fitting up. "This may well be an early and modest work of Charles Lanyon, who became County Surveyor in the year when the decision to build was taken. It is a simple but very pleasing court house with a classical feeling, its pyramidal arrangement reminiscent of Hillsborough. The lower layer is five bays wide and deep, of basalt blocks with brick dressings to the windows and to the pilaster-like projections by which they are divided. The central doorway, at the head of seven stone steps, is framed in plain stone pilasters, with Greek-key ornament incised in the lintel. The door and fanlight are inappropriate. The upper storey, three bays wide and deep, is of the same pleasant brownish basalt, with quoins and lugged architraves of freestone, topped by a pyramidal roof. The whole building stands on a plinth behind a stone parapet wall" (Brett, 1973).

Writing in the same year, Girvan accorded it an 'A' and described it as "an interesting building somewhat unfortunately placed in a cramped site". Incredibly, it seems not to be listed officially, though it is within the conservation area. Designed in the year of Queen Victoria's accession to the throne, it well exemplifies the transition from Georgian to Victorian and, if indeed (as I surmise but cannot prove) it is by Charles Lanyon, then it is a fascinating example of one of the first exploratory works of a very young architect whose arrival in Ireland coincided with the change of reign.

Photograph: Michael O'Connell.
Situation: Charlotte Street, Ballymoney; td, Town Parks; Parish, District Council, Ballymoney; Grid ref. C 945 258.
References: Not listed; in conservation area. GJ records, 1837-8, in PRONI; Brett, 'Court houses and market houses', UAHS, 1973, p 28; Girvan, 'North Antrim', UAHS, 1972, p 41.

Court House, Ballymena

220. "A handsome building of black basalt in the Tudor Revival style. It first came before the Grand Jury in 1844, but the County Surveyor, Charles Lanyon, had to delay work 'in order to meet the views of the proprietor of the town with regard to other improvements'. In 1845, work was to proceed 'according to the original arrangement jointly with the building of a hotel adjoining the Court house by Sir Robert Adair.' The Court house was finally completed in 1846 at a cost of £3,000; the hotel cost £3,650. There used to be a covered corridor linking the two buildings, so that the judge could roll straight from bed to bench, and from bench to board" (Brett, 1973).

It is implicit in the Grand Jury records, but not actually explicitly stated, that both buildings were designed by Charles Lanyon himself. The front doorcase, very tall and very Tudor, has a good deal in common with the near-contemporary work of the same architect at Queen's University. At either side of the central projection containing the doorway is "a two-arched arcade, an interesting half-way house between the open market-arch tradition and that of the cloister". Two fine heads, representing blindfold justice, serve as corbels for the dripstone of the central segmental-pointed windows above the door. "The architect ... has devised a facade full of light and shade" (Williams).

Pilson, in the very last entry in his Annals of the County Antrim, comments on this (then exciting) example of the contemporary architecture of 1846 - "The interior of this building is most conveniently constructed: no other build-ing in the county, of the same description, is capable of affording so much accommodation. The wooden boxes, or stables, in front or along side the bench, being at once well-arranged and roomy. The whole of the interior forms an oblong parallelogram, with entrances to the boxes from the side, as well as from the body of the court. It is capable of containing 1,500 persons, with a small gallery along the back wall, facing the bench. The gothic windows in the sides, are found to answer their purpose well, and two fire places at either side, with grates, the lower bars of which are placed at a height of seven feet from the ground, add, in the winter season, considerably to the comfort of the place." However did they tend the fires? It is no good going to look, for the gothic windows and the fire places have alike disappeared, to be replaced by a nondescript modern court-room.

At the time of writing, surrounded by tall security fencing. The exterior is well cared-for and in good shape; the too-tall extension at the rear is in an unsympathetic modern style.

Photograph: Michael O'Connell.
Situation: Nos. 9 to 13, Ballymoney Road, Ballymena; td, Town Parks; Parish, Kilconriola; District Council, Ballymena; Grid ref. D 106 034.
References: Listed B1. GJ reports, ANT 4/4/10-13, 1844-7, in PRONI; Pilson, 'History of Belfast', 1846, p 172; Girvan, 'Antrim & Ballymena', UAHS, 1969, p 19; Brett, 'Court houses and market houses', UAHS, 1973, p 28; Williams, 'Architecture in Ireland', 1994, p 2.

Old Schoolhouse, Ballintoy

221. A whitewashed and harled one-and-a-half storey cottage, with small window in the gable-end; four bays of paired round-headed windows, a round-headed doorway with radial fanlight; quoins; chimneys at the gable-ends: set at the top of a steeply sloping hillside lawn.

Shown on the first Ordnance Survey map of 1832, though possibly then disused: Thomas Fagan, writing up the fair sheets of the Memoir for the parish, says that Ballintoy, Master Daniel McNeill, pay school, annual income 15 pounds, has "no house, 150 pounds about to be laid out"; and indeed the 'new' schoolhouse nearby was built only a few years later. H A Boyd asserts that "This was the school founded under the terms of Mrs Jane Stewart's Will, but may be even older than 1760." In my opinion, it is more probable that this is the schoolhouse "built by George Alexander Fullerton Esq. and supported by him and partly by the scholars", on an "exposed" site, valued at £4.12.11 in the valuation of 1834-5.

The former schoolroom has for many years served as the local Orange Hall; the master's accommodation has for many years been occupied by the sexton.

Photograph: Michael O'Connell.
Situation: 130 White Park Road, Ballintoy; td, Parish, Ballintoy; District Council, Moyle; Grid ref. D 038 445.
References: Listed B. OS map, 1832; VAL 1B/131 in PRONI; T Fagan, OSM, 1838, Antrim, IX, p 35; Girvan, 'North Antrim', UAHS, 1972, p 32; H A Boyd, in 'Northern Constitution', 17 June 1978.

Craigs Schoolhouse (now Church Hall), Cullybackey

222. "Immediately opposite to the Church, a very hand-some parochial school-house has been erected, by means of a grant from the Governors of Erasmus Smith's Schools, and nearly the same sum from Mr John McNeile, of Parkmount" (1843). The "accompanying view" (by Thomas Turner) of both church (50) and schoolhouse shows that the buildings were designed to complement each other; as Samuel Lewis remarks, "the Church and School house correspond in architecture". An uncommonly nice little schoolhouse of squared blackstone with sandstone trim, a symmetrical facade centred on a Tudor doorcase, two pretty metal ventilators (like pierced onions) on the roofline; teacher's house at the right-hand end. Girvan accorded this building an A, and commented "Probably by Charles Lanyon".

No longer used as a school; the ugly barn-like structure erected at the rear serves as a parish hall; the sexton lives in the former schoolteacher's house. The school play-ground has been tarmacadamed to provide car parking for the church. Apart from a pair of nice, low, clipped yews at the front door, the present appearance of the group is distressing.

Photograph: Michael O'Connell.
Situation: Opposite Craigs Parish Church; td, Craigs; Parish, Craigs, formerly Ahoghill; District Council, Ballymena; Grid ref. D 047 079.
References: Listed B. Lewis, TD, 1847, I, p 418; Ewart, 'Down & Connor & Dromore', 1886, p 88; 'Last report of the Down and Connor Church Accommodation Society', 1843, p 27; Girvan, 'West Antrim', UAHS, 1970, p 29; Pierce and Coey, 'Taken for granted', 1984, p 51.

The Causeway School, The Aird

223. Built in 1914-15, to a design by Clough Williams Ellis, "In memory of Lord Macnaghten of Runkerry" inscribed, beside "The Causeway School", on slate inset in elliptical lunettes. Most distinguished member of a distinguished legal family, born 1830, he was a Lord of Appeal in Ordinary from 1887 until his death in 1913.

An admirable building, white-painted roughcast, black paint, and slate: smaller-than-usual slates used in a sculptural way, so that even the curves of the octagonal cupola or bell-cote, and its very louvres, are of slate throughout. The main hall has seven bays of tall windows: at the front, great arched openings, originally unglazed, now with 38-pane radially-glazed windows: upstairs, library reached by an outside staircase: entrance hall with, outside and inside, excellent bronze panels commissioned from Rosamund Praeger by Lord Macnaghten's daughters; chimneys, offices and lavatories skilfully incorporated into the north-facing front, tucked not far below the skyline of the Causeway Heads. Now a much-used show-place for schoolchildren; owned and managed by the North

Eastern Education and Library Board, and in excellent order.

In my view, by far the best of this architect's Irish ventures - better certainly than his school in Bushmills, for the same family; than Glenmona House for Lord Cushendun; even, in my judgement, than the Square and the Maud Cottages at Cushendun (214). This building is, plainly, of the Celtic fringe: it might not seem out of place in Wales, the Hebrides, Cornwall, or Brittany: Girvan thinks it "as eccentric as it is unexpected", and comments that "the building seems to take a light-hearted attitude to the grandeur of the surrounding scenery"; but to my eye, it fits perfectly into this dramatic landscape.

Photograph: Michael O'Connell. (See also colour-plate XVb)
Situation: North of the road from the Causeway Head to Dunseverick; td, Ardihannon; Parish, Billy; District Council, Moyle; Grid ref. C 946 440.
References: Listed B. Drawings RAN 32/H/2/1-10 in RIBA Library, London; 'Coleraine Chronicle', 7 August 1915; Girvan, 'North Antrim', UAHS, 1972, p 26.

War Memorial Hall, Ballinderry

224. "Foundation stone laid by Alfred Sefton Esq., 5th July 1924", according to a stone to one side; "Ballinderry War Memorial Hall, Erected 1924", inscribed in a lunette under the segmental-curved hood of the porch, with Tuscan columns, of this pleasing, symmetrical, neo-Georgian composition. Designed by R H Gibson, later to be the owner of Ballinderry Glebe (113), rather in the manner of, and every bit as good as, the work of Clough Williams Ellis. "Among the halls he has designed is a very fine one - a war memorial - at Ballinderry; and the Heyne Memorial hall" (at St Mark's, Dundela) "in the design of which he and Mr Seaver were associated".

All the detailing is confident - the over-sailing eaves; the central oculus topped by stylised pediment and square cupola; the Georgian-glazed windows; the curved screen walls with square piers, spherical knops, and wrought iron gates in the doorways. Roughcast, this delightful little building is painted crisply white, with cherry-red detailing, all on a black plinth.

One feels that architect and client were here in uncommonly close, and happy, accord. The building is a real ornament to an already pretty village.

Photograph: Michael O'Connell.
Situation: 10A North Street, Upper Ballinderry; td, Derryscollop; Parish, Ballinderry; District Council, Lisburn; Grid ref. J 163 673.
References: Listed B1. IB, 29 August 1931, p 753; P Larmour in 'Perspective', July/August 1995, pp 75-77.

Orange Hall, Lisburn

225. Dated 1871 on the string-course above the entrance. A pleasing stuffy stucco classical facade, the generous detailing nicely picked out in two shades of grey, dull red, blue, and white. It has excellent triple round-headed windows with cable-moulding eyebrows, and barley sugar cast-iron dividers, above the central doorway. The side walls are of more economical random rubble with brick dressings.

It is a pity that the rather unsuitable modern brick wall and wrought iron gates detract from the effect of this flamboyant piece of work.

Photograph: Michael O'Connell.
Situation: Railway Street, Lisburn; td, Lisnagarvey; Parish and District Council, Lisburn; Grid ref. J 266 645.
References: Not listed; in conservation area.

Colane Orange / Black / Masonic Hall, Aghalee

226 (right). Can this pleasing, cottage-like, little hall really, as seems to be the case, accommodate the orange, black and masonic orders all three? If so, it must be nearly unique. On the gable of the porch, in a circle, the masonic dividers, L-square, and a purple-painted capital G; in a larger circle, on the main gable, a seven-pointed golden star, with the inscription "Colane Primrose RBP No 249 1914". Down below, a stone inscribed "This stone was laid by Master Chs R Chapman 8th July 1914". There are fluted pilasters at the corners of porch and main hall; fancy architraves; all the stucco-work neatly painted in cream, grey, yellow, purple and white: roof of red tiles and ridge-tiles, with a chimney at the opposite gable to the porch. Three openings in each side wall.

Photograph: Michael O'Connell.
Situation: Colane Road, Aghalee; td, Poobles; Parish, Aghalee; District Council, Lisburn; Grid ref. J 141 628.
References: Not listed. Datestone inscriptions.

Masonic Hall, Clough

227. A remarkable outburst of classicism in the middle of a small, somewhat depressed, village: a two-storeyed pebble-dashed hall, five bays deep, whose pedimented facade has two pairs of Corinthian columns supporting architrave and dentilled cornice: between the columns, a pair of round-headed windows. Described by Pierce and Coey as "A strange, mainly plain, roughcast two-storey building with a classical facade consisting of an out-of-scale pediment over a heavy cornice and architrave, all supported on two pairs of unfluted Corinthian columns".

According to an appeal on behalf of Clough Masonic Lodge No 574, circulated in January 1922, "About two years ago the Brethren secured the necessary ground free of rent (through the generosity of one of the members) to erect a Hall, and on this they have erected a large and commodious hall, which is admitted by all who have seen it to be one of the best for its situation in Ireland". But, unfortunately, "the cost of the building and furnishing is about £3,000. The members have paid about £1,200, and an effort is now being made to raise the balance of £1,800".

Photograph: Michael O'Connell.
Situation: Broughshane Road, Clough; td, Cloghgaldanagh; Parish, Dunaghy; District Council, Ballymena; Grid ref. D 098 145.
References: Listed B1. Girvan, 'West Antrim', UAHS, 1970, p 32; Pierce and Coey, 'Taken for granted', 1984, p 51; information from Mr T Young, Broughshane.

Crosskeys Inn, Ardnaglass

228. A white-washed one-and-a-half storey thatched public-house, possibly 17th-century, quite unspoiled. Although it stands on the old main road from Dublin to Coleraine, it could hardly have been a coaching-inn, since it has not enough space for bedrooms or stabling. It was probably more of a comfort-stop, evidently combining the functions of shop, post-office, and bar, with perhaps a spirit-grocer's licence. The oldest part of the building has very small Georgian-glazed windows; the projecting part towards the road, probably an early 19th-century addition, has one rather larger window, with ten panes in each sash.

The windows have shutters, upon one of which the crossed keys of the name are painted. There is also a panel with a delightful primitive painting of St Patrick casting out the snakes from Ireland. Although the keys rightly belong to St Peter, not St Patrick, it has been suggested that both name and pictures may refer back to a period when the pub was used as a place of meeting by two near-by lodges of the Hibernians.

This must be "the noted publick house where the Misses Boyds live", a "good stone and lime farm house" with ten acres of land, "in the townland of Ardnaglass, in Grange, and county of Antrim, near the navigable river Bann and in the heart of a pleasant country where the linen manufacture flourishes in the greatest degree, and near many market towns" (16 March, 1771). The names of the earliest proprietors have been lost; but a Mr McErlean was postmaster here in the 1850s; he was followed by Mr Neeson; then by three or four generations of Kennedys. The last John Kennedy left the pub to his housekeeper, Tilly McKeever, from whom the father of the present owner bought it in 1965.

Photograph: Michael O'Connell.

Situation: 40 Grange Road, Ardnaglass at the cross-roads of the Money-glass-Ahoghill and Grange Corner-Portglenone roads; td, Ardnaglass; Parish, Grange of Ballyscullion; District Council, Ballymena; Grid ref. J 016 965.

References: Listed B1/Q. Taylor and Skinner, 'Roads', 1778, p 18; Wilson, 'Post-chaise companion', 1803, p 55; advertisement of 1771 cited in O'Laverty, 'Down and Connor', III, 1884, p 340 n, and in Bigger 'Ulster land war', 1910, p 129; OS map, 1832; Girvan, 'West Antrim', UAHS, 1970, p 22; Pierce and Coey, 'Taken for granted', 1984, p 36.

Thatch Inn (formerly O'Neill Arms), Broughshane

229. "William Weir has this day opened the long established Inn, in Broughshane, known by the name of the O'Neill Arms, where gentlemen will meet with good entertainment. 19th May, 1789." An unexpectedly rustic survival in the middle of the main street of Broughshane: two-storey, six bays wide, roughcast, whitewashed, and thatched, with original (rather narrow) Georgian-glazed 12-pane sashes; the entrance off-centre with a modestly-pleasing shopfront-label over the door. "A primitive royal coat of arms is said to recall the impromptu visit of some English sovereign" (Girvan); of this there seems to be no record; but Prince Charles sampled Black Bush on the premises on 7th July 1994.

Photograph: Michael O'Connell
Situation: 57 Main Street, Broughshane; td and Parish, Skerry and Racavan; District Council, Ballymena; Grid ref. D 153 066.
References: Listed B+. BNL, 29 May 1789; Girvan, 'Antrim & Ballymena', UAHS, 1969, p 32; Pierce and Coey, 'Taken for granted, 1984, p 36.

Antrim Arms, Ballycastle

230. So early as 1816, a year after Waterloo, the Rev. Luke Connolly writes of the Ballycastle tourist trade, "When an exclusion from the continent obliged the English gentry to seek for attractions in their own dominions, the Giant's Causeway became a place of fashionable resort to many British visitants of distinction ... during the summer months, handsome carriages with coronets have been often observed to drive up to the door of an ill-regulated inn, where the chambers were in disorder, the attendants slovenly, and the larder almost empty ... A considerable alteration, however, for the better has lately taken place ... There is now a decent inn kept by a person of the name of Fullarton, who has carriages for hire ... opposite the church." Now a fine 5-plus-one-bay three-storey building, with basement, on a steeply sloping corner site, stuccoed and with Victorian glazing, of uncertain antiquity: the previous inn of the same name on the same site was leased in the mid-18th century by Alexander Boyd to Robert

McCarroll, surgeon. According to Dr Alexander Knox, author in 1845 of Irish Watering Places and "late physician and surgeon to the Ballycastle Dispensary, Fever Hospital, and Poor House", Ballycastle "has two hotels, one of which, the Antrim Arms, has a very good posting establishment connected with it". In 1858, it was stated to have been owned by Mr R McDonnell.

The present building probably dates from around 1835; certainly such a date would seem plausible for the excellent porch with elegant fluted Ionic columns, the best feature of the building. However, W A Green's photograph, from the turn of this century, shows the same columns but quite a different pediment - note also the slated gable, and the use of pointed slates in place of chimney-pots. By 1861, the hotel comprised two large houses of three storeys with basement, at the corner of Castle Street and Fair Hill, one the property of John McGildowney Esq. and the other that of Mrs Rosetta McGildowney, both leased to John McDonnell, all together valued at £38. A woodcut of it, looking very much as now, accompanies a full-page advertisement for the hotel in 1888, when it is described by R Hunter, proprietor, as "established over half a century".

In 1831, Lt Robe had remarked, with feeling, "considering the great number of visitors who pass through Ballycastle in the course of the summer, in the tour of the coast of Antrim, the accommodations for travellers are wretched, the only inn being dirty in the extreme." In 1835, James Boyle added: "There is but 1 inn in the town, and it affords but indifferent accommodation for trav-

ellers; but it may be expected that the great numbers of visitors who now pass through Ballycastle, in the tour of the Antrim coast, will shortly lead to improvement". The present hotel, one hopes, represented this improvement.

Photographs: Michael O'Connell; W A Green, Ulster Folk Museum WAG 826.
Situation: 75 Castle Street (at the junction with the Diamond), Ballycastle; td, Townparks; Parish, Ramoan; District Council, Moyle; Grid ref. D 115 407.
References: Listed B1; in conservation area. L Connolly, in Mason, 'Statistical account', II, 1816, p 504; T C Robe, OSM, 1831, and J Boyle, 1835, Antrim, IX, pp 89, 94; VAL 2B/1/28C, p 53, in PRONI; Knox, 'Irish watering places', 1845, p 281; Carroll, 'Tourist's illustrated handbook', 1853; Bassett, 'Antrim', 1888, p 92: H A Boyd, in 'Coleraine Chronicle', 1 July 1967; Brett, 'Glens', UAHS, 1971, p 47; Mullin, 'Causeway coast', 1974, p 171.

Londonderry Arms, Carnlough

231. In 1835, according to James Boyle, the principal support of the inhabitants of Carnlough "seems to be derived from letting lodgings to the crowds of the lower orders who swarm here in summer from the inland country for the benefit of sea bathing"; but there was no hotel for the better class of visitor. By 1845, there was still no hotel, though Dr Knox remarked that "the neat little villas lying along the beautiful white beach of Carnlough bay" were much resorted to for bathing. It fell to Lady Londonderry to remedy the deficiency.

This agreeable hotel, built by her about 1850, has the appearance of an earlier Georgian coaching inn. The main building has various ornamental flourishes - quoins, a porch with Doric columns, pediments to some of the windows, and open pediments at the eaves. The five bay extension next door is much simpler: both admirably painted in black and white, the older part now generously clothed in ivy. Drawings by one Patrick Mahon, unfortunately undated, but apparently of about 1852 to 1854, provide for four additional bedrooms upstairs in the extension, and for a "Gentleman's Bath Room Hot and Cold" with "plunge and shower bath", and a Ladies' ditto, on the ground floor, to the left of the fan-lighted hall doorway.

The specification, and a tender for £570 excluding leadwork, both likewise maddeningly undated, also survive.

In 1859 it was held by James McVickers on lease from her ladyship, rent-free for the first two years, afterwards at £30 a year. This caused some puzzlement to the valuer, who wrote "This is a very good concern with a very fine yard and offices and altogether a capital house - but there is no business doing and I could not put on more than £25 - it is set for that money but I would not mind the rent as, if a proper person had it, there might be a fair business done in it". And: "I would be a good deal more on the Hotel and offices but I believe we cannot raise the valuation ... There is no business to support so fine a concern".

Happily, business has improved since then, and the establishment is now a popular and successful one.

Photograph: Michael O'Connell. (See also colour-plate Xb)
Situation: 20-24 Harbour Road, Carnlough; td, Carnlough South; Parish, Ardclinis; District Council, Larne; Grid ref. D 288 180.
References: Listed B1; in conservation area. J Boyle, OSM, 1835, Antrim, IV, p 6; VAL 2B/1/38, pp 77, 78, and D 2977/37/5/1, in PRONI; Knox, 'Irish watering places', 1845, p 280; Brett, 'Glens', UAHS, 1971, p 19.

McCollam's Pub, Cushendall

232. Two three-storey houses, perhaps of 1830-40, one rather taller than the other and with a coach arch; all windows with original Georgian glazing-pattern, and heavy stucco architraves; and a very pleasant fascia-board with raised white squiggly lettering: all admirably painted.

Owned in 1856 by John and Margaret Barry; his widow remarried John McAllister, whose niece Nancy, having married one Joseph McCollam of Armoy, came to live here, and was by 1908 the holder of the spirit licence. "Nancy Joe, as she was known to her customers, was of formidable proportions, and is reputed to have been at least 18 stone. She was respected for her ability to remove the most obstreperous customer by the scruff of the neck, yet she was also renowned as a generous lady ... Nancy's daughters, Mary Ann and Grace, helped their mother run a very busy boarding house and restaurant, catering for large parties of residents as well as a passing trade." The business was carried on, first, by her son Johnny Joe, then her grandson Joe.

Photograph: Michael O'Connell.

Situation: 21-23 Mill Street, Cushendall; td, Cushendall; Parish, Layde; District Council, Moyle; Grid ref. D 237 276.

References: Listed B; in conservation area. Brett, 'Glens', UAHS, 1971, pp 35-6; Pierce and Coey, 'Taken for granted', 1984, p 18; Connon and McNaughton, 'Days gone by', 1991, pp 62-3.

Joymount Arms (also known as 'The Wee Red Bar', also 'Ow'nie's'), Carrickfergus

233. Described in 1978 as "a two-storey, two-bay public house, very imaginatively painted in red and white, held together by quoins". In fact, three-bay, as the surviving window-sill to the left of the door demonstrates; not disproved by the fact that the door is well off-centre. At present, very imaginatively painted in red and black, with white linings and glazing bars. On the front facade, the legend "Joymount Arms, Established 1846"; the date seems unverifiable, but perfectly convincing. Originally the house faced the sea and its battery wall, before the interposition of the Marine Gardens and Highway in the 1950s.

The name of the original owner is lost in the mists of antiquity; but for very many years the house belonged to the Crowe family; passing then to Owen McCullough ("Ow'nie") and his widow, formerly housekeeper, Kathleen; before being bought in 1989 by its present owners.

This public house has for many years been the preferred resort of archaeologists excavating in the town. Sentimentalists among their number will regret many of the changes to the interior, especially in the extension, but the outside of the pub is still charming.

Photograph: Michael O'Connell. (See also colour-plate XIc)
Situation: 9 Joymount Place, Carrickfergus; td, Parish, District Council, all Carrickfergus; Grid ref. J 416 877
References: Not listed; not in conservation area. Campbell and Crowther, 'Carrickfergus', UAHS, 1978, p 33; information from owners and customers.

McAuley's Pub, Carnlough

234. Just at the river bridge. Charles McAuley's, dated 1912: "an extravagant and hilarious example of fine ornate Art Nouveau lettering, ornament and painting; incongruous to the older part of the town, but not to the resort atmosphere of the front" (Brett, 1971). The gable freshly painted in vividly contrasting black and white, the raised lettering of the word 'Hotel' having been tactfully painted out in black. This represents the rebuilding of a much older inn, in the ownership of the McAuley family since the mid-18th century, burned down in 1912. It was reported to have been the meeting-place of the local United Irishmen before they assembled, under the leadership of a 19-year old Presbyterian minister (Rev. Robert Acheson), at Bellair Hill above Glenarm on 7th June 1798.

Photograph: Michael O'Connell.
Situation: 2-4 Bridge Street, Carnlough; td, Carnlough South; Parish, Ardclinis; District Council, Larne; Grid ref. D 288 179.
References: Listed B1; in conservation area. Brett, 'Glens', UAHS, 1971, pp 19, 26; McKillop, 'Glenarm', 1987, pp 32-33.

Shop (now Post Office), Roses Lane Ends, Ballinderry

235. A nice old two-storey whitewashed-and-slated late-Georgian shop and dwelling, perhaps of about 1820; a bit shabby, in need of whitewashing, the black paint of the woodwork in need of refreshment, but almost unspoiled; a small two-storey extension, one window altered, the windows (three upstairs, three plus two doors downstairs) otherwise Georgian-glazed in appropriately differing patterns according to varying size.

This may or may not be the public house and general shop valued at £4 and occupied by Edward Devlin in 1861. Bassett in 1888, says that "Rose's Lane Ends is a rural post office on a hill commanding a beautiful view of Lough Neagh ... Post Master: H Patterson."

Photograph: Michael O'Connell.
Situation: At Roses Lane Ends crossroads, on the road from Crumlin to Lurgan; td, Ballymacrevan; Parish, Ballinderry; District Council, Lisburn; Grid ref. J 133 704.
References: Listed B2. OS map, 1832; VAL 2B/1/55A, p 11; Bassett, 'Antrim', 1888, p 252.

Shop Front and Facade, Etam, 27 - 29 High Street, Ballymena

236. In 1969, Girvan wrote of Montgomery's Furniture Shop, 27-29 High Street: "A first-rate late Georgian block, five bays by three storeys, with an exceptionally fine classical shop front along its entire length; built of basalt with brick trim and Georgian glazed windows above the ground floor. The shopfront has a long entablature supported on five fluted Ionic columns that are finely carved. They are irregularly spaced and between each column is a tripartite Georgian window, an extremely elegant late 18th century door in a curved segmental recess, then the main shop front, a central door with curved glazed windows on either side, and finally a coach entrance to the yard behind. This shopfront must be one of the best remaining of its period anywhere in Ireland and ought to be preserved".

The Montgomerys were long established in the town as coach-builders, cabinet-makers, and purveyors of furniture; William, carpenter, Matthew, coach-maker, and Hugh, cabinet-maker appear in the Directories from 1852 on, but the shop front is certainly earlier. According to James Boyle, "High Street and Wellington Street are still in progress" in 1835; "High Street is tolerably uniform and wide, the houses being of good size and either 2 or 3-storeys high. They are suitable for business or for families of moderate income, and let at from 10 to 30 pounds per annum."

In 1976, the building was listed in the rare Category A (as its remains still are), and soon after was purchased under blight notice by the Government. In 1981 listed

building consent for its demolition was refused, but it collapsed on 20th August 1981, and there was a further collapse (after work carried out too close to it) in January 1982. In the course of that year the whole building was taken down and rebuilt, brick by brick, on almost exactly its original site. The restoration was carefully done, and the building's use, as bar and restaurant, was quite appropriate, as also the colours of the paintwork, which repeated those - dark green and cream - which had been applied, by the same decorator, thirty years before. Unfortunately, in November 1989 permission for change of use was given to the London chain of Etam shops, but without adequate development control conditions to protect the building's character. Now the front doors do not open, strip lights are all too visible through the front windows, one front window gives depressing views of some kind of junk store, plate glass has been inserted in the back windows, and the colour scheme is inappropriate. As custodians of a first-rate building, Etam should be ashamed of themselves: not a good advertisement for that company.

Photograph: Michael O'Connell.
Situation: 25-29 High Street, Ballymena; td, Town Parks; Parish, Kilconriola; District Council, Ballymena; Grid ref. D 034 108.
References: Listed A. J Boyle, OSM, 1835, Antrim, VIII, pp 96, 97; Bassett, 'Antrim', 1888, p 291; Girvan, 'Antrim & Ballymena', UAHS, 1969, p 18 and front cover; Pierce and Coey, 'Taken for granted', 1984, p 37; information in MBR.

Shop (now Post Office), 39 Toberwine Street, Glenarm

237. A three-storey three-bay house and shop, roughcast and painted, with quoins, slated roof and chimney stacks all complete, next door to the courthouse. The ground floor facade is divided by pilasters: there are two broad and handsome 15-pane windows, separated by double-doors to the shop with an elaborate geometrical fanlight above; to the right, the separate entrance to the house over the shop, with similar but narrower doorway and geometrical fanlight.

This building may be the one reputed to have been built before 1700 by a retired ship's captain named Wilson; or it may be a later rebuilding on the same site, said to have been that of the earliest post office in the village. The present appearance of house and shopfront would suggest a date between 1825 and 1845, but shopfronts are notoriously liable to alteration. Some such date would tend to be confirmed by the Ordnance Survey memoir which records that, in 1835, "Glenarm consists of 1 long street of tolerable regularity and 2 smaller ones branching off from it. It contains 145 houses, of which 1 is 3-storeys, 97 2-storeys and the remainder 1-storey." It is possible, but not very likely, that the present post office is

the solitary 3-storey house of the 1835 description. In 1779, a map of the village shows this site in the occupation of Margery Burgess; the Valuation book of 1861 shows the name of Samuel Dick struck out, and the word "vacant" - the house was in category 1B and valued at £15. Between 1861 and 1866, it was occupied first by William, then by Ellen Allen. For many years this was the principal shop in the village: in 1901, taken on by William Tuppen, maternal grandfather of the present owner, who conducted a groceries, hardware and general merchandise shop on the left-hand site of the shop door, while his wife conducted a drapery establishment on the right-hand side. In 1959, the shop was taken on as a Post Office by Richard Pullins, father of the present owner.

Photograph: Michael O'Connell.

Situation: 39, Toberwine Street, Glenarm; td, Town Parks; Parish, Tickmacrevan; District Council, Larne; Grid ref. D 311 152.

References: Listed B1; in conservation area. J Boyle, OSM, 1835, Antrim, IV, 1835, p 128; VAL 2B/1/41B, p 11, and VAL 12B/7/9A, p 71, in PRONI; J Irvine, 'A map of Glenarm 1779', in 'Glynns', IX, 1981, p 59; Brett, 'Glens', UAHS, 1971, p 16; information from owner.

Threshing Barn, Leslie Hill, Ballymoney

238. A seven-bay two-storey building as unusual as it is attractive. Cruciform in shape, it has in effect four gables, the roof of king-post construction, airy and Piranesian. Part is roughcast and freshly whitewashed, part is of random blackstone with red brick dressings. There are tall louvred openings for ventilation, over low arched openings (some blocked); the composition is topped by a little bell-cote. The cross-block was designed to provide threshing-floor below, grain storage above.

Apparently of the same date as Leslie Hill house (72), for it appears on both the surveys of 1774 by Hans Sloane and 1776 by John O'Hara. On 3rd August in that same year Arthur Young recorded that he went to "Lesly Hill, where I met Mr Lesly, a warm admirer of husbandry, and practising it on a scale not often met with. I have no where met with any person more inclined, or better able, to

inform me minutely on every object ... Mr Lesly's granary is one of the best contrived I have seen in Ireland; it is raised over the threshing-floor of his barn, and the floor of it is hair-cloth for the air to pass through the heap, which is a good contrivance. The whole building is well executed and very convenient, and contains two large bullock sheds". And: "I would remark that Mr Leslie's crops of wheat were the finest I had seen in Ireland, nor do I remember finer in England." And: "In cattle, Mr Lesly has been equally attentive; he procured one of Mr

Bakewell's bulls two years ago, and has bred many calves by him." And: "In drainage he has made considerable exertions, principally by hollow [pipes]." Mr Leslie must have been a notable agriculturist indeed.

Photographs: Michael O'Connell.
Situation: In the farmyard at the rear of Leslie Hill house; td, Ballypatrick; Parish and District Council, Ballymoney; Grid ref. C 935 259.
References: Listed B+. Surveys, H Sloane, 1774 and J O'Hara, 1776, in possession of owner; Young, 'Tour in Ireland', 1780, pp 132-139.

Gilbert's Dam, Aghagallon

239. A remarkable group of buildings, perhaps mid-18th century, perhaps earlier, probably a bit later, in the process of restoration. The mill-dam, with artificial crannog for the resident swans, powers a large, beautifully-restored breast wheel; which in turn powers every kind of necessary device from threshing-machine to turnip-cutter, from sharpening-stone to butter-churn. The wheel is housed in a brick extension to a long, airy, slated blackstone 'barn'; on the side facing the dam, and the gable, pierced by three rows of circular port-holes for purposes of ventilation; on the other side, four large arches are carried on square columns with rounded corners, all of red brick. Various grain stores and ancillary buildings stand nearby; a two-storey cottage; and the former mill-owner's house, of five-

bays, two-storey, covered in Virginia creeper: with a couchant lion white-painted on top of the porch, and a supernumerary oculus window on the ground floor.

The old mill-house has been supplanted by a late-Victorian stucco villa, yellow-painted, across the road; to which is attached a most extraordinary garden of gravel, *rocaille* and water, laid out by the present owner's grandfather between 1880 and 1920, incorporating, concealed inside a stone turret, a primitive shower-bath for the use of workmen overcome by the dust of the threshing or the mill.

The Gilbert family, its present and (they claim) original owners, bought the property back in 1989, after most of it had lain vacant for forty years: and are now busily engaged in the formidable task of setting all to rights again. 'Gilbert's Bridge' is shown on the Ordnance Survey map of 1832; though T C Hannyngton, in his Memoir of 1835, says ominously "Mills: none: the parish has not a sufficient fall for the erection of a mill". He also records that "the late Mrs Ann Gilbert of Drumaleet gave birth to 24 separate children, the offspring of 3 husbands. Her first marriage took place between the 15th and 17th years of her age and she was often called into her house from jack-stone play among other children after her first birth, and by much flattery got to give her child suck. She died about 30 years back at an advanced age." Jonathan, then James Gilbert and Stephen Gilbert, had houses and farms in the

townland in 1834, as also did Thomas Gilbert in 1859; some of the buildings valued were two-storey, but it is not possible with any confidence to identify the buildings here illustrated. Also of this robust stock is W Stephen Gilbert, the Belfast seed merchant and novelist.

Photograph: Michael O'Connell. (See also colour-plate VIa)
Situation: Riverdale, Gilbert's Bridge, west of the road from Aghalee to Aghagallon; td, and Parish, Aghagallon; District Council, Craigavon; Grid ref. J 110 641.
References: Not listed. OS map, 1832; T C Hannyngton, OSM, 1835, and T Fagan, Antrim, VII, pp 4, 21; VAL 1B/165A, p 21, and VAL 2B/1/54, p 33, in PRONI; information from owners.

Camellia House, Shane's Castle

240 (right). During a visit to Shane's Castle in 1783 Sarah Siddons noted "a fine Conservatory, ... where the waves of the superb lake wash'd its feet ..." Thomas Milton, in 1793, published a print of Shane's Castle with loughside conservatory; the accompanying text says that "within these few Years an Embank-ment was made, on which is built a Green House, the Castle Wall forming one Side, and the Glass projecting into the Lake on the other": but the present Camellia House appears to be to designs by John Nash, built between 1812 and 1816, and very closely resembling the long conservatory which Nash had built for himself a few years earlier at his home, East Cowes Castle in the Isle of Wight. It is thirteen bays long, each wide round-headed window with a fanlight-like radial top; the timbers of the glass roof supported on Nash's 'standard' cast-iron trusses; between the windows, slim stone colonettes supporting fluted arches (Boyle says, "a handsome front of 13 Saxon windows separated by moulded columns of sandstone"); battlements at the top of each wall. Originally stocked with "rare exotics besides some remarkably fine orange and lemon trees"; now full to the brim with mature camellias of several varieties. Beneath, "a double row of twenty six segmental vaults leading to

two water gates for the purpose of taking in coals" for the heating furnace. But this description much understates the extent and complexity of the labyrinth of dark and rather menacing tunnels, passageways, rooms, stores and a great basement kitchen, the sandy floors channelled by the water running down the walls, which underlie the loughside terrace.

The whole structure, with a rather later telescopic tower and battlemented bastion kitted out with a suite of naval cannon, is built on a platform, extending out into Lough Neagh. Since then, the successive lowerings of the water level of the Lough have deprived the group of the picturesque effect which Nash had intended; especially if it was intended to furnish a dock for the sail or steam yachts of the dashing proprietor.

It appears that, after the death of the first Viscount O'Neill at the Battle of Antrim in 1798, his successor, elevated to an Earldom on the Act of Union in 1800, called in Nash, then working at Killymoon, to design a completely new house for him. Two drawings survive; the new house was far from complete when most of the old house, the family records, and contents were destroyed by an accidental fire in 1816; such work on the house as

Detail from a painting of Shane's Castle by Felix Kelly, completed in 1988 - a speculation on the appearance of the Castle if the designs by John Nash had been completed after the fire in 1816

proceeded does not accord with Nash's surviving drawings. Most of the relevant papers and buildings, alike, were destroyed in another fire in the Victorian castle, this time the work of Sinn Fein, on 25th May 1922. Doubt has been cast on the extent of Nash's involvement in the work at Shane's Castle. According to Robin Fedden, quoted by Colvin, Thomas Hopper was employed to arbitrate between Nash and Lord O'Neill, "who began to rebuild the house after a fire had destroyed the old castle in 1816, but stopped the work before it was finished". There can, I think, be no doubt about the attribution of the Camellia House itself to Nash.

The O'Neill family were considerable builders. Apart from the Camellia House, it is worth recording their other contributions to the architecture of County Antrim. Two gate-lodges of around 1850, with Puginesque bargeboards, are attributed by Dean to James Sands. The very grand Randalstown gateway and lodge (196), in a flamboyant Jacobethan style, may be by Sands or may be by Charles Lanyon, by whom the new castle of 1862 was designed. The present house at Shane's Castle is of 1958, by Arthur Jury. Other O'Neill ventures were: Tollymore Lodge, Broughshane - a sort of dower-house, now burned down and its site submerged in the modern buildings of a hotel; Rockport at Cushendun (155), still standing, and Glenmona (or possibly Glendun Lodge, 154), likewise at Cushendun, the former rebuilt, the latter still standing; Raymond Cottage - beside Lough Beg, a charming thatched cottage orné, "walls all of wood, plastered and

pebble-dashed outside", of which a plan and elevation survive (see page 217), but not the cottage; Cleggan Lodge at Aghafatten (89), still standing but no longer thatched; Deerpark Cottage, a rustick building of blackstone with mock tree trunks all round, and an oval reception room, "in miniature imitation of the lodge of the ranger of Windsor Forest", demolished by the Department of Agriculture though it could have been saved; the cottage on Ram's Island, thatched, with pretty lattice windows, bought by Lord O'Neill from a Liverpool merchant named James Whittle, burned down, it is said by Americans from Langford Lodge, during the second World War; and the mysterious Charlotte Cottage referred to in Lord O'Neill's private flag-code-book for his yacht - but nobody seems to know where that was. There are also various estate workers' cottages, lodges and farm buildings of some interest.

Photograph: Michael O'Connell. Painting: reproduced by permission of Lord O'Neill.

Situation: In the grounds of Shane's Castle demesne; td, Shane's Castle Park; Parish, Drummaul; District Council, Antrim; Grid ref. J 116 879.

References: Listed A. Siddons, 'Reminiscenses', 1942, p 27; Milton, 'Seats and demesnes of Ireland', pl XXII, 1793, p xliii; J Boyle, OSM, 1838, Antrim, VI, p 48; EM Jope, 'Nash in Northern Ireland', in UJA, 3rd series, XIX, 1956, p 121; Davis, 'John Nash', 1966, p 50; Girvan, 'West Antrim', UAHS, 1970, p 21; Colvin, 'Dictionary', 1978, footnote pp 434-5; Mansbridge, 'John Nash', 1991, p 180; Girvan, unpublished notes; information from the family.

Grain Lofts and Warehouses (now Ballinderry China / Antiques), Upper Ballinderry

241. A remarkable series of vernacular commercial buildings in the late-Georgian style. For the most part, built of random rubble, whitewashed, but there have been many alterations, and one gable is of brick. Originally these were four buildings, probably not all built at the same time, with extensive yards and out-offices at the rear.

The Ordnance Survey Memoirs are specific: Upper Ballinderry at the date of survey (before 1838) consisted only of "2 public houses, a smithy, and a few neat-looking cottages ... the new church and a neat cottage built by one of the innkeepers give a very pleasant appearance to the place. One of the innkeepers, or indeed both, sell groceries ... the road from Glenavy to Moira runs through the village." According to the Valuation book compiled in 1837, Thomas Walkington owned the corn mill, kiln, houses etc. at Lower Ballinderry to a value of £14.11.3; and house, offices and stores at Upper Ballinderry, to a value of no less than £58.4.10. The Walkingtons were also the owners of Oatland Cottage next door until both were acquired by the present owners in 1950.

The 'house' nearest the cross-roads is the most sophisticated, also - judging from the unrecessed window-frames - perhaps the earliest, three-storey and four-bay, with three wide sixteen-pane Georgian windows on the ground floor; the corner is canted up to the second storey, and has a square-headed doorway in the angle. The next 'house' is of three bays and three storeys, all eight windows Georgian-glazed but this time set back behind reveals. These houses underwent considerable external refurbishment in 1994; although they certainly stood in need of tidying up, or at least whitewashing and repainting, something has been lost in the rather stark replastering.

The third 'house' is of four bays and three storeys; all

the openings are segmental-headed, but only the two windows on the ground floor, flanking the doorway, are Georgian-glazed; the upper openings have louvres not glass. The fourth 'house' has a slightly lower roofline, but yet manages to cram in four storeys - again, all the openings are segmental-headed, none are glazed, and there is no window, only a central doorway, at ground level: this contained grain-drying lofts, and the chimney-stacks are in fact ventilators designed to extract the moist air.

Tempting as it is to date them earlier, it seems likely that these buildings are not much earlier than 1837, and were the extensive outbuildings appurtenant to Oatland Cottage next door (172), itself enlarged only in 1903. Mrs Sally MacIntyre, *née* Walkington, born there in 1908, recalls loose-boxes for hunters; a byre for four cows to supply cream to the cottage; piggeries; harness-room; and a corn mill, turned latterly by a steam engine, but before that by a circular horse-walk. In the troubled times of 1912, there was a shooting range in the haggard, and Mrs MacIntyre recalls watching from the billiard-room window whilst her father and Colonel Pakenham drilled the volunteers in the upper yard. During the second World War, there was a camp at the rear housing first British, then American, soldiery; then prisoners-of-war.

Photograph: Michael O'Connell: after 1994 refurbishment.
Situation: 2-4 Lower Ballinderry Road, Upper Ballinderry; td, Bally-scolly; Parish, Ballinderry; District Council, Lisburn; Grid ref. J 163 672.
References: Listed B2 (only?). OS map, 1833; G Scott, OSM, n.d., and T Fagan, 1838, Antrim, VII, pp 45, 49; VAL 1B/167, and VAL 2B/1/55A, in PRONI; F W Hamond, notes in MBR, 3 March 1995; information from Mrs MacIntyre.

Counting House and Thread Factory, Hilden

242. "Now the seat of the most extensive thread factory in Ireland" (Fagan, 1837); "The largest manufacturers in the world of tailors' thread and shoemakers' thread for hand and machine sewing" (Bassett, 1888). No identifiable building remains from the first development of the site by William Barbour in 1823; but, amidst a vast expanse of industrial buildings of many dates, these two stand out. The whole complex is still in use, and for pretty much its original purpose: and is accordingly quite a rare survival for County Antrim; though by no means unique, it is less altered than most others.

The counting-house is a five-bay two-storey stucco block, three bays deep, with windows and doorway set back in recesses; four tall chimney stacks on the parapet. Next to it, and set forward by one bay, the thread factory of 1861 (dated on keystone), also of five bays, of red-painted random stone, with brick dressings: originally the same height as the counting-house, but an extra one-and-a-half storeys have been added, with pediment and a kind of chevron brick ornament. These appear to have been added some time after the adjoining blocks, similarly raised at a later date, which bear a panel with the date 1851.

There are remarkable keystones on both buildings, several of which look as if they are actual portraits (see page 242): one Victorian worthy with a prominent beaked nose, another with a fashionable Dundreary: unfortunately no folk-memory seems to survive as to the identities of their subjects, though a Barbour family photograph-album might be helpful. A similar group of keystone-heads adorns the former engine-house, evidently of much the same date, whose side wall accommodates also a lion's head, a boar's head, and the head and trunk of a playful elephant.

Photographs: Michael O'Connell.
Situation: Hilden Mill, Lambeg; td, Lambeg South; Parish, Lambeg; District Council, Lisburn; Grid ref. J 283 653.
References: The above parts of the complex listed B1. Bayly, 'Lisburn', 1834, p 51; T Fagan, OSM, 1837, Antrim, VI, p 139; Bassett, 'Antrim', 1888, pp 218, 219; McCutcheon, 'Industrial archaeology', 1980, pls 83.7, 89.1, 91.8; reports in MBR.

Former Ulster Bank (now Flixton Place), Ballymena

243. The building known as Flixton Place, now the office of James Ballentine & Son, solicitors, is an effectively-sited and dignified two-storey five-bay ashlar classical block commanding one whole side of the Pentagon at the heart of Ballymena: the rear incorporates three storeys beneath the same roofline. Central porch with Tuscan columns *in antis:* quoins: string-course; dentils; and architraves to the downstairs windows incorporating the hand of Ulster in a little projection on top of each. The building is topped by a hipped roof behind cornice and parapet, not provided for in the architect's drawings; surmounted by prominent stone chimney stacks of which the most prominent is, for obvious but disconcerting reasons, off-centre. Flixton Hall, Bungay, Suffolk was one of the English seats of the Adair family.

Originally designed as the Ballymena office of the Ulster Bank, which in 1874 covenanted within three years to build on the site "a good and substantial Bank and Dwelling House ... at least 18 feet to the eave". The Ulster Bank archive retains two sheets of elevation drawings, undated, stamped 'Thomas Jackson & Son, Plough Buildings, Belfast', and a plan, dated 14th December 1874, and stamped 'Thomas Jackson, 5 Corn Market'. This is probably Thomas Jackson's last work, before he died, aged 83, in 1890. The banking hall, with dentilled cornice, is very grand and spacious. The branch moved here in 1879 from Wellington Street; the manager was the formidable William Hogg, in charge from 1846 until his death in 1887, for whom it was locally known as "Hogg's Bank". He was in the habit of rising at seven each morning, extracting the bank's books from the strongroom, milking

FRONT ELEVATION

his cow in a field nearby, breakfasting, and then attending to business: which did not, however, if he could avoid it, include correspondence. It was no doubt to suit his requirements that the single-storey service range at the rear was designed with spaces for coal; knives, shoes, etc; potatoes; car-house; stabling for two horses; and byre for two cows. In 1963, the Ulster Bank moved back to Wellington Street, to a much inferior new building; the Ballymena Council used the premises as offices until 1987, when they were acquired by the present owners for use as solicitors' offices

- a function they serve admirably.

Photograph: Michael O'Connell. Architectural drawing: reproduced by courtesy of Ulster Bank Ltd, premises department.
Situation: The Pentagon, 38 George Street, Ballymena; td, Town Parks; Parish, Kilconriola; District Council, Ballymena; Grid ref. D 105 033.
References: Listed B1. Lease of 6 April 1874, Baron Waveney to Ulster Bank, in possession of owners; Knox, 'Decades of the Ulster Bank', 1965, pp 34, 35; Girvan, 'Antrim & Ballymena', UAHS, 1969, p 18; H Dixon, in 'Proceedings and reports of BNHPS', 2nd series, IX, 1970/77, pp 25, 26, 29; drawings in Ulster Bank, premises department.

Police Station, Bushmills

244. One of the few survivors still in use of the series of police stations designed for the RUC by T F O Rippingham in the 1920s. This must be regarded as an outstandingly successful example of architectural good manners, with its wide-eaved hipped roof, gable-end chimney stacks, Georgian sashes, and round-headed recesses, fitting politely alongside neighbours of every date in the main streets of the small towns and villages of Northern Ireland, though sadly disfigured of recent years by defensive screens and blast-walls. The recessed arches in the ground floor evoke recollections of buildings such as Randalstown market house (218) and Caledon court house;

it would be hard to imagine a simpler means of linking the modern with the past, but when I sought to introduce the same idiom, for occasional emphasis, into Housing Executive terraces, my suggestion was disallowed, both on grounds of cost and of good taste!

Opened on 29th April, 1938; photograph taken in the mid-1960s before fortifications became necessary.

Photograph: RUC Museum, Brooklyn, Belfast.
Situation: Main Street, Bushmills; td, Magheraboy; Parish, Dunluce; District Council, Moyle; Grid ref. C 941 407.
References: Not listed. Dixon, 'Introduction', UAHS, 1975, p 80.

Rope Bridge, Carrick-a-Rede

245. A fishermen's bridge, erected in May of each year, giving access from the mainland to an island off whose point is a fruitful salmon net. The earliest description known to me is that of the Rev. William Hamilton, in a letter of 3rd August 1784:

"In riding from Ballycastle to Portrush, I went a short way off the beaten track to see a whimsical little fishing rock, connected to the main land by a very extraordinary flying bridge; it is called Carrick-a-Rede (or the rock in the road) ... I was quite delighted with the appearance of this fanciful fishery ... The fish generally swim pretty close to the shore - but how to get at the rock is the question. - A chasm full sixty feet in breadth, and of a depth frightful to look at, separates it from the adjacent land ... In this perplexity there is really no resource, except in attempting to throw a bridge of ropes from the main land to the island, which accordingly the fishermen every year accomplish in a very singular manner. Two strong cables are extended across the gulph by an expert climber, and fastened firmly into iron rings, mortised into the rock on either side; between these ropes a number of boards, about a foot in breadth, are laid in succession, supported at intervals by cross-cords - and thus the pathway is formed."

Unfortunately, Mr Hamilton (who met an untimely end when murdered in County Donegal in March 1797, "Victim to the brutal fury of an armed Banditti") does not advert to the antiquity of the bridge. Dr Beaufort, in his journal of a tour in August 1765, made no mention of the bridge; but then he was pressed for time; and he made no mention of it either on a return visit in 1807.

In 1792, the Rev. W H Barnard of Oxon made two pretty drawings of it, now in the Ashmolean Museum, and wrote in his business-like accompanying note:

"The bridge consists of 3 cables strongly attached to the rocks on both sides by iron rings; across these cables at 3ft distance are short spars of about 3ft long and the path-way is formed of 2 boards in breadth laid loosely on these spars and so irregularly that in many places the ends not joining leaves a long space with but one narrow plank to support the passenger. The undulation of the bridge upon the first step is tremendous and increases considerably at the centre, forming always an angle at the point where the weight rests. Few of the natives around except the fishermen employed ever venture to cross, ... but even they seldom take an unnecessary trip ... The bridge is up for 4 months of the year from 1st July until November after which time nothing remains except a rope left purposely to extend in the ensuing season."

By 1835, James Boyle was writing: "The bridge which connects this island with the mainland is one of the lions of the coast. It is about 100 feet long and is made of ropes suspended from either side of the chasm, at an elevation of about 80 feet above the water. Its breadth is about 3 feet. Narrow boards are laid across the ropes at some distance from each other and a rope serving as a sort of guide is suspended across about 3 feet above the bridge. No dependence or weight must be laid on it, as it will immediately swing away for some distance from the bridge to which it is but slightly fastened ..." "said to have been erected about 80 years back" (i.e., before 1755) ... "very narrow and dangerous to pass over ... dogs in passing over it have been often carried over by the wind and killed in their fall ..." (Boyle). "Six fishers and one clerk reside on this rock during the fishing season: the fishers receive one-third of the fish taken, for their wages; a third goes for the boats and nets, and the remainder to the proprietor" (M'Skimin). "The bridge is stored in winter, and renewed once in every three years. In stormy weather the wind rushing through the chasm makes the bridge dangerous for strangers: at such times lives have been sacrificed in attempts to cross" (Bassett). "Until recently there was only one slight rope elevated to the

hand" (Forde).

The second hand-rope, like its mate now fixed to the bridge itself, seems to have been added about 1918; since then the whole contraption, though still alarming, has been much less so than previously. The mere thought of humping great loads of fish or sea-wrack over that swaying pathway, using no hands, is quite terrifying. Since 1830 a bag-net has been used instead of the previous draft-net. In 1967, the bridge and island were bought by the National Trust, and free access was restored, a charge having been previously levied by a neighbouring farmer for access over his land.

Water-colours: W H Barnard, Ashmolean Museum, Oxford. Photograph: R J Welch, Ulster Museum W01/08/7.
Situation: Access from Larrybane (National Trust); td, Knocksoghy; Parish, Ballintoy; District Council, Moyle; Grid ref. D 062 449.
References: National Trust property; not listed. D A Beaufort, Journals, 1765 (Ms 4024) and 1807 (Ms 4033) in TCD Library; Hamilton, 'Antrim', 1822, pp 71-74; W H Barnard, drawings in Ashmolean Museum, and accompanying description, EDB 322, 1792; Dubourdieu, 'Antrim', 1812, pp 564-5; S M'Skimin, 'Guide to the Causeway', in Hamilton, 'Antrim', 1822, p 245; J Boyle, OSM, 1835, and T Fagan, 1838, Antrim, IX, pp 14, 34-5; Bassett, 'Antrim', 1888, p 97; Forde, 'Round the coast', 1928, p 81; Welch, 'Ireland's eye', 1977, p 86; M'Cahan, 'Local histories', 1988; Gallagher and Rogers, 'Castle, coast and cottage', 1992, pp 102, 161.

Bush (Upper) Bridge, Palmer's Mill, Nos 1, 3, and 5 Bridge Street, Bushmills

246. An uncommonly attractive group which would be more attractive still if the corner building between Palmer's corn mill and the river were to be restored.

The bridge is of four arches, basalt, and looks quite early: the river flows below it, broad and peat-coloured, joined upstream by mill laids or flumes - two mill wheels are still in place, though no longer in working order. In 1683, Richard Dobbs writes "and soe to Bushmills a small towne with a fayre stone bridge over the Bush water, and soe to Dunluce Hall, the Earl of Antrym's howse." Whether this is still the same bridge is uncertain; as it is whether this is the bridge shown on Herman Moll's map of Ireland of 1714, but it was still the only bridge over the Bush in 1835 when James Boyle described it as "a clumsy old structure 52 feet long and 18 feet wide"; evidently by then, however, it had been widened by some six feet, and was widened again at a later date.

Palmer's Mill, originally a corn mill, seems to have been built between 1835 and 1857; later, flax scutching machinery was introduced, but subsequently removed, and the buildings have recently been very nicely restored as a dwelling.

Curry's flax mill on the opposite bank is, at the time of writing, also in course of restoration. The tall stone house nearest the river, two-storey-and-attic to the road but three-storey-and-attic to the waterside, with a good Georgian-glazed window below the road level and console brackets at the front door above, was once the Northern Bank; with its neighbours, equally worth restoring also.

Photograph: Michael O'Connell.
Situation: Bridge Street, Bushmills; tds, Magheraboy and Ballaghmore; Parishes Billy and Dunluce; District Council, Moyle; Grid ref. C 940 408.
References: 1 to 5 Bridge Street, listed B1; others listed B; all in conservation area. R Dobbs, D162/6, 1683, in PRONI; H Moll, 'New map of Ireland', 1714, in Linen Hall Library; Taylor and Skinner, 'Roads', 1778, p 272; J Boyle, OSM, 1835, Antrim, V, p 45; Girvan, 'North Antrim', UAHS, 1972, p 18; notes by F W Hamond of 11.8.1994 (bridge) and 16.7.1989 (Palmer's Mill) in MBR.

▷

Photographs: Michael O'Connell.
Situation: Curry's Bridge, on Slaght Road; tds, Tullynamullan / Appletree; Parish, Connor; District Council, Ballymena; Grid ref. J 015 971. Slaght Bridge, on Whitesides Road from Ballymena to Toome; tds, Slaght/Downtallybegs; Parishes, Connor/Ahoghill; District Council,

Ballymena; Grid ref. J 090 998.
References: Curry's Bridge: Listed B1 (IA). Taylor and Skinner, 'Roads', 1778, p 17; Lendrick, map, 1780; Girvan, 'West Antrim', UAHS, 1970, p 30; McCutcheon, 'Industrial archaeology', 1980, p 31, and pl 3.1. Slaght Bridge: Not listed. Williamson, map, 1808.

Curry's Bridge, and Slaght Bridge, Kells

247. Curry's Bridge (above) is a very pleasing six-arch hump-backed bridge, of basalt rubble with piers at the abutments, carrying the county road from Randalstown to Ballymena over the Kells Water shortly before the latter falls into the River Main. A bridge here is shown both on Lendrick's map of 1780 and in Taylor and Skinner, and it seems almost certain that this is the same, possibly rebuilt and repaired many times over the years.

Slaght Bridge (below), less than two miles away, carries the new road from Toome to Ballymena over the river Maine; it does not appear on the late 18th-century maps of Taylor and Skinner or Lendrick, turning up for the first time on Williamson's map of 1808; but I have not succeeded in finding any reference to it in the Grand Jury presentments between those dates. With four principal arches and no less than nine subsidiary flood arches on the east side, Dr Hamond considers it "a fine example of a causeway bridge ... it parallels Drum Bridge on the Upper Malone Road in this respect".

Most of the splendid 18th-century bridges on the river Main above Ballymena were swept away as part of the, environmentally disastrous, drainage scheme of the 1980s; these two are amongst the best, and the most characteristic, remaining in the district.

Glendun Viaduct, Glendun

248. A very tall and impressive stone three-arch bridge, the central arch taller and wider than its companions, carrying the coast road high above the Glendun river and the roadways up the glen. Inscribed, in a panel at the centre of the southern parapet, 'Glendunn Bridge 1839'. By the youthful county surveyor, Charles Lanyon, then aged only 22. He was obviously very proud of his work, and not without reason: "The whole height of the bridge will be 80 feet and will form a handsome and noble structure", he told the Grand Jury. He was assisted by the equally youthful R M Young, then his apprentice. "The stones were quarried in Layde, taken by boat to Cushendun and then transported by cart to the bridge ...... A labourer's pay was ten pence a day; barrowmen, and they were very numerous, and cartmen were paid a shilling a day ...... The scaffolding was supported by ship's masts". Samuel Lewis, in 1847, describes "the royal military road lately completed ... The baronies of Carey and Glenarm are united by a splendid viaduct thrown across the romantic valley of Glendun". So late as 1854, Doyle wrote "the tourist may proceed to Ballycastle by the new and very splendid road

constructed by the Board of Works, under the direction of Mr Bald. The great object of attraction is the magnificent bridge which connects the sides of Glendun; the central arch stands 80 feet above the river; two smaller arches, one on either side, span the roads which run parallel to the river".

It is of reddish dressed stone, the central arch carried between tapering pylons of rusticated ashlar. The trees have now grown up to such an extent that, from most angles, the imposing dimensions of the work are masked; it has now melted into the landscape, but must have stood out very bare and raw when it was new.

Photograph: R J Welch, Ulster Museum W01/54/9.
Situation: The viaduct carries the main coast road from Cushendall to Ballycastle; tds, Clegnagh/Irragh; Parish, Layde; District Council, Moyle; Grid ref. D 215 322.
References: Listed B+; not in conservation area. GJ records, 1837-1839 in PRONI; Lewis, TD, 1847, I, p 427; Doyle, 'Tours in Ulster', 1854, p 223; Brett, 'Glens', UAHS, 1971, p 40; 'The Big Bridge', in 'Glynns', VII, 1979, p 18; McCutcheon, 'Industrial archaeology', 1980, pp 30, 33; Hamond, 'Antrim coast & glens', 1991, p 79.

Bridges over River Main, Randalstown

249. The two bridges over the River Main, side by side, provide a striking contrast.

The older, the road bridge, probably 18th-century, has nine segmental arches divided by angled piers; widened in 1818, 1834 and again in 1864. In 1838, "The bridge over the river Main is a clumsy old structure and must be of some antiquity, as it seems to have been twice widened, though it is in tolerable repair ... It is supported by nine circular-segment arches of unequal span ... formerly very narrow". In July 1847, Charles Lanyon advised the Grand Jury that "I find it to be in so bad a state of repair, that I have no hesitation in saying it would be desirable to build a new bridge ... I propose to erect the new bridge a little higher up the river, so as to place it in a direct line with the approaches on either side, and thus avoid the awkward and dangerous turn which exists at the western end." But his recommendation seems not to have been accepted, despite his advice that "the traffic over this bridge is very considerable, and it may reasonably be anticipated that it will be importantly increased on the opening of the Randalstown branch of the Ballymena Railway"; the original terminus of this branch being on the east bank of the river.

The later railway viaduct, of 1855-6, (now cut short) is much higher; there are eight skewed brick-vaulted arches carried on very tall squared basalt piers, with rusticated voussoirs. "Built in 1855 by William Dargan to a design by Charles Lanyon, the viaduct has not been in use since 1959 but remains an impressive and durable reminder of the railway age" (McCutcheon). Girvan calls this "A triumph of 19th century engineering and undoubtedly the most impressive feature of Randalstown".

Photograph: W A Green, Ulster Folk & Transport Museum WAG 1732.
Situation: Across river Main as it passes through Randalstown; tds, Randalstown/Ballygrooby/Shane's Castle Park; Parish, Drummaule; District Council, Antrim; Grid ref. J 084 903.
References: Both listed B1. J Boyle, OSM, 1838, and G W Hemans, Antrim, VI, pp 44, 81; Lewis, TD, 1837, II, p 484; GJ presentments, 1847, ANT 4/4/13, in PRONI; Girvan, 'Antrim and Ballymena', UAHS, 1969, p 27; McCutcheon, 'Industrial archaeology', 1980, caption to pl 38.4; notes in MBR of September 1994 and February 1995 by F Hamond.

Railway Bridges, Whiteabbey

250. Three concrete railway bridges, side by side, over the Glenville Road, each at a different height and each with a different gradient, creating a quite extraordinary pattern of complex solid geometry. The bridges are dated 1931, 1932, and 1933; the first carries the down line from Belfast to Larne; the second, the double line between Belfast and Antrim; the third, the up line from Larne to Belfast.

Designed by W K Wallace CE for the LMS Railway Company; he was also responsible for the two nearby concrete viaducts which together form a flying junction, or, as McCutcheon calls it, "burrowing junction". This scheme was intended to combat unemployment, as well as to overcome the problem of the steep gradients encountered above Whiteabbey on the face of the Antrim escarpment; it involved 17,000 cubic yards of concrete and 700 tons of steel reinforcement. McCutcheon describes this complex as forming part of "one of the most significant examples of modern railway architecture in the British Isles".

"The line was opened in 1934 and operated until 1978, when regular passenger traffic was withdrawn, Antrim-bound trains being redirected through Lisburn and Crumlin" (Hamond); but there are plans to reopen it as a result of the link between York Street and Central Station.

Photograph: Michael O'Connell.

Situation: At former Bleach Green Halt, Glenville Road, Newtownabbey; td, Croghfern; Parish, Whitehouse; District Council, Newtownabbey; Grid ref. J 355 833.

References: Listed B1. McCutcheon, 'Industrial archaeology', 1980, pp 166, 215; Barry, 'Across deep waters', 1985, pp 15, 23; notes by F Hamond, December 1994, in MBR.

East Light, Rathlin Island

251. The most dramatic of the seven lighthouses in the county still in use: built by George Halpin senior between 1849 and 1856 at a cost of £17,140. The lower light was discontinued in 1894. Three lightkeepers' houses survive within a stone-walled enclosure: one handsomely built of dressed basalt, the others architectural oddities: above each front porch is a water-tank, neatly stuccoed and with an ornamental wreath appliqué, completely masking all daylight from the bedroom window. It was here that Marconi carried out early experiments in wireless telegraphy between Rathlin and Ballycastle in 1898. Now, sadly, unmanned and automatically operated.

Of the two other Rathlin lights, the Bull was completed in 1919, at a cost of £400,000, to designs by C W Scott who deliberately sited it 100 feet below the top of the cliff; and, the Rue, an automatic light first installed in 1915, swept away by a gale in 1919, and replaced by the present tower in 1920. The twin lights on the Maiden Rocks were built in 1829, again to the designs of George Halpin senior, but the West Tower was abandoned in 1903. The light at Ferris Point on Islandmagee dates from 1839, but the present modern complex, looking like an airport control tower, is of 1957; it controls also the Maidens, and the light to the west of the entrance to Larne Lough, in the Chaine memorial tower, adapted for use as a lighthouse in 1899. The granite lighthouse on Black Head was completed in 1902. All these, save Ferris Point, are now unmanned and under automatic controls.

To a landsman it seems strange that, whilst there have been plenty of wrecks, there has never been a light on any of the three most conspicuous headlands of this north-east corner of Ireland - Fair Head; Tor Head; and Garron Point.

Photograph: R J Welch, Ulster Museum W01/83/7.
Situation: On top of the headland at the north-east corner of Rathlin Island; td, Ballycarry; Parish, Rathlin; District Council, Moyle; Grid ref. D 162 520.
References: Not listed. Brett, 'Rathlin', UAHS, 1974, p 17, 18, 19; R Callwell, Ms History (Irish Lights Commission); Wilson, 'Irish Lighthouse Service', 1968; Long, 'Bright light, white water', 1993.

Former Coastguard Station, Ballycastle

252. An excellent terrace of seven two-storey whitewashed houses, with dressed stone long-and-short surrounds to Georgian-glazed windows, 8 panes to each sash; the centre house a tower, all of dressed stone, with a strange brick pierced parapet (possibly dating from the second World War? but Hamond says, "used as an anti-submarine look-out during World War I") topped by a little round turret. It has been suggested that the tower, which to some extent resembles the Napoleonic signal towers on the coast of Donegal, may be earlier than the rest of the terrace. Chimney stacks of yellowish brick.

The terrace is oddly disposed east and west, looking out from its hillside towards Fair Head: the gables are blank, and no window commands a view of the open sea, even though the northernmost house (with grander windows than the others) was apparently intended for the Chief Officer. In 1837, "Here is a station of the constabulary police; also a coast-guard station, which is the head of a district comprising also the stations of Port Rush, Port Ballintrae, Port Ballintoy, Rathlin Island, Tor Head, Cushendun and Cushendall, under the charge of a resident inspecting commander."

This group of buildings seems to be considerably earlier than most of the stations around the coast - I thought around 1845, the listers think around 1855 - and is quite lacking in the warlike pistol-loups and murder-holes provided elsewhere: cf Whitehead (253). There is no mention of a coastguard station in the Ordnance Survey Memoirs; in 1835, Boyle reports that Captain Gilbert, RN, inspecting commander of coastguard; Captain Blois RN; Captain Sampson; and Lieut Shatt, RN, chief officer of coastguard: all, like the curate and the doctor, "live in plain, substantial houses, mostly 2-storeys high and without anything in their architecture or appearance worthy of description." But by 1861, "Coast Guard Station, House and Garden; Watch house; and Boat house", all occupied by the Board of Admiralty, were together valued at £6.5.0, unless "quere exemption?".

Photograph: Michael O'Connell.
Situation: In a cul de sac, off North Street, Ballycastle; td, Town Parks; Parish, Ramoan; District Council, Moyle; Grid ref. D 119 415.
References: Listed B1; not in conservation area. Lewis, TD, 1837, I, p 127; VAL 2B/1/28C, p 79, in PRONI; Brett, 'Glens', UAHS, 1971, p 51; Hamond, 'Antrim coast & glens', 1991, p 73; 'Buildings at risk', II, 1995, p 8.

Former Coastguard Station, Whitehead

253. A terrace of seven redbrick coastguard cottages with dressed-stone trim, built in 1870-1 at a cost of £1,732.18.2. The earlier coastguard cottages are shown on the site of the present yacht club in the 1858 Ordnance Survey map. There survive drawings for similar, but not identical, coastguard stations at Ballycastle, Co. Mayo (1871) and Rathmullan, Co. Donegal (1873), both to designs by Enoch Trevor Owen, one of Sir Charles Lanyon's architect brothers-in-law. The Board of Works records in Dublin indicate that the prototype was built at Dun Laoghaire in 1859; "over 60 new stations were built during the following twenty years." The terrace at Craigavad appears to be broadly similar. Restored as dwellings c 1989, when acceptable additions were made at the rear. No 5 incorporates a three-storey square tower; at the other end of the terrace, No 10 has at some date been stuccoed and painted, while leaving the stone trim uncovered. The

watchtower at one end was occupied by the officer, that at the other end by the boatman. Each of the end houses has either two or three triangular oriels, supported on strange mannerist geometrical consoles and incorporating carved stone pistol-loups and murder-holes, and, with additional upper-floor pistol-loups,

commanding the approaches from every point of the compass.

Part of the extensive series of "stations" erected in the mid-19th century all around the coastline of Antrim, and of Ireland. The Coastguard was at this period administered by the Admiralty: "a naval force maintained in Great Britain and Ireland to suppress smuggling, aid shipwrecked vessels and serve as a reserve to the navy". This station is exceptionally defensible, like a 15th-century tower-house: so, were the smugglers on this stretch of coast exceptionally aggressive? Or was this, as in near-contemporary fortification of the Channel Islands, intended as a defence against French naval aggression? Or, perhaps most plausibly, was the perceived threat from the Fenians? But there were never many Fenians in this part of County Antrim!

Denis Mayne observes: "It would seem that all coastguard stations built in Ireland between the late 1850s and the late 1870s incorporated these defensive measures. Besides the pistol-loups and murder-holes, the oriel windows were protected by bullet-proof metal shutters and the houses had intercommunicating doors which allowed the crews access to the whole terrace at a time of attack. I have always assumed that, as agents of the British government, coastguard personnel were perceived as potential targets, and the isolated positions of most stations was considered to increase their vulnerability ... They are monuments to a unique group of men and their wives who lived in lonely places and experienced an uneasy and ambivalent relationship with the local population."

Photographs: W A Green, Ulster Folk and Transport Museum WAG 769; Michael O'Connell.
Situation: 5-10 Beach Road, Whitehead; td, White Head; Parish, Templecorran; District Council, Carrickfergus; Grid ref. J 475 914.
References: Listed B1; in conservation area. OS map, 1858; article on 'Coastguard', Encyclopaedia Britannica, 11th ed., 1910; Green, 'Tour of east Antrim', 1990, p 34; 'Public works', 1988, p 30; copy drawings for Co. Mayo in MBR; information from Denis Mayne.

Railway Station, Whitehead

254. Opened in 1877 to designs (costing £875) by John Lanyon for the Carrickfergus and Larne Railway; managed from the outset, and subsequently taken over, by the Northern Counties Railway Co.; additions of the 1890s by John Hanna, architect.

"In the early part of 1870 a request was received for a new station better appointed and more central to the heart of the developing township ... Howell of the Belfast and Northern Counties produced plans ... but the C and L found these too expensive. Quarrels with the owners of the land ensued, and it was not until September 1875 that John Lanyon submitted a revised plan which, costing between £600 and £700, was also found too expensive. A month later it was proposed that sleeping accommodation be provided in the new building as local bedrooms for visitors were 'limited'; but this, it was found, would cost £1,500 and, however desirable, was rejected, and Lanyon's plan was adopted ... Opened in June 1877" (Currie).

A pleasing group comprising waiting room and canopy with carved shamrocks, station-master's house, porter's office, signal box, refreshment room, bar, shelter, and a particularly fine cast-iron foot-bridge by McFarlanes. (According to Doreen Corcoran, the original station foot-bridge has been dismantled, that still in place having been designed to give access to the beach from Cable Road).

Mostly of red and black brick, slate roofs (pyramidal on the signal box), and fancy bargeboards: all in good shape. One of the very few County Antrim stations to survive unscathed the passion of NI Railways for modernisation, perhaps in part because of the proximity of the premises of the Railway Preservation Society of Ireland; restored 1993, by Design II Architects.

Photographs: Michael O'Connell.
Situation: Cable Road, Whitehead; td, White Head; Parish, Islandmagee; District Council, Carrickfergus; Grid ref. J 475 918.
References: Listed B1; in conservation area. Currie, 'Northern Counties Railway', I, 1973, p 143, II, 1974, p 39; Green, 'Tour of East Antrim', 1990, p 28; notes in MBR of 15 October 1991 by F Hamond; 'Perspective', March/April 1994, p 24.

Railway Station, Carrickfergus

255. A nicely vigorous set of buildings of 1895 by Berkely Deane Wise, after the earlier station had been gutted by fire; a blown-up version of the station to be found in a boy's Hornby set. Described by Currie as "an exceptionally fine mock Tudor style erection, with a main and island platform". Where Tudor - and Stockbroker's Tudor - are usually black and white, this is painted red and cream - Railwayman's Tudor, perhaps?

The main block presents to the street a frontage of warm brickwork, red beams, and cream panels; the front to the lines brings the roof, of greenish tiles, sweeping down to a canopy, carried on ornate cast-iron columns, over the platform. In the booking-hall, a free-standing stone and bronze war memorial records the names of all those employees in Northern Ireland of the Midland Railway Company who served and returned, as well as those who laid down their lives: this originally stood in the much-to-be-lamented York Street terminus of the Northern Counties line.

The shelter on the opposite platform is less imposing, but delightfully toy-like. There is a signal-box of traditional shape. There is also a nicely traditional station garden.

Photograph: Michael O'Connell.
Situation: Victoria Street, Carrickfergus; td, Middle Division; Parish and District Council, Carrickfergus; Grid ref. J 413 877.
References: Listed B1/IA; outside conservation area. Currie, 'Northern Counties Railway', I, 1973, p 227; Campbell and Crowther, 'Carrickfergus', UAHS, 1978, p 28.

Power Station, Kilroot

256. A series of massive free-standing and interlocking cubes, variously painted green, light grey and dark grey, with the intention of breaking up the mass; and three cylinders, with almost no taper; the whole group as geometrical as if built from a child's box of blocks. The tallest chimney is enormous, 650 feet high, with four so-to-speak chimney-pots on top; the middling one, at less than half the height, is slimmer and lighthouse-like; the smallest one seems truncated by comparison. There is yet another, subsidiary, chimney round the corner, designed to heat and so keep moving the sluggish oil pumped ashore at the Cloghan Point jetty. Originally, the station was designed for oil-firing; converted in 1989 to dual purpose oil or coal-firing. There are now sixteen oil burners and sixteen coal burners serving each boiler and generator.

All these enormous creatures of the late 20th century are surrounded by cranes, avenues of pylons, low conical-topped oil-tanks, inclined chutes, and miscellaneous hardware. Built between 1973 and 1981 to the designs of Kennedy and Donkin, well-known Manchester consulting engineers, and Clifford, Tee and Gale, architectural consultants, of London. By the time the power station was completed, it had already been overtaken by the 1974 oil crisis. Forecasts of demand plummeted. In the end, Units 1 and 2 were converted so as to be capable of using coal; and Units 3 and 4 have never been completed at all. Privatised in 1993.

No building in the county has more impact on the landscape - whether from the west, where it completely overshadows the castle keep and spire of Carrickfergus; from the north, where Islandmagee is trapped between the smoke-stacks of Ballylumford and those of Kilroot; from inland and the east, where the network of pylons and power-lines adds to the visual mischief; or most of all, from the County Down shores of Belfast Lough, where many a householder considers his view to be ruined. Moreover, fumes from the great chimney, carried on the prevalent westerly winds, have been blamed for the acid rain afflicting the forests and tundra of Scandinavia - whether justly or unjustly, I cannot say.

Photograph: Michael O'Connell.
Situation: Between the village of Eden and the shore of Belfast Lough; td and Parish, Kilroot; District Council, Carrickfergus; Grid ref. J 445 890.
References: Not listed (yet?); NIE, information booklets.

Elliott's Hill Windfarm, Tildarg

257. Up on the 300-metre high hill-tops of the ridge dividing the valley of the Six Mile Water from Glenwhirry, there suddenly appeared, in January 1995, a flock of ten tall white windmills. With their great three-bladed propellers humming, they look poised, just ready for take-off; one wonders how they are anchored to the moorland. The design, by Nordtank, is Danish. Slim, elegant and sculptural, each 125 feet tall, they are at first glance attractive and exciting: although their proliferation would no doubt be a different matter. For the present, they still have rarity and novelty value. Just as the older kind of windmills, the older kind of redbrick factory chimneys, lighthouses, and obelisks still please the eye, so do these; in contrast to electricity pylons, satellite dishes, wireless masts, shiny tin chimneys, and high-rise flats or offices, with which we have become surfeited.

Whatever the future may hold, I think I shall continue to prefer these elegant artefacts on the skyline to the cruder (if more productive) bulk of the power stations at Kilroot (256) and Ballylumford. Some people find upland windfarms offensively obtrusive, but I find them endlessly fascinating: especially when their ghostly white shapes stand out against the black clouds of a thundery sky. To stand amongst them (by permission) on a squally day is an eerie experience: they turn their heads, they mop and mow, they hum and haw, like the musical statues which guarded the pass through the mountains to Erewhon. Cows and calves, dwarfed to the size of tittle-mice, graze at the feet of the pylons. The larks soar and sing on all sides, miraculously unscathed by the slashing blades that mince the upper air. And all around is spread the whole county, from Cave Hill to Lough Neagh, from Drumbulkin to Orra, from Trostan to Slemish.

Photograph: Michael O'Connell.
Situation: Reached by a private road near Whappstown, off Tildarg road; tds, Whappstown, Tildarg; Parish, Connor; District Council, Ballymena; Grid ref. J 221 968.
References: Not listed. Publicity leaflets published by B9 Energy Services Ltd, Larne; 'Ulster architect', May/June 1995, pp 28-29; CEB Brett, in 'Ulster architect', August 1995, pp 10-11.

CHAPTER EIGHT

FOLLIES, MONUMENTS
AND MEMORIALS

From their nature, neither follies, nor monuments, nor memorials, lend themselves easily to generalisations. So there is little to be said by way of introduction to this chapter, except that each of the buildings described is *sui generis.*

It is perhaps relevant to add that there appears to be no particularly strong tradition of stone carving in the county: not surprisingly, for its native stones are not easily worked. By far the most important monument, the 17th-century Chichester memorial in Carrickfergus parish church, was certainly imported, and is ineligible for its own entry anyway as being within doors: despite the fact that Homan Potterton describes it as "the most elaborate and exquisite of its type surviving in Ireland".[1] There are some pleasing 18th-century tombstones in the graveyards of Rathlin and the Route, probably from the hand of one Alexander McDonnell who wrought a monument for his own family at Bonamargy (14) in 1764.[2]

References: 1. Potterton, 'Irish church monuments', UAHS, 1975, pp 17, 88-9. 2. Brett, 'Glens', UAHS, 1971, p 53, and back cover; 'Rathlin', UAHS, 1974, pp 14, 15.

Chichester tomb in St Nicholas's church, Carrickfergus (24), about 1616. Photograph: MBR

Templetown Mausoleum, Templepatrick

258. "The burial ground in the village of Templepatrick is situated on its northern side and is supposed to have been that of the Priorate of St John, and of the Temple erected here in the 14th century. The Upton or Templetown family bury here and have a handsome and spacious mausoleum in the centre of the ground" (Boyle).

Built 1789, in part execution of a design by Robert Adam: at once, severe and richly detailed. The side walls are almost plain, with only entablature, fluting, and simple panels; but the front is an elegant ashlar composition of semi-circular arch, two niches with urns (one of which has unfortunately lost its knop), medallions in lunettes, and a panel inscribed 'Sacred to the Memory of the Right Honourable Arthur Upton', all topped by garlands, square urns for ashes, and a single vase-shaped urn on the summit. The roof is a pyramid of ashlar. The interior is austere in the extreme, apart from the inscription in the tympanum of the recessed arch at the rear - 'This building is erected/by Sarah Upton/to perpetuate the memory/of an husband she loved and esteemed/He was born January the IX MDCCXV/and departed this life/September the XXVIII/MDCCLXVIII.' (For this lady's predilection for crayfish, see page 290). There are five small later memorial tablets in memory of other members of the Upton family. "The emptiness of the interior ... is both solemn and moving" (Howley).

The original plan envisaged that not only the front should be decorated, but that the north side wall should have a central doorway with niches flanked by pairs of coupled columns. "Though not as grand as Adam had intended, the Mausoleum is still one of the most complete examples of European neo-classicism left in Ireland" (Girvan). "Its entrance facade has more decoration than any of Adam's other mausoleums" (King). "It has the peculiar poise associated with Adam's work: classical sarcophagi and urns, leafy swags, circular reliefs, and exquisitely carved Roman letters all blend into a harmonious whole" (Dixon). "A calm and restrained building of great beauty and delicacy" (Howley). Dr Craig considers it the finest mausoleum in the country, and remarks that it is, also, "the only actual Adam building in Ireland" (except, presumably, the Castle Upton stable block?, 68). Set in a regrettably overcrowded old graveyard - later tombstones hem in the Mausoleum on every side; the Mausoleum itself in the care of the National Trust since 1965.

Photograph: Michael O'Connell.
Situation: In graveyard beside stables of Castle Upton, off main Belfast-Antrim road in village of Templepatrick; td, and Parish, Templepatrick; District Council, Antrim; Grid ref. J 228 859.
References: Listed A. Adam drawings, XLIV, Nos 85 and 86, in Sir John Soane's Museum; J Boyle, OSM, 1838, Templepatrick, as yet unpublished; Girvan, 'West Antrim', UAHS, 1970, pp 17, 31; Dixon, 'Introduction', UAHS, 1975, p 46; Curl, 'Mausolea in Ulster', UAHS, 1978, p 7; Craig, 'Architecture of Ireland', 1982, p 322; King, 'Complete works of Robert and James Adam', 1991, pp 359-60; Gallagher and Rogers, 'Castle coast and cottage', 1992, p 123; Howley, 'Follies and garden buildings', 1993, pp 179, 180.

date of 1821, suggested by McSparran, Irvine and Dallat, seems a lot more plausible. They assume that it was built with stone brought from the Red Arch, opened up about 1817.

"The Tower was the great object of Mr Turnly's thoughts; among his papers were instructions to Dan McBride, an army pensioner whom he appointed its guard. It was always to be provisioned for a year; it was to have a permanent 'garrison of one man' who was not to leave it night or day; it was to be armed with one musket, a bayonet, a case of pistols, and a pike, thirteen feet long, having a cross of wood or iron on its handle, so that it could not be pulled through the hole guarding the doorway. The guard was to ring the bell at nine o'clock every night, and it was not to be rung at any other time except as an alarm bell" (O'Laverty). Bassett says, however, "From March to November, the caretaker rings a bell at 7 am and 9 am, and at 1, 2, 6 and 9 pm. From November to March, she rings it at 9 am, 1, 2 and 9 pm. In this way some of the purposes of a public clock are effectively served": and adds "the lower storey is used as a reservoir for the village water supply, which comes from a rock spring a quarter of a mile away." As to this, Hamond, surprisingly, describes the building itself as 'Water Reservoir', and says that, after its original construction, "a spring-fed reservoir was built into the ground floor. This supplied a now-defunct fountain in the Tower's east wall, inscribed with the initials F, S, J, and T."

Turnly's Tower, Cushendall

259. "Among the new buildings in and around [Cushendall], the most extraordinary and conspicuous is a tall, square tapering tower, at the crossways in the centre of the village, erected as a place of confinement for idlers and rioters" (1845). Intended presumably as a folly or eyecatcher, James Boyle of the Ordnance Survey thought "It is not at all ornamental in its structure and is said to have been built after the model of some Chinese tower." Built by the village's "energetic and patriotic proprietor" Francis Turnly (or Turnley), "a gentleman who went out in early life to China in 1796. He remained in China and the East till 1801, but during his stay he realised £70,000 or £80,000, and on his return he purchased two estates, one at Cushendall, for which he paid £24,000, and another at Drumnasole" (88) "for which he paid £9,500. Though eccentric, and perhaps demented, he effected extraordinary improvements in buildings and roads on his property." Both Boyle and O'Laverty firmly date the Tower to 1809. But it seems from the deeds that it was only in 1813 that Francis Turnly bought the Cushendall estate from "William Richardson, Esq, of the City of Dublin, a captain in the Co. Antrim militia", for £19,485; so the

building itself as 'Water Reservoir', and says that, after its original construction, "a spring-fed reservoir was built into the ground floor. This supplied a now-defunct fountain in the Tower's east wall, inscribed with the initials F, S, J, and T."

In 1834, the Tower was valued at £3.10.0, with the comment "unsuitable for a dwelling and only one small room in the same storey"; occupied in that year, nonetheless, by one Bernard Murphy. The Tower is five storeys high (though one storey is almost invisible externally), of local red sandstone, with a battlemented parapet, projecting window-cases on each outer wall (the lowest with murder-holes), a narrow round-headed doorway with mock-medieval door, and a windowless dungeon. James Howley remarks: "This ... presents us with the argument that bona fide follies can be found in urban as well as rural settings". Restored and modernised as a (very unusual) dwelling by Hearth Revolving Fund, 1992-3; the original curfew bell having gone missing, was replaced by one from a London fire station.

Apparently now the property of an eccentric London pop group and publishers: perhaps a suitably bizarre fate.

The Traill Crest, Billy

260. A most curious and enigmatic monument, of uncertain date. According to Boyd, "The Traill family crest is a column, or pillar, a representation of which may be seen in the form of a stone structure on the rising ground in a field near the hamlet of Castlecatt, Bushmills, and fairly convenient to the family seat - Ballylough"; but Burke says the crest is "a column or pillar set in the sea"! Three cubes of squared basalt, of diminishing size, set each at right angles to the one below, to a height of some 25 feet, topped (until lately, for it has recently fallen into disrepair) by iron flag and weathervane. The monument stands, isolated, on a grassy knoll (reserved from the sale under the Land Acts) overlooking the road from Dervock to Bushmills,on the opposite side from Ballylough House (118). One local account has it that it was built to provide employment during the Famine of 1845-50. Another has it that it was built to commemorate a horse killed in the Crimean War of 1854-56. Neither of these agreeable tales holds water, since it is clearly marked, and described as 'spire', on the first Ordnance Survey map of 1832, though, surprisingly, it receives no mention in the unusually detailed Ordnance Survey Memoir for this parish. Perhaps the most plausible explanation is that it was never meant for anything but an eye-catcher or folly, most probably erected at the same time as the similarly-constructed quadrant walls at Ballylough House, which can be securely dated to 1815.

Photograph: Michael O'Connell. (The farmer had spread lime on his field the day this photograph was taken).
Situation: To the east of the main road from Dervock to Bushmills; td, Cavan, Parish, Billy; District Council, Moyle; Grid ref. C 957 380.
References: Listed B. OS map, 1832; Burke, 'Landed gentry of Ireland', 1958, p 702; Girvan, 'North Antrim', UAHS, 1972, pp 29, 38; H A Boyd, in 'Northern Constitution', 8 April 1978.

◁

Photograph: Michael O'Connell.
Situation: At the cross-roads at the centre of Cushendall village; td, Cushendall; Parish, Layde; District Council, Moyle; Grid ref. D 237 277.
References: Listed B+; in conservation area. T 1750/4/A to G, and VAL 2B/1/40B, in PRONI; J Boyle, OSM, 1835, Antrim, IV, p 46; PG, I, 1845, p 559; O'Laverty, 'Down and Connor', IV, 1887, pp 538-9; Bassett, 'Antrim', 1888, p 133; Brett, 'Glens', UAHS, 1971, pp 35-6; Pierce and Coey, 'Taken for granted', 1984, pp 84-85; Hamond, 'Antrim coast & glens', 1991, p 479; Howley, 'Follies and garden buildings', 1993, p 66; 'HEARTH review', 1994, p 45.

Stephenson Mausoleum, Kilbride

261. The exotic Stephenson family mausoleum, like a miniature granite Mogul tomb overlooking the valley of the Six Mile Water, commemorates no less than four Ulster medical men, and other members of the family. They include: Samuel Martin Stephenson, MD of Belfast, d. 1833 aet. 91; Samuel Martin Stephenson, Superintending Surgeon, Madras Presidency, d. 1834 aet. 50; George Alexander Stephenson, late surgeon 3rd Dragoon Guards, d. 1864 aet. 76; Robert Stephenson, MD of Wellington Place, Belfast, d. 1869 aet. 75; also Paul Stephenson, d. aged 92, and his wife, d. aged 96.

J Bleakly of the Ordnance Survey says "There is an ancient graveyard in this parish, in the townland of Kilbride, in the centre of which stood a church which is said to have been dedicated to St. Bridget. Not a vestige of this edifice remains ... Near the centre of the graveyard there stands a very fine monument, erected in 1837 to the memory of the Stephenson family, in which 13 of that family are interred. It was built at the expense of the late Dr Stephenson (author of an Historical Essay on the parish and congregation of Templepatrick) and cost 300 pounds. It is built of Tardree cut stone and displays much architectural beauty." His book, published in 1824, is long, learned, and for the most part distinctly dry; but ends with the following charming flourish: "The lady of the late

Arthur Upton introduced a stranger into our river, called crawfish; crefish; by the French, crevice; by some, the fresh water lobster, and by Linnaeus, astacus. It was put into the brook of Templepatrick; it descended into the Six-Mile Water, where it found a situation perfectly suited to its nature: deep water and banks of loam, which they excavate as lodgings for themselves and their young: they have increased to a very great multitude. Finis."

The date is no longer decipherable on the iron door; presumably erected by the surgeon of dragoons in memory of his medical father and brother. Curl says "the date is about 1838, but the architecture owes something to the spirit of the Brighton Pavilion as well as to the funerary buildings of Moslem India". The ivy which covered the mausoleum in 1970 was cut back, but it is once again in poor order: pieces of stonework are beginning to lean and tumble: it well deserves a thorough restoration, but who is to do that?

Photograph: Michael O'Connell. (See also colour-plate Vb)
Situation: In the graveyard adjoining Kilbride Presbyterian church, north of the road from Coggrey to Holestone; td, and Parish, Kilbride; District Council, Newtownabbey; Grid ref. J 248 915.
Reference: Listed, B1. Stephenson, 'Templepatrick', 1824; J Bleakly, OSM, 1838, Antrim, XI, p 153; Girvan, 'West Antrim', UAHS, 1970, p 20; Curl, 'Mausolea in Ulster', UAHS, 1978, p 18.

O'Connor Memorial, Ballycastle

262. In the centre of the Diamond, usually surrounded by cars, a tall slim monument on a granite plinth containing drinking fountains for man and beast. The principal structure is of sandstone, incorporating eight polished marble colonettes, carrying on pointed arches the rather elegant spire. One panel displays Dr O'Connor's arms and motto; the opposite one says:

> 'In memory of George Matthew O'Connor MB. Born 1st June 1817, died 20 November 1897. A faithful friend and upright citizen and a skilful practitioner, who during 53 years of earnest and kindly labour in his profession in this place endeared himself to all classes of the community. Erected by public subscription, 1899.'

Designed by S Kelway Pope, MSA, of Southampton; executed by Charles Darragh and Andy Verdon, stone masons; cost £352.15.10. Happily, the incongruous brick planter by which the memorial's base was surrounded in 1971 has been removed.

Photograph: W A Green, Ulster Folk Museum WAG 826. (Note the use of the fountain for its intended purpose; also the prevalence of frilly lace curtains at the turn of the century).

Situation: The Diamond, Ballycastle; td, Town Parks; Parish, Ramoan; District Council, Moyle; Grid ref. D 115 407.

References: Listed B; in conservation area. Richardson, 'Guide to Ballycastle', 1905; Brett, 'Glens', UAHS, 1971, pp 46, 48.

Wallace Fountain, Lisburn

year to the Borough of Shoreditch, which gave it to the Wallace Collection in 1959.

Dated 1872, and signed by the foundry, Val d'Osne, Château le Bourg. The sculptor, born in Nantes in 1829, died in Paris in 1906; a pupil of Rude, he hardly lived up to his early promise, a large proportion of his surviving work being in the museum of his native town. However, he was described at the time as "un véritable artiste, ... le sculpteur consciencieux et élégant bien connu par ses envois à chaque exposition"; and was the author of slightly florid marble busts of Lord Hertford and of Lady Wallace, still displayed in the Collection. The word 'wallace' no longer appears in modern French dictionaries amongst the very small number of words beginning with W; it seems to have been replaced by 'walkman'! The fountain, now painted blue-green with gilded details, but not just lately, has four caryatids with arms upraised bearing aloft the domelet which shelters the waterspout. The very first installed, at the end of an alley of plane trees, in the boulevard de Combat in the suburb of La Villette, was poetically described at the time: "quatre caryatides de bronze aux formes rigoureusement dessinées sous les draperies, soutiennent de leurs bras étendus un dôme écaillé ainsi que la carapace d'un dauphin - Au centre de ce dôme s'élève un filet d'eau claire qui tombe avec le murmure cher aux poètes dans une vasque entre les caryatides ..." The article ends with the suggestion that Sir Richard should have provided supplies of sugar and slices of lemon alongside each drinking fountain - by implication, rum or whiskey too? ... "Une petite requête d'utilité publique: ne serait-il pas possible de mettre auprès des fontaines du sucre et du citron?"

263. In 1969, the then Director of the Wallace Collection wrote: "Immediately after the siege of Paris, M. Richard Wallace (as he then was) had fifty drinking fountains designed in the French Renaissance style by the sculptor Charles Auguste Lebourg, and presented them to the City ... These fountains had the distinction of adding a new word - 'Wallace' - to the French language. Many of these street monuments have been removed from their original sites. Within a few years it is likely that they will have disappeared entirely. Fortunately ... there are several in Rotterdam, two in Sir Richard Wallace's former parliamentary constituency at Lisburn in Northern Ireland (where three were sacrificed to the wartime demand for scrap metal), another is at Ilfracombe," - and one in the Wallace Collection, London. It appears that, after the first fifty commissioned by Sir Richard, the city of Paris had another 30 cast at its own expense, and subsequently the foundry marketed the design world-wide on its own account, so that examples turn up all over the place. The London example was cast c. 1904 and presented in that

Photograph: Michael O'Connell. (Note the Castle gateway of 1677 in the background).

Situation: Castle Gardens, Lisburn; td, Lisnagarvey, Parish and District Council, Lisburn; Grid ref. J 264 642.

References: Listed A. 'La Vie Parisienne', Septembre 1872, p 573; 'Times literary supplement', 16 January 1969, p 63; Brett and Dunleath, 'Lisburn', UAHS, 1969, pp 2, 10; J F Burns, in 'Lisburn Historical Society journal', III, 1980, p 14; B Mackey, in 'Ulster Star', 8 November 1990; Aulet, 'La fuente Wallace', 1993: information from B Mackey of the Lisburn Museum and Peter Hughes of the Wallace Collection.

Mementos of John Carey, Toome and Duneane

264. The surviving mementos comprise: John Carey's highly extraordinary memorial in Duneane Presbyterian

churchyard; the pump he installed on the outskirts of Toome; and the gate, with ornate gate pillars, outside his home, Rarity Cottage, Duneane (the cottage itself is no longer there).

John Carey was born in 1800; licensed as a Presbyterian minister in 1832; suspended for 'prevarication' and forgery in 1842; charged with attempted murder of another Presbyterian minister, whilst in the pulpit, by shooting him with a musket through the church window, but released on (suspect) evidence of an alibi; disappeared from view for seven years; returned, mysteriously prosperous, and set up house in Rarity Cottage in 1850; erected his 'Fountain Free to All', and his own tomb, in 1860; after a tempestuous life, died in his 91st year, in 1891, in Rarity Cottage; and left an eccentric will which gave rise to years of litigation.

His most substantial (but not most durable) memorial he built in 1866 on the far side of the River Bann, just over Toome Bridge. According to the inscription on the florid facade, it was 'The Temple of Liberty, Learning and Select Amusement. Dedicated, Erected and Endowed by John Carey - a Free Gift to his Country.' It had a hall to seat 1,500 people, a library of 5,000 books, statues (or busts) of gods and goddesses, of Grattan, Cobden, and Kosciusko, Columbus, Washington and Wilberforce, a fifty-candle chandelier, and a fine organ. It was alas burned down, probably maliciously, in 1911; but lingered until recently in the memory of those still living. "It is said that he also erected a tall tower beside the Temple, but that it was blown down on a stormy night".

The surviving wrought-iron gate outside his home incorporates three human faces, and a delightful cat; it hangs between strange white-and-yellow-painted gateposts, reminiscent of the bulbous domes of St Basil's Cathedral, Moscow.

The pump stands at the side of the Randalstown Road, above "a well which never ran dry"; behind it an iron placard is firmly grasped by a cast-iron arm and hand, with convincing fingernails; and proclaims it 'the Design and Gift of John Cary, 1860.'

The same, or similar, arms, wrists and hands (painted grey, but rusting) appear in the railings around what Girvan has described as the "almost surrealist" memorial which Carey erected, ostensibly to his parents, in fact to his ancestry and himself, in Duneane Presbyterian churchyard. An essay of some 1500 words, ending up 'See Burke's landed gentry', describes his and their virtues; the bizarre composition of marble and cast-iron is topped by urn and hand, with pointing-upwards index finger, inscribed on the back of the hand - "The Bar Above"!

"In life he was most ingenious, persevering, and benevolent; in death an example to all for these great moral virtues". Or so he maintained.

Photographs: W A Green, Ulster Folk Museum WAG 1742; Michael O'Connell. (See also colour-plate XIb)
Situation: Rarity Cottage gates, td, Ballymatoskerty; Grid ref J 005 968; pump, td, Toome; Grid ref. H 993 904; memorial, td, Ballylenully; Grid ref. J 023 905; all in Parish, Duneane; District Council, Antrim.

References: Memorial, listed B+; fountain, listed B1. D 1583, in PRONI; Girvan, 'West Antrim', UAHS, 1970, p 22; 'John Carey', 1991, passim; Howley, 'Follies and garden buildings', 1993, p 205; Blair, 'County Antrim characters', 1993, pp 48-49; Polly Devlin, in 'Irish Times', 21 July 1994.

Chaine Memorial, Larne

265. Built in 1887 to designs by S P Close who, only nine years earlier, had designed the Olderfleet Hotel for the citizen so remarkably commemorated: also the neighbouring mansions of Clonalis and Magheramorne House. Above the door, a plaque inscribed:

'This Tower was erected ... by the contributions of every class in this mixed community irrespective of creed or party All cordially united in esteem and affection for the memory of

JAMES CHAINE

of Ballycraigy and Cairncastle Co Antrim who represented this county in the Imperial Parliament of Great Britain and Ireland from February 1874 till 4th May 1885 when his early and lamented death in his 44th year of his age deprived his native county of one who had worked indefatigably for its interests ...'

According to the unpublished reminiscences of W R Young of Galgorm, James Chaine "had induced the Admiralty to make Larne the port of departure" for the Prince and Princess of Wales. "... So anxious was Mr Chaine that the arrangements should be perfect that he spent the whole of a cold April night on the quay, supervising the preparations. Everything went off splendidly, but Mr Chaine contracted pneumonia of which he died days after the royal departure".

Ninety-two feet high, his memorial is fairly closely modelled on the round tower at Antrim (4) (near Chaine's home at Ballycraigy), but the squared Annalong granite of which it is built is much harsher than the fieldstones of the original. Of the three pencil-like cylinders, this one would be HH, St Patrick's Jordanstown (65) HB, and The Steeple at Antrim BB. After its completion, the Commissioners of Irish Lights agreed to instal navigation lights on the seaward side, first lit in 1899. The legend that Mr Chaine was buried, standing upright, in his memorial tower is, unhappily, unfounded.

Photograph: Michael O'Connell. (See also colour-plate XVI)
Situation: To seaward of Tower Road, Larne; td, Curran and Drumaliss; Parish, Inver; District Council, Larne; Grid ref. D 415 030.
References: Listed B. W R Young, unpublished reminiscences, 1932; Green, 'Tour of East Antrim', 1990, p 17; M Close, in 'The Curran', 1987, p 9, and 1988, p 12; Howley, Follies and garden buildings', 1993, p 58.

Knockagh Monument, Greenisland

266. The second most prominent sea-mark of Belfast Lough, after the power station chimney at Kilroot (256): a dignified memorial, in the form of an obelisk, to the men of County Antrim who lost their lives in the two World Wars. The site was only chosen after consideration of various alternatives, including the top of Slemish mountain and the Giant's Causeway. Designed by Henry Seaver, a not unscholarly architect, it is a scaled-down version of the Wellington Testimonial in the Phoenix Park, Dublin, the 205-foot high obelisk designed by Sir Robert Smirke, completed in 1817 at a cost of over £26,000.

Unfortunately, though Henry Barton (originator of the project) had hoped to raise £25,000 for a monument 110 feet high, by 1935 he had managed to raise only £3026, mainly because of the understandable wish of many towns and villages to have their own memorials to their own dead. The consequence is that, however imposing it may look from a distance, the Knockagh monument is rather a sad thing from close up. It is built not of stone, but of concrete blocks, and the concrete has not worn well; condensation (or worse) oozes from numerous weeping-holes bored near the base; vandalism and graffiti are not uncommon; rather obtrusive safety railings divide the viewer from the view, though the latter is stunning on a good day. The upper part of the obelisk bears the dates 1914-1918 and 1939-1945 enclosed within bronze appliqué laurel wreaths. On the south face of the base, there is a simple and moving inscription, though not in the words proposed by Mr Barton, of lead set into cement.

Restored in 1985 by Kirk, McClure and Morton, consulting engineers, at the shared expense of the eight district councils which had then replaced Grand Jury and County Council. An under-rated, but by no means an insignificant, component in the fabric of the county.

Photograph: Michael O'Connell.
Situation: On the top of the 270-metre-high Knockagh hill, reached by a lane running southward from the road from Woodburn to Ballyhowne; td, West Division; Parish, and District Council, Carrickfergus; Grid ref. J 368 868.
References: Listed B1. 'Belfast Telegraph', 9 October 1922; D Corcoran, in 'Journal of Carrickfergus Historical Society', II, 1986.

This bibliography relates only to printed books. Citations from newspapers and journals; particulars of maps, guides to individual buildings, deeds, documents, letters, private papers and unpublished material, will be found in the references appended to the entries for the buildings concerned. Where no such particulars are given, it may be assumed that the authority in question is in private hands and unavailable for public access.

Akenson, D.H. *The Irish education experiment: the national system of education in the nineteenth century,* London, 1970

Antrim, Angela, Countess of *The Antrim McDonnells,* Belfast, 1977

An archaeological survey of County Down. Ed. by E.M. Jope, Belfast, 1966

The architecture of Richard Morrison and William Vitruvius Morrison. Ed. by A.M. Rowan, Dublin, 1989

Armstrong, Robert *Through the ages to Newtownabbey,* Muckamore, [1979]

The arts in Ulster: a symposium. Ed. by S.H. Bell, London, 1951

Atkinson, A. *Ireland exhibited to England in a political and moral survey of her population,* 2 vols, London, 1823

Atkinson, A. *Ireland in the nineteenth century ... seats and scenery of the north west district,* London, 1833

Aulet, J-L. *La fuente Wallace,* Ferrol, 1993

Ballywalter Park. Ed. by Peter Rankin, UAHS, Belfast, 1985

Barr, W.N.C. *Derriaghy: a short history of the parish,* Belfast, 1974

Barrow, John *A tour around Ireland ... in ... 1835,* London, 1836

Barry, M. *Across deep waters: bridges of Ireland,* Dublin, 1985

Bassett, G.H. *The book of County Antrim,* Dublin, 1888

Bayly, Henry *A topographical and historical account of Lisburn,* Belfast, 1834

Beaufort, D.A. *Memoir of a map of Ireland,* Dublin, 1792

Bence-Jones, Mark *Burke's guide to country houses, Vol I: Ireland,* London, 1978

Bigger, F.J. *The Ulster land war of 1770,* Dublin, 1910

Blair, S.A. *County Antrim characters,* Ballymena, 1993

Blair, S.A. *In the midst of the village: history of Dunloy Presbyterian Church,* Drumreagh, 1991

Borlase, W.C. *The dolmens of Ireland,* 3 vols, London, 1897

Boyd, H.A. *A history of the Church of Ireland in Dunluce parish,* Coleraine, 1937

Boyd, H.A. *A history of the Church of Ireland in Ramoan parish,* Ballycastle, 1930

Boyd, H.A. *The parishes of Craigs, Dunaghy and Killagan,* Ballymena, 1991

Brett, C.E.B., and Dunleath, Dorinda *Borough of Lisburn,* UAHS, Belfast, 1969

Brett, C.E.B. *Buildings of Belfast, 1700-1914,* London, 1967; Belfast, 1985

Brett, C.E.B. *Court houses and market houses of the province of Ulster,* UAHS, Belfast, 1973

Brett, C.E.B. *The Glens of Antrim,* UAHS, Belfast, 1971

Brett, C.E.B. *The island of Rathlin,* UAHS, Belfast, 1974

Brett, C.E.B. *Roger Mulholland, architect, of Belfast,* UAHS, Belfast, 1976

Buildings at risk: a catalogue of historic buildings at risk in Northern Ireland, UAHS, Belfast, 1993, 1995

Burke's Irish family records, London, 1976

Burke's landed gentry of Ireland, London, 1958

Camac, Thomas *History of Derrykeighan parish,* Coleraine, [1908], reprinted 1930

Camblin, Gilbert *The town in Ulster,* Belfast, 1951

Campbell, Gordon and Crowther, Susan *The town of Carrickfergus,* UAHS, Belfast, 1978

Carmody, W.P. *Lisburn Cathedral and its past rectors,* Belfast, 1926

Carroll, J. *Tourist's illustrated handbook,* London, 1853

Chambers, George *Faces of change: the Belfast and Northern Ireland Chambers of Commerce and Industry, 1783-1983,* Belfast, [1984]

Clergy of Connor, Belfast, 1993

Colvin, Howard *A biographical dictionary of British architects, 1600-1840,* London, 1954; 1978

The complete peerage, 13 vols, London, 1910-1959

Connon, A. and McNaughton, A.M. *Days gone by,* Dungannon, 1991

Cox, R.R. *The parish of Kilbride,* Doagh, 1959

Craig, Maurice *The architecture of Ireland,* London, 1982

Craig, Maurice *Classic Irish houses of the middle size,* London, 1976

Curl, J.S. *Mausolea in Ulster,* UAHS, Belfast, 1978

Currie, J.R.L. *The Northern Counties Railway,* 2 vols, Newton Abbott, 1973, 1974

Davis, Terence *John Nash, the Prince Regent's architect,* London, 1966

Dean, J.A.K. *The gate lodges of Ulster: a gazetteer,* UAHS, Belfast, 1994

Delany, Mary *Letters from Georgian Ireland: the correspondence, 1731-68.* Ed. by Angélique Day, Belfast, 1991

Dixon, Hugh *An introduction to Ulster architecture,* UAHS, Belfast, 1975

Dixon, Hugh *Ulster architecture 1800-1900,* UAHS, Belfast, 1972

Donaldson, Dixon *An historical, traditional and descriptive account of Islandmagee,* [1928]

Dowlin, Avy *Ballycarry in olden days,* Belfast, 1963

Doyle, J.B. *Tours in Ulster: a hand book to the antiquities and scenery of the north of Ireland,* Dublin, 1854

Drew, Thomas *The ancient church of St. Nicholas, Carrickfergus,* Dublin, 1872

Dubourdieu, John *Statistical survey of the county of Antrim,* 2 vols, Dublin, 1812

Egerton, T. and Bigger, F.J. *A local illustrated, historical and antiquarian guide for tourists in ... the district between Carrickfergus and Larne,* Belfast, [1906]

Ewart, L.M. *Handbook of the United Diocese of Down & Connor & Dromore,* Belfast, [1886]

Fair, J.A. *To this you belong,* Belfast, [1980]

Ferguson, M.C. *Sir Samuel Ferguson in the Ireland of his day,* 2 vols, Edinburgh, 1896

Forde, Hugh *Round the coast of Northern Ireland,* Belfast, 1928

Gage, Catherine *A history of the island of Rathlin (1851).* Transcribed by J.M. Dickson, Coleraine, 1995

Gailey, Alan *Rural houses of the north of Ireland,* Edinburgh, 1984

Gallagher, Lyn and Rogers, Dick *Castle, coast and cottage,* Belfast, 1986; 1992

Galloway, Peter *The cathedrals of Ireland,* Belfast, 1992

Gibbs, James *A book of architecture,* London, 1728

Girvan, W.D., Oram, Richard and Rowan, A.J. *Antrim & Ballymena,* UAHS, Belfast, 1969

Girvan, W.D. *North Antrim,* UAHS, Belfast, 1972

Girvan, W.D. and Rowan, A.J. *West Antrim,* UAHS, Belfast, 1970

Glassie, Henry *Passing the time: folklore and history of an Ulster community,* Dublin, 1982

Glenravel: a local history. Ed. by Joan O'Boyle, Ballymena, 1993

Green, E.R.R. *The Lagan valley 1800-1850: a local history of the industrial revolution,* London, 1949

Green, W.A. *A tour of east Antrim.* Compiled by Doreen Corcoran, Belfast, 1990

[Greene, W.J.] *A concise history of Lisburn and neighbourhood,* Belfast, 1906

Hamilton, J.B. *Ballymoney and district ... prior to the twentieth century,* Ballycastle, 1957

Hamilton, William *Letters concerning the northern coast of the county of Antrim,* Belfast, 1822

Hamond, Fred *Antrim coast & glens: industrial heritage,* Belfast, 1991

HEARTH: a review of projects completed 1978-1993, Belfast, 1994

Hill, George *An historical account of the Macdonnells of Antrim,* Belfast, 1873

Hill, George *The Stewarts of Ballintoy,* Coleraine, 1865

Historic monuments of Northern Ireland. Ed. by Ann Hamlin, Belfast, 1983

Hoare, R.C. *Journal of a tour in Ireland, A.D. 1806,* London, 1807

Howley, James *Follies and garden buildings of Ireland,* New Haven, 1993

Ingham, Richard *A history of Gracehill,* 1977

Inglis, H.D. *Ireland in 1834: a journey,* 2 vols, London, 1834, 1835

John Carey. Ed. by Euell Dunlop and B. Foy, Ballymena, 1991

Johns, A.A. *Derrykeighan,* Derrykeighan, 1981

Johnston, Roy *All his own work: Newton Penprase,* Belfast, 1977

King, David *The complete works of Robert and James Adam,* Oxford, 1991

Knox, Alexander *The Irish watering places,* Dublin, 1845

Knox, W.J. *Decades of the Ulster Bank, 1836-1964,* Belfast, 1965

Larmour, Paul *Belfast: an illustrated architectural guide,* Belfast, 1987

Lawlor, H.C. *Dunluce Castle and the Route,* Belfast, 1919

Lewis, Samuel *A topographical dictionary of Ireland,* 3 vols, London, 1837; 1840; 1847

Long, Bill *Bright light, white water: the story of Irish lighthouses,* Dublin, 1993

Lyons, Mary C. *Illustrated incumbered estates: Ireland, 1850-1905,* Whitegate, 1993

Macartney of Lisanoure, 1737-1806. Ed. by Peter Roebuck, Belfast, 1983

M'Cahan, Robert *M'Cahan's local histories, (1923): a series of pamphlets on north Antrim and the Glens,* Cushendall, 1988

McCallin, J. and Delargy, N. *Survey of Layde graveyard,* Coleraine, [1992]

McCutcheon, W.A. *The industrial archaeology of Northern Ireland,* Belfast, 1980

McKillop, Felix *Glenarm: a local history,* Belfast, 1987

McLean, M. *Dunloy past and present,* Ballycastle, 1990

Macnaghten, A.I. *The chiefs of Clan Macnachtan,* Windsor, 1951

McNeill, T.E. *Anglo-Norman Ulster,* Edinburgh, 1980

McNeill, T.E. *Carrickfergus Castle,* Belfast, 1981

M'Skimin, Samuel *The history and antiquities of the county of the town of Carrickfergus,* Belfast, 1811; 1823; 1832/39; 1909

Magill, Paul *Garron Tower,* Belfast, 1990

Maguire, W.A. *Living like a lord: the second Marquis of Donegall, 1769-1844,* Belfast, 1984

Malins, Edward and The Knight of Glin *Lost demesnes: Irish landscape gardening, 1660-1845,* London, 1976

Mallory, J.P. and McNeill, T.E. *The archaeology of Ulster,* Belfast, 1991

Mansbridge, Michael *John Nash: a complete catalogue,* London, 1991

Marshall, H.C. *The parish of Lambeg,* Lisburn, 1933

Mason, W.S. *A statistical account, or parochial survey of Ireland,* 3 vols, Dublin, 1814, 1816, 1819

Milton, Thomas *The seats and demesnes of the nobility and gentry of Ireland,* London, 1783-1794

Mitchell, G.R. *Guide to St Nicholas' church, Carrickfergus,* Carrickfergus, 1962

Moody, T.W. and Beckett, J.C. *Queen's, Belfast, 1845-1949,* 2 vols, London, 1959

Mullin, Julia *The Causeway coast,* Belfast, 1974; Coleraine, 1982

Mullin, Julia *History of Dunluce Presbyterian Church,* Bushmills, 1995

Mullin, Julia *The Presbytery of Coleraine,* Belfast, 1979

O'Kane, P. *Sweet Drummaul,* Randalstown, 1991

O'Laverty, James *A historical account of the Diocese of Down and Connor,* 5 vols, Dublin, 1878, 1880, 1884, 1887, 1895

The oldest register of the parish of Derriaghy ... 1696-1772. Ed. by W.N.C. Barr and W.C. Kerr, Derriaghy, 1981

Ollerenshaw, Philip *Banking in nineteenth-century Ireland: the Belfast banks, 1825-1914,* Manchester, 1987

O'Neill, C.H. *Antrim Castle,* Dublin, 1860

Ordnance Survey memoirs of Ireland. Ed. by Angélique Day, Belfast, 1990 - [in progress]

The parliamentary gazetteer of Ireland, 3 vols, Dublin, 1845-1846

Petrie, George. *The ecclesiastical architecture of Ireland anterior to the Anglo-Norman invasion,* Dublin, 1845

Pierce, Richard and Coey, Alastair *Taken for granted,* Belfast, 1984

Pilson, J.A. *History of the rise and progress of Belfast, and annals of the County Antrim,* Belfast, 1846

Plumptre, Anne *Narrative of a residence in Ireland during ... 1814 ... and 1815,* London, 1817

Pococke, Richard *Tour in Ireland in 1752.* Ed. by G.T. Stokes, Dublin, 1891

Potterton, Homan *Irish church monuments 1570-1880,* UAHS, Belfast, 1975

A preliminary survey of the ancient monuments of Northern Ireland. Ed. by D.A. Chart, Belfast, 1940

Proctor, E.K. *Belfast scenery in thirty views 1832.* With a modern commentary by Fred Heatley and Hugh Dixon, Belfast, 1983

Public works: the architecture of the Office of Public works, 1831-1987. Ed. by C. O'Connor and J. O'Regan, Dublin, 1988

Rankin, D.H. *A short history of the parish of Kilroot,* Belfast, 1982

Reeves, William *Ecclesiastical antiquities of Down, Connor and Dromore,* Dublin, 1847

Richardson, Alfred *A guide to Ballycastle and neighbourhood,* [Belfast], 1905

Richardson, J.N. *The Quakri at Lurgan & Grange,* Bessbrook, 1877; [1899]

Richardson, J.N. *Reminiscences of 'Friends' in Ulster,* Gloucester, [1911]

Robinson, Philip *Carrickfergus (Irish historic towns atlas, 2),* Dublin, 1986

Robinson, Tim *Stones of Aran: labyrinth,* Dublin, 1995

Rutherford, George *Old families of Carrickfergus and Ballynure,* Belfast, 1995

Sadleir, T.U. and Dickinson, P.L. *Georgian mansions in Ireland,* Dublin, 1915

Shaw, William *Cullybackey: the story of an Ulster village,* Edinburgh, [1913]

Sheehy, Jeanne *The rediscovery of Ireland's past: the Celtic Revival, 1830-1930,* London, 1980

Siddons, Sarah *The reminiscences ... 1773 - 1785.* Ed. by William Van Lennep, Cambridge, Mass., 1942

Simpson, Jonathan *Annals of my life, labours and travels,* Belfast, 1895

Slater's national commercial directory of Ireland, Manchester, 1846

Smyth, Alastair *The story of Antrim,* Antrim, 1984

Speers, Sheela *Under the big lamp ... Carrickfergus,* Belfast, 1989

Stephenson, S.M. *Historical essay on the parish and congregation of Templepatrick,* Belfast, 1824

Stewart, A.M. *Royal Hibernian Academy of Arts: index of exhibitors and their works, 1826 to 1979,* 2 vols, Dublin, 1985, 1986

Stewart, A.T.Q. *The summer soldiers: the 1798 rebellion in Antrim and Down,* Belfast, 1995

Summerson, John *The life and work of John Nash, architect,* London, 1980

Taylor, George and Skinner, Andrew *Maps of the roads of Ireland,* London, 1778; 1783

Thompson, J. *The story of Finvoy Presbyterian Church,* Finvoy, 1990

Todd, Richard *Caught in the act,* London, 1986

Totten, Jean *Gleanings from Glenavy parish,* Newcastle, 1980

Wakefield, Edward *An account of Ireland, statistical and political,* 2 vols, London, 1812

Watson, Charles *The story of the united parishes of Glenavy, Camlin and Tullyrusk,* Belfast, 1892

Welch, R.J. *Ireland's eye.* Commentary by E.E. Evans and B.S. Turner, Belfast, 1977

Wesley, John *The journal.* Ed. by N. Curnock, 8 vols, London, 1909-1916

West, Thomas *A historical sketch of First Antrim Presbyterian Church,* Antrim, 1902

White, Rosalie *History of Gracehill Moravian Settlement,* 1996

Williams, Jeremy *Architecture in Ireland, 1837-1921,* Dublin, 1994

Wilson, T.G. *The Irish Lighthouse Service,* Dublin, 1968

Wilson, William *The post-chaise companion ... through Ireland,* Dublin, 1784; 1786; 1803; 1813

Young, Amy *Three hundred years in Innishowen,* Belfast, 1929

Young, Arthur *A tour in Ireland in the years 1776 ... [to] ... 1779,* London, 1780

Young, R.M. *Belfast and the province of Ulster in the twentieth century,* Brighton, 1909

Youngson, A.J. *The making of classical Edinburgh, 1750-1848,* Edinburgh, 1966

Clare Park, Ballycastle, in its prime; now in the last stages of dereliction. Photograph: R J Welch, Ulster Museum W01/66/3

INDEX
(to page numbers)

Glenarm Castle and Barbican (86) in winter:
"... the horns of elfland faintly blowing"? Photograph: Michael O'Connell

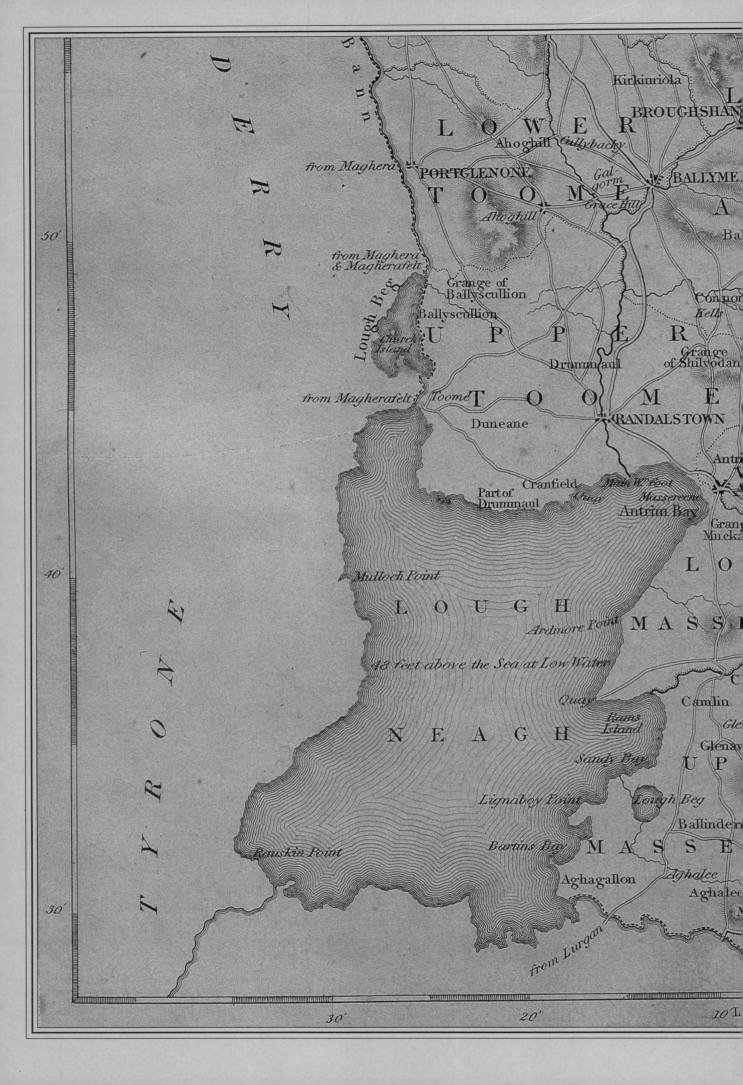